JEWS, GENTILES AND ETHNIC RECONCILIATION: PAUL'S JEWISH IDENTITY AND EPHESIANS

Much recent scholarship has focused on Paul's insistence on Gentile membership of the people of God equally with Jews. Dr Yee's study of Ephesians 2 reveals how the distinctively Jewish world view of the author of Ephesians underlies this key text. He explores how the Ephesians' author provides a resolution to one of the thorniest issues regarding two ethnic groups in the earliest period of Christianity: can Jew and Gentile, the two estranged human groups, be one (people of God) and if so, how? Setting Ephesians 2 as fully as possible into its historical context, he describes some of the relevant Jewish features and demonstrates them, revealing many explosive but hidden issues. This book provides an important contribution to the continuing reassessment of Christian and Jewish self-understanding in regard to each other during the critical period of the latter decades of the first century CE.

TET-LIM N. YEE is a Lecturer in New Testament Studies at the Theological Centre for Asia, Singapore. He is also Research Director, City and Culture Research Centre, Malaysia, and Honorary Research Associate, Divinity School of Chung-Chi College at the Chinese University of Hong Kong.

SOCIETY FOR NEW TESTAMENT STUDIES

MONOGRAPH SERIES

General Editor: Richard Bauckham

130

JEWS, GENTILES AND ETHNIC RECONCILIATION:
PAUL'S JEWISH IDENTITY AND EPHESIANS

SOCIETY FOR NEW TESTAMENT STUDIES

MONOGRAPH SERIES

Titles in the series

117. Jesus and Israel's Traditions of Judgement and Restoration
STEVEN M. BRYAN
0 521 81183 X

118. The Myth of a Gentile Galilee
MARK A. CHANCEY
0 521 81487 1

119. New Creation in Paul's Letters and Thought
MOYER V. HUBBARD
0 521 81485 5

120. Belly and Body in the Pauline Epistles
KARL OLAV SANDNES
0 521 81535 5

121. The First Christian Historian
DANIEL MARGUERAT
0 521 81650 5

122. An Aramaic Approach to Q
MAURICE CASEY
0 521 81723 4

123. Isaiah's Christ in Matthew's Gospel
RICHARD BEATON
0 521 81888 5

124. God and History in the Book of Revelation
MICHAEL GILBERTSON
0 521 82466 4

125. Jesus' Defeat of Death
PETER G. BOLT
0 521 83036 2

126. From Hope to Despair in Thessalonica
COLIN R. NICHOLL
0 521 83142 3

127. Matthew's Trilogy of Parables
WESLEY G. OLMSTEAD
0 521 83154 7

128. The People of God in the Apocalypse
STEPHEN PATTEMORE
0 521 83698 0

129. The Exorcism Stories in Luke-Acts
TODD KLUTZ
0 521 83804 5

130. Jews, Gentiles and Ethnic Reconciliation: Paul's Jewish Identity and Ephesians
TET-LIM N. YEE
0 521 83831 2

Jews, Gentiles and Ethnic Reconciliation: Paul's Jewish Identity and Ephesians

TET-LIM N. YEE

Theological Centre for Asia, Singapore
City and Culture Research Centre, Malaysia
Divinity School of Chung Chi College, the Chinese University of Hong Kong

CAMBRIDGE
UNIVERSITY PRESS

PUBLISHED BY THE PRESS SYNDICATE OF THE UNIVERSITY OF CAMBRIDGE
The Pitt Building, Trumpington Street, Cambridge, United Kingdom

CAMBRIDGE UNIVERSITY PRESS
The Edinburgh Building, Cambridge, CB2 2RU, UK
40 West 20th Street, New York, NY 10011–4211, USA
477 Williamstown Road, Port Melbourne, VIC 3207, Australia
Ruiz de Alarcón 13, 28014 Madrid, Spain
Dock House, The Waterfront, Cape Town 8001, South Africa

http://www.cambridge.org

First published 2005

Printed in the United Kingdom at the University Press, Cambridge

Typeface Times 10/12 pt. *System* LaTeX 2_ε [TB]

A catalogue record for this book is available from the British Library

Library of Congress Cataloguing in Publication data
Yee, Tet-Lim N.
Jews, Gentiles and ethnic reconciliation: Paul's Jewish Identity
and Ephesians / Tet-Lim N. Yee.
p. cm. – (Monograph series / Society for New Testament Studies; 130)
Includes bibliographical references and index.
ISBN 0-521-83831-2
1. Bible. N.T. Ephesians II – Criticism, interpretation, etc. 2. Jews in the New Testament. 3. Gentiles in the New Testament. I. Title. II. Monograph series (Society for New Testament Studies); 130.
BS2695.6.J44Y44 2004
227′.5067 – dc22 2004045737

ISBN 0 521 83831 2 hardback

To Jin Kuan
and to our beloved children
Opheleia Tse-Shiuan and Phil Fei-Wu

In memoriam
Zhi Cheng

CONTENTS

FOREWORD

The relation of Judaism to Christianity has always been a question heavy-laden with negative and threatening overtones. The term 'Christianity' was initially used (by Ignatius) to define Christianity by way of contrast with 'Judaism'. And the long centuries of Christian imperialist disdain for Judaism persisted well into the second half of the twentieth century. However, the attempt to achieve a healthier and more just appreciation of Judaism on the part of Christian scholarship is now well under way.

The New Testament has been at the heart of this reappraisal: understandably, since some of its own more antithetical statements have contributed to the rise of Christian anti-Judaism. But the renewed appreciation of Judaism as a religion of covenant and atonement as well as of law and obedience, and of Christianty's Jewish origins, of Jesus the Jew, of the New Testament as largely written by Jews, and of the Jewish character of the Christianity therein expressed has more and more counteracted such polemical passages. The new perspective on Paul in particular has made it much clearer that terms like 'Jew', 'Judaism' and especially 'Israel' reflect a much more complex reality (historical, social, religious) than a too simplistic reading of the antithetical statements has hitherto recognised.

The discussion aroused by this new perspective on Paul has focused principally on the two letters of Paul which deal most fully with the Jew/Gentile issue – Romans and Galatians. Somewhat surprisingly, comparatively little attention has been given to Ephesians – understandable, since the Pauline authorship of Ephesians remains in dispute, but surprising nonetheless since Ephesians 2 is arguably one of the most expressive statements of Paul's view of the Jew/Gentile issue.

It is this lack which Dr Yee addresses. He sets himself the task of checking to what extent the new perspective sheds light on Ephesians and vice versa. He sees the letter, chapter 2 in particular, as providing an answer to two basic questions: 'Can Jew and Gentile, two estranged human groups, be one people of God? And if so, how?' He notes and analyses the distinctively Jewish, the *still* distinctively Jewish, attitude expressed in 2.11–12. The problem is that this has become an expression of 'covenantal ethnocentrism'; religious identity and ethnic identity have become too much bound up in each other. So the solution is not a simple absorption of Gentiles into ethnic Israel. But neither is the solution to regard the 'Church' as a new and quite separate entity from 'Israel', as though the chapter could be entitled 'Israel and the Church'. The critique of ethnic Israel ('covenantal ethnocentrism') does not extend to Israel as still reflected in the rest of chapter 2. The chapter's vision is of an inclusivist 'Israel' rather than Israel defining itself in narrow exclusivist terms. The primary christological solution cannot be adequately appreciated without also recognising the author's attempt to deconstruct the more traditional Jewish identity and to re-express it in the terms which he himself still affirmed and embraced.

This is but the core of the thesis. It is developed and documented in fine detail and the repercussions for our understanding of other parts of the letter are well drawn out. This book will provide an important correction to the course steered by both older and more recent studies of Ephesians. I commend it warmly.

JAMES D. G. DUNN
Emeritus Lightfoot Professor of Divinity, University of Durham

PREFACE

This study is a slightly revised version of my doctoral thesis submitted to the Department of Theology, Durham University in June 1999. It was examined by Professors William S. Campbell and Loren Stuckenbruck, to both of whom I am much indebted for their encouraging reception of the thesis and their helpful comments. None of these scholars is responsible for whatever deficiencies remain in the present work.

I am especially grateful to my advisor, Professor James Dunn, not only for his wise guidance, insightful comments and patience, but also for his warm friendship and hospitality at Durham. It is a great privilege that I can study with one who has spent decades on Paul and Christian origins and is still producing substantial works on the subjects. Connoisseurs of Dunn's work will find its 'echoes' in this study.

Among other friends and colleagues who helped and supported me over these years of research and teaching, I should like to thank: Linda and Steve Wright, Vicki and Andy Carver, Steve Barton, Walter Moberly, Rob Hayward, Scot McKnight, Murray Harris, Ezra Kok, Lo Lung Kwong, Michael Fuller, Jenny and Mike Gilbertson, Márta and András Csepreg, Diana and Danny Koh, Marcus Conti, Yong-Qiang Zong, Hanry Yu, Derek Tan, Chris Dippenaar, Alan Harkness, Chin Ken Pa, Choong Chee Pang, Liew Yoo Kiang, Caleb Soo, Chong Chin Chung, Wong Chiau Yau, Clement Chia, Chan Yew Ming, Chen Dong-Feng, and Chan Juin Ming. One of my students, Cynthia Choo Bee Lay, has given invaluable assistance in the preparation of this work.

During my studies in Durham, I enjoyed and profited enormously from my lessons with two foreign language teachers, Frau Wollfraund Coles of the Department of German, Durham University and Margaret Gough of St Nick's Church who taught me French. I also must express my heartiest thanks to the helpful staff of Durham Palace Green Library: Alisoun Roberts, Carol Simmons, Barbara Johnson, Colin Gorman. I wish to thank Margaret Parkinson and Anne Parker, the secretaries for postgraduates in theological studies.

Many friends provided substantial financial support during my research in Britain. I should like to record my heartiest gratitude to Nancy and Richard Song and Huang Kuei-Mei, without whom my years of research would not have been possible. My warmest thanks to family friends Angel Yen and Shou-Chern, Elizabeth and Richard Brigg, and to James Lu and San-San Pan. Members from the Church of the Living Water in Taipei, Taiwan have been immensely generous to our family. I also received a grant from The Langham Scholarships Trust (1995); thanks are due especially to Jeff Gardner and Paul Berg of the Trust for their memorable kindness.

Finally I want to thank my loving wife Jin Kuan whose unconditional support given to me remains a constant inspiration. This book is dedicated to her and to our children, Opheleia Tse-Shiuan and Phil Fei-Wu, as well as to the memory of our beloved Zhi Cheng ('Our *politeuma* is in heaven').

TET-LIM N. YEE
Kampar, Perak, West Malaysia

ABBREVIATIONS

In general, the conventions followed for the abbreviations of the titles of journals and reference works are those of the *Journal of Biblical Literature*, 107 (1988), 579–96.

AB	*Anchor Bible*
ABD	*Anchor Bible Dictionary*
AFLNWG	Arbeitsgemeinschaft für Forschung des Landes Norrhein Westfalen-Geisteswissenschaften
AGAJU	Arbeiten zur Geschichte des Antiken Judentums und des Urchristentums
AHAWPHK	Abhandlungen der Heidelberg Akademie den Wissenschaften, Philosophisch-historiche Klasse
AnBib	Analecta Biblica
ANRW	*Aufstieg und Niedergang der Römischen Welt*
ARW	*Archiv für Religionswissenschaft*
AS	*Ancient Society*
BAGD	W. Bauer, W. F. Arndt, F. W. Gingrich and F. W. Danker, *Greek-English Lexicon of the NT*
BASOR	*Bulletin of the American Schools of Oriental Research*
BBB	Bonner Biblische Beiträge
BDF	F. Blass, A. Debrunner and R. W. Funk, *A Greek Grammar of the New Testament*
BGBE	Beiträge zur Geschichte der biblischen Exegese
BHTh	Beiträge zur historischen Theologie
BI	*Biblical Interpretation*
Bib	*Biblica*
BibLeb	*Bibel und Leben*
Bijdragen	*Bijdragen, Tijdschrift voor Filosofie en Theologie*
BJRL	*Bulletin of the John Rylands University Library of Manchester*

BJS	Brown Judaic Studies
BL	Biblical Languages
BT	*Bible Translator*
BU	Biblische Untersuchungen
BZ	*Biblische Zeitschrift*
BZAW	Beihefte zur ZAW
BZNW	Beihefte zur ZNW
CBET	Contributions to Biblical Exegesis and Theology
CBQ	*Catholic Biblical Quarterly*
CBQMS	Catholic Biblical Quarterly Monograph Series
CCWJCW	Cambridge Commentaries on Writings of the Jewish and Christian World
CIG	*Corpus Inscriptionum Graecarum*
CIJ	*Corpus Inscriptionum Judaicarum*
CJZC	*Corpus jüdischer Zeugnisse aus der Cyrenaika*
CNT	Commentaire du Nouveau Testament
CP	*Classical Philology*
CPJ	*Corpus Papyrorum Judaicarum*
CR	*Classical Review*
CRINT	Compendia rerum Iudaicarum ad Novum Testamentum
DDDB	*Dictionary of Deities and Demons in the Bible*
A.-M. Denis	*Concordance grecque des pseudépigraphes d'Ancien Testament*
DGLR	*A Dictionary of Greek and Latin Legal Terms in Rabbinic Literature*
DHA	*Dialogues d'histoire ancienne*
DPL	*Dictionary of Paul and His Letters*
DSS	Dead Sea Scrolls
EDNT	*Exegetical Dictionary of the New Testament*
EFN	Estudios de Filología Neotestamentaria
EGGNT	Exegetical Guide to the Greek New Testament
ENT	Erläuterungen zum Neuen Testament
EthG	*Ethnic Groups*
EvQ	*Evangelical Quarterly*
ExpT	*Expository Times*
FB	Forschung zur Bibel
FBBS	Facet Books, Biblical Series
FHJA	*Fragments from Hellenistic Jewish Authors*
FRLANT	Forschungen zur Religion und Literatur des Altes und Neuen Testaments

GLAJJ	*Greek and Latin Authors on Jews and Judaism*
GNT	Grundriße zum Nueen Testament
GTJ	*Grace Theological Journal*
HJPAJC	E. Schürer, *The History of the Jewish People in the Age of Jesus Christ*
HNT	Handbuch zum Neuen Testament
Hoppe	R. Hoppe, *Epheserbrief, Kolosserbrief*, Stuttgarter Kleiner Kommentar, Neues Testament 10 (Stuttgart: Katholisches Bibelwerk, 1987)
HTR	Handwörterbuch für Theologie und Religionwissenschaft
HTR	*Harvard Theological Review*
HUCA	*Hebrew Union College Annual*
IB	*The Interpreter's Bible*
IBM	*Ancient Greek Inscriptions in the British Museum*
IBS	*Irish Biblical Studies*
ICC	The International Critical Commentary
IDB	*Interpreter's Dictionary of the Bible*
IDBSup	*Supplementary volume to IDB*
IEJ	*Israel Exploration Journal*
IG	*Inscriptiones Graecae*
IGRR	*Inscriptiones Graecae Res Romanas Pertinentes 1911–27*
ILS	*Inscriptiones Latinae Selectae*
Int	*Interpretation*
IVLPU	*Indicem Verborum in Libris Pseudepigraphis Usurpatorum*
JBC	*New Jerome Bible Commentary*
JBL	*Journal of Biblical Literature*
JE	*Jewish Encyclopedia*
JETS	*Journal of the Evangelical Theological Society*
JHS	*Journal of Hellenic Studies*
JIGRE	*Jewish Inscriptions of Graeco-Roman Egypt*
JJS	*Journal of Jewish Studies*
JQR	*Jewish Quarterly Review*
JRS	*Journal of Roman Studies*
JSJ	*Journal for the Study of Judaism*
JSNT	*Journal for the Study of the New Testament*
JSNTSS	Journal for the Study of the New Testament Supplement Series

JSPSS	Journal for the Study of the Pseudepigrapha Supplement Series
JSS	*Journal of Semitic Studies*
JTS	*Journal of Theological Studies*
KEK	Kritisch-exegetischer Kommentar über das Neue Testament
Lat	*Latomus*
LCL	Loeb Classical Library
LEC	Library of Early Christianity
LEH	J. Lust, E. Eynikel and K. Hauspie, *A Greek-English Lexicon of the Septuagint*
LSJ	Liddell, H. G., R. Scott, H. S. Jones, *A Greek-English Lexicon*
LUÅ	Lunds Universitets Årsskrift
LVTA	*Librorum Veteris Testamenti Apocryphorum Philogica*
MEΛ	MEΛETHMATA
M-M	J. H. Moulton and G. Milligan, *The Vocabulary of the Greek Testament, Illustrated from the Papyri and other Non-Literary Sources*
NA[27]	Nestle Aland
NBC	*New Bible Commentary*
NBD	*New Bible Dictionary*
NCB	New Clarendon Bible
NDIEC	*New Documents Illustrating Early Christianity*
NEBE	Die Neue Echter Bibel Ergänzungs
NEBNT	Die Neue Echter Bibel Neues Testament
Neot	*Neotestamentica*
NIBC	New International Biblical Series
NICNT	The New International Commentary on the New Testament
NIDNTT	*The New International Dictionary of New Testament Theology*
NIGTC	The New International Greek Testament Commentary
NJB	New Jerusalem Bible
NJBC	*New Jerome Biblical Commentary*
NovT	*Novum Testamentum*
NTD	Das Neue Testament Deutsch
NTG	New Testament Guides
NTOA	Novum Testamentum et Orbis Antiquus
NTS	*New Testament Studies*

NTTS	New Testament Tools and Studies
OCD	*The Oxford Classical Dictionary* (3rd edition)
ODJR	*The Oxford Dictionary of the Jewish Religion*
OGIS	*Orientis graeci inscriptiones selectae*
OJRS	*Ohio Journal of Religious Studies*
OPTAT	*Occasional Papers in Translation and Textlinguistics*
OSCC	Oklahoma Series in Classical Culture
ÖTKNT	Ökumenischer Taschenbuch-Kommentar Neuen Testament
OTL	Old Testament Library
OTP	*The Old Testament Pseudepigrapha*
PA	Philosophia Antiqua
PCB	*Peake's Commentary on the Bible*
PCPhSS	Proceedings of the Cambridge Philological Society Supplementary Volumes
PGL	*A Patristic Greek Lexicon*
PGM	*The Greek Magical Papyri in Translation*
PS	Phoenix Supplementary Volumes
QD	Quaestiones disputatae
RECA	*Paulys Real-Encyclopädae der Classischen Alterumwissenschaft*
ResQ	*Restoration Quarterly*
RevQ	*Revue de Qumran*
RGG^3	*Die Religion in Geschichte und Gegenwart: Handwörtbuch für Theologie und Religionswissenschaft*
RheM	*Rheinisches Museum für Philologie*
RST	Regensburger Studien zum Theologie
SANT	Studien zum Alten und Neuen Testament
SB	Subsidia Biblica
SBG	Studies in Biblical Greek
SBLDS	Society of Biblical Literature Dissertation Series
SBLMS	Society of Biblical Literature Monograph Series
SBLSBS	Society of Biblical Literature Sources for Biblical Study
SBS	Stuttgarter Bibelstudien
SBU	*Symbolae Biblicae Upsalienses*
SCI	*Scripta Classica Israelica*
SCP	*Studies in Classical Philology*
SE	*Studia Evangelica*
SEG	*Supplementum Epigraphicum Graecum*
SEJE	*Studies in Early Jewish Epigraphy*

SGA	*Sammelbuch Griechischer urkunden aus Ägypten*
SIG	*Sylloge Inscriptionum Graecarum*
SIGC	Studien zur Interkulturellen Geschichte des Christentums
SJLA	Studies in Judaism in Late Antiquity
SJSJ	Supplements to the Journal for the Study of Judaism
SJT	*Scottish Journal of Theology*
SNovT	Supplements to Novum Testamentum
SNT	Studien zum Neuen Testament
SNTSMS	Society for New Testament Studies Monograph Series
SPB	Studia Post-Biblica
SSEJC	Studies in Scripture in Early Judaism and Christianity
ST	*Studia Theologica cura Ordinum Theologicorum Scandinavorum*
StPB	Studia post-biblica
Str-B	H. Strack and P. Billerbeck, *Kommentar zum Neuen Testament*
SUNT	Studien zur Umwelt des Neuen Testaments
SVF	*Stoicorum Veterum Fragmenta*
TDNT	*Theological Dictionary of the New Testament*
TH	Théologie Historique
THNT	Theologischer Handkommentar zum Neuen Testament
TLNT	*Theological Lexicon of the New Testament*
TLOT	*Theological Lexicon of the Old Testament*
TRE	*Theologische Realenzyklopädie*
TS	*Theological Studies*
TSAJ	Texte und Studien zum antiken Judentum
TThS	Trier Theologische Studien
TU	Texte und Untersuchungen
TWAT	*Theologische Wörterbuch zum Alten Testament*
TynB	*Tyndale Bulletin*
TZ	*Theologische Zeitschrift*
UBSGNT	The United Bible Societies Greek New Testament
UNT	Untersuchungen zum Neuen Testament
VT	*Vetus Testamentum*
WBC	Word Biblical Commentary
WMANT	Wissenschaft Monographs zum Alten und Neuen Testament
WUNT	Wissenschaftliche Untersuchungen zum Neuen Testament

ZAW	*Zeitschrift für die altetestamentliche Wissenschaft*
ZB	Zürcher Bibelkommentare
ZBNT	Zürcher Bibelkommentare Neuen Testament
ZNW	*Zeitschrift für die neutestamentliche Wissenschaft*
ZTK	*Zeitschrift für Theologie und Kirche*

1

INTRODUCTION

1.1 The problem

One of the crucial but almost neglected questions in New Testament research is that of the Jewish attitudes toward the Gentiles in the epistle to the Ephesians. The main reason for the neglect of this ethnic factor, unfortunately, has been the uncritical reading of some of the statements about the Gentiles in Ephesians itself, which I hope to rectify in the present study. Still more importantly, the neglect of the factor is closely associated with the hermeneutical 'grid' through which Pauline Christianity was portrayed. A brief comment on the framework mentioned above is appropriate.

New Testament scholarship on Pauline Christianity since the second quarter of the nineteenth century, as widely recognised, has been dominated largely by the philosophy of dialectics, epitomised by the works of Hegel. The founder of the Tübingen School, F. C. Baur, and a chorus of scholars who depended upon this philosophy, had read the history of earliest Christianity in dialectic terms.[1] Baur and his followers, as we shall see, have had a continuing sway in subsequent New Testament scholarship not only in the area of Paul's earlier letters but also in such letters as Ephesians. The heritage of the dialectic philosophy with which Baur was associated may also account for the tendency to interpret Pauline Christianity in terms of conflict between Jews and Gentiles or between Jewish Christianity and Hellenistic Christianity (see my review of Percy and Fischer below).[2] Suffice it to say that works of the proponents of this school of thought reveal a fundamental problem of the paradigm. With its emphasis on 'conflict' or ecclesiastical polemic, the paradigm mentioned above has led in no small degree to the underestimation of other

[1] Baur, *Paul*, 59, 125–8; cf. Baur, *History*, 43, 61, 122–8 ('Christianity as a universal principle of salvation: the conflict between Paulinism and Judaism, and its adjustment in the idea of the catholic church').

[2] The dichotomy between 'law' and 'faith', a theological presupposition of much Lutheran scholarship, often exhibits logical similarity with the dialectic theory.

factors which are germane to our understanding of Pauline Christianity. Indeed the major deficiency of the foregoing paradigm is its failure to penetrate more fully into the historical context within which the Pauline letters were written and to which these letters were addressed. But with the introduction to New Testament studies of the 'new perspective on Paul', it has now become quite clear that an opportunity to reconsider the question of Pauline Christianity, and more importantly to set the epistle to the Ephesians within the 'new perspective', can now be undertaken. The works of E. Sanders (1977) and J. Dunn (1988, 1990)[3] in particular have been valuable contributions in this direction.

Sanders has built up a different presentation of Palestinian Judaism at the time of Paul from a massive analysis of much of the relevant Jewish literature for that period. His main contention is that Judaism during the Second Temple period has always been first and foremost a religion of grace, with human obedience understood as response to that grace. He has shown with sufficient weight of evidence that for the first-century Jew, Israel's covenant relation with God was fundamental: God had chosen Israel to be his peculiar people, to enjoy a special relationship under his rule. The covenant had been given by divine initiative. The law had been given as an expression of this covenant and provided the framework for life within it (thus, 'covenantal nomism').[4] The perspective-shifting work of Sanders is hailed by Dunn, who has made a fresh assessment of Paul's earlier letters (Romans and Galatians) and theology with the 'new perspective'.[5] One of the values of the 'new perspective' is that it allowed the fundamental problem of the relationship of Christianity to Judaism to re-emerge on centre stage.[6] It also allowed exegetes to penetrate inside the historical context, a major part of which is the self-understanding of Jews and Judaism in the first century, and the life setting in which Paul's letters were first read and heard.[7] We may add that one of the benefits we can gain from fresh insights provided by the 'new perspective' is that of a greater critical distance from the methodological presuppositions of Baur and his successors.

The present study seeks to bring the significance of the 'new perspective' to bear on Ephesians, in the hope of being able to read Ephesians within the context which it provides (see my discussion in Chapter 2 below). It is my contention that previous work on Ephesians has seriously

[3] Dunn, *Romans 1–8*, lxiii–lxvi; Dunn, 'New Perspective'.

[4] Sanders, *Paul*, 75, 420, 544.

[5] For Dunn's reappraisal of Sanders's 'new perspective', see his 'New Perspective', here 186–8; cf. Dunn, *Romans 1–8*, lxvi; Dunn, *Galatians*; Dunn, *TPA*, esp. 335–40.

[6] Dunn, *TPA*, 335–340.

[7] Dunn, *Romans 1–8*, xiv–xv.

undermined the degree of continuity between Israel and the church which it expresses. The 'new perspective' mentioned above has given us an opportunity to look at some of the old issues afresh. What is the relation of the author's theology to that of first-century Jews and Judaism? What picture of Judaism can we draw from the writing of Ephesians? Was Judaism simply the foil of the author's theology of the church? How does he relate the church to Israel's heritage in terms of continuity and discontinuity? To what extent do we see a distinctively Jewish view of the Gentiles? Do we easily see Jewish atitudes toward the Gentiles in Ephesians? What was at issue between Jews and Gentiles? It is my conviction that these questions can be understood only if the historical context of first-century Jews and Judaism is fully appreciated.

1.2 The justification of the present study

Despite the fact that Ephesians has been the locus of intense scholarly interest and, with reference to 2.11–22 in particular, a lively arena of debate, no full-scale treatment of the theme of Jewish attitudes toward the Gentiles and ethnic reconciliation in Ephesians 2 against the backdrop of the Jewish perspective has yet been undertaken. The present study is thus an endeavour to fill that gap. Before proceeding with an account of the Jewish attitudes toward the Gentiles, which takes into account the ethnic factors and the issue of ethnic reconciliation closely associated with it, a review of some of the major contributions of previous scholars would be appropriate.

The scholarly investigation of our letter is quite vast, and an adequate treatment of its history would require a sizeable monograph.[8] For our present purposes only the studies of representatives of the major hypotheses will be reviewed. In addition to this, most of the arguments and counter-arguments advanced in these hypotheses do not concern us except in three respects, in the hope that this will help us to gain some orientation in what is otherwise a baffling mass of conflicting theories. First, we are interested in what has already been said in these studies about the Gentiles and Jews in Ephesians. Secondly, we are also interested in the virtual absence of reference in such studies to the purpose of Ephesians against the backcloth of the Jewish perception of the Gentiles which is the chief concern of this study. Thirdly, we are concerned with the virtual

[8] Useful surveys of scholarship can be found in Merkel, 'Diskussion'; Rader, *Hostility*; Schnackenburg, 'Exegese'; Bruce, *Ephesians*, 229–46; Moore, 'Ephesians'; Lincoln, 'Church'; Schnelle, *History*, 299–314.

absence of reference in such studies to the connections between Jewish attitudes toward Gentiles and ethnic reconciliation.

1.2.1 A 'Gentile Christianity' drifted from its mooring in the Jewish tradition?

There is an influential school of thought which suggests that Ephesians addressed a concrete crisis created by the success of 'Gentile Christianity' and its drift from its moorings in the Jewish tradition. The influence of this is well illustrated in the works of E. Käsemann and a chorus of scholars who followed this theory.

Käsemann[9] assumed that the specific historical situation addressed by the author of Ephesians is disclosed in Ephesians 2.11ff. He argues that the letter/tractate was written to urge the Gentile Christian majority to accept a Jewish Christian minority and to retain its ties with the ancient Hebrew tradition. What was mentioned as a possibility by Paul in his earlier letter (i.e. Rom. 11.17ff.) has now become an actuality: Gentile Christians are looking with disdain upon Jewish Christians. The thought-provoking thesis of Käsemann thus envisages a situation in which Gentile Christians were feeling a certain unease about the historical linkage of their faith with Israel and were rejecting the Jewish Christians' emphasis on salvation history. He thus theorises that the Gentiles were looking to some timeless Gnostic myths about creation and redemption to fill the vacuum created by this rejection of the Old Testament. The net result of this move was not only a severance of Gentile Christianity from its historical moorings but an effective dissolving of Christian community, since, according to Käsemann, Gnosticism is a religion which had little room for the notion of a church/community.[10] This accounts for the author's insistence on the place of the church as the new creation, and his bringing Jews and Gentiles

9 Käsemann, 'Ephesians'; Käsemann, *Perspectives*, 109–10.

10 There has been a long tradition of speaking of Ephesians as countering a pre-Christian Gnostic soteriology/christology. See, e.g., Pokorný, 'Mysterien'; cf. Pokorný, *Gnosis*, 82ff. Pokorný, however, has argued with some hesitation in his later work, cf. Pokorný, *Epheser*, here 22–4. Since Schlier's *Christus* (1933), much of the discussion of Ephesians has centred upon the relationship between Ephesians and Gnosticism (145); cf. Käsemann, *Leib*, 145; Fischer, *Tendenz*, 173–200; Conzelmann, *Epheser*, 87; Lindemann, *Epheserbrief*, 121; Köster, *Introduction*, 267–72, argued that 'Ephesians was unable to enter into a theological controversy with Gnosticism, for it was from Gnosticism that the author drew the theological categories that made his universalism possible' (271). For an overview of how the recent history of interpretation has sought the key to Ephesians in Gnostic background, see esp. Merkel, 'Diskussion', 3176–95; cf. Arnold, *Ephesians*, 7–13; Bruce, *Ephesians*, 236.

into one body where each needs the other not only in the cosmos but in history. The author of Ephesians therefore offers a sustained apologetic for the necessity of the church as a historical entity in which the Gentiles in particular have their place as part of redeemed creation with links connecting them to Israel.[11]

Käsemann also sees the ecclesiology of Ephesians as typical of an institutionalised Christianity which had subordinated christology to a 'high' view of the church.[12] In this way, he is able to acknowledge an important development of Pauline theology in the ecclesiology of Ephesians, and relegates Ephesians to a post-Pauline era when a degenerated form of the apostle's theology set in.

It must be said that Käsemann's assertion, presumably driven along by the force of his internal dialogue (i.e. between his reading of Ephesians and himself), despite its increasing detachment from the author's own emphases, is made with no exegetical backing. His thesis that at the time when Ephesians was written the 'concrete situation' was that 'the Gentile Christians were pushing the Jewish Christians aside' is difficult to prove.[13] The reasons why the *continuity* of the people of God (Israel) was thwarted and therefore needed to be energetically stressed must be sought elsewhere.

[11] Käsemann, 'Epheserbrief', 518; cf. Käsemann, 'Ephesians', 291; Käsemann, *Perspectives*, ch. 5, esp. 109–10.

[12] For the development of the Pauline movement in terms of 'ongoing process of institutionalisation in the early church', see esp. MacDonald, *Pauline Churches* (1988). MacDonald contends that the stage of development evident in Ephesians is 'community-stabilizing institutionalization', reflecting notably the 'social situation in the Pauline sect after the disappearance of the Apostle' in which the issue concerning the means through which Gentiles enter the body of those being saved, characteristic of those early community-building days, had been resolved (89, 155). MacDonald's thesis is based on the assumption that the unity of Gentiles and Jews is a *fait accompli*: the concern was then to harmonise in the predominantly Gentile church relations between Gentile Christians and the Jewish Christian minority (95, 155). The obvious merit of MacDonald's study is that the 'body' language is transposed into a sociological terminology which enables her to claim that the transformation of 'the symbol of the body' may be related to a need to underline the authority of Christ and of the 'authority structures' in order to stabilise community life (156). The second half of MacDonald's statement, however, is ill judged. To be sure, MacDonald's thesis lacked a convincing survey of the Jewish perspective against which the 'body' symbol was brought to view. The same failure is also reflected in her treatment of the motif of heavenly enthronement: is MacDonald correct in suggesting that the motif is introduced to deal with 'an awareness of the delay of the parousia' (149–53, esp. 153)? MacDonald's reconstruction of the social reality underlying Ephesians and of the realised aspect of eschatology leaves us wondering whether the 'social situation' of the communities can be fully appreciated without giving Jewish attitudes toward the Gentiles their due weight.

[13] Käsemann, *Perspectives*, 110.

P. Sampley also contends that Gentile Christianity was threatening to lose its connection with Jewish Christianity.[14] He concludes that the use of the OT in the letter reflects the author's intention to reply to Gentile Christians who were in danger of divorcing themselves from their Jewish Christian heritage.[15] R. Martin argues that in a church predominantly made up of Gentile Christians the danger presented a new face: it was not that Gentile believers would succumb to Judaising practices (such as circumcision). Rather, the threat was that Gentile Christians would want to cast off all association with the Old Testament faith and disown their origins in Israel's salvation history. Thus, the Gentiles need a salutary reminder that 'salvation is of the Jews' and that Paul's 'salvation history' theology never displaced the significance of Israel as the people of God who have now come to full realisation in the 'one body' of a world-wide church in the author's day. For Martin, 'the separation of Christianity and Judaism is recognised; Jewish Christianity has passed into history as a once-posed threat to the audience of Ephesians';[16] and the 'recall' to that continuity is the main theme in Ephesians 2.11–22.[17] D. Smith, like Martin, finds in Ephesians a Gentile Christianity which was threatening to lose its connection with Jewish Christianity, but he argues that the author refers to certain 'Gentile-Jewish-Christians' who displayed contempt toward natural Jews who have become Christians.[18] These Christians were syncretistic in disposition, representing 'a fascinating synthesis of esoteric elements drawn from Judaism, Christianity and Hellenistic religion in general'.[19]

It may fairly be claimed that Käsemann and others depend too heavily upon the theory pioneered by Baur, who contends that the history of 'primitive' Christianity, like all human history, was determined by the interplay of human conflict and actually took place within the nexus of such an interplay.[20] It has become quite obvious that the 'conflict' theory outlined above has exerted enormous influence on subsequent studies and spawned multiple permutations and hybrids. Nevertheless, the common deficiency of the studies outlined above is its failure to move beyond speculation about the negative attitude of Gentile Christians toward Jewish Christianity. Baur, Käsemann and others who followed in their footsteps have ignored the presence of obvious Jewish features which provide clues concerning the Jewish attitudes toward the Gentiles, let alone the author's representation of these attitudes.

[14] Sampley, *One Flesh*, 160. [15] Ibid., esp. 158–63.
[16] Martin, *Reconciliation*, 160. [17] Ibid. [18] Smith, 'Heresy'.
[19] Ibid., 103. [20] See Kümmel, *History*, 127–46, esp. 129–32.

1.2.2 The equalising of the Gentiles with the Jews?

Moving in a rather different direction from the theses outlined above, E. Percy has proposed a different kind of crisis which gave rise to the writing of Ephesians.[21] Like Käsemann, Percy also insists that Ephesians 2.11–22 is the centre of the epistle, but he argues (*contra* Käsemann) that the passage in Ephesians 2.11–22 is primarily a proclamation of Gentiles who participate in the promise of salvation in the same way as the Jews ('daß die Heiden in gleicher Weise wie die Juden am Heil teilnehmen').[22] The prerequisite of the equal partnership is based on the Christ-event described in vv. 14–15. Percy, who wrote in a pre-Sanders era, contends that the Law as the means of salvation is the sole obstacle which separated Jews from the Gentiles. Once this stumbling block is removed, their equal share in salvation will be gained.[23] Yet Percy has given no real attention to the ethnic factor by which one may account for Jewish attitudes toward the Gentiles. More importantly, the connections between ethnocentrism and the need to stress the motif of equal partnership between Jew and Gentile are not adequately dealt with in Percy's monograph.

1.2.3 Israel, Gentiles and the Church: continuity or discontinuity?

A new stage in the discussion of Ephesians is marked by the well-known hypothesis of M. Barth, who contends that the theme in Ephesians 2 (especially vv. 11–22) is the 'naturalisation of the Gentiles'. He has argued in a very straightforward manner in a number of publications that there is only one people of God, Israel, of which Gentile Christians are members.[24] He however maintained that the statement in Ephesians 2.12 describes 'a status of strangership' rather than 'an event leading to estrangement'. The expression 'strangers and sojourners' (v. 19) is the authentic interpretation of Gentiles being 'excluded' from Israel. These terms prove that the Gentiles had not been 'naturalised'; the author does not intend to say that at an earlier moment they were 'expatriated'. Never before have the Gentiles been fellow-citizens and members of Israel.[25] The naturalisation and adoption of Gentiles, according to Barth,

[21] Percy, *Probleme*.

[22] Ibid., 278–86, esp. 279; Percy, 'Probleme', esp. 187–8, here 187. See also Mouton, 'Communicative Power', 291.

[23] Percy, *Probleme*, 280.

[24] Barth, *Wall*, 122, 128; cf. Barth, 'Conversion'; Barth, *People*, esp. 29–49; Barth, 'Traditions'; Barth, *Ephesians 1–3*, esp. 253–62.

[25] Barth, *People*, 45–6; Barth, *Ephesians 1–3*, 257.

presupposes the destruction of the wall, built up by an interpretation of the law 'in statutory ordinances', which separates the people of God from the nations.[26]

Barth's approach is different from those studies mentioned in the foregoing section and begins to take the Jew–Gentile problem seriously. His basic concern is the identity of Israel as the one people of God, and the identity of Christianity which is to be defined in that light. However, the one significant issue that Barth has failed to clarify in his study of Ephesians is whether Israel could become so entangled with a particular ethnic identity that one can only speak of the 'naturalisation of the Gentiles' as tantamount to turning them into proselytes or an ethnically based Judaism. Suffice it to say that Barth has given no real attention to the ethnic factors that had led to Gentiles being 'excluded' from the Israel of God.

Barth's 'laology', however, has come under severe attack in studies which opt for the theories of substitution in which Israel is replaced by the church. The church, according to some scholars, is the 'true Israel'.[27] M. Rese, for example, has raised the issue of Israel and the 'relationship of church and Israel' in his essay entitled 'Die Vorzüge Israels in Röm 9,4f. und Eph 2,12: Exegetische Anmerkungen zum Thema Kirche und Israel' (1975).[28] He advances his study with the assumption that the views of 'Israel' in Romans 9.4f. and Ephesians 2.12 are very different and that the writers of these letters have opposite views about the relationship between the church and Israel: 'While the advantages of Israel are spoken of directly in Rom. 9.4f., they are in view only indirectly in *Eph. 2.12* and then in such a way that the Gentile Christians are reminded of their relationship to Israel in their pre-Christian heathen past.'[29] Rese then argues that the dark description of the Gentile Christians' past is nothing else than the dark background against which the bright present stands out all the more. In this bright salutary present there is no room for any thought about the unbelieving Israel. Something like the unbelieving and hardened Israel, whose existence and fate bothered and moved Paul in Romans

[26] Barth, *People*, 46.

[27] E.g., Stuhlmacher, 'Peace'; Beck, *Mature Christianity*, 82, contends the anti-Jewish polemic that is present in Ephesians is 'not in virulent anti-Jewish statements but in the claim, characteristic of the formative and normative writings of most militant religions, that the new religious community successfully and gloriously supersedes its antecedents' (82).

[28] Rese, 'Vorzüge', esp. 219–22; cf. Rese, 'Church', esp. 23–9.

[29] 'Während in Röm. 9,4f. direkt von den Vorzügen Israels gesprochen wird, geraten sie in *Eph.2,12* nur indirekt in den Blick, und zwar so, daß die Heidenchristen an ihr Verhältnis zu Israel in ihrer vorchristlichen heidnischen Vergangenheit erinnert werden.' (Italics his, Rese, 'Vorzüge', 219; Rese, 'Church', 26.)

9–11, does not exist for the author of Ephesians. He concludes that Israel has found her genuine prolongation exclusively in the church of Jewish and Gentile Christians: 'The peculiarity of Israel is thereby transferred to the Church of Jesus Christ and therefore only mentioned indirectly. After Christ the Church and Israel are one and the same thing; the unbelieving Israel is outside the horizon of the Church, is simply unimportant.'[30] For Rese, the differences between Romans and Ephesians go beyond anything that might be explained simply as a result of differences between times and audiences addressed in these letters.[31]

Rese's thesis so much hinges on his interpretation of the tiny phrase in Ephesians 2.12 (ὅτι ἦτε τῷ καιρῷ ἐκείνῳ χωρὶς Χριστοῦ) that Christ is understood as 'not yet in his flesh' ('der Zeit vor Christus').[32] It is at this point that it becomes clear that Rese's thesis is inadequate as an explanation of the 'opposite views about the relationship between the church and Israel' in Romans and Ephesians. It is less than clear that the author's concern is the 'salvation-historical difference between Jews and Gentiles that was in force in the time before Christ'.[33] It is also far from true that the alleged 'opposite views' necessarily reflect the different viewpoints of the writers of the two letters (according to Rese, Paul and his pupil). Rese has taken Ephesians 2.12 out of its original context (esp. v. 11!) and more importantly he has failed to ask whether the statements about the Gentiles in Ephesians 2.12 consist of 'echoic utterances' or the perception of *other* Jews about the Gentiles. What we miss in Rese's work, therefore, is a careful analysis of the Jewish perspective (or Judaism), on which our explanation of 'Israel's privileges which make up the past deficiencies of the Gentiles' (and the 'differences' between Romans and Ephesians) ought to be based.

[30] 'Die Besonderheit Israels geht damit auf die Kirche Jesu Christi über und kommt deshalb auch nur indirekt zur Sprache. Nach Christus sind Kirche und Israel ein und dasselbe; das ungläubige Israel aber ist außerhalb des Gesichtskreises der Kirche, ist schlicht uninteressant' (Rese, 'Vorzüge', 222).

[31] Ibid., 219.

[32] Ibid., 219, 222. Rese is not alone in this view: see, e.g., Lincoln, 'Church', 610, who argues that the advantages of Israel 'pertain only to the time prior to Christ'; Mußner, *Tractate*, 25; Bruce, *Ephesians*, 293–4; Roloff, *Kirche*, 240–1, et al.

[33] Rese, 'Vorzüge', 220–1; cf. Rese, 'Church', 28. The emphasis on the 'salvation-historical difference between Jews and Gentiles' derives from Schlier's influence on Rese, see Schlier, *Epheser*, 120. Rese has failed to see that in Eph. 2.11–12, ποτέ and τῷ καιρῷ ἐκείνῳ χωρὶς Χριστοῦ are interchangeable, denoting the 'time' before the conversion of Gentiles. As far as we can tell, the adverb χωρίς is never used to designate the 'pre-incarnate' state of a person: see, e.g., Gen. 46.26; Num. 16.49; Judg. 20.15, 17; 1 Kgs 5.16; 1 Esd. 4.17; 5.4; Judith 7.2; 5.8; *Arist.* 123. See further LSJ, s.v.; BAGD, s.v. See my discussion of Eph. 2.12 in chapter 3, section 3.3.1.2 below.

A major challenge to Barth's notion of 'laology' is that of A. Lincoln. Writing on the church and Israel in Ephesians,[34] Lincoln has rightly observed that the pericope in Ephesians 2.11–22 stands parallel to 2.1–10. This is confirmed by a formal analysis of the contrast schema of 'then' and 'now' which provides a major structural element for the pericopes of 2.1–10 and 2.11–22, respectively, and shapes also the key summarising verse later (v. 19).[35] He argues that the primary purpose of the 'then–now' schema (and therefore of the pericope of vv. 11–22) is not a general depiction of the relationship between Gentiles and Jews, nor is it primarily an answer to the question, 'How can Jews and Christians (*sc.* Gentiles) be the eschatological people of God?' (*contra* Merklein),[36] nor is it even a discussion of the place of the Gentiles in the history of salvation. Instead, Ephesians 2 involves *a comparison* between these particular Gentile readers' pre-Christian past in its relation to Israel's privileges, and their Christian present in the church, on which attention is focused at the end of the chapter in vv. 19–22. The mention of Israel, then, only functions as part of this comparison and serves the purpose of bringing home to the readers the greatness of their salvation.[37] The irony in Lincoln's proposal, however, is that the more he speaks about the deprived status

[34] Lincoln, 'Church'; cf. Lincoln, *Ephesians*, xliii–xciii; Lincoln, 'Theology', 158–61. Lincoln also argues that Ephesians simply does not contain references to a specific setting or problems, and therefore other external data cannot be brought to bear in the same way as with other letters to build up a more detailed picture of the particular situation being addressed. The lack of specificity in Ephesians has prompted Lincoln to suggest an investigation of the communicative function of the letter through the letter's 'rhetorical situation', which, according to Lincoln, may help to avoid some of the pressures and frustrations imposed by the demand to discover immediately a specific historical life-setting: 'The rhetorical situation can be defined in terms of the rhetorical occasion to which the text is understood as a fitting response, and in terms of the rhetorical problem or problems that the author has to overcome in order to win the recipients over to his or her point of view. Investigation of the rhetorical situation will not ignore the historical life-setting but directs attention first and foremost to what can be inferred both from the picture of the implied writer and recipients that emerge from a text and from the text's rhetorical genre and strategies' (lxxiv). Lincoln therefore concludes that '[t]he general aspects of the purposes of the letter which emerged from the analysis of its rhetorical situation indicate why Ephesians so easily transcends its original setting and has had such a broad and universal appeal' (lxxxi, lxxiv–lxxix), cf. Lincoln, 'Theology', 79–83.

[35] Lincoln, 'Church', 608. Lincoln's 'schema' depends heavily on the work of Tachau, see his *Ephesians*, 84–8.

[36] Lincoln, 'Church', 608, has misquoted Merklein's thesis: 'Wie können Juden *und* Heiden eschatologisches Gottesvolk sein?' (*Christus*, 28, 71, 76), but see his *Ephesians*, 132.

[37] Lincoln, 'Church', 609; Lincoln, 'Theology', 159. Lincoln's theory is very close to that of Dahl, 'Gentiles', 38, who writes: 'Ephesians simply reminds Christian Gentiles of their former status as excluded aliens in order to demonstrate the magnitude of the blessings which God in his mercy has extended to them.' Like Rese and Mußner, Lincoln reads the adverbial phrase 'apart from Christ' (χωρὶς Χριστοῦ) predicatively as the first of the Gentile

of the Gentiles against the backdrop of Israel's privileges,[38] the more distant/estranged the Gentiles and Israel have become. Lincoln also overstates the discontinuity of Israel and the church.[39] His proposal gives very little attention to the question of whether the author's statements about the Gentiles' past also tell us as much about the Jews as about the Gentiles. He has failed to ask whether the author of Ephesians also reveals the Jewish attitudes toward the Gentiles by means of the 'then–now' schema, i.e. the mindset that is not necessarily that of the author himself, but which forms the basis of his argument, let alone some of the pertinent issues which are concealed in these attitudes.[40] These issues, significant as they must be for our understanding of the purpose of Ephesians 2, are not adequately dealt with in Lincoln's work. What appears to be most important for Lincoln is that the author of Ephesians has underlined the *discontinuity* in the relationship of Israel and the church.[41]

Roman Catholic scholarship, on the other hand, continues to take the view that the author of Ephesians advocates a 'remnant theory', the basic tenet of which is that a partial continuity between the old and new peoples of God is maintained through Jews who believe in Christ. R. Schnackenburg, while devoting much space to the 'relationship of Israel and the church' in his writing on the subject,[42] does not, however, make full use of the evidence which throws light on the Jewish attitude toward the Gentiles.

Moving in a different direction from that of Schnackenburg, H. Merklein[43] raises an important question in his study of Ephesians 2.11–18, namely that the passage is meant to be an answer to the question 'How can Jews and Gentiles be the eschatological people of God?'[44] He argues that the Church, the 'eschatological Israel' which has become the realm of

Christians' former disadvantages (*Ephesians*, 136). He concludes on the basis of this reading that 'whereas in Rom. 9–11 the advantages of Israel still play a role in the time after Christ, in Ephesians, in contrast . . . they pertain only to the time *prior to* Christ' (Lincoln, 'Church', 610, italics mine; see also 616).

[38] Lincoln, 'Church', 616–17; Lincoln, *Ephesians*, lxxvi.

[39] Lincoln, *Ephesians*, xciii.

[40] See also Best, *Ephesians*², 268, who concludes: 'AE [*sc.* the author of Ephesians] must have known there were unbelieving Jews yet says nothing about them' (268).

[41] Lincoln, 'Theology', writes: 'What appears to be most important for the writer is to underline the discontinuity in the relationship [*sc.* to Israel]' (107, 133–4); cf. Lincoln, 'Church', 608, 615.

[42] Schnackenburg, 'Politeia'; cf. Schnackenburg, 'Bau'; Schnackenburg, 'Exegese'; Schnackenburg, *Ephesians*, 321–5.

[43] Merklein, *Christus*, esp. 16–61, 99–102, 63–5 (on vv. 1–10); cf. Merklein, 'Komposition'; Merklein, *Amt*, 118, 128; Merklein, 'Rezeption'.

[44] Merklein, *Christus*, 28, 71.

salvation, is the answer to the question.[45] Such expressions as 'in Christ' and 'far from Christ' are all ecclesiological formulae,[46] and the train of thought of Ephesians 2 is utterly unequivocal if one comprehends it under and from the author's concept of the Church or ecclesiological perspective.[47] It is also from this perspective that the antithesis between Jew and Gentile, the relevance (or irrelevance) of such categories as the Jewish Law and Israel's other privileges, all become discernible.[48] As regards the connections between Israel and the Church, Merklein contends that 'Israel' denotes the 'Congregation of Israel' *in the OT sense* and at the same time the Church as the 'eschatological people of God', but insists that there is no constructive connection between the two entities.[49]

There is some justification for such an interpretative move, and Merklein's 'consistent ecclesiology' can provide a link between 'Israel' and the 'Church' as the people of God. There are, however, difficulties with Merklein's thesis as well. When asked, why must the author then discuss the Church in terms of Israel if there is no constructive connection at all between the two?, Merklein concludes that 'to a post-Pauline Gentile Christianity the salvation-historical provenance of the Church from Israel must be put before its eyes'.[50] It is at this point that it becomes clear that Merklein's thesis is inadequate. For Merklein, 'Israel', alongside other distinctive features of Judaism (such as the Jewish Law, Jewish circumcision, etc.), functions solely as a foil for the author's positive theology of the Church.[51] The result of Merklein's study has left us wondering whether he has dressed up the Church as a separate entity from Israel. For us the salient question is, does the author of Ephesians, as Merklein would like to think, attest a form of triumphalist ecclesiology in which the Church now 'sits upon' Israel, making Judaism obsolete? The more fundamental issues such as, why didn't (or couldn't) Jew and Gentile become the one people of God?, are left unexplored in the work of Merklein.

1.2.4 The alienation between Jews and Christians?

K. Fischer (1973) has offered an alternative reading to that of the theory of substitution. He embeds Ephesians in a very concrete historical situation: the apparent issues of the post-apostolic period being the alienation between Jews and Christians.[52] Of special interest to us is his

[45] Ibid., 23. Merklein, 'Rezeption', claims that in Ephesians soteriology has become a function of ecclesiology (48, 62). He also claims that Ephesians 'does not write ecclesiology next to Christology, but rather an ecclesiological Christology' ('Rezeption', 62).

[46] Merklein, *Christus*, 21. [47] Ibid., 99. [48] Ibid., 23, 74; cf. Merklein, *Amt*, 128.

[49] Merklein, *Christus*, 21, 72–6, esp. 74. Merklein's definition of Israel has come under severe attack in Schnackenburg, 'Exegese', 471.

[50] Merklein, *Christus*, 76. [51] Ibid., 76–8. [52] Fischer, *Tendenz*, 79–94.

argument that the solidarity of Jewish and Gentile Christians after Paul is broken down. A ramification of this is that it is no longer possible for Jewish Christians to confess Christ and simultaneously to continue living as Jews.[53] Ephesians was therefore written to address this crisis against the background of an increasingly sharp anti-Judaism among Gentile Christians who were in danger of repudiating the Jewish tradition, advocating the equality of the Jewish Christian inheritance within the predominantly Gentile community. Fischer's thesis is clear, namely that Israel is the people of God and has its covenant promises. The Gentiles had nothing. The church is not the continuation of Israel, a boundless Judaism, but the heir of Israel, of her promise and the covenants. The history of Israel is therefore also the history of the church.[54] As regards the motif of continuity and discontinuity between Israel and church, Fischer contends that the church is in continuity with Israel's promise but in discontinuity with it in terms of realisation. Repudiating the idea of the church as a 'third race', Fischer maintains that there is not one people comprising both old and new, but old and new covenant partners. Any contempt for the old covenant partners will then be a disdain of the love of God toward Israel.[55]

The bedrock of Fischer's thesis is the assumption of the success in Gentile mission in the earliest church. Fischer (among many others) may be accused of concocting conflict between Jew and Christian which is not the concern of Ephesians. It is true that the emphasis on the oneness of the church may well suggest that there was tension between Jew and Gentile. However, it is less than clear that the alleged tension is necessarily the outcome of an increasing anti-Judaism disposition among Christian Gentiles. Fischer has paid no real attention to the Jewish features in Ephesians or attempted to read these features against the backcloth of the Jewish perspective on Gentiles, and, most importantly, he has failed to ask whether the author of Ephesians intended to expose the Gentiles to the exclusivistic Jewish attitudes toward them echoed in Ephesians 2.11f.

Fischer is not alone in latching on to a supposed crisis in which unity between Jewish and Gentile Christians in the church is threatened. His theory of 'a concrete crisis' is hailed by C. Roetzel, who goes so far as to suggest that the author of Ephesians uses Paul's name to argue for the inclusion of Jewish Christians in the community dominated by a Gentile majority without assimilation to the views of the latter: '[w]hile Paul had argued for the inclusion of Gentiles *qua* Gentiles, the author of Ephesians argues for the inclusion of Jewish Christians *qua* Jewish Christians'.[56]

53 Ibid., 210, also 93. 54 Ibid., 80. 55 Ibid., 81.
56 Roetzel, *Conversations*, 142–3.

Roetzel concludes that the weakness of the form of spirituality advocated by the author is evident, for the unity he envisaged in transcending the 'Law of the commandments' would necessarily lead to the assimilation of the Jewish Christians to the ways of Gentile Christianity.[57]

Like Fischer, Roetzel does not present us with yet another novel view of the 'relationship' between Gentile and Jewish Christians. His thesis that 'the author of Ephesians writes to urge the Gentile Christian majority to accept a Jewish Christian minority and to retain its ties with the ancient Hebrew tradition' is based solely on his conjecture of the 'climate of vehement ill will' that affects that relationship.[58] The issue before us is whether this 'climate' best explains the evidence. It is also less than clear that that relationship can be confidently hypothesised on the amount of information given in the letter itself, or that the Gentile attitude has become the focus of attention to any degree. The many Jewish features which allow us to understand the theme of 'attitude' from a perspective different from Roetzel's are ignored and underplayed (e.g., 2.11–12; 4.17–19).

In his more recent study of the relationship between Jews and Gentiles in the church, J. T. Sanders also opted for the view that Jews and Gentiles were the 'two denominations' which were not united in the church and that 'the author regards the implication of Christ's death to be that there should be unity in the church'.[59] Nevertheless, it is less than clear that Ephesians is meant to be an argument for corporate unity between Jews and Gentiles in the church.[60]

1.2.5 Ethno-cultural conflict between Jews and Greeks?

E. Faust also envisages a specific situation in Asia Minor in his monograph *Pax Christi et Pax Caesaris* (1993). He advances his study of Ephesians with two basic assumptions: (1) Ephesians 2.11–22 is meant to be understood against the background of a lively ethno-cultural conflict between Jew and *Greek* in Asia Minor, and (2) the issue in Ephesians 2.14–16 (also 1.20–3; 2.19b; 4.15f.) is meant to be examined against the backdrop of the ideology of the dominion of the Roman imperialism which serves as an antithetical parallel to *pax Christi*.[61] Faust starts

[57] Roetzel, 'Relations', 88. [58] Roetzel, *Conversations*, 141–2.

[59] Sanders, *Schismatics*, 200–1.

[60] Roetzel, 'Relations', 88; Sanders, *Schismatics*, 200; Mitton, *Ephesians*, 101.

[61] Faust has provided an impressive reconstruction of the relationship between Jew and Greek from the period of the early emperors to Titus, who reacted against Jewish nationalism which endangered the stability of the Roman empire (*Pax*, 226–79, 325–59).

out from these assumptions by arguing that the passage in Ephesians 2.11–12 refers to the separation of the former Gentiles from the Jews and their God: the Gentiles were regarded from the point of view of the Jewish *politeia* as ethno-cultural aliens in the antique political sense, whereby socio-political and cultic foreignness were coordinated.[62] He also argues that Ephesians 2.13 portrays a 'Jewish theology of conversion' ('judische Konversionstheologie').[63] More importantly, an *imperial ideology* is expressed in Ephesians 2.14–18: namely, the peace-making work of Christ betrays a structural analogy to that of the (Roman) emperor who is the leader/head and the soul of the state and who inspires the right ethical attitude of peace on the part of his subjects (= the emperor's body).[64] The *finis ultimus* of the author's argument is to portray Christ as an alternative model (i.e., *pax Christi*) to the integration of Jews in *pax Romana*, i.e., the 'intercultural unity of the overall empire'.[65]

The following criticism, however, can be levelled against Faust's ingenious reconstruction of the ethno-cultural conflict of the time. First, had the author intended to lay stress upon 'a lively ethno-cultural conflict between Jew and *Greek* in Asia Minor' (italics mine), we would expect him to indicate these ethnic groups in more explicit terms (cf. e.g., 1 Cor. 12.13; Gal. 3.28).[66] Although Faust is aware of the fact that the Gentiles were perceived from a Jewish viewpoint (v. 12), he has made no obvious attempt to read Ephesians 2.11–13 consistently against the backdrop of the *Jewish* attitude toward non-Jews in general (*not* 'Greek', but 'the nations', cf. 2.11; 4.17–19), let alone against the theology/ideology which is concealed in this attitude. Since there is no hint in Ephesians of the response of the 'Greek' (to use Faust's word), it is difficult to tell whether the theory of ethno-cultural conflict mentioned above could throw any positive light on Ephesians. Second and more importantly, Faust, who argues along socio-political lines for the positive correlation between *pax Christi* and *pax Caesaris*, has considerably romanticised the nature of *pax Caesaris* which is marked by seduction, coercion, bloodshed and brutality and which fails categorically to assess properly the means by which Christ (or the Roman emperor) concluded peace.[67] Faust's tendentious

[62] Ibid., 104, 111, 179. [63] Ibid., 111.

[64] Ibid., 164–81, 280–314, 315–24, esp. 321. Faust contends that the Christ-hymn in Eph. 2.14ff. can be paralleled in the Hellenistic encomium of the emperor (e.g., Philo, *Legat. Gaium*, 143–7).

[65] Faust, *Pax*, 372.

[66] For a more accurate analysis of the conflict between Jew and Greek, see esp. Stanley, 'Conflict'.

[67] See, e.g., Tacitus, *Ann.* 1.2.1. For a more helpful assessment of *pax Romana*, see esp. Wengst, *Pax*.

thesis ignores the challenge of such passages as Ephesians 2.13 and 2.15 which seem to present an insurmountable obstacle to his 'imperial ideology'.

1.2.6 The form-critical analysis of Ephesians 2.1–22

There is an influential school of thought which suggests that the interest of the author of Ephesians is not concerned with the historical development of the church. P. Tachau, a pupil of E. Lohse, has argued in his monograph *'Einst' und 'Jetzt' im Neuen Testament* (1972) that a schema whose content is a contrast between the pre-Christian past and the Christian present is usually (but not always) signalled by the use of ποτέ and νῦν.[68] He concludes that the schema which occurs in the NT has no clear antecedent in the OT or intertestamental Judaism[69] and that the original life-setting for it is to be sought in the context of early Christian preaching which may have been in connection with baptism or recent conversion. He concedes that these original connections are no longer accessible because the schema is found in a variety of different contexts in the NT.[70]

There can be little doubt that Tachau has put NT scholarship considerably in his debt by his study of the 'then–now' schema. His thesis has also influenced subsequent studies of Ephesians.[71] Of special interest to us is Tachau's analysis of the usage of the schema in our epistle (2.1–4, 11–13; and 5.8).[72] He concludes that (a) Ephesians 2.1–10 must be seen as an *incomplete* argument by itself, since the νῦν aspect of the schema

[68] Tachau, *Einst*, 52–8, 80, 133. However, Tachau also claims that the presence of the adverbs 'then' and 'now' is not constitutive of the schema, but merely characteristic (*Einst*, 51, 69, 86 and 96). The 'then–now' schema can exist without these adverbs. Is Tachau correct in ignoring the fact that the OT authors who *do not use these two adverbs* could also have such schema in mind? But Tachau, who searched the prehistory of the adverbs through the Hebrew concordance or its equivalents in the Greek, proved otherwise (21, 58)! See n. 81, below.

[69] Tachau, *Einst*, 21–70. The exception, according to Tachau, is *Joseph & Aseneth* 55.13ff. (*loc. cit.*, 52–8). He discovered the 'then–now' schema in Batiffol's edition of the text. The 'then–now' schema is omitted in the Philonenko edition of the book. Nevertheless, Tachau seems to assume in the instance of *Joseph & Aseneth* that the two adverbs are *constitutive* of the schema!

[70] Tachau, *Einst*, 129–34, esp. 130. We may note, however, that Greek writers had already employed the 'then–now' schema to attach positive valence to the 'present' age: see, e.g., Hesiod, *Theogony*; Strabo, *Geog.*; Epictetus, *Diatr.* 4.4.7. On the significance of the structural properties of ancient Greek ethnographies to the contact with and control of 'barbarian' peoples, particularly the 'then–now' temporal structure in Strabo, see esp. Clavel-Lévêque, 'Strabon'. For Strabo, the 'past' of the non-Greeks was 'barbaric'.

[71] See, e.g., Lindemann, *Epheserbrief*, 42–3; Conzelmann, *Polemics*, 46; Borgen, 'Synagogue', esp. 57–8; Lincoln, *Ephesians*, 86–8, et al.

[72] Tachau, *Einst*, 134–43.

is absent.[73] However, Ephesians 2.11f. begins with Gentiles being characterized from a *Jewish* standpoint and should be seen as 'a *new* train of thought as this particular form of speech is *not* found in 2.1–10' (italics mine). (b) The 'then–now' schema serves to bring to view *only* the past of the Gentiles and their new Christian existence, highlighting salvation as a present reality effected by God through the Christ-event; and (c) the 'then–now' schema relates only to the contrast of contents but not to the contrast of the two 'periodisations' of history.[74] In short, Ephesians 2.11–22 is not about a historical development from 'then' to 'now', but the mention of the past serves simply to qualify the present.

The following observations, however, tell fairly decisively against Tachau's proposal.

(1) Tachau rightly observes that a Jewish aspect is clearly present in vv. 11–12 in which the 'then-now' schema is overlapped by a Jew–Gentile theme.[75] But the difficulty for Tachau is that the 'non-Jewish past and Christian present are not themselves corresponding contrasts' ('nichtjüdische Vergangenheit und christliche Gegenwart sind keine sich entsprechenden Gegensätze').[76] It is at this point that it becomes clear that Tachau's thesis is inadequate. He is constrained by the parameters of his own thesis that the schema can only reflect a contrast of the pre-Christian past and the Christian present and that the schema serves only to make explicit the removal of Christians from their sphere of origin.[77] The issue for us is why the author writes what he does about the Gentiles in Jewish terms. Is Tachau correct in ignoring the fact that the author does not conceive of Christian Gentiles without a connection to Israel, as if they

73 Ibid., 138–9. This view, however, is modified by Lincoln, *Ephesians*, 87, who argues that the νῦν-aspect is implicit in vv. 4, 5 and that the 'real' contrast which deals with salvation is complete in v. 7.

74 Tachau, *Einst*, writes: 'Es ist ein Schema der sich kontrastierenden Inhalte, kein Schema des Kontrastes zweier Geschichtsepochen. So auch hier' (141–2). Tachau's theory is followed by Lincoln, who writes: 'What this use of the schema involves, then, is not a general contrast between Gentiles and Jews, but, more specifically, a contrast between the pre-Christian past in its relation to Israel's privileges and the Christian present of these particular Gentile addressees' (*Ephesians*, 125).

75 'Die Vergangenheit der Adressaten wird jetzt betont vom Standpunkt der Juden aus anvisiert (vom Verhaltnis Juden – Heiden war bisher noch nicht die Rede): Einst seid ihr keine Juden gewesen' (137).

76 Tachau, *Einst*, 141, who also writes: 'So liegt das eigentliche Thema der verse 11–22 nicht etwa in dem Gegenüber von Juden und Heiden, sondern in dem vom vorchristlichen und christlichen Zustand der Heiden. Dabei wird der vorchristliche Zustand z.T. von jüdischen Gesichtspunkten aus geschildert.'

77 But see the critique by Schnackenburg, who argues that the same schema also occurs in the letter's paraenesis ('Paraklese-Abschnitten') to describe 'the confrontation of the Gentiles with their pagan past, with which the Christians are surrounded on all sides' ('Exegese', 473–4).

(and their Christian 'present') can be separated entirely from the Jewish root? It seems clear that Tachau does not know quite what to make of the 'then–now' schema (or, at least the 'then' aspect of the schema), which can be used to fulfil other functions, such as the 'past' of the Gentiles perceived from the perspective of the Jews![78]

(2) The contention that Ephesians 2.11f. should be seen as 'a new train of thought as this particular form of speech is not found in 2.1–10' is wide of the mark.[79] Tachau does not follow through his insight of the 'non-Jewish past' of the Gentiles far enough or with sufficient consistency by failing to ask whether there the author *also* talked about the 'non-Jewish past' of the Gentiles from a Jewish perspective (esp. vv. 1–2). Is Tachau correct in ignoring a certain self-confident Jewish perspective which the author embedded in his argument within the 'then–now' schema?

(3) Tachau also underplayed the *significance* that 'echoic utterances' (to use Sperber's word) could have for the author and/or Gentiles: he failed to recognise that the expressions about the 'past' of the Gentiles communicate more than 'content' (and therefore do not necessarily represent immediate information about them).[80] What is curiously unexplored in his 'then–now' schema is that the author of Ephesians could have exposed the Gentile readers to an attitude, an opinion, a judgement, and emotion which follows from this.[81] Is Tachau correct in ignoring the *affective* power of these statements which the author embedded in the 'then–now' schema? The possibility of echoic utterances (or a 'straight reportage' – J. Barclay) by which the author, apart from his own perspective, alludes to the perspective of other Jews and, not least, their attitudes toward the Gentiles, remains unexplored in Tachau's work.[82]

[78] Cf. 5.8, at which the author continues to speak of the Gentiles from a Jewish perspective. Tachau is well aware of the dilemma that exists in his ποτέ-νῦν schema: 'Doch führt das den Verfasser alsbald vor logische Schwierigkeiten, da sich die Antithesen "einst keine Juden – jetzt in Christus" nicht entsprechen' (*Einst*, 137).

[79] Ibid., 135.

[80] By 'significance' I mean the relation of meaning between the sense of an utterance and the author's 'world' or some aspect of that world, see esp. Cotterell and Turner, *Linguistics*, 93.

[81] Tachau contends that the NT usage of the schema is far more than rhetorical and involves the important element of the contrast between pre-Christian past and Christian present (*Einst*, 94).

[82] Ibid., 142–3; Lincoln, *Ephesians*, 86–9, 91–9, 124–6, 134–9. Lincoln has also downplayed the ethnic dimension which is depicted in Eph. 2.11–22, esp. vv. 11–13. He contends that the ποτέ-νῦν schema serves as reminder to the Gentiles of the privileges they *now* enjoy in Christ (125–6); Lindemann, *Epheserbrief*, 42–3; Conzelmann, *Polemics*, 46. For a helpful discussion of 'echoic utterances' in modern linguistics, see esp. Sperber and Wilson, *Relevance*, here 237–43.

In nuce, the function of Tachau's 'then–now' schema needs to be tempered to some degree if it is to avoid becoming a too constrictive scheme which confines its use only to the 'twofold contrast between believers' past, unredeemed situation and their present privileged experience of salvation'.[83]

1.2.7 The cancellation of time in Ephesians?

Among the commentaries and monographs which advocate the discontinuity between the church and Israel, A. Lindemann's *Aufhebung der Zeit* (1975) stands at one extreme.[84] His is a study of the notion of history and eschatology in Ephesians in which he goes so far as to suggest that Ephesians is not concerned with any particular history or situation. He wishes to confirm the dehistoricisation of the thought of Ephesians especially with regard to its eschatology, which in his opinion almost completely eliminates the future dimension.[85] Time and history are cancelled 'in Christ'.[86] The 'present' of Christian existence in the church is what the author of Ephesians is really interested in, and he conceives of this in a time-less fashion. Of special interest to us is Lindemann's thesis that a historical cause is not outlined in Ephesians 2 (esp. vv. 11–22).[87] Lindemann argues that Ephesians employed mythical materials to establish 'Christianity',[88] and that the theological argument in Ephesians 2 is developed with the aid of a Gnostic *Vorlage* (esp. vv. 14–16) which describes the restoration of the unity between the divine and the human realms/spheres as the foundation of cosmic reconciliation.

The extreme thesis of Lindemann is truly to eliminate completely any possible interest in the continuity between the church and Israel.[89] When asked, why then does the author mention such categories as circumcision,

[83] The same criticism can be levelled against Lincoln, *Ephesians*, 86–8, who depends heavily upon Tachau's theory. It is beyond the scope of the present study to assess other NT passages which are alleged to have exhibited a 'then–now' schema. We may note, however, that the wider usage of the schema can be found in some NT passages: see, e.g., Gal. 4.8, in which Paul describes the 'past' of the Gentiles from a *Jewish* perspective: 'Formerly, when you *did not know God*, you were in bondage to beings that by nature are not gods; but *now* that you have come to know God, or rather to be known by God, how can you turn back again to the weak and beggarly elemental spirits, whose slaves you want to be once more?' (NRSV). The same Jewish perspective is also found in Eph. 4.17–19.

[84] Lindemann, *Aufhebung*, esp. 106–92; Lindemann, 'Bemerkungen', here 246–9; Lindemann, *Epheserbrief*, here 34–56.

[85] Lindemann, *Aufhebung*, 191–2, 252; see also 146. [86] Ibid., 248. [87] Ibid., 248.

[88] Ibid., 172–3, where he opposes the view of Schlier (*Christus*, 23) that our epistle has interpreted the mythical tradition historically.

[89] Lindemann, *Aufhebung*, 253.

Israel, the covenants of promise, hope and God?, Lindemann's answer is that these categories served only as a symbol for the 'sphere' of salvation in the early part of the author's passage (i.e., Eph. 2.11–12).[90]

Despite Lindemann's extreme attempt to dehistoricise the thought of Ephesians, his thesis must be read as a protest against those studies which set forth to explain the connections between the church and Israel in a straightforward manner (e.g., Barth) or to emphasise the salvation-historical precedence of Jew over Gentile on flimsy exegetical grounds (e.g., H. Chadwick, F. Mußner and others).[91] For Lindemann, 'Eph. [esp. 2.14–15] is not about the God–man relationship or about the issue of the relationship of Jews and Gentiles, but it is about the situation of Christians, about the effect of the act of Christ's salvation on the cosmos and on the *individuals*' (italics mine).[92] Lindemann's tendentious thesis (*sc*. a form of Gnosticism which lays stress upon individuals rather than person-in-community or 'dyadic personality'?) denies that the author had thought at all of the concrete groups within the church: accordingly, had the author had Jewish Christians in mind, he would not only have denied in his arguments each of their salvation-historical privileges but also seriously jeopardised before all else their present identity and their status within the church, for, according to Lindemann, in the author's massive argument on the elimination of the law, the actual nature of Jewish Christianity, its loyalty to the law, had been rejected as Christian-unfriendly (*christuswidrig*).[93]

But the thesis that the author has opted for, a 'timeless ontology of the church', is an overstatement. Lindemann has sidetracked into a peculiar theological slant and based his conclusions more on his ingenious theory than on an actual reading of the primary text. He neglects the challenge of various passages which suggest that the tension between 'already' and 'not yet' is clearly retained in Ephesians.[94]

[90] See further Lona, *Eschatologie*, 71–80, who rejects Lindemann's thesis outright; Schnelle, *History*, 313.

[91] Chadwick, 'Absicht'. See further Lindemann, *Aufhebung*, 145, 148–9, who criticises Mußner (*Christus*, 77).

[92] Lindemann, *Aufhebung*, 173; also 53.

[93] Lindemann, *Epheserbrief*, writes: 'So erweist es sich erneut als sehr fraglich, Eph. 2, 14–18 überhaupt im Zusammenhang des Themas "Juden und Heiden" (oder gar "Israel und Kirche") zu sehen' (52–3). He even questioned whether the 'both' language in vv. 14ff. can be answered with certainty: 'Möglicherweise ist die Frage, wen oder was der Verfasser mit den "Zwei", den "beiden", den "Fernen" und "Nahen" im einzelnen gemeint hat, *gar nicht beanwortbar*' (*Epheserbrief*, 53, italics mine).

[94] See, e.g., 1.13–14, cf. 4.30; 1.21; 2.21–2; 3.19; 4.13–16; 5.5; 6.8, 13, et al. For a helpful review of Lindemann's proposal, see esp. Lona, *Eschatologie*, 71–80; Schnelle, *History*, 312–13. See further Lincoln, *Paradise*, here 167; cf. Lincoln, *Ephesians*, lxxxix–xc; Lona, *Eschatologie*, 442–4.

It should also come as no surprise that Lindemann's theory has failed to give to the Jewish perspective its due weight, and more importantly, he has also misconstrued the letter of Ephesians as a deliberate retraction of the (*sc.* Jewish!) perspective of Romans 9–11.[95] There is no real attention given to the ethnographic categories which are evident in our author's statements about the Gentiles and which throw light upon our understanding of the Jews and their attitude to the Gentiles.[96]

1.2.8 *Weltangst* in Asia Minor

The suggestion that the tension between the 'now' and 'not yet' is muted in the eschatology of Ephesians has come under severe attack in recent years.[97] Of special interest to us is the dissertation by H. Lona on the subject of (ecclesiological) eschatology in Ephesians in his *Die Eschatologie im Kolosser- und Epheserbrief* (1984).[98] His aim is to discover the authorial intent concerning the unique accent of the eschatology of Ephesians. For this Lona has made a serious attempt to relate the eschatology of Ephesians to the situation facing the churches in western Asia Minor: despite the apparent unity Rome was bringing to the empire, individuals felt alienated. The cosmos had become unstable and became the embodiment of evil and full of demonic 'powers'. He therefore contends that the author of Ephesians is addressing this scenario of *Weltangst*, viz. a fear of the influence of malignant forces,[99] and that his eschatological statements are meant to strengthen Christians who encountered the mounting threats of their own environment.[100] The presence and future of salvation, however, are spoken of in connection with the reality of the church. Lona sees soteriology as a function of ecclesiology: the church represents the presence of salvation.[101]

Lona's description of alienation experienced among the ancients is very useful. Nevertheless, there is no real attention given to the connections between the alleged alienation and the Jewish attitude toward the Gentiles. He has made no attempt to associate the realised aspect of eschatology with the attitude mentioned above. To be sure, Lona does not deal with the connections between the transposition of the Gentiles (and Jews

95 Lindemann, *Aufhebung*, writes: 'Die Kirche steht nicht in geschichtlicher Kontinuität zu Israel, mit dem "Gottesvolk" des Alten Testament hat sie nichts zu tun . . . So wirkt der ganze Epheserbrief beinahe wie eine gezielte "Zurücknahme" von Röm 9–11' (253); cf. Lindemann, *Epheserbrief*, 43, 46.

96 Lindemann, *Aufhebung*, 106, 147–51.

97 Käsemann, 'Ephesians'; Lindemann, *Aufhebung*.

98 Lona, *Eschatologie*, 241–441, 442–8, esp. 256–67 (on. Eph. 2.11–13) and 360–74 (on Eph. 2.6f.).

99 Ibid., 425–6, 428–48. 100 Ibid., 442–4. 101 Ibid., 364, 442.

alike) into the heavenly realm – one of the most significant aspects of (realised) eschatology in Ephesians[102] – and the negative valence which was attached to the Gentiles who were deemed 'out of place' in the perception of the Jews. Neither has Lona adequately considered whether the author's language of the realised aspect of eschatology is indeed that of relocation, meaning by that that those (i.e., the Gentiles) who were reduced to the category of the false or 'out of place' have 'now' overcome their status of estrangement (vv. 1–2).

1.2.9 Linguistics and metalinguistics

In a number of publications N. Dahl has argued that Ephesians was written to give newly formed Gentile churches instructions on the meaning of their baptism.[103] Of special interest to us is his essay entitled 'Gentiles, Christians, and Israelites in the Epistle to the Ephesians' (1986),[104] in which Dahl observes that most early Christians perceived the world in which they lived as a world of Jews and Gentiles. He recognises that there are explicit statements about the Gentiles in Ephesians which represent an excessively negative attitude toward non-Christian Gentiles, the non-Jewish part of humanity. He argues that the picture of the Gentiles and their way of life draws upon Jewish and Christian stereotypes.[105] In addition to this, Dahl insists that Ephesians never speaks about Jews except in statements about Gentiles: 'Ephesians never uses the term "the Jews" but the "circumcision" to describe "Israelites".'[106] He then concludes that 'the designation the "so-called circumcision" carries disparaging connotations which are reinforced by the pejoratives "in the flesh" and "made with hands"'.[107]

Dahl's study of the statements about Gentiles or Israelites reflects the bare study of language outside the social relations in which it occurs. The weakness of this approach is made more apparent when the following question is posed: do we easily see Gentiles self-designate themselves as the 'uncircumcision' or designate the non-Jewish world as the 'nations' (cf. 4.17–19)? The question is really whether the designation 'the uncircumcision' tells us much about the ethnicity of the language

[102] Ibid., 245–56, esp. 246–50.

[103] Dahl, 'Adresse', here 263–4; cf. Dahl, 'Creation', esp. 436–7; Dahl, 'Gentiles', 38. The connection of Ephesians with baptism is also emphasised by Kirby who studies the relation between the writing and Christian rites which he argues were influenced by Jewish liturgical traditions, see his *Pentecost*, 144–6; Coutts, 'Ephesians 1.3–14,' here 125–7. Lincoln describes Ephesians as a liturgical homily for a baptismal occasion, see his *Paradise*, 135–6, but changed his mind later in his *Ephesians*, lxxix. For a helpful review of the various baptismal theories, see esp. Arnold, *Ephesians*, 135–6.

[104] Dahl, 'Gentiles,' 31–9. [105] Ibid., 32. [106] Ibid., 35. [107] Ibid., 35–6.

user.[108] Dahl has failed to acknowledge that the 'speech type' (genre) here is clearly that of an ethnographic description which indicates none other than a Jewish perspective and can only be understood against the backcloth of that perspective. This means that any attempt at a more complete study of the statements about the Gentiles would require us to address such questions as the 'utterance meaning' (who is speaking, and to whom?), and thus to describe, in addition to merely 'sentence meaning', the relation of the utterance to its social context, its speaker's 'plan' or 'speech will', and above all its 'location' in a dialogue.[109]

Although Dahl rightly observes that 'the author of Ephesians had a keen interest in the Jewish roots and origin of the church',[110] he fails to acknowledge that the early Christians who 'perceived the world in which they lived as a world of Jews and Gentiles' were Jews.[111] The inadequacy of Dahl's study (as of those who advocate the theory of substitution) is therefore that he has failed to recognise that the author's statements about the Gentiles also reveal Jewish attitudes to Gentiles. There is also no real attention given by Dahl to those statements which unequivocally underscore the perspective of Jews.

Like Dahl, E. Best contends that the author of Ephesians has made no attempt to associate Christian Gentiles and non-Christian Jews: 'AE [*sc.* the author of Ephesians] must have known there were unbelieving Jews yet says nothing about them.'[112] Accordingly, there are no statements about the ultimate fate of the Jews: 'since his main purpose is to build up the church and maintain its unity, he has no need to refer to the continuance of Israel'.[113] As far as Best could discern, Ephesians contains no sign of tension between Jews and Gentiles and it is unlikely that there were *actual* strains between these two groups. He, however, concedes that there is a discussion of the relation between Jewish and Gentile Christians. Like Käsemann, Best attributes this discussion to the fact that '[p]erhaps Gentile Christians were in danger of forgetting their Jewish inheritance and a suitable theology of their *relationship* to Jews needs to be given' (italics mine).[114]

108 Dahl, ibid., writes: 'In general, Ephesians yields very little information about the Israelites with whom the Gentile Christians have been united' (36). Dahl's theory is endorsed by Lincoln, *Ephesians*, lxxxiv.

109 See further Dentith, 'Language', esp. 33; Cotterell and Turner, *Linguistics*, ch. 2 (on Dimensions of the Meaning of a Discourse), esp. 93–5.

110 Dahl, 'Gentiles', 37.

111 See esp. Hartog, *Mirror*, passim; Hall, *Barbarian*, passim; Balsdon, *Aliens*, passim.

112 Best, *Ephesians*², 268.

113 Ibid., 268–9.

114 Best, 'Judaism' [= *Essays*, 87–101]; cf. Best, *Ephesians*¹, 92; Best, *Ephesians*², 267–9.

As far as we can tell, Best has underplayed the most apparent Jewish features in Ephesians 2 which contain some significant clue to the purpose of the letter. His 'Christian view of Judaism' is not only anachronistically unnecessary (i.e., 'Christian' as opposed to Jews (and Gentiles)), but also disregards the author's Jewish perspective about the Gentiles, let alone some ethnographic categories which clearly reveal the way Jews perceived the Gentiles. (Do we easily find 'Christian' Gentiles labelling Jews as the 'circumcision' or the Gentiles as the 'uncircumcision'?) Since Best has paid only scant attention to the author, who perceives the Gentiles from a native Jewish point of view in which some crucial (if not explosive) issues are concealed, it must be said that his interpretation of Ephesians constitutes no real advance.

1.2.10 The language of 'powers' in Ephesians

A quite different interpretative tack has been taken more recently by some scholars who find appropriate background to the language of 'powers' in the NT. The most comprehensive analysis of the language of 'powers' is provided recently by W. Wink in his 'trilogy'.[115] The exegetical and hermeneutical foundations are well laid in his earliest volume in which Wink analyses not just 'principalities and authorities' but a whole range of terminology for 'power'.[116] To this Wink also adds the following observation: '*Unless the context further specifies* (and some do), *we are to take the terms for power in their most comprehensive sense*, understanding them to mean both heavenly *and* earthly, divine *and* human, good *and* evil powers' (italics his).[117] In this light, Wink contends that in the NT the 'powers' frequently refer to actual spiritual agencies, but he also makes room from within the NT itself for modern reinterpretation whereby the cosmic powers are both 'the inner and outer aspect of any given manifestation of power'.[118] It is also from this interpretative principle that Wink asserts that the language of power in Ephesians (especially Eph. 2.1–2), alongside other 'disputed passages' in the NT, 'has been demythologised, although it remains highly metaphorical'.[119]

[115] Wink, *Naming*; cf. Wink, *Unmasking*; Wink, *Engaging*.

[116] Wink, *Naming*, 13–35. [117] Ibid., 39, 100.

[118] '[T]he "principalities and powers" are the inner aspect and outer aspects of any given manifestations of power. As the inner aspect they are the spirituality of institutions, the "within" of corporate structures and systems, the inner essence of outer organisations of power. As the outer aspect they are political systems, appointed officials, the "chair" of an organisation, laws – in short, all the tangible manifestations which power takes' (ibid., 5).

[119] Ibid., 60–4, 82–96, here 83.

Wink's interpretative move is flawed on at least two counts: (a) it is true that a word can have a wide range of meaning (e.g., 'dictionary' meanings), but it would be linguistically flawed to assert that this principle is applicable to a 'power' vocabulary which occurs in a specific context. Instead, one should assume, unless a double entendre is intended, that one or other meaning is likely to be intended in most contexts; Wink seems to point this procedure in the opposite direction. (b) To this we must add that even when the context clearly specifics the sense of the 'powers', Wink himself does not follow his own interpretative key consistently.[120] There is also no clear evidence which supports Wink's thesis that the 'language of power' in Ephesians is 'extremely imprecise, liquid, interchangeable', or that its author has not been able to keep the 'powers' and the order of human society as distinct categories.[121]

It is also surprising to gather from a study which understands the language of 'powers' as 'a means for developing a Christian social ethic from within the language of the NT'[122] that no real attention is given to the question as to whether the language mentioned above could have been used as a measure of social distance (between different ethnic groups), or as a label to reinforce the distancing of 'us' from 'them'.

C. Arnold has brought new light to the interpretation of the 'powers' from a different perspective. He argues that 'a knowledge of Hellenistic magic may very well be the most important background for understanding why the author highlights the power of God and the "powers" of evil in Ephesians'.[123] Arnold's goal has been to acquire an understanding of the nature and motivation for the inclusion of the power-motif in Ephesians by studying the author's development of the theme against the backdrop of the spiritual environment of western Asia Minor in the first century AD. He contends that the common feature in the religious and/or magical traditions of western Asia Minor in the first century AD 'is an acute and thriving belief in and fear of the evil spiritual "powers", and the most pressing question facing the believers at Ephesus and throughout western Asia Minor was the position of Christ in relation to these hostile powers'.[124] The first half of Ephesians 2 is included alongside other

[120] This fallacy is repeated in Wink's analyses, see, e.g., Eph. 6.12, at which the author clearly 'specifies' the powers as those which are 'in the heavenly realms', but certainly not as those which are 'not only divine but human, not only personified but structural . . .' (ibid., 85). See also Wink's exegesis on Col. 1.16 (ibid., 64–77), in which Wink concludes that the 'powers' include both things visible and things invisible. This conclusion is unlikely, for the author clearly qualifies the 'things invisible' immediately with the following addition: 'whether thrones or dominions or rulers or principalities'.

[121] *Contra* Wink, ibid., 82–4, who argues that the 'power' is lined up with human sin.

[122] Ibid., 5.

[123] Arnold, *Ephesians*, 39.

[124] Ibid., 5–41, 50, 123.

passages in his study because of its pivotal importance for understanding the author's message regarding the power of God and the 'powers of evil'.[125]

Arnold has produced by far the most literal reading of the 'powers' language in Ephesians.[126] He challenges the demythologising trend that other advocates[127] see in the first century CE by contending that an objective or substantive concept of power prevailed throughout the Hellenistic world of the first century CE.

Arnold's substantive concept of the 'powers' can be seen as a protest against the view which imposes a post-Enlightenment mindset on the first-century writers.[128] A major deficiency in Arnold's work, however, remains his failure to go beyond semantic representation of the language of 'powers' (i.e., what do the 'power' terms mean?) which takes no sufficient account of such non-linguistic properties as, for example, the identity of the author/speaker and his speech plan (i.e., how does the author (a Jew) *use* the language of 'powers'? What does *he* mean by the 'powers'?). Do the author's statements regarding the 'powers' tell us as much about the author as about what he says about the Gentiles (e.g., his belief, attitude, proposition, thought, and so forth)?[129] Given that the ancients embraced the reality of the 'spirit world' (*Geisterglauben*),[130] there are such salient questions that need to be addressed as, for example, what is communicated via the language of 'powers'? Does the author use the 'powers' language to attach negative valence to the Gentiles, reinforcing thus a

125 Ibid., 59–62, 134–7, 150. 126 See esp. ibid., esp. 41–69.

127 See, e.g., Berkhof, *Powers*, who comments: '[T]he apocalypses think primarily of the principalities and powers as heavenly angels, Paul as structures of earthly existence. This new burden of meaning is, so far as we can see, Paul's own creation . . . One can even doubt whether Paul conceived of the powers as personal beings. In any case this aspect is so secondary that it makes little difference whether he did or not' (18). See also Caird, *Principalities*, who does not maintain a clear distinction between the 'powers' and human institutions, but argues that Paul's 'principalities and powers' *include* the state (16). Caird, however, modified his position, maintaining that Paul was referring to spiritual beings which operate in and within the structures (*Letters*, 149, n. 47). See also Yoder, *Politics*, 136–9; Ellul, *Subversion*, 76.

128 One of the great contributions of the post-Enlightenment mentality is to belittle (consciously or unconsciously) the ability of the 'primitive' mind to make distinctions between 'myth' and 'reality'. I suspect the 'natural' and 'supernatural' (like 'myth' and 'reality') in modern jargon are a post-Enlightenment construct and have very little to do with the symbolic universe of the ancients. For the dilemma of western Christianity in the post-Enlightenment period, see esp. Lincoln, 'Liberation'.

129 See in particular Dentith, 'Language', 20–40, esp. 33; Sperber and Wilson, *Relevance*; Searle, *Expression*; Cotterell and Turner, *Linguistics*, 16, 296.

130 Arnold, *Ephesians*, 170. See further Everling, *Angelologie*, 109; Dibelius, *Geisterwelt*, 5; Charlesworth, *OTP* 1.66; cf. Charlesworth, 'Scrolls', esp. 13; O'Brien, 'Principalities', esp. 135–6; Malina, *Anthropology*, 110–12; Lincoln, 'Liberation', 338.

negative counterimage to the positive ideal of God's people according to an already well-established *social* 'code' (say, of the Jews)? Although Arnold acknowledges 'some aspects of Judaism in Asia Minor',[131] he has given no real attention to the perspective of a Christian Jew, who would consider the language of 'powers' a useful means to reinforce his own conviction in the 'one God' and, more importantly, a conviction which would probably provide 'the most important background' for determining the way he would caricature the Gentile world and the 'spirit world'. There is also no serious attempt in Arnold's work to relate the 'power' language in Ephesians to the religious and/or sectarian quarrels in certain (not all) early Judaism*s*[132] which assumed the reality of *Geisterglauben* but would employ the 'powers' language (insolently) as a means of dividing, establishing the differences between human groups, reinforcing where their 'otherness' lies (e.g. *Jub.* 15.31–4; 1QS 3–4; John 8.44–7, 48–53; 2 Cor. 4.3; 1 Tim. 4.1; Rev. 3.9; *Mart. Isa.* 2.2–4, etc.).[133]

As far as we can tell, Arnold has given by far the narrowest definition for such words as, for example, 'demonic' and 'demon' (= 'evil' or pernicious spirit).[134] Clearly the notion of demon/'daemon' (δαίμων in its original sense) in the wider philosophical tradition of the Graeco-Roman world reflects a far broader spectrum of interpretations of these terms than Arnold would like to envisage.[135]

In 1993 J. H. Roberts also presented a short treatment on the emphasis in Ephesians on powers, coupled with the equally important emphasis on the unity of Jewish and Gentile Christians in the church.[136] He ventured the theory that there is a theological connection between the themes of unity of the church and of the power of God over the powers of evil. Indeed, he suggested that the context of Ephesians was one where the enmity between Jewish and Gentile Christians in the church was carried over from the age-old strife that existed between Jews and Gentiles in Asia Minor, and was understood to be the work of the evil spiritual beings,

131 Arnold, *Ephesians*, 29–34. He, however, concludes that 'there is substantial evidence of Jews practicing magic' (30).

132 But see, e.g., Smith, 'Powers'; Johnson, 'Slander'; Segal, 'Ruler'; Kee, 'Membership', esp. 105–6, 115; Rokeah, *Jews*, esp. 133–67.

133 The weakness of Arnold's thesis is also repeated in some more recent studies of the 'powers' in Ephesians: Carr, *Angels*, 25–43, 100–11; Wink, *Naming*, esp. 89–96; Lee, 'Powers'. There is also no real progress in Lincoln, 'Liberation', whose sweeping conclusion is that 'discussion of the interpretation of the powers turns out to be a subheading under the topic of evil' (337).

134 See, e.g., Arnold, *Ephesians*, 51. For Arnold, 'demonic' and magical are synonyms (33). We must note that the two terms do not occur in Ephesians.

135 See my discussion of 2.2 in chapter 2, section 2.3.1 below.

136 Roberts, 'Enigma', 103.

the existence of which was accepted by all in that society. According to Roberts, this has necessitated the author of Ephesians to pose unity of the church as the outcome of God's victory over opposing powers of evil, and he asserts that the above statement of faith would be negated if disunity prevailed. This understanding inclines Roberts to surmise that any schismatic movement – and even the existence of strife between the two groups of believers within the church – carries with it the implication that the forces of evil have the power to withstand the conquering might of God. That is, it would be in direct opposition to the accepted statement of faith. Such an understanding also implies that the readers were under compulsion to utilise God's power to preserve and promote the unity within the one body of Christ (105).

It is not clear for Ephesians whether the sociological and political enmity of Jews and Greeks in the Hellenistic world, and especially in the Roman province of Asia (western Asia Minor), spilled over into the church once its membership became mixed and even predominantly Greek.

As far as I can tell, study of the motif of 'powers' in relation to ethnography (and therefore Jewish ethnographic apology) has not advanced very far. It is curious why, in their debates on the language of 'powers', scholars have rarely paused to ponder whether the 'powers' in Ephesians had been used to forge an external identity of the Gentiles in accordance with the *self*-confidence of a certain Judaism (not all) which is bold enough to reduce 'another' to the category of the false through such language.

1.2.11 Locating Ephesians within a Jewish context

At this point it is appropriate to mention some important contributions in the study of Ephesians which locate the latter within a Jewish context.[137] K. Kuhn (1968), for example, has examined the similarities between the general style of Ephesians and the language of Qumran. With reference to the language and style of Ephesians Kuhn concludes that 'Semitic syntactical occurrences appear four times more frequently in the Epistle to the Ephesians than in all the remaining letters of the *corpus Paulinum*.'[138] The many-sided and close connections between the language and style of Ephesians and Qumran texts have led Kuhn to the conclusion that the close relationship cannot be explained by the fact that both texts 'reflect,

[137] See also Merkel, 'Diskussion', 3195–220.

[138] Kuhn, 'Ephesians', here 116. See also Braun, *Qumran*, 215–25; Deichgräber, *Gotteshymnus*, passim.

each independently of the other, the style of the *Old Testament*'. Such a relationship, he believes, is best accounted for 'on the basis of a continuity of tradition'.[139]

F. Mußner also observes in his *Tractate on the Jews* (1984) that the statements in Ephesians 2.12 concern the theological situation of the Gentiles made 'within the horizon of Israel, of the "circumcision"'.[140] He makes three main points. Like Schlier and Rese, Mußner argues that the author is concerned with the salvation-historical difference prior to Christ, whom he also regarded as the privilege of Israel, i.e., 'the hope of *the* Messiah'.[141] The author 'does not say that Israel had lost its privileges enumerated in 2.12' and 'does not leave out the fate of salvation of that Israel which had not found the path to the gospel',[142] and 'there is no ecclesiology without reference to Israel'. However, Mußner, like Kuhn, has not given adequate attention to the issues which are concealed within the 'horizon of Israel' and to the Jewish attitudes toward the Gentiles.

1.2.12 The new perspective on Ephesians

Mention should be made of studies which provide a useful analogy to the kind of investigation proposed in the present study. I would draw particular attention to Dunn's two important essays, 'Anti-Semitism in the Deutero-Pauline Literature' (1993) and 'Deutero-Pauline Letters' (1995), since the theme of Dunn's work runs parallel to the theme of the present study on the Jewish categories and expressions of the Jewish perspective. I shall indicate three main points. First, the characteristic Jewish language throughout Ephesians cannot be put down simply to a contrived or even learned familiarity with the Jewish scriptures. Rather, we have to speak of a writer whose own thought processes are thoroughly impregnated with characteristic Jewish thought and manners of speech.[143] Second, the Jewish features and the strongly Semitic language in Ephesians are not appropriated in polemical fashion;[144] and third, the passage in Ephesians 2.11–22 gains its fullest significance within the Jewish context as the author's perspective is again wholly Jewish.[145]

The 'new perspective' provided by Dunn, which deals with the overtly Jewish character of Ephesians and defines the 'context' of the latter in broad categories of Jewish thought and praxis, represents a significant

139 Mußner, *Epheser*, 120.
140 Mußner, *Tractate*, 23–6; cf. Mußner, 'Contributions'.
141 Mußner, *Tractate*, 261, nn. 85, 87, 91; Mußner, *Epheser*, 70–1.
142 Mußner, *Tractate*, 25.
143 Dunn, 'Deutero-Pauline Letters'.
144 Dunn, 'Anti-Semitism', 156–9.
145 Dunn, 'Deutero-Pauline Letters', 139.

advance on that of Kuhn and Mußner. Its value can be summed up thus. The Jewish perspective implies that due weight must be given to such questions as the identity of the speaker and his perception and attitudes toward non-Jews. However, Dunn does not address such salient questions as whether the author's language also intended to expose the Gentiles to exclusivistic Jewish attitudes, whether Jews had reduced the Gentiles to the category of the false, and whether these attitudes are closely related to the theme of ethnic estrangement and reconciliation. Dunn's 'new perspective' could therefore be strengthened by devoting close attention to the following areas: (1) discussion of the Jewish perspective turns out to be a subheading under the topic of communication. If communication includes not simply semantic representation but such non-linguistic properties as the identity of the speaker (and thus the author's *Jewish* perspective), what is communicated, then? Why does the author write what he does about Gentiles? What is the author's 'utterance meaning'? What significance could his utterance have for the author himself or his Gentile readers? (2) Since there are sufficient clues in Ephesians 2 which show that the author had entered into dialogue with *other* Jews by exposing the Gentile readers to the Jewish attitudes toward them, we must take into account the fact that Ephesians consists of the perspective of *other* Jews which the author had disclosed or alluded to.[146] Does the author then echo the perception/attitude of other Jews about the Gentiles in such a way as to make this interpretable and usable for his own communicative purposes? What explosive issues are concealed in his representaion of this perspective, then? How does the Jewish perspective (and the various Jewish categories which underscore that perspective) relate to the theme of ethnic estrangement and reconciliation? Briefly, then, we will need to engage with the representation of the Gentiles from the Jewish perspective in which some crucial, if not explosive, issues are concealed, and the various ethnographic categories in Ephesians 2, which gain their fullest significance within the Jewish 'context'.

1.3 The need for this study

We are now in a position to sum up our discussion to this point. A fair amount of research has been variously undertaken on the relationship of the church and Israel, the continuity or discontinuity of the church and

[146] Dunn clearly acknowledges a similar kind of dialogue in his 'Echoes', here 461, where Paul (a Jew) uses insiders' code to distinguish himself from other Jews in a way analogous to the distinction between Jew and Gentile.

Israel, the conflict between Jewish and Gentile Christians, ethno-cultural conflict between Jews and Greeks, the ongoing process of institutionalisation in the post-Pauline churches, the cancellation of time and, not least, the 'powers' against the background of *Weltangst* or Hellenistic magical traditions. More can be said about the proposals put forth by Ephesians scholars,[147] but it is not necessary, since the main representatives of the various hypotheses which spawned multiple permutations and hybrids have been mapped out quite sufficiently.

Our brief survey of the relevant scholarly literature has shown that in spite of the fact that there has been a steady stream of studies on the different *motifs* in Ephesians, relatively little work has been done on the specific theme of the Jewish attitudes toward the Gentiles and ethnic reconciliation against the backcloth of such a Jewish perspective.[148] Work by Dunn, in the course of examining Ephesians' 'context' in broad categories of Jewish thought and praxis, has opened up what appears to be a fruitful line of enquiry, one likely to confirm that the impression given by the letter is of a native (Hellenistic) Jewish perspective. Since Dunn has not pursued the connections between the exclusivistic Jewish attitudes toward the Gentiles and ethnic reconciliation there would appear to be scope for a contribution to research in this area along the following lines: a re-examination of Ephesians 2 with critical response to recent studies, by taking account of such salient questions as, for example, were there ethnic factors which had led to the exclusion of Gentiles from the Israel of God? Did the author of Ephesians intend to communicate these factors to his Gentile readers? Do his statements about the Gentiles also tell us about himself and about Jewish attitudes toward the Gentiles? The thesis of the present study is that Jewish attitudes toward the Gentiles had become the main factors which had led to Gentiles being excluded from the purpose of God before the latter had any positive connection with Christ. The Gentiles were excluded from Israel's God-given blessings on the basis of a particular *ethnos*. To make sense of these exclusive attitudes and

[147] See, e.g., Kitchen, *Anakephalaiosis* (1988); Jeal, *Theology and Ethics* (1990); Hui, *Holy Spirit* (1992); McVay, *Ecclesial Metaphor* (1995); Hinkle, *Peace* (1997).

[148] In this study I do not use 'ethnic' as synonymous with 'racial'. An ethnic unit is a 'population whose members believe that in some sense they share some common descent and a common cultural heritage or tradition or practice, and are so regarded by others'. The term 'race' or 'racial' refers to an aggregate whose members are objectively distinguished from others by certain gross hereditary phenotypical features (see esp. Smith, 'Ethnicity', 192). Therefore the conception that Judaism is *racially* exclusive should be avoided. Circumcision, for example, is a Jewish practice rather than a racial characteristic, and so Gentiles could become Jews by undertaking the rite of circumcision and what it entailed. See further Barclay, *Jews*, 438; Cohen, *Jewishness*, 107–238.

of a self-confident Judaism which is bold enough to reduce the Gentile 'other' to the category of the false or 'out of place', the author does not just expose the Gentiles to these attitudes, but also re-presents what the Jews perceived about the Gentiles in such a way as to make it interpretable and usable for his own communicative purposes. His representation of the Gentile 'other' from a Jewish perspective is meant to underscore the exclusivistic Jewish attitude which has led to ethnic alienation. The antidote to the alienation or ethnic estrangement is that the Messiah Jesus, who is eulogised as the peace-maker, and whose reconciling work is marked by his undisguised inclusivism, has come disinterestedly between Jews and Gentiles to overcome the barrier between the two and to create a people that is marked by the acceptance of the ethnic 'other'.

1.4 Aims, plan and presuppositions of the present study

Our justification outlined above also brings us to the five specific aims of the present study. The first of these is basically descriptive and is concerned with identifying as precisely as possible some of the most obvious Jewish features in Ephesians. To what extent does Ephesians show a continuity with Jewish tradition? Does the author of Ephesians embrace a Jewish world view? Does he perceive the world 'without' from the perspective of a Jew? My task is to show whether Ephesians 2 can be best explained by the hypothesis that the author describes the Gentiles from a Jewish perspective.

The second aim follows on from the first and is primarily explanatory and attempts to account for the author's Jewish perspective by commenting on the passage in 2.1–10.

The third aim seeks to demonstrate, on the basis of our findings in chapter 2, the major writing concern of the author in vv. 11–13.

The fourth aim comes from the first three and is concerned with the question of how Jew and Gentile could be one.

The fifth aim of this study is to describe some of the implications of *pax Christi* for the Christian Gentiles and, not least, for their relationship with the Jews.

The first two aims are taken up in chapter 2, in which I shall argue that the passage in 2.1–10 gains its fullest significance within a Jewish context. I will also show the way in which the author employed the 'powers' language and the rhetoric of admission to heighten such issues as the social distance between Jews and Gentiles.

The third aim is taken up in chapter 3, which is devoted to a detailed exegesis of 2.11–13. This is informed throughout by the findings of chapter 2 about Jewish categories and the Jewish attitudes toward the Gentiles.

The fourth and fifth aims are taken up in chapters 4 and 5, respectively. Chapter 4 will show that the author of Ephesians has proffered a christological solution to an estranged humanity (vv. 14–18). Chapter 5 will show some of the implications of Christ's reconciling work for the Christian Gentiles and, not least, for their relationship with the 'holy ones' which is redefined within the framework of *pax Christi* (vv. 19–22).

In the final chapter of the present study I will gather and summarise the conclusions, in which I also draw together some of the implications of this study for future research.

The presuppositions concerning the letter to the Ephesians upon which this study stands are proposed as follows: (1) Ephesians will be understood as written by a (Christian) Jew, who never ceased to be a Jew.[149] We will not presuppose Pauline authorship as a basis for the study, however. (2) Ephesians will be examined in its own right. The affinity of Ephesians with its 'sibling' letter, Colossians, and the undisputed letters of Paul, means that the terminology and concepts in Ephesians will be frequently compared to those in the earlier Paulines and Colossians. (3) Ephesians was written to Christian Gentiles. The author of Ephesians has this specific group of persons in mind and speaks to them in the second person (of the verbs he uses).

[149] This study does not intend to delve into the complex scholarly exchanges concerning the Pauline or Deutero-Pauline authorship of Ephesians, although clarification on this particular issue will help determine more accurately the *historical context* of our text. For a helpful discussion of the issue of authorship, see esp. Best, *Ephesians*², 6–44; Kümmel, *Introduction*, 350–66; Schnelle, *History*, 300–3; Barth, *Ephesians 1–3*, 36–41; cf. Barth, 'Traditions'; Porter and Clarke, 'Perspective', et al. The conclusion of Mitton, *Ephesians*, 264, that the author of Ephesians 'was of Gentile birth' is self-condemned and falls by the wayside on the grounds of the weight of evidence which points in the other direction; also Goodspeed, *Meaning*, who writes: 'The writer is a Greek Christian' (32).

2

CONTINUITY OR DISCONTINUITY? THE NEW PERSPECTIVE ON EPHESIANS, WITH REFERENCE TO EPHESIANS 2.1–10

2.1 Introduction

There is now a broad consensus that most NT writers – including the author of Ephesians – were Christian Jews.[1] The significance of this consensus on Ephesians, however, has not been fully appreciated.[2] But with the 'new perspective on Paul' which helps us to gain a clearer view of the first-century Jews and Judaism, a fresh assessment of Ephesians within the 'new perspective' can now be made possible and is necessary.[3]

The present chapter, which sets Ephesians within the 'new perpective', is to penetrate into the historical context of first-century Judaism within which our epistle was written. Since a major part of that 'context' is the self-understanding of the first-century Jews and Judaism, the following questions can therefore be posed at the outset of this study. Did the author of Ephesians see the world as a Jew? Can sufficient evidence be culled from the letter itself as regards his Jewish attitude toward the Gentiles? What picture of Judaism can we draw from Ephesians? Was there an interaction going on between our author with the self-understanding of the Jews and Judaism? What significant bearing does this self-understanding have upon our study of Jewish attitudes toward the Gentiles? Our first

[1] Despite the complex scholarly exchanges concerning the Pauline or Deutero-Pauline authorship of 'Ephesians', the suggestion that the author is a Jew is accepted without demur by most scholars. For a helpful discussion of Ephesians from a Jewish background, see, e.g., Merkel, 'Diskussion,' here 3195–212; Barth, 'Traditions'; Dunn, 'Anti-Semitism'; cf. Dunn, 'Deutero-Pauline Letters', 138. Lincoln, 'Theology', 86–90, concludes that a Hellenistic Judaism should prove the most plausible background for Ephesians' own thought (90). Gnilka, *Epheserbrief*, 33–45, concludes that Hellenistic Judaism provides most illumination for some of the main concepts in Ephesians.

[2] See esp. Kuhn, 'Ephesians'; Mußner, 'Contributions'; cf. Mußner, *Tractate*, 29ff.; Dunn, 'Antisemitism', 156–9; Dunn, 'Deutero-Pauline Letters', 136–9.

[3] Sanders, *Paul*, 449, who provides the 'new perspective', has for some reason given almost no attention at all to Ephesians. Even his analysis of Eph. 2.11–22 is largely constrained by the parameters of his own thesis that 'those who already belong to Israel must still join *the new movement*' (see his *Law*, 172, italics mine). For a helpful assessment of Sanders, see esp. Dunn, 'New Perspective', 184–8.

interpretative move is therefore an attempt to go inside the historical context of the author of Ephesians, leaving aside some of the questions which will be dealt with in the course of this study. Our major purpose at the moment is to examine how far and in what way the author of Ephesians shows a particular relationship to the Jewish heritage as regards language, terminology, thought and ideas, and most importantly to lay bare the significant bearing of this Jewish context upon his attitude toward the Gentiles. To demonstrate my case I shall also focus particularly on 2.1–10 and attempt to set it as fully as possible into this context. This chapter concludes with the conviction that the passage in Ephesians 2.1–10 can be best explained by the hypothesis that the author not only perceives the non-Jewish world as a (Christian) Jew but also speaks in reconciliatory terms of Jews and Gentiles who were both in need of God's gracious attitude and act toward them.

2.2 Locating Ephesians within a Jewish context

The author uses characteristic Jewish language at the outset of his letter.[4] He describes the recipients as the 'saints' with a view to identifying the Gentile believers with Israel's heritage (see also my discussion on 2.19; 3.18). His introductory eulogy ('Blessed be the God and Father of our Lord Jesus Christ . . .', 1.3–14) is deeply rooted in the Jewish scripture where the word ברוך and its cognates occur no less than five hundred times.[5] It shows a remarkable similarity to the terminology and motif of early Judaism(s) which eulogises the one God in its most common

[4] Caragounis, *Mysterion*, 44, who rightly observes that the eulogy in Ephesians, like the eulogies found in the Apocrypha, the Qumran Hodayoth and the NT, is 'inspired by the common Israelite-Jewish background, which has left more than mere traces of religious devotion in the Psalms, and in the eulogies of the OT and Judaism'; Dunn, 'Deutero-Pauline Letters', 136; Gibbs, *Creation*, 93–138.

[5] See, e.g., 1 Kgs 8.15; Pss 18.47; 28.6; 31.21; 66.20; 68.19; 119.12, etc. See further Westermann, *Praise*, 87–9, who argues that the earliest form of *berakah* occurred in individual response to an act of God's deliverance and provision. It became associated with the cult and with Israel's corporate worship later. To find in our present *berakah* a reference to 'baptismal-eulogy' is not only needlessly anachronistic, it is to forfeit the undisguised inclusivism of God's election, which the author leads us to expect at the outset, *pace* Dahl, 'Adresse', who writes: 'Tatsächlich spielen in Eph 1: 3–14 Taufmotive eine grosse Rolle' (264). It is, however, possible to suggest that there is a close correlation between the eulogy and the contents of the letter, and thus Dahl, who aptly labelled the introductory eulogy as 'Briefeingangs-Eulogie', 'Adresse', 261. Dahl's 'baptismal' theory is followed by Coutts, 'Ephesians 1.3–14', who argues that a liturgical prayer connected with baptism lies behind the *berakah* of Eph. 1; Kirby, *Pentecost*, 40ff.; Schlier, *Epheser*, 72. For a detailed discussion of the 'epistolary function' of the eulogy, see esp. O'Brien, 'Unusual Introduction', esp. 510–12. See also Caragounis, *Mysterion*, who comments: 'One must neither expect the Eulogy as if the Eulogy were merely the announcement of

prayer, the *berakah*.[6] Striking parallels are found in hymns and prayers from Qumran texts which carried on this tradition (e.g., 1QS 11.15; 1QM 13.2; 14.4, 8; 18.6; 1QH 5.20; 10.14; 11.27, 29, 32; 16.8).[7] Such eulogies remained dominant in the synagogal benedictions and prayers such as the *Shemoneh 'Esreh* (1, 18, Palestinian rec.).[8] The thought world behind these blessings is clearly the common value shared by our author and other devout Jews that the 'one God' is the real bestower of blessing and initiator of every step towards its realisation (1.10).[9] The introductory eulogy-language in Ephesians can therefore be seen as an effective means by which such common value is conveyed or sustained (cf. 1 Cor. 1.3; Luke 1.68–75; 1 Pet. 1.3). What is new in Ephesians with respect to the Jewish tradition is such expressions as 'the Father of our Lord Jesus Christ' and the repetition of such formulae as 'in Christ' or 'in him'. Nevertheless, the incorporation of these expressions into the Ephesians eulogy is one of Ephesians' distinctive contributions, highlighting the christological intensification of the eulogy-motif rather than 'the distinctive Christian content of this berakah in comparison with its Jewish counterparts'.[10] It means that the grounds for the broad sweep of God's plan and the manifold spiritual blessings to both Jew and Gentile in Christ can be comprehended by taking the common value mentioned above as their starting point.

But the eulogy mentioned above is composed also with a view to presenting Christ as having integrally 'participated' in God's electing purpose 'before the foundation of the world'.[11] There can be little doubt that the author of Ephesians is obsessed with the idea of Christ as the

a sermon's contents (since it has instructive function itself), nor must one think, on the other hand, that the points of contact between the Eulogy and the rest of the Epistle are rather hazy and undefined' (50).

[6] See, e.g., Tobit 8.5, 15; Judith 13.17–18; Pr. Azar. 3, 29–34; 2 Macc. 1.17; 1 Esd. 4.40, 60; 3 Macc. 7.23.

[7] The extent of Semitisms in Ephesians is observed by Kuhn, 'Ephesians', who argues that 'one cannot fail to notice the striking similarity between a sentence such as the one we find in Eph. 1.3–14 and the typical Hebrew sentence structure of the Qumran Texts' (117); Deichgräber, *Gotteshymnus*, 72–5, esp. 75; Braun, *Qumran*, 215–25. See also Flusser, 'Psalms', here 551–2; O'Brien, 'Unusual Introduction', here 507–9; Caragounis, *Mysterion*, 44.

[8] See further Schürer, *HJPAJC*, II, 455–63; Str-B, IV, 616ff., 627ff.; van Roon, *Authenticity*, 182–90.

[9] Thus in *m*. Ber. 35a, we read: 'It is forbidden to a man to enjoy anything of this world without a benediction, and if anyone enjoys anything of this world without a benediction, he commits sacrilege.'

[10] *Pace* Lincoln, *Ephesians*, 11, 21.

[11] The phrase πρὸ καταβολῆς κόσμου also appears elsewhere in the NT: see, e.g., John 17.24; 2 Tim. 1.9; 1 Pet. 1.20.

mediator of God's election and redemption (e.g., ὁ εὐλογήσας . . . ἐν τῷ Χριστῷ, v. 3; ἐξελέξατο ἡμᾶς ἐν αὐτῷ πρὸ καταβολῆς κόσμου, v. 4; προορίσας ἡμᾶς . . . διὰ Ἰησοῦ Χριστοῦ κτλ., v. 5; ἐχαρίτωσεν ἡμᾶς ἐν τῷ ἠγαπημένῳ, v. 6; ἐν ᾧ ἔχομεν τὴν ἀπολύτρωσιν διὰ τοῦ αἵματος αὐτοῦ, v. 7; προέθετο ἐν αὐτῷ, v. 9; ἀνακεφαλαιώσασθαι τὰ πάντα ἐν τῷ Χριστῷ . . . ἐν αὐτῷ, v. 10; ἐν ᾧ καὶ ἐκληρώθημεν προορισθέντες κατὰ πρόθεσιν . . . αὐτοῦ, v. 11; ἐν τῷ Χριστῷ, vv. 10, 12).[12] The key to understanding the author's message here is the recognition that the *berakah* that has come to pass 'in' and 'through' Christ was God's own predetermination from the beginning.[13] His thesis about Christ is bold enough, but it in no way poses any threat to his monotheism (cf. 4.5–6; see my discussion below). Indeed his manner of speech and thought world are akin to those of the Jewish wisdom tradition in which such concepts of 'wisdom' or 'Logos' were often employed to speak of God's activity and his nearness to his creation (cf. Prov. 3.19/Ps. 103.24, LXX; 8.22–31; Sir. 1.4; 24.9; Wis. 6.22–8.1; 11QtgJob 30.1–5; 11Q5 26.14–15; *Gen R.* 1.1; Philo, *Opif.* 16–24).[14] The category of divine 'wisdom' which is now applied to Christ enables our author to speak with certainty of the 'one God' in his elective and redemptive *immanence*.[15] By saying that Christ is 'involved' in God's electing activity, the author of Ephesians is able to lay bare his claim that Christ is indeed the definitive self-expression of God's original purpose in electing his people.[16] His

[12] Allan, 'In Christ', suggests that the 'in Christ' formula in Ephesians is 'the formula of God's activity through Christ' (59). The extensive repetition of such prepositional phrases as 'in Christ' and 'through Christ' (or a variation of these phrases) throughout the eulogy suggests strongly that the author has intended his readers to give heed to the role of Christ in God's electing activity.

[13] See further Hofius, 'Erwählt', who argues that the idea of God's election 'before the creation of the world' has already been developed in early Judaism (128).

[14] See esp. Dunn, 'Monotheistic Faith', here 318–21; cf. Dunn, *Christ*, 15–16; Gilbert, 'Wisdom', esp. 284–8; Nickelsburg and Stone, *Faith*, 203–31; Hengel, *Judaism*, 153ff. See also Wilckens, 'σοφία'; Fohrer, 'σοφία', with extensive further bibliography.

[15] The older standard works have taken our expression in v. 4 *literally* to mean Christ's real pre-existence: see, e.g., Schlier, *Epheser*, 49 who speaks of the Christian adaptation of the Jewish theologoumenon of the pre-existence of the Messiah and the people of salvation. It is, however, dubious that such a 'Jewish theologoumenon' can be found in pre-Christian Judaism(s). Lincoln, *Ephesians*, 24 claims that 'probably the notion of the election of believers in Christ has been combined with that of the preexistence of Christ'. Hamerton-Kelly, *Pre-existence*, concludes that 'both Christ, and, in him, Christians, must have enjoyed "ideal pre-existence" before the world' (here 181–2); Beker, *Heirs*, 89–91. Schnabel, 'Wisdom', here 970–1, argues that such prepositional phrases as 'in him' – be it understood as in an instrumental sense or the 'sphere' within which the work of creation took place – only make sense if Christ was present at creation (970–1), et al.

[16] This claim almost certainly goes beyond that of the earlier Pauline letters. Strangely enough, the 'wisdom' language (vv. 3–4) is not discussed in Dunn's *Christology*, 235–6; cf. Dunn, *TPA*, 266–88; *Christ*, 15–16, 17–18.

'wisdom' language could easily evoke in the Gentile readers a deep sense of assurance of God's purpose for them: 'In/through him (Christ) even you (Gentiles) . . . were sealed with the promised Holy Spirit, which is the guarantee of our inheritance until we acquire possession of it, to the praise of his (God's) glory' (vv. 13–14, my own translation). The language of divine wisdom, which is found quite often in Jewish apologetic in which Jewish particularism and the belief in the one God are held together, is now employed by our author to lay bare the conviction that God's choice is 'in Christ'. Despite his christological claims, it is safe to say that the 'wisdom' language in the introductory eulogy can be located within the Jewish 'wisdom' tradition.

The same characteristically Jewish character lies behind the author's statements about God. Although the idea of God as Father is familiar enough in Greek,[17] the language here, that of the 'God-Father'[18] who chooses a people 'to be holy and unblemished before him',[19] is exclusively Jewish: it refers to God's relationship with the people of Israel (Deut. 7.6; 14.2; 32.6; Isa. 63.16, twice; 64.8; Jer. 31.9; Mal. 1.6; 2.10).[20] To be sure, the connection between 'God' and 'Father' is a clear reminder of Israel's self-understanding as the people that is bounded by God's

[17] See, e.g., Homer, *Od.* 1.28; *Il.* 1.544, 15.47; Plato, *Tim.* 28C; Pindar, *Ol.* 2.17; Epictetus, *Diatr.* 1.3.1, et al. See further Schrenk, 'πατήρ,' 945–59, with extensive further bibliography.

[18] My own translation. The non-use of a second definite article in the expression ὁ θεὸς καὶ πατὴρ may have been *theo*logically significant: the author of Ephesians may deliberately regard the two terms (i.e., 'God' and 'Father') which he placed in one regimen as belonging naturally together as a unit in concept or reality. Be that as it may, the author, unlike the Greek, does not recognise the designation 'Father' as a mere 'manifestation' of the one God. Thus, Eph. 1.3 may need to be paraphrased more accurately as 'Blessed be the God-Father of our Lord Jesus Christ . . .' (e.g., 1.3; also, 5.20: 'always and for everything giving thanks in the name of our Lord Jesus Christ to the God-Father' rather than, *contra* NRSV: '. . . to God the Father'); cf. 1.2, 17; 6.23.

[19] The LXX has already chosen ἄμωμος as the translation value for תמים, 'perfect', and defines this term in relation to sacrificial animals generally as meaning 'without a blemish'. The basic idea of 'holy and unblemished' is derived from the OT cult, denoting that which has been set apart or consecrated to God, e.g., Exod. 29.1; Lev. 1.3, 10; 22.21; Num. 6.14; Ezek. 43.22–5, etc. The parallel is particularly close with Col. 1.22; see also 1QS 3.7–9; 8.4–9; CD 20.1–2 (תמים קדש), 20.5 and 7 (תמים תקדש); cf. 1QS 2.1. The author of Ephesians has probably 'transcoded' the 'holy and unblemished' language of its ordinary cultic use by suggesting that moral and religious blamelessness are fundamentally essential, just as the physical perfection of a sacrifice is an unnegotiable presupposition of cultic use. The same transcoding can also be seen in 5.27, at which the presentation of the wife to Christ is likened to an unblemished 'sacrifice' offered to God. See further Dunn, 'Deutero-Pauline Letters', 137; cf. Dunn, *Colossians and Philemon*, 109–10.

[20] See also *Joseph & Aseneth* 8.9; *midr.* Ps. 74.1; 93.3; *Gen. R.* 1.5.

gracious election, covenant and the promise of salvation. God is the 'Father of corporate or national Israel'.[21] This well explains why Jews – both of the diaspora and of Palestine – could easily invoke God as their Father: 'Look upon the descendants of Abraham, O Father, upon the children of the sainted Jacob, a people of your consecrated portion who are perishing as foreigners in a foreign land' (3 Macc. 6.3, cf. 5.7; Tobit 13.4; Wis. 2.13–20; 14.3; Sir. 23.4; 51.10 (Hebr.); *Jub.* 1.23–5, 28; 1QH 9.35–6; 4Q373 1.16; 4Q460 5.6; Josephus, *A. J.* 5.93). The author of Ephesians has certainly shared the same 'semantic universe' (to use Mußner's words) with other devout Jews when he evoked the electing love of God in his eulogy, despite his undisguised inclusivism in which the Gentiles can also invoke the God of Israel as their Father (1.2, 3–14, 17; 3.14–15; 5.20; 6.23).[22] Not unrelated to this invigoration is the author's recitation of the Jewish *Shema*, the confession that 'God is one': 'One God-Father of all, who is above all and through all and in all' (4.6).[23] For anyone who is familiar with the Jewish scriptures evocation of the *Shema* would immediately evoke the characteristic talk of the 'one God', namely 'the Lord God of Israel' (e.g., Deut. 6.4–9; 11.13–21; Num. 15.37–41; *2 Baruch* 48.24; *Sib. Or.* 3.11; 4.30; Philo, *Spec. Leg.* 1.67; *Opif.* 171; Josephus, *A. J.* 4.201; *C. Ap.* 2.193; *Shemoneh 'Esreh* 18).[24] It is safe to say that our author does not advocate a *new* God. His confession of the 'one God' here is obviously the natural result of the (Jewish) monotheistic tradition which he embraces and a manifesto of a Jew's faith in the one God of Israel.[25] One may add that his affirmation of the 'one God' and 'one Lord' (4.5–6; cf. 1 Cor. 8.6), the risen and ascended Christ and mediator between God and humankind, still exhibits Jewish features by following the Jewish tradition of exclusively monotheistic belief rather than an infringement of that belief – he clearly acknowledges that the 'one God'

21 Fitzmyer, *Paul*, 53; Michel, 'πατήρ', 54; Hofius, 'πατήρ', here 617–18.

22 The most fundamental Jewish belief of God as Father is shared by other NT writers. The 'God-Father' designation is a typically Pauline expression: out of 11 times, 8 are found in Pauline letters, see, e.g., Rom. 15.6, 24; 2 Cor. 1.3; 11.31; Gal. 1.4; 1 Thess. 3.11, 13; see also Jas. 1.27; 1 Pet. 1.3; Rev. 1.6.

23 The translation of Eph. 4.6 in NRSV, i.e., 'one God and Father of all', is less accurate. See further Harris, 'Prepositions', 1178.

24 This basic declaration and manifesto of Judaism is found elsewhere in the NT, see, e.g., Rom. 3.30; 1 Cor. 8.4; Gal. 3.20; 1 Tim. 2.5. See further Str-B, IV, 189–207; Schürer, *HJPAJC*, II, 454–5; Dunn, *TPA*, §2.2; Neufeld, *Confessions*, 34–41, 44 n. 4; Borgen, 'Unity'; Schrenk, 'πατήρ', 978, n. 206.

25 That Christians and Jews believed in the same God did not go unrecognised by the 'outsider', see, e.g., Origen, *Cels.* 5.59. See further Dunn, *TPA*, §2.2. See also Neufeld, *Confessions*, 36.

is 'the God and Father of our *Lord Jesus Christ*' (1.3, 17; 1.19–22, par. Ps. 110.1).[26]

The foregoing observation is important for our study, for, as we shall see, it is precisely the author's fundamental belief in the oneness of God that provides the best explanation for the way in which he perceives and assesses the world 'without' (τὰ ἔθνη, cf. 2.11; 3.1; 4.17), and in particular the way in which he caricatures the 'world of this darkness' (see my discussion of 2.2, 11–12 below; see also 6.10–12). This can be easily justified when we refer to his ethical argumentation in which the Gentiles' moral conduct was scrutinised exclusively from the perspective of a Jew: 'and you must no longer *walk* as the *Gentiles* do . . .' (4.17, lit.). The Gentiles' deep-rooted ignorance, according to this perspective, is due to the fact that they had lopped themselves off from the source of life, i.e., they were 'alienated from the life of the (one) God' (4.18–19).[27] His language here is a clear reflection of traditional Jewish polemics against the Gentiles with respect to the moral standard of the latter.[28] It is safe to say that the author's concept about God is essentially a reflection of his

[26] *Contra* de Lacey, 'One Lord', who contends that 'Jesus' lordship can almost threaten the Father's godship' (201). See further Dunn, *TPA*, §10.3, esp. 246–65, esp. 254; Neufeld, *Confessions*, 67. Hurtado, *One God*, 99–103, argues that 'early Christian devotion constituted a significant mutation or innovation in Jewish monotheistic tradition' (99). He rightly observes that Christ is the object of hymnic praise in the context of Eph. 5.19, i.e., 'making melody *to the Lord* [*sc.*] with all your heart' (102–3, italics his). Such veneration to Christ, according to Hurtado, would have been perceived as an infringement on monotheism by Jews, while the Christians themselves retained monotheism in a permutated form ('binitarian monotheism'). Hurtado has drawn a clear line of discontinuity between Jewish concepts and 'Pauline Christianity' in Ephesians. However, we would need to note (a) that the object of thanksgivings in Ephesians is not the glorified Christ, but God (5.20) and (b) that the'veneration' given to Christ is only an attendant circumstance (expressed by the participial εὐχαριστοῦντες; cf. λαλοῦντες, ᾄδοντες; ψάλλοντες, v. 19): it did not appear until the Ephesian readers were urged to be 'filled by the Spirit (of God!)' (5.18). The venerative statement in Eph. 5.19 is therefore subordinate to the idea of the nearness of God to humankind (through his spirit) and therefore cannot be perceived as an infringement of traditional Jewish monotheism. For a critique of Hurtado's 'binitarian monotheism', see esp. Stuckenbruck, *Angel Veneration*, who argues that the veneration of angels in early Judaism provided a kind of structure or paradigm for Christians by/through which they expressed their monotheistic faith once they were showing veneration to Christ (7–9, 200–4).

[27] Moritz, *Mystery*, 24 n. 3, argues that the author no longer equates the Gentile readers with the nations. This observation, however, is ill judged, for the author's statements in 4.17–19 tell us more about the author's attitudes toward the non-Jewish world, i.e., the 'nations', than about his Gentile readers.

[28] See, e.g., Isa. 1.17–25; 41.8–9; 44.9–20; Job. 18.21; Ps. 79.6; Jer. 10.25; 1 Macc. 1.27; 3 Macc. 4.16; Wis. 13.1; 14.23–6; 2 Esd. 7.48; Judith 8.20; Pr. Azar. 22; Ep. Jer. passim. See also Rom. 1.21–5; 1 Thess. 4.5; 2 Thess. 1.8. See further Dunn, 'Deutero-Pauline Letters', 139; Johnson, 'Slander'; Schürer, *HJPAJC*, II, 454–5, 481–2; Kobelski, 'Ephesians', 889.

self-understanding which gives us an inkling of his own awareness of his own relationship to God.

The use of the 'mystery' language in Ephesians is extensive (1.9; 3.3, 4, 9; 5.32; 6.19). There is now a broad consensus that the idea of divine secrets and purposes, which were once hidden but have been revealed or made 'seen' by divine agency, is clearly a reflection of the Jewish apocalyptic thought in which God is the revealer of mysteries (Dan. 2.18–19, 27–30; 1QpHab. 7.4f.; 1QH 4.27f.; 1QS 3.23; 4.18; 11.5–7; 1QMyst; 2 Esd. 10.38; 14.5; *1 Enoch* 51.3; 103.2; *2 Bar.* 81.4, et al.)[29] This is the sense of 'mystery' clearly in view in 1.9 – 'For he has made known to us in all wisdom and insight the mystery of his will, according to his purpose which he set forth in Christ.' God's 'manifold wisdom and insight' is focused largely on God's plan to unite all things in Christ, and this includes the incorporation of the Gentiles into the body of Christ: namely that 'Gentiles are fellow-heirs, members of the same body and partakers of the promise in Christ Jesus' (cf. 1.17–19).[30] In 3.3–6, the holy apostles and prophets lay bare the execution of a 'mystery', hitherto known only to God, but now made known to humankind. The 'mystery' language in Ephesians 6.19 can also be read in the same light, where the 'mystery of the gospel' (6.19; cf. 6.15) refers, most probably, to the gospel of reconciliation (6.15). Here again the author's thought process is impregnated with characteristic Jewish apocalyptic ideas, for the gospel is probably a divine revelation which could be proclaimed only when the (divine) utterance was given to the steward of the mystery (cf. 1.17–18; 1QH 1.21; Luke 1.64).[31] Perhaps most striking of all is the author's

[29] I am grateful to Dr. Loren Stuckenbruck for suggesting that there are 'good' and 'bad' mysteries in early Judaism (cf. 1Q23 9 + 14 + 15; *1 Enoch* 15–16). See also Brown, *Semitic Background*, 22–9, 57 n. 168; Bockmuehl, *Revelation*, 199–205; Mußner, 'Contributions', here 159–63; Kuhn, 'Ephesians', here 118–19; Braun, *Qumran*, 215–25; O'Brien, 'Mystery', 622; Dunn, *Colossians and Philemon*, here 119–21; Schlier, *Epheser*, 60; Lincoln, *Ephesians*, 30–1.

[30] *Pace* Dahl, 'Cosmic Dimensions', 69–70, who rightly observes that the theme of revealed knowledge is much more prominent in Ephesians than in any other Pauline letter, including Colossians, but he ignores in his exegesis of Eph. 3.18 that the focus therein is not on the 'immeasurable dimension of the universe' or the 'revelation of cosmological mysteries' but on the theme of God's 'mystery' in which God's purpose is to include Gentiles in his saving purpose. For a summary of interpretations of the dimensional language in 3.18, see esp. Barth, *Ephesians 1–3*, 395–7.

[31] The 'mystery' in 5.32 is difficult. The most plausible explanation, according to Bockmuehl, is that 'we are dealing with an *exegetical* mystery: a deeper (in this case either allegorical or prophetic) meaning of a Scriptural text which has been elicited by means of some form of inspired exegesis. In other words, the deeper meaning of Gen 2: 24 points typically to Christ and the church' (*Revelation*, 204, italics his). For a different interpretation, see, e.g., Lincoln, 'Use', 33.

statement in 3.9, where 'the plan of the mystery' which is hidden for ages in God might be made known to the 'powers' in the heavenly places.

The same conclusion can also be drawn from the author's use of the Jewish scriptures, which clearly shows the continuity of Ephesians with the Jewish tradition and, not least, our author's debt to the tradition. This has long since been recognised by many scholars,[32] albeit the citation of the Jewish scriptures is not often prefaced by explicit introductory formulae.[33] To these we must add the various allusions of differing strength to the Jewish scriptures. These are 'quotations' or covert references without formal invocation.[34] 'We cannot therefore speak of literary artifice so much as of a mode of thought and speech whose very language and metaphors have been shaped by life-long familiarity with the Jewish scriptures.'[35]

Especially characteristic of our epistle is the author's frequent appeal to the Jewish scriptures to consolidate his ethical arguments.[36] He has often resorted to the scriptures to link the Jewish tradition to his ethical injunctions by allowing the words of the scripture to influence the shaping of his teaching. We may note, for example, the author's perspective on the husband–wife relationship, which is clearly informed by the Jewish scripture (5.31; Gen. 2.24; cf. 4Q416 2.4.1–13; Matt. 19.5). The oneness of husband and wife, which is perceived as a microcosm of the oneness of

[32] See in particular Lincoln, 'Use'; Hübner, *Vetus Testamentum*, 425–79; cf. Hübner, *Biblische Theologie*, 374; Barth, 'Traditions'; Moritz, *Mystery*, passim; Dunn, 'Deutero-Pauline Letters', here 137–8. It is incorrect, *contra* Beker, *Heirs*, 93, to say that there is a 'nearly complete neglect of the Old Testament' in Ephesians; cf. Lindemann, *Aufhebung*, who minimises the significance of the role of the Jewish scriptures in Ephesians: 'Es hat sich gezeigt, daß der Verfasser des Epheserbriefes über einen "Schriftgebrauch" im spezifischen Sinne nicht verfügt' (89).

[33] Strictly speaking, there is only one passage in Ephesians with an explicit introductory formula: 4.8/Ps. 68.19, MT(?)). The following examples are obviously direct quotations from the OT which appear without any formal quotation formula: 1.20/Ps. 110.1; 1.22/Ps. 8.7; 2.17/Isa. 57.19; 5.31/Gen. 2.24; 6.2–3/Exod. 20.12; Deut. 5.16). To these the passage in 5.14 must also be added, where an introductory formula clearly refers the readers to the 'scripture', but the exact location of OT text is not certain (Is. 26.19; 51.17(?)).

[34] There are no less than 30 allusions which can be conveniently detected in Ephesians. Passages which appear in Ephesians are written in bold letters: **4.14**/Isa. 57.20; Sir. 5.9; **4.24**/Gen. 1.26–7; Wis. 9.3; **4.25**/Zech. 8.16; **4.26**/Ps. 4.5; Prov. 4.5; Deut. 24.15; **4.30**/Isa. 63.10; **5.2**/Exod. 29.18; Ps. 40.6; Ezek. 20.41; **5.5**/Wis. 14.12; **5.16**/Dan. 2.8; Amos 5.13; **5.18**/Prov. 23.31; **5.26**/Isa. 61.10/Ezek. 16.9; **5.31–2**/Gen. 2.24; 1 Cor. 6.16; Matt. 19.15; Mark 10.7–8; **6.2–3**/Exod. 20.12; Deut. 5.16; Matt. 15.4; Mark 7.10; Luke 18.20; **6.4**/Prov. 2.2; 3.11; **6.7**/2 Chr. 19.6; **6.9**/Lev. 25.43; **6.10**/Isa. 40.26; **6.13**/Wis. 5.17; **6.14**/Isa. 11.5; 59.17; Wis. 5.18; **6.15**/Isa. 52.7; Nahum 2.1; **6.16**/Wis. 5.19, 21; **6.17**/Isa. 49.2; 59.17; Hos. 6.5. See also Dunn, 'Deutero-Pauline Letters', 137–8.

[35] Dunn, 'Deutero-Pauline Letters', 138.

[36] Sampley, *One Flesh*, 159–63, concludes that '[t]he theological and ethical perspectives of the author of Ephesians are informed by and grounded in the OT' (160).

Christ and his church-body, is now reinforced with the Jewish scripture as its vehicle (vv. 23, 28, 29, 30). Scriptural reference also stands behind the command to honour parents (6.2–3), which is a non-formal invocation to Exodus 20.12 (cf. Deut. 5.16; Col. 3.20).[37] The 'commandment of God' here not only shows the common value which our author shared with other Jewish writers (cf. Sir. 3.3–16; 4Q416 2.3.15–19 (= Sapiential Work A); Philo, *Spec.* 2.261; *Decal.* 1.121; *midr.* Deut. 6 on Deut. 22.6; Col. 3.20) but also provides a good starting point for religious dialogues (if not quarrels) among the Jews.[38] The 'volume' of the allusion to the Jewish scriptures becomes even louder when the author attaches to the commandment God's 'promise', echoing the original promise of the land (i.e., Canaan) to Israel – even though the 'earth' here may have become a well-tempered word which enables our author to broaden the scope of the promise to include the Gentile readers as its bearers: 'that it may be well with *you* and that *you* may live long on the earth' (6.2b–3; cf. Deut. 5.16).[39] In all these ways the author's use of the Jewish scriptures reveals facets of Ephesians' setting within Judaism. The Jewish scriptures provide the best possible interpretative context for the ethical teaching in Ephesians.

The reason for the heavy use of the Jewish scripture in Ephesians is obvious enough: it shows the continuity of Ephesians with the Jewish tradition to such an extent that the Jewish scriptures had become part of the author's tacit dimension, forming the 'grid' of his theological and ethical weaving.[40] The underlying indebtedness to the scriptures best explains why such formal 'introductory' formulae as 'in accordance with the scriptures' are scarcely required in Ephesians.[41] The author's use of the scriptures may not have conformed to our modern ideas and criteria

[37] See also Freund, 'Decalogue', 140–1, who concludes that the Decalogue may have been seen as a vehicle for the expression of relevant and immediate ethical, societal or religious concerns, and that the citations of differing orders and commandments by key Hebrew Bible and NT figures imply that 'they saw the Sinaitic revelation as something more than a one-time appearance and declaration' (140–1).

[38] See, e.g., the 'in-house' dispute between Jesus and the 'Pharisees and the scribes' (e.g., Matt. 15.4; Mark 7.10; 10.19).

[39] Lincoln, 'Use', 39, who rightly observes that the promise has been introduced by the writer to reinforce the commandment, but it is far from the truth that 'as a consequence the writer may have failed to integrate its Jewish this-wordly perspective consistently with his earlier interpretation of inheritance' (39).

[40] I am indebted to Polanyi, *Personal Knowledge*, 87. See also Dodd, *Scriptures*, who concludes that the OT scripture is the 'substructure' of all Christian theology (127); cf. Dunn, *TPA*, §7.2.

[41] Schrage, *Ethics*, writes: 'The Jewish tradition of the OT is rather already an integral part of the Christian tradition' (248).

for quoting scriptures,[42] but it does conform to the contemporary Jewish way of interpreting them and must be judged in that light.[43] It also means that we (hearers) will be able to discern (by hindsight) the 'echo' of the original voice if due attention is given first and foremost to the language of scripture which our author has uttered.[44]

Two further indicators of the Jewish character of Ephesians are also worth mentioning before we conclude our present analysis. The directions to slaves and masters (Eph. 6.5–9) are based presumably on two Jewish motifs: the 'fear of the Lord'[45] and God's impartiality,[46] which are peculiarly Jewish ideas. In his exhortation to the 'masters'[47] our author also uses characteristic language of Jewish apocalyptic thought, where the heavenly realm above had a number of regions (Deut. 10.14; 1 Kgs 8.27; 2 Chr. 2.6; Neh. 9.6; *1 Enoch* 60.8; 61.12; 70.3; *2 Enoch* 8.1; *Apoc. Mos.* 37.5).[48] The implication is that the author views the present (social) reality from the perspective of God's cosmic majesty (2 Macc. 15.4; Judith 9.12).[49]

The exhortation on the battle against the 'powers', which forms the final part of the paraenesis in Ephesians (6.10–20), uses characteristic Jewish language. The *topos* of 'warfare' is familiar enough in classical

[42] See further Koch, *Schrift*, 11–23, who sets forth in a methodologically precise way the criteria used to determine a direct quotation; Thompson, *Clothed with Christ*, esp. ch. 1.

[43] See further Fitzmyer, 'Quotations'; cf. Carson and Williamson, *It is Written*, passim.

[44] *Pace* Moritz, *Mystery*, who concludes that the subtle use of Israel's Scriptures is best explained on the presupposition that there was a not insignificant Jewish-minded contingent – perhaps ethnic Jews or Gentile God-fearers – among the addressees and that a significant portion of the recipients had sufficient knowledge of these Scriptures to appreciate the thrust of the quotations and allusions employed (25, see also 54 and 126). What Moritz has overlooked, however, is the more fundamental aspect of the *speaker's* perspective. It is more likely that the Jewish Scriptures reveal the continuity of Ephesians with the Jewish tradition and, more importantly, the author's indebtedness to that tradition which provides the proper basis for establishing some of the taken-for-granted assumptions of the author. For a helpful discussion of the social function of allusions, see, e.g., Dunn, *1 Corinthians*, here 101; Barth, 'Traditions', 5. See further Giles, 'Ethnicity Markers'; Holmes, *Sociolinguistics*, 190–201.

[45] 5.21; Judith 14.3; Wis. 17.10; 2 Esd. 15.33, 37. The same motif is echoed in the NT: see, e.g., Phil. 2.12–13. In our present context, it is Christ rather than the earthly masters that slaves should fear.

[46] See, e.g., Deut. 10.17; 2 Chr. 19.7; Sir. 35.12–16; cf. Acts. 10.34; Rom. 2.11; Col. 3.25; Jas. 2.1.

[47] The word-play κύριοι/Κύριος (paronomasia) is conceived in the original.

[48] *Pace* Lincoln, 'Heavenlies', who suggests that the author of Ephesians was not concerned about the number of heavens, nor dependent on apocalyptic or rabbinic speculation in this regard (479–80).

[49] See esp. Gibbs, *Creation* 131, who points out that the significance of heaven is that it is where God's throne is.

Greek (and Roman) literature,[50] but the idea of 'putting on the armour of God' is wholly and exclusively Jewish.[51] The author has alluded to the Jewish scriptures (Isa. 11.5; 59.17; Wis. 5.18). He uses characteristic Jewish language throughout: 'flesh and blood', a well-established Jewish expression for humanity (Hebr. בשר ודם, 6.12; Sir. 14.18; *1 Enoch* 15.4; *b.* Sanh. 91a; Matt. 16.17; 18.23; 1 Cor. 15.50; Gal. 1.16; Heb. 2.14);[52] 'having girded your loins' (6.14; Exod. 12.11; Jer. 1.17; Judith 4.14); 'having put on the breastplate of righteousness' (6.14; Isa. 11.5; Wis. 5.18); 'the helmet of salvation' (6.17; Isa. 59.17);[53] 'the sword of the Spirit, the word of God' (6.17; Isa. 49.2; Hos. 6.5); and, 'open my mouth' (6.19; Ezek. 3.27; 29.21; Wis. 10.21; Sir. 15.5; 24.2; 2 Esd. 9.28; 14.37–41; 1QH 10.7).[54] Given the various Jewish features in the expressions mentioned above, we cannot but admit that these are significant clues to the author's ethnicity and that his thought processes are impregnated with characteristic Jewish thought and manner of speech.[55]

2.3 The new perspective on Ephesians 2.1–10

It should be clear by now how far and in what way the author has spoken as one who perceives the world as a Jew, echoing typically Jewish language, terminology, thought and ideas. The various Jewish categories mentioned in the foregoing are but a starting point for our exploration of Ephesians within a Jewish context. As we shall see, the spectacle of the Gentile 'other' in 2.1–22 gains its laden significance within this Jewish context. I shall show in our exegesis of vv. 1–10 that our passage provides some of the most important information about the Gentile 'other' from a Jewish perspective.

[50] See in particular Burgess, 'Epideictic Literature', here 209–14. Burgess contends that warfare furnishes a theme for speeches common to almost all writers in history, and that the conditions under which a general's speech is supposed to be delivered are those of an army at the moment of conflict; Shelton, *Romans*, esp. ch. 11.

[51] See in particular Neufeld, *Armour*.

[52] The phrase πρὸς αἷμα καὶ σάρκα, in which the preposition πρὸς governs the two nouns in one regimen, suggests that the author perceives the 'blood' and 'flesh' as conceptually one. See also Behm, 'αἷμα', who concludes that 'Greek authors who bring the words together think more of the actual constituents of the human body' (172); Böcher, 'αἷμα', here 38.

[53] *Pace* Lincoln, 'Use', 42–3, who concludes that the homily of Eph. 6 is inspired by the Pauline depiction of the believer's armour in 1 Thess. 5.8. He does not, however, indicate whether 1 Thess. 5.8 *also* uses typical Jewish language.

[54] It is likely that the author has likened himself to the prophets of the Jewish scriptures, proclaiming 'the mystery of the Gospel'.

[55] See also Holmes, *Sociolinguistics*, esp. ch. 8.

2.3.1 A Jewish representation of the Gentile 'other'

The Gentiles ('you',[56] over against 'we also' in v. 3)[57] 'were dead in their trespasses and sins', meaning by that that they were in 'false steps' or unintentional blunders (cf. 1.7),[58] and that they deliberately deviated from the right way or failed to achieve God's standard.[59] The net result of both their unintentional errors and their deliberate unacceptable conduct is the same: their faults had led them to (spiritual) death. The theology behind such caricature is typically Jewish (Gen. 2.15–17; Ezek. 3.20; 14.11–13; 18.21–2, 26; cf. *1 Enoch* 103.5; Col. 2.13).[60] With the prepositional clause 'in which (*sc.* sins) you walked . . .' (v. 2a),[61] the former state of the Gentile readers is put beyond question in Jewish terms. For the metaphor 'walk' (= 'the walk of life' or the way one conducts himself) is typically Jewish (הלך),[62] and atypical of Greek thought. Indeed the

[56] The pronoun stands in the accusative case, but there is no expressed verb to which it forms the object. The verb implied is probably 'make alive' in v. 5 below: 'But God . . . brought us to life'.

[57] Lincoln, *Ephesians*, 91–2, who contends, and quite rightly so, that 'the readers are primarily Gentile Christians (cf. 2:11)', but concludes that 'this is not deducible either from the force of the καί or the use of the second person plural as over against the first person plural'. Lincoln's claim is pedantically unnecessary, for it can only be sustained when vv. 1–10 are read in isolation from the subsequent paragraph – which is not likely in the original (written without accents, breathings and paragraph divisions in a modern sense). But more importantly, Lincoln also failed to detect the various Jewish features in Eph. 2.1–22 which show that the author speaks of the Gentiles from a Jewish viewpoint in which 'you' is understood as the ethnic 'other'. See further Kuhn, 'Ephesians'; Mußner, 'Contributions', 162–3, 166–7, 171, 175–6; Braun, *Qumran*, 216–17; Dunn, 'Deutero-Pauline Letters', here 138; Bruce, *Ephesians*, 283.

[58] See, e.g., Rom. 6.23; 7.10, 24; 8.10; Col. 2.13; *Pss. Sol.* 3.7; 13.5, 10; Polybius, *Hist.* 15.23.5. See further Bauder, 'παράπτωμα'; Wolter, 'παράπτωμα'; Michaelis, 'παράπτωμα'; BAGD, s.v., 2αα.

[59] See Günther, 'ἁμαρτία'; Fiedler, 'ἁμαρτία', 66.

[60] In Hellenistic Jewish thought, 'death' is usually seen as a metaphor for a life of wickedness; hence, the epithet 'corpse-bearers': see, e.g., Philo. *Leg.* 1.105–6, 107–8 (on Gen. 2.17); *Post.* 45; *Det.* 48; *Her.* 309. See further Wedderburn, *Baptism*, 63.

[61] *Pace* Lincoln, *Ephesians*, 93–4, who claims that the feminine relative pronoun αἷς in v. 2a refers not to its most immediate antecedent ταῖς ἁμαρτίαις but to the whole phrase 'your trespasses and sins'; Patzia, *Ephesians*, 177. If the two nouns, 'trespasses' and 'sins', are to form a hendiadys to expressing one concept, we would expect the author to drop the definite article of the second noun (see, e.g., 4.24; 6.4; 6.5; 6.12). See further Bruce, *Ephesians*, 280 n. 14; Harris, 'Prepositions', 1178; Zerwick, *BG*, no. 117.

[62] See, e.g., 2 Kgs 20.3; Prov. 8.20/Eccles. 11.9; 28.18; Eccles. 4.15; Isa. 33.15; 59.9; Sir. 13.13; *Jub.* 21.22; *T. Abr.* 10.13; *Mart. Isa.* 3.3; *T. Iss.* 3.1; 4.1, 6; 5.1; *T. Jud.* 24.3; 1QS 1.6, 8; 3.20–1; 5.10; $1QS^b$ 3.24; CD 2.15–16; 7.4–7; 9.4; 1QpH 11.13–14; 1QM 13.12, et al. There can be little doubt that the typically Jewish way of articulation was inherited by our author and other NT writers: see, e.g., Eph. 4.1, 17 (twice); 5.2, 15; Rom. 6.4; 8.4; 13.13; 1 Cor. 7.17; 2 Cor. 4.2; 5.7; Gal. 5.16; Col. 1.10; John 8.12; 11.10; 12.35/1 John 1.6 and 2.11; 2 John 4/3 John 3, et al. The corresponding Hebrew verb הלך gives

expression here provides one of the most obvious linguistic clues to the author's ethnicity.[63]

Although the author does not provide a detailed catalogue of the Gentiles' 'sins' (cf. Col. 3.7),[64] their 'sins' are made plain in his subsequent argument in vv. 2b, 2c:

2.2a (ἐν αἷς ποτε περιεπατήσατε)
2.2b κατὰ τὸν αἰῶνα τοῦ κόσμου τούτου,
2.2c κατὰ τὸν ἄρχοντα
τῆς ἐξουσίας
τοῦ ἀέρος
τοῦ πνεύματος
τοῦ νῦν ἐνεργοῦντος
ἐν τοῖς υἱοῖς τῆς ἀπειθείας

The massing together of various genitival phrases after the prepositional phrase 'according to the prince' (κατά τὸν ἄρχοντα) suggests, most probably, that the author intends to describe the various characteristics of the 'prince' by means of an expanded *gemination*:[65] if so, the first genitival phrase (τῆς ἐξουσίας) fulfils its role as an adjective, 'the powerful prince' (otherwise, 'the prince of power');[66] the 'air' denotes the domain/realm of this powerful 'prince'; the prince is a spirit-being

rise to the technical term 'halakhah' to denote rabbinic rulings on how the Torah should be interpreted in daily life: see, e.g., Exod. 16.4; Lev. 18.4; Jer. 44.23; Ezek. 5.6–7. See further Seesemann, 'πατέω', 944; Dunn, *Romans*, 315–16; cf. Dunn, 'Echoes', 461–2; Dunn, *Colossians and Philemon*, 71; Caird, *Letters*, 51; Schnackenburg, *Ephesians*, 91 n. 11; Barth, *Ephesians*, 213; Ebel, 'περιπατέω', 943–4; Lincoln, *Ephesians*, 94; Patzia, *Ephesians*, 177; BAGD, s.v. περιπατέω. The development in the paraenesis with the use of the verb περιπατέω (e.g., 4.1, 17 (twice); 5.2, 15) is a well-known rhetorical device in rabbinic writing, which, significantly, indicates the author's debt to Jewish convention. See further Kitchen, *Ephesians*, 17.

63 Cf. Mark 7.5; Acts 21.21. See further Holmes, *Sociolinguistics*, 190–201.

64 The intertextual connections between our present expression in v. 2a and Col. 3.7 (ἐν οἷς καὶ ὑμεῖς περιπατήσατε κτλ.) are clear enough. In the latter, the dative relative pronoun οἷς looks back to the neuter ἅ in v. 6a and the 'sins' include 'fornication, impurity, passion, evil desire, and greed, which is idolatry'. The language of Col. 3.6–7 shows a typical Jewish impression of the non-Jewish world: see, e.g., Wis. 14.12, 30; Judith 8.18–20; *2 Enoch* 2.2; 10.6; 66.1, 5; *Sib. Or.* 3.235; 4.5ff.; *T. Nap.* 3.3; *T. Jud.* 16.2; *T. Sim.* 5.3; *T. Ash.* 5.1; 1 Pet. 4.3.

65 The second κατά-phrase in v. 2c *repeats* the first (v. 2b) by virtue of its syntactical structure: the second κατά-phrase is almost identically inside the same sentence by attaching extra information to the first from a new slant. See further Wills, *Repetition*, 418ff.

66 Best, *Ephesians*², 204; cf. Rom. 13.1–3; 2 Cor. 10.8; 2 Thess. 3.9; also John 5.27; Acts. 26.10; Rev. 13.4–5, 7, 12; 17.13; Tobit, 7.10; 1 Macc. 10.38; Josephus, *A. J.* 247; Philo, *Legat.* 26, 54, 190; *Opif.* 17; *Cher.*, 27.

or a 'middle being' betwixt earth and heavens;[67] and the final genitival phrase τοῦ νῦν ἐνεργοῦντος κτλ. can then be seen as an 'incomplete' epiphoric (unit-final) multiplication which is 'unfinalizable' (to use M. Bakhtin's word) and which could still open to further multiplications (if required), or otherwise as leading to the climax of the author's characterisation of the 'prince'. The pleonastic nature of the whole phrase in v. 2c would not be out of accord with the author's style and denotes he is searching for befitting expressions by which he could represent the 'prince'/ruler as precisely as possible.[68] Suffice it to say that one of the effects of massing together the various genitival phrases in asyndeton (τῆς ἐξουσίας, τοῦ ἀέρος, τοῦ πνεύματος, του κτλ.) is probably emphasis or intensification, making the author's utterances appear vigorous and, not least, creating an impression of vehemence (cf. Quintilian, *Inst.* 9.3.53–4).

Still more importantly, what is at stake is the author's perception about the Gentiles: they walked in sins according to the 'aeon' of this world. Scholars who lay a great deal of weight on the Jewish apocalyptic conception which understood the world history as a sequence of 'ages', especially 'this age' and 'the age to come', often opt for a spatio-temporal reference here.[69] Thus, it is alleged that the Gentiles, instead of being oriented to the life of the age to come, had been dominated by this present evil age and this world ('this world-age'). Their sinful activities were simply in line with the norms and values of a spatio-temporal complex which is wholly hostile to God.[70]

[67] *Pace* Lindemann, *Aufhebung*, 110, who sees the 'prince' and the 'spirit' (*geistige Atmosphäre*) as two separate entities; cf. Lindemann, *Epheserbrief*, 36; Carr, *Angels*, 103, who sees the spirit in v. 2c as a reference to a spiritual influence other than the 'prince'; and the suggestion of the 'world atmosphere' or *Zeitgeist* by Wink, *Naming*, 84. The use of the term 'spirit' (Heb. *ruach*), as designating angels who belong to the heavenly realm, is very frequent in Jewish apocalyptic literature: see, e.g., 1 Sam. 6.1; 1 Kgs. 22.21; Job 4.15; Heb. 1.14; 1QS 3.21–3; 1QH 10.8; *Jub.* 1.25; 2.2; 15.31–32; *2 Enoch* 12.1–2; 16.7; *T. Levi* 4.1; 2 Esd. 6.41; *Apoc. Abr.* 19.6. See also *1 Enoch* 15.4, 6–8, 10, which refers to the disembodied giants who are 'spirits'. In any case, in *1 Enoch* 15–16, the 'spirits' are no longer in the heavenly realm as such. In Qumran 4Q530 column ii line 2 they are called 'princes'; cf. *Jub.* 10. See further Davidson, *Angels*, 155–6; Sekki, *Ruah*, 145–71; Davidson, *Angel*, 55, 152–6, 203–4, 219–20; Sjöberg, 'πνεῦμα', 375–6.

[68] For other epiphoric and anaphoric (unit-initial) multiplications in Ephesians, see, e.g., the use of such formulae as 'in Christ' and 'in whom' in the introductory eulogy of our epistle (1.3–14; 4.4; 4.11; 4.13; 6.10–12). See further Wills, *Repetition*, 418–26; Bullinger, *Figures*, 70; Turner, *Style*, 85. For a brief discussion of the different interpretations of v. 2c, cf. Carr, *Angels*, 100–3.

[69] Thus Gnilka, *Epheserbrief*, 115; Bruce, *Ephesians*, 281 n. 18; Lincoln, *Paradise*, 170; cf. Lincoln, *Ephesians*, 94–5, 'this world-age'; Carr, *Angels*, 100; Arnold, *Ephesians*, 59; Page, *Satan and Demons*, 185; Best, *Ephesians*^{2}, 203, et al.

[70] See, e.g., Lincoln, *Ephesians*, 95.

The foregoing reading, however, is by no means conclusive.[71] It makes good sense when we regard the reference in v. 2 as signifying an alien or 'another' deity Αἰών (i.e., a deity 'without beginning middle and end, without change', *SIG*³ 1125.5–6) which had already acquired religious significance in the Hellenistic period,[72] since in the same location we also find 'another' supernatural being like the 'prince of the air' or the 'spirit that is now at work in the sons of disobedience' (vv. 2b, 2c). The concern here is not so much that there is 'a penetration into Christian thinking of a mythological conception of syncretism which came to play a most important part in Gnosticism'[73] or a personal evil power which is the apposition of the prince of the realm of air.[74] Nor is the concern here a personified 'World-Age' who is the antagonist of God's good creation and of God himself.[75] Still less is there a 'demonification of the aeon-concept'.[76] Rather, the author's statement is ethnographic: he was putting himself in the shoes of a typical Jew who looked at 'the rest' as outside the realm of God. Moreover, his statement resembled

[71] The syntax of Eph. 2.2b is unique in the NT, namely, the two lexical items, αἰών and κόσμος, as they now stand, are not necessarily interchangeable. They are more likely to exhibit not a synonymic but rather a hyponymic relationship, meaning the noun αἰών *unilaterally* entails the second noun κόσμος, where ὁ αἰών is a hyponym of ὁ κόσμος τούτου, and by the same token, ὁ κόσμος τούτου is a superordinate of ὁ αἰών. This follows that the genitive phrase τοῦ κόσμου τούτου may have the force of restriction, it confines the αἰών to this world (order). For a helpful discussion of 'hyponym' in modern linguistics, see esp. Cruse, *Lexical Semantics*, 88–92, 123–4.

[72] See, e.g., *SIG*³ 1125.8 (74–73 BCE); *SIG*³ 757 (1st CE) has recorded an inscription dedicated to Αἰών as a deity, cited in M-M, s.v.; *IG* 2.4705; Ps-Callisthenes, *Alexander* 1.30.6, 1.33.2; Epiphanius, *Panarion* 51.22; *PGM* 1.200; cf. Macrobius, *Sat.* 1.19.14; Lydus, *De Mensibus*, 64.6–14. The present view was originally proposed by Reitzenstein, *Erlösungsmysterium*, who concludes that αἰῶνος is 'the endless time' and is a deity with a real cult (171–207); cf. Nock, 'Mandulis Aion', 78–99, esp. 83–9; Colpe, *Schule*, 209–16; Stambaugh, *Sarapis*, 84–5; Gnilka, *Epheser*, 114; Lindemann, *Aufhebung*, 56–9, 108–11; cf. Lindemann, *Epheserbrief*, 35; Schlier, *Epheser*, 103–4; Mußner, *Christus*, 26; Pokorný, *Epheser*, 99; Schnackenburg, *Ephesians*, 91 n. 2; Zepf, 'Aion'; Winston, *Wisdom*, 257; Sasse, 'αἰών', 198, 203 n. 20, 207–8; BAGD, s.v., 4. By far the most detailed study of the subject is undertaken by Zuntz, who investigates how the dedication to Aion came to be made at Eleusis in the time of Augustus. Zuntz's main contention is that Aion became a god – an activator and preserver of the universe – when Augustus 'proclaimed' the god Aion for the Greek world, and that Augustus did this with the same intention and at the same time (17 BCE) as he announced the start of a new Aera (*saeculum*) by celebrating the Secular Games (56–8). It must be said that scholars who opt for the personal reference here did not necessarily depend on the later Gnostic myth for its support, cf. Nock, 'Mandulis Aion', 90. For the meaning of 'Aion' in late antiquity, see, e.g., Parker, 'Aion'.

[73] *Contra* Pokorný, *Epheser*, 99; Sasse, 'αἰών', 207–8; Schweizer, 'Kirche'. Chronologically the link with Gnostic or Hermetic literature is tenuous.

[74] Kobelski, 'Ephesians', 887; also Lindemann, *Epheserbrief*, 35.

[75] Barth, *Ephesians*, 214.

[76] Gnilka, *Epheserbrief*, 114–15; Schnackenburg, *Ephesians*, 91 n. 9; also BAGD 28.4.

the language of typical Jews who disagreed with the Gentiles' religion and who would speak dismissively against the Gentiles, who lay outside the orbit of God. The main gist of the author's message is to reduce the Gentile religion to the category of the false (cf. 4.1–6 and 4.17–19). Thus his statement tells as much about the sort of people the Gentiles were as about the sort of person the author might be. His statement can be best explained by the hypothesis that exclusive monotheism, one of the 'pillars' of early Judaism (or 'common Judaism'), is for him a pertinent factor in the pre-conversion situation of the Gentiles.[77] The naming of a foreign deity reveals more about his religious convictions than about his personal interest in the deity.[78]

The author's method of argument is very similar to that of Hellenistic Jewish polemics against Gentile idolatry. Philo, for example, named several Hellenistic deities in order to underscore their 'otherness' and discredit their validity (*Decal.* 54–5, 59, 64, 66; *Spec.* 1.20). According

[77] For the author's characterisation of the Gentiles in 2.12 – 'having no hope and without God in *the* world' (ἄθεοι ἐν τῷ κόσμῳ), see my discussion in 3.3.3, below. The connection between Jewish identity and their monotheistic faith is profoundly clear throughout the history of the Jewish people, see Exod. 20.3; Deut. 4.39; 6.4; Isa. 45.20–5; Josephus, *A. J.* 5.1, 17, 112; also Philo, *Decal.* 65. Jewish monotheism was well recognised by 'outsiders', see in particular Tacitus, *Hist.* 5.5.4; Origen, *Cels.* 1.24. See further Dunn, *Partings*, 21; Cohen, *Maccabees*, 81–5.

[78] The method of argument of the Ephesians author is probably closer to that of Philo, who named many alien deities to reinforce his dismissive attitude toward worthless Hellenistic idols, e.g., Hera (air), Kore (the goddess who gave birth to Aion), Demeter, Pluto (earth), Poseidon (sea), Hephaestus (fire), Apollo (sun), Artemis (moon), Aphrodite (morning star) and Hermes (glitterer). Philo's main aim was to expose the fact that the names of these 'foreign' deities were 'misleading titles'. Possibly in his view is the Jewish presumption regarding the sublimity of its idea of God which underlay Philo's disparagement of Gentile religion. These alien deities were assigned to underscore the objects of worship by those who have intentionally hidden the true God from their own sight (παρεκαλύψαντο ψευδωνύμους προσρήσεις ἐκείνοις ἐπιφημίσαντες ἑτερας ἕτεροι, *Decal.* 53). Since these names represent barely the componential elements of the universe (τῶν τοῦ κόσμου μερῶν), they should not be equated with the one omnipotent God (*Decal.* 58); cf. Philo, *Spec.* 1.14; *Contempl.* 3, 131. See also Deut. 4.19; 17.2–3; Wis. 13.1–2; *Sib. Or.* 3.1–38; *1 Enoch* 75.1; 80.6–7; *Jub.* 2.2. However, one must concede that the evidence that Aion was venerated in Asia Minor is wanting in our extant literature other than Ephesians. Therefore our author may have provided a fresh piece of evidence in his representation of the reality of Gentiles' religion. The following NT passages can be understood in thc same light: see esp. 2 Cor. 4.4; Gal. 4.3; Col. 2.8. A similar 'rhetoric of ridicule' is also found in Philo's *QG* 1.100, where he condemned those who idolised 'time' (Gk. Χρόνος) as their god. Philo's argument is based on the assumption that 'God's life is not a time, but eternity, which is the archetype and pattern of time; and in eternity there is no past, nor future, but only present existence' (*Deus.* 31–2); see also *Mut.* 267; *Mer* 165; *Plant.* 47–53; cf. Philo, *Decal.* 52–7, 64, 66; *Abr.* 69, 71, 77, 84; *Mos.* 2.193–6; *Spec.* 1.13–31, 32–5, 331–2, 344–5; *Fug.* 180; Wis. 13.1–2; *1 Enoch* 80.6–7; *Sib. Or.* 3.1–38; cf. Deut. 4.19; Rom. 1.18–25; 2 Cor. 4.3–4; Gal. 4.3; 1 Pet. 4.3; Ep. Jer., et al. See further Pfeiffer, 'Polemics'; Winston, *Wisdom*, 248; Pettazoni, *Aion-(Kronos) Chronos*, 171–207; Brandon, 'Time as God'; cf. Brandon, *Deity*, 31–64.

to Josephus, Jews had a reputation for slighting the divinity of what others professed to venerate (*A. J.* 3.179; Wis. 13.1–9; *Joseph & Aseneth* 7.3). The 'Aion of this age' can therefore be understood as castigating terms underscoring the incongruity of Gentiles who walked according to the creation rather than following the Creator *par excellence*. His language is therefore a reflection of the attitude of typical Jews who were bold enough to ridicule those who did not acknowledge their exclusively monotheistic piety (e.g., Philo, *Decal.* 53, 58, 64; *Congr.* 103–5; Wis. 14.12–14; cf. 2 Cor. 4.4). The implication is that the Gentiles who 'walked in sins' ('Gentile sinners', cf. Gal. 2.15) had failed to recognise the one true God but lived in accordance with the norms set by a foreign 'god' whose totality of existence is limited to 'this world' (cf. 1.3–4). It should come as no surprise that the 'Aion of this world' is almost equivalent to an epithet of denigration: the Aion that pertains to this (created) world.[79] The point is that our author (a Jew) was well able to 'borrow' the name of a foreign deity and to put it to the service of his exclusive monotheism. In portraying the 'divine space' of a foreign deity ('the Aion *of this world*'), he was able to underscore the *otherness* of the Aion, the outer limits of his 'world' in which the axiom of exclusive monotheism is a pertinent factor (see my discussion in the previous section), and more importantly to lay bare the 'otherness' of his Gentile readers.[80]

It should be clear by now that the idea of a personal Αἰών and a Jewish context, when taken at face value, seem to be in gross tension with one another but in fact are not. In his ethnographic statements about the Gentile, our author lays bare the fact that the otherness of a 'foreign' deity and the otherness of his Gentile readers are inextricably bound, each shedding light upon the 'otherness' of the other.

In addition, the Gentiles are said to be under the control of 'the powerful prince of the air' (κατὰ τὸν ἄρχοντα κτλ.).[81] The basic idea is clearly

[79] I therefore disagree with Schlier, *Epheser*, 102, who argues that the author refers to 'this world encountered as a unified and personified god of eternity'; Bruce, *Ephesians*, 282; Merklein, 'ἀήρ'; Lincoln, *Ephesians*, 95; Best, *Ephesians*^{2}, 203–4; Holtz, 'αἰών', 46. Lindemann, *Epheserbrief*, 35, aptly concludes that 'the dominion of this timeless Αἰών is this world (*Das Herrschaftsgebiet dieses Äons ist diese Welt*)'. Cf. 1 Cor. 3.19; 5.10; 7.31.

[80] *Pace* Roberts, 'Enigma', who suggests a situation which held true for all mankind, *both* Jews and Gentiles suffered the fate of being under the rule of evil powers (100).

[81] *Pace* Merklein, 'ἀήρ', who identifies the 'prince' with the 'aeon of this world'. Three major interpretations are proposed regarding the meaning of the term ἄρχων: (1) For scholars who desire to explain the origins of evil in the universe, the 'prince' is often read as a demonic or evil spirit that delights in determining what humankind will do by bending them to his will (Schnackenburg, *Ephesians*, 90). Hence, the term ἄρχων has often been interpreted as Satan (Caird, *Letters*, 51; Aune, 'Archon', 156; Page, *Satan and Demons*,

that human destiny is in some sense controlled by mysterious agencies and influences.[82] The idea outlined above is not peculiarly Jewish and has ancient lineage traceable at least as far back as the Greek belief in a scale of living creatures who reside in different regions (earth, water, air (or ether), fire) of the universe in ascending order of perfection (e.g., Plato, *Leges* 4.713C–D; cf. Plato, *De loide* 272E; Plato, *Politicus* 109B–C; Plato, *Cratylus* 397D; Plutarch, *De fato* 572F–573B; cf. Plutarch, *Isis et Osiride* 361B; *De Defectu Oraculorum* 415A–B; *De tranquillitate animi* 474B–C; Cicero, *De divinatione* 1.30.64; Celsus, *Aretes Logos* 5.25). The author of *Epinomis* (Philippus of Opus?), for example, has given an elaborate sketch of a cosmic system of five spheres (fire, ether, air, water, earth) in which the cosmic soul is filled with living creatures (θεογονία καὶ ζῳογονία). The second and the third domains are the abode of the daemons or 'air-borne race' (ἀέριον γένος) which had their existence and activity betwixt mortal and immortal: they 'interpret all men and all things both to one another and to the most exalted gods' (984A–985B; cf. Plato, *Symposium* 202D). The same line of argument is pursued in Hellenistic Judaism in which such middle beings as 'daemons' and the 'unbodied souls', like the angels in the Jewish tradition, are believed to be situated

185–6; Wink, *Naming*, 83), the Evil One (Schnackenburg, *Ephesians*, 91; Bruce, *Ephesians*, 282), or an 'ultimate personal power of evil' behind the principalities and powers (Lincoln, *Ephesians*, 95). Foerster, 'ἀήρ', 165, has gone so far as to suggest an organised kingdom which comes under the single ruler Satan. (2) Others have surmised that the DSS provide sufficient parallel ideas to those in our epistle and have identified the figure Belial with ἄρχων (Carr, *Angels*, 102). Our present term occurs quite often in the NT and whenever it is believed to refer to the devil or Satan there are always sufficient clues to confirm the referent (e.g., Matt. 9.34, ἄρχων τῶν δαιμονίων; see also 12.24; Mark 3.22; Luke 11.15; or, ἄρχων τοῦ κόσμου τούτου, as in John 12.31; 14.30; 16.11. See further BAGD, s.v., 3; Delling, 'ἄρχω'. (3) It is more likely that the word ἄρχων denotes an angelic figure (e.g., Dan. (Theod.) 10.13, 20–1; 12.1; 1QS 3.20; CD 5.18; 1QM 13.10; 17.5–6; *1 Enoch* 6.3, 7, 8; 98.46; *Joseph & Aseneth* 14.8; *T. Sim.* 2.7; *T. Jud.* 19.4; *T. Benj.* 3.4; *2 Enoch* 29.4; b. Yoma 77a; *b.* Pesahim, 111b; *Asc. Isa.* 7.9–12; 10.20; *PGM*, I, 97–194; IV, 2699. See further Str-B, IV, 516; Mußner, *Christus*, 16f.; Rokeah, *Jews*, 150–1, 155–6; Schürer, *HJPAJC*, III, 882–3; Kasher, 'Angelology', 168–91. See also Winston, *Wisdom*, 250; Davidson, *Angels*, 147–8; Gnilka, *Epheserbrief*, 64–6; Collins, 'Prince'; Sekki, *Ruah*, 145–71.

[82] The most famous instance of the idea can be found in Hesiod, *Opera et dies*, who writes: 'For upon the bounteous earth Zeus has thrice ten thousand spirits, watchers of mortal men, and these keep watch on judgments and deeds of wrong as they roam, clothed in mist, all over the earth' (252–3; cf. 122–3). Plato, *Pol.*, 271D–E, claimed that in the early times the world and all its creatures were divided among daemons, who acted as divine shepherds, caring for all the needs of the creatures entrusted to them; cf. *Symposium* 202D–203A; Euripides, *Alc.* 1003; Plato, *Cratylus*, 398B; Plutarch, *Gen. Socr.*, 593D; Lucian, *Peregr.* 36. See further Dietrich, *Fate*, 327–37; Boeft, *Fate*, 8–20; cf. Boeft, *Demons*, here 1–6; Robertson and Dietrich, 'Fate'; Stewart, *Myths*, 434–50; Brenk, 'Moon', 2087; Cargal, 'Heavenlies', esp. 805–8.

in the domain of the 'air' (Philo, *Somn.* 1.134–5, 141; *Gig.* 6–8, 58; *Conf.* 176 and 174; cf. Philo, *Flacc.* 123).[83] It should occasion no surprise that the Gentile readers could have no difficulty in comprehending the author's 'sentence meaning': the 'powerful prince of the air' is a 'middle being' who dominates and constitutes the 'air' and whose existence is betwixt earth and heaven.[84]

But we must not lose sight of the fact that the author is speaking about the Gentiles from the perspective of a Jew (cf. vv. 11a; 3.1). What is ingrained in his statements is therefore the spectacle of the 'other'. The question that needs to be addressed is therefore the significance his 'utterance' could have for him and his readers: what does *he* (a Jew) mean (instead of, what does he mean by his sentence in v. 2?) by saying that the Gentiles walked in sins according to this 'middle being'? The answer is probably that the author's characterisation of the Gentiles here is, like his previous statement, a way of positioning 'another'.[85] I am inclined to think that he has harnessed the language of 'angelology' (or daemonology) as a means to measure the religious and social distance between himself (or other Jews) and the Gentiles and, simultaneously, to affirm the cosmic majesty of his own God.[86] This theology was well rooted in the Jewish scriptures: 'When the Most High apportioned the

[83] The Hellenistic Judaism mentioned here may be contrasted with the disembodied demons/spirits version in the Enochic traditions in which the spirits are not placed within a stratified supra-terrestrial cosmos (i.e., in the air). Rather, they dwell essentially on the earth as a kind of punishment for the evils they committed before the great flood. See further the following passages on 'demon' or 'daemon': Hesiod, *Op.*, 122–3, 252–3 (i.e., human beings who transmuted into the spirits, cf. Plutarch, *Def. orac.* 415B); Plato, *Symp.* 202E (i.e., demon = Eros who is a great god!); [Plato], *Epin.* 984a–985c (i.e., the middle beings who dwell in the realms of ether and air, acting as interpreters of all things, to one another and to the highest gods); Plutarch, *Def. orac.* 417A (i.e., the 'daemons' are the guardians of the sacred rites of the gods and prompters of the mysteries), cf. 417C; *Is. Os.* 360D–361A (i.e., demigods), 361B (i.e., 'holy deities'). See further Boeft, *Fate*, esp. 1–7; Stewart, *Myths*, here 434–50; Brenk, 'Moon'; Böcher, 'Däemonen'; Versnel, 'Daimôn'. See also Rist, 'Daimonion', who argues that the 'daimonion' is a spirit-guide or a 'voice' within a person; Darcus, 'Daimon'.

[84] Cf. *T. Levi* 3.3–8. See also Dibelius, *Geisterwelt*, 158–64; Schlier, *Epheser*, 180f.

[85] The 'spirit'/powers language had become a powerful weapon in early Christian polemics, probing human groups, establishing the differences between them and reinforcing where their 'otherness' lay: see, e.g., John 8.44–7, 48–53; 2 Cor. 4.3; 1 Tim. 4.1; Rev. 3.9; *Mart. Isa.* 2.2–4, et al. See further Smith, 'Powers'; Johnson, 'Slander'; Segal, 'Ruler'; Kee, 'Membership', esp. 105–6, 115; Rokeah, *Jews*, esp. 133–67; Dunn, *Partings*, 21; Cohen, *Maccabees*, 81–5. This aspect of the language has been missed by most commentaries: Lincoln, *Ephesians*, 123–4, 167–8; Carr, *Angels*, 25–43, 100–11; Wink, *Naming*, 89–96; Lee, 'Powers'; Arnold, *Ephesians*, passim.

[86] See particularly Dunn, *Galatians*, 192.

nations, when he divided humankind, he fixed the boundaries of the peoples according to the number of the gods' (Deut. 32.8–9).[87] There the concern is not simply with *how* Israel came to have a unique relationship with God, but also with the way in which the unmatched position of Israel in the whole cosmos over against the nations could be defined.[88] The boundaries on which the distinctive identity of Israel as the chosen people of God depends must have given Israel a profound sense of privilege (cf. Exod. 19.5–6; Deut. 7.6–8; 10.15; 29.13; 32.9; 33.29).

The thought world mentioned above is enshrined by the author of *Jubilees*, who harnessed the 'spirit' language to reinforce the *set-apartness* of Israel: while 'other' supermundane powers rule over all the nations and lead them astray, Israel is God's choice and is not subordinated to any angel or spirit-being (15.28–32).[89] Similarly with Philo, who consistently referred to Deuteronomy 32.8–9 to accentuate the distinctive identity of Israel as God's portion over against the nations: accordingly, the difference between Israel and the nations has already been made explicit in the Law, for the boundaries between Israel and other nations 'were fixed not by the creation to which we belong, but on principles which are divine and are older than we and all that belong to earth' (*Post.* 89–92, 167–9; *Plant.* 58–60; *Congr.* 58; *Virt.* 73–4). Philo's endeavour to find a theological rationale to uphold the distinctiveness of Israel is well within the thought world of other Jews who perceived themselves as the chosen people of God. No different are the covenanters at Qumran, for whom the 'spirits' had played an important role in aiding them to sharpen the boundaries of their own group over against an 'other': while their own community has come under the supervision of God with the Prince of Light,[90] the 'sons of perversity' were 'sub-let' to the Angel of Darkness or Belial (1QS 3.20–1; 1QM 13.4, 7–13; 15.2–3; 4Q286 7.2.6;

[87] The LXX Deut. 32.8–9 reflects the Hebrew *bene elim* (*sc.* ἀγγέλων θεοῦ) instead of *bene yisrael*, cf. 4QDeut.[q]; Philo, *Post.* 89–92; *Plant.* 59–60; *Congr.* 58.

[88] von Rad, *Deuteronomy*, 197; Preuss, *Theology*, esp. 38, 105, 256. Skehan, 'Structure', suggests that the *bene El* in Deut. 32 are associated with the celestial bodies which are taken as the types of real spiritual beings, the guardian angels of the individual nations, who are subject to the Lord and take charge of the nations at his bidding. Israel, however, is governed by no angel, but by the Lord himself, directly (154); cf. Skehan, 'Song of Moses'; Meyer, 'Dtn 32', 197–209.

[89] Meyer, 'λαός', 41, has gone so far as to suggest that the use of 'lead them astray' points clearly to heathen idolatry: non-Jews were seduced to apostasy from Yahweh (i.e., idolatry) by their national genii. Meyer's argument is based on the assumption that the 'gods' stand behind the national genii; cf. Collins, 'Prince', 1250; Clements, *Deuteronomy*, 47; Mach, *Engelsglauben*, 257–62.

[90] So the self-designation of the Qumran members as the 'sons of light': see, e.g., 1QS 3.13, 24, 25; cf. 1QS 1.3; 2.6; 1QM 1.1, 3, 9, 11, 13.

11QMelch. 2.12–13(?)).[91] Despite the fact that the Qumran sectarians did not always walk perfectly in the ways of light (e.g., 1QS 3.21–3), this does not deter them from using the 'spirit' language to assert that humankind is in either one category or the other.[92]

If our analysis is correct, the author's characterisation of the Gentiles in v. 2c is a negative verdict on the Gentiles. His language and style are reminiscent of a certain self-confident Judaism that is bold enough to promulgate the Gentiles' defects by positioning them within the domain of 'another' power (cf. 6.11–12(?)).[93] His characterisation of the Gentiles suggests, most probably, that he sees himself as one of God's choice.[94]

Suffice it to say that the author was able to heighten the boundary between different human groups by attaching the Gentiles to the 'Aion of this world' and the 'prince of the power of the air'. Indeed one cannot fully appreciate the language of 'powers' in v. 2 (*pace* Arnold, Carr, Wink) without taking into account the author's Jewish perspective in which Gentiles were truly 'out of place' on the basis of his monotheistic piety and self-perception as God's elect. But why then did he choose to represent the Gentile 'other' in such a manner of speech? The wider picture of his formulation may seem odd at this point, but its intention will be clearer later.

[91] See also 4Q390 fr. 1.11: 'And the Angels of hostility (i.e., Mastemoth) will *rule over them* and [. . .] they will turn aside and do [. . .] what I consider evil, *walking* in the stubbornness of their hearts.' Although the present text contains several lacunae, its general sense is clear. The sect also adduced different epithets to describe those beyond its pale; see for examples 1QM 18.1, 3: 'the whole horde of Belial' which includes the Kittim (either a Greek or Roman ruler) and the 'army' under Belial's dominion. This is contrasted to 'the God of Israel' and 'the holy ones' (i.e., angels *and* the community itself); cf. Dan. 10.13, 20, 21; 12.1; *1 Enoch* 20.5; 4Q390 2.1.4, 6–7; 2.1.8–10; 1QpHab 9.5, 12; 8.11, 12.6–9; 4Q286–7 Plate 12 fr. 3.2.6.

[92] The dualism at Qumran was always within the framework of monotheism: see, e.g., Pryke, 'Spirit and Flesh', 346–7, 350; May, 'Cosmological Reference', 4; Davidson, *Angels*, 160, 166; Licht, 'Two Spirits'; Sekki, *Ruah*, 213–15; Anderson, 'Ruah'; Kee, 'Membership', 115; Nitzan, '4QBerakhot^{a-e}', 495. Treves, 'Two Spirits'; and Werner-Møller, 'Two Spirits', both suggest that the 'two spirits' are simply 'tendencies or propensities which are implemented in every man's heart'. This view, however, is rejected by most scholars, see esp. May, 'Cosmological Reference', 1–3.

[93] Cf. Sir. 17.17, which I have not included as evidence in our present discussion. For it is more likely that the author of *Sirach* has in mind a human 'ruler', rather than an angelic being: cf. 33.19; 41.17. See also Carr, *Angels*, 31.

[94] Cf. Plutarch, *De fato* 572F–573A, who claimed that humankind is conformed to different 'grades' of providence (πρόνοια): the providence which belongs to the daemons stationed in the terrestrial regions as watchers and overseers of the actions of mankind would reasonably be called tertiary, as opposed to the primary providence of God in the strictest sense and to the highest degree (πρόνοια ἡ ἀνωτάτω καὶ πρώτη τοῦ πρώτου θεοῦ); cf. 574A.

Further evidence that the author perceives the world as a Jew is found in the designation of the 'prince' who energises his power among the 'sons of disobedience'.[95] This Semitising expression suggests a whole class of persons who are disobedient to God.[96] The same designation also occurs in Ephesians 5.6. There the author refers to those who indulged in voluptuous acts and lewd conversations (5.1–6).[97] Here the 'disobedient' are still held under the angelic 'prince' (hence the use of the adverb νῦν).[98]

To sum up. If we have 'heard' our author correctly, we cannot avoid the conclusion that his statements about the Gentiles mean more than the passing on of information about the latter. What is mirrored in these statements is, indeed, the deep sense of chosenness which enabled him to translate the Gentiles into the Jewish world through his rhetoric of 'otherness'.[99] The otherness of the foreign deity and the 'prince', according to whom the Gentiles walked, are simply euphemisms for the otherness of the Gentiles. The naming of these 'powers' thus provides an adequate point of reference for his Gentile addressees. As ethnographic categories the 'Aion' or the 'prince' is like a landmark in space confirming the Gentiles in a preordained class/category according to the author's Jewish perceptions.

2.3.2 The rhetoric of admission and conciliation

It is premature, however, to suggest that the negative verdict on the Gentiles is the ultimate end of the author's argument. We should not allow the author's vigorous language to distract us from careful investigation

[95] The Jewishness of the present expressions is beyond doubt: see, e.g., Eph. 3.5 ('sons of men'); also 1 Sam. 26.16; 1 Macc. 2.47; Sir. 16.1; Matt. 23.15; Luke 16.8; 20.36; 1 Thess. 5.5; 1QH 5.25: 'sons of disaster'; 'sons of sin': 1QH 6.30; the 'sons of darkness': 1QS 1.10; 1QM 1.1, 7, 16; 3.16; *1 Enoch* 10.9; *Apoc. Mos.* 3; et al. See further Braun, *Qumran*, 216–17; Wink, *Naming*, 82; Blässer, 'ἀπειθέω'; Zerwick, *BG*, no. 43; Moule, *Idiom*, 174–5.

[96] See also Rom. 2.8; 10.21; 11.30–2; 15.31; Heb. 4.6, 11; *Ps. Sol.* 17.20; Josephus, *A. J.* 3.316.

[97] The prepositional phrase διὰ ταῦτα in Eph. 5.6 is anaphorical in its usage: it looks back to those sinful behaviours which the author describes in 5.1–5: fornication, impurities, covetousness, filthiness, obscene talks, levity, etc.; cf. Col. 3.5. Indeed these behaviours are typical Jewish charges against the Gentile world, cf. *T. Reub.* 1.6; 3.3; 4.6–8; Wis. 2.16; *1 Enoch.* 10.11; *T. Jud.* 14.5; *Arist.* 152.

[98] The 'form-critical' analysis of Tachau, *Einst*, 134–43, ignores the challenge of the adverb νῦν in v. 2, which clearly suggests that the schema (at least the 'now' aspect of the schema) can be used to denote not only the Christian 'present' but also those who *are* disobedient to God.

[99] See also my discussion of vv. 11–12 in chapter 3, section 3.2.1–3.2.3 below.

of the underlying issues at stake between Jews and Gentiles. The dismal image of the Gentiles is but a preamble to a vigorous self-assessment of the author himself, whose aim is (re)conciliatory, seeking to mitigate the (social) distance between Jews and Gentiles, and more importantly to confront both human groups with the grace of God which is brought about by or through Christ. This he has done by turning the tables on himself and his fellow-Jews: 'Among them we also, all, once lived in the passions of our flesh, following the will of the flesh and mind' (lit.).[100] Possibly the self-indictment is aimed at what the author perceives to be a typical Jewish attitude of polemic against Gentile idolatry, which would applaud Jewish condemnation of Gentile religion and miss the wider relevance of the broader list of vices into which Jews could slide without being fully aware. The implication is clearly that the Jews were not quite 'set apart' from the 'sons of disobedience'.[101] They were among the latter[102] and lived 'in accordance with the desires of the flesh'.[103] Given that the author is conscious of his own ethnicity when he speaks of himself and his fellow-Jews, we cannot rule out that he may be referring to the insatiable desires which are forbidden by the Law (e.g., Num. 11.4, 34; 15.39; 33.16, 17; Deut. 9.22; Ps. 105.14; Prov. 6.25; Sus. 8–12, 32; cf. Sir. 18.30–1; Rom. 7.7–8, et al.)[104]

Although the term 'flesh' does not necessarily carry with it negative overtones (e.g., 2.11b; 2.14; 5.29; 6.5, 12), its neutral sense can certainly be ruled out here. Indeed the 'flesh' has now been perceived as a kind of 'power' under which Jews indulged in its desires, fulfilling its 'will' (cf. 4 Macc. 7.18; Gal. 5.16, 24). The additional conjunctival phrase καὶ τῶν διανοιῶν probably suggests that *even* (epexegetic καί) their thoughts or dispositions were filled with desires which crave for the satisfaction

100 *Pace* Richardson, *Israel*, who contends that 'there is no contrast between Jewish and Gentile Christians, for the statement in 2: 11 has not been made yet, but rather an application to a particular instance from general experience' (150).

101 Thus the emphatic καὶ ἡμεῖς ('even we'). See further Abbott, *Ephesians*, 43; Bruce, *Ephesians*, 283.

102 *Pace* Robinson, *Ephesians*, 155 who argues that the relative pronoun οἷς denotes the trespasses and sins of v. 2; Ramaroson, 'Éphésiens 1, 15–2, 10', here 397. The relative pronoun οἷς, most probably, looks back to the the 'sons of disobedience' as its antecedent.

103 The author may well suggest that the Jews were within the sphere of influence of the flesh; for this usage of the preposition ἐν, cf. Porter, *Idioms*, 157. The term ἀνεστράφημέν here has much the same sense as περιπατέω in v. 2, cf. the related noun ἀναστροφή, in 4.22; also Gal. 1.13; 2 Pet. 2.7, 18; Prov. 20.7; 2 Macc. 6.23; Tobit 4.14; *Arist.* 130, 216; *Test. Ash.* 6.3; Josephus, *A. J.* 18.359; 19.72; BAGD, s.v.; M-M, s.v.

104 In Hellenistic Jewish thought, 'desires' refer quite often to the lustful portion of the soul: see, e.g., Philo, *Leg.* 115; *Decal.* 142–53; *Mos.* 2.23–4; cf. 4 Macc. 1.22–7; 2.4–5; 3.11–16.

of mortal appetites and propensities (cf. Num. 15.39; Sir. 3.24; Baruch 1.22; 4.28; *Arist.* 292; *T. Ben.* 5.1). It should come as no surprise that the author could pass a negative verdict on himself and his fellow-Jews: 'and we (too) by nature children of wrath, like "the rest"'.[105] Again the rhetoric of the author is that of admission, although his manner of speech is characterstically Jewish (5.8; Sir. 16.1; 41.6; Rom. 9.8; 1 Pet. 1.14; 2 Pet. 2.14).[106] The underlying assumption of this vigorous language is probably that God is the sustainer as well as the author of the moral law and that Israel had breached this law (e.g., Isa. 30.9–11; 59.12–13; 63.10; 65.2; cf. Rom. 10.21). In short, the author does not speak in commendatory fashion or with great confidence about his and his people's own 'nature'.[107]

2.3.3 The saving grace of God in Christ

The author's self-portrait above rings oddly, until we realise that his vigorous language is that of admission and of conciliation: the Jews, too, had fallen short of God's standard, as much as 'the rest', and were worthy of God's wrath.[108] In so doing, he has taken an essential step in mitigating the difference between himself (his fellow-Jews included) and his Gentile readers. The aim of his argument is to reveal a much deeper insight, namely that there is a way of release from the hopeless condition of humankind: 'But God, who is rich in mercy, out of the great love with which he loved us . . .'. There can be little doubt that the author has in mind both the Gentile readers and Jews here.[109] The characterisation of God as 'rich in mercy' clearly echoes earlier voices of the Jewish scriptures

[105] *Pace* Lincoln, *Ephesians*, who is of the opinion that 'what was once true of the readers (vv 1, 2) was also once true of all believers (v 3a), and what was once true of all believers is also true of the rest of humanity' (99).

[106] See further Zerwick, *BG*, no. 43; Mußner, *Epheser*, 60–1; Lincoln, *Ephesians*, 98; Schnackenburg, *Ephesians*, 92; Schneider, 'τέκνον', 341.

[107] It is worth noting that our author has parted company from not a few Jewish writers who had spoken with great certainty of their good 'nature': see, e.g., Josephus, *A. J.* 4.193; cf. 5.317; 6.294; 7.130; 14.13; Philo, *Decal.* 59; also *Spec.* 2.42; *Prob.* 160; *Abr.* 6. It is precisely this confidence which enables Josephus (and other Jews) to speak in negative terms about the bad nature of the rest of mankind: see, e.g., Josephus, *A. J.* 5.215; 6.59, 136; *B. J.* 1.255; cf. Wis. 13.1f. The passage in Gal. 2.15 can probably be read in the same light.

[108] See esp. Exod. 32.10–12; Num. 25.1–4; Deut. 29.16–28; 2 Chr. 24.18; Jer. 7.16–20; Isa. 30.1, 9; Ezek. 22.1–4. It is far more likely (*pace* MacGregor, 'Wrath', 105–6) that 'wrath' is an *effectus* ('feeling,' 'emotion'), God's eternal opposition to sin and sinners, than an *affectus* ('action,' 'activity'), an impersonal principle of retribution or law of cause and effect in a moral world; see esp. Harris, *Colossians and Philemon*, 147.

[109] *Pace* Lincoln, *Ephesians*, 99–100, who argues that the author 'returns to the thought begun in v.1 interrupted by his expression on what it means to be dead through trespasses and sins in vv.2, 3'.

(e.g., Exod. 34.6–7a; 102.8; Jonah 4.2; Wis. 9.1; Sir. 2.11; Pr. Man. 6–7, 14). With God's mercy is conjoined his love. For anyone who is familiar with the Jewish scriptures, God's mercy and love are tightly knitted with his election of Israel, underscoring his faithfulness to his covenantal relationship with Israel (e.g., Deut. 7.7–10; Neh. 9.17, 19; Hos. 3.1; 11.1; Baruch 3.36; 2 Esd. 4.23; 5.27; 1QS 4.4; 1QH 10.14; 1QM 14.4; 4QM[a] 8.3; *T. Mos.* 4.1, 5).[110] It is probably the deep sense of chosenness which enables our author to use the 'covenant' language to underscore God's steadfast love and mercy (cf. Ps. 32.18–19; Tobit 8.16; Judith 7.30; Wis. 3.9; 15.1; Sir. 36.12; Pr. Azar. 19).[111] The contribution of our author is that the scope of God's mercy and love is now broadened out to embrace both Jews and Gentiles (cf. 1.3–4).[112]

There can be little doubt that the author continues to speak of God who 'made alive the dead' in characteristically Jewish terms.[113] C. Burchard has observed that 'around the beginning of the common era, he who gives life to the dead had become all but a definition of God in Judaism'.[114] Indeed we cannot understand the author's language (and therefore his faith) except in terms of Jewish thought. The contribution of our author is that the immeasurable greatness of God's power in making the dead alive is heightened through the Messiah,[115] the agent of God's mercy and

[110] *Pace* Barth, *Ephesians 1–3*, 219, who concludes that 'Ephesians does not make use of specific covenant language'; Schlier, *Epheser*, 109 who concludes that the love of God mentioned here is associated with the event of baptism; cf. Pokorný, *Epheser*, 102.

[111] Cf. Ps. 77.68; 2 Macc. 7.37; Wis. 3.9; 4.15; Sir. 36.17; 2 Esd. 8.45; *Shemoneh 'Esreh* 1, 19; 11QPs 19.1–18.

[112] See further Bruce, *Ephesians*, 285.

[113] See, e.g., Tobit 13.2; Wis. 16.13; 2 Macc. 7.22–3; 1QH 3.19; 4Q521; *Joseph & Aseneth* 8.3, 9, 12.1; 15.5; 20.7; *Arist. 16.5*; *T. Gad* 4.6; *T. Aser* 5.2; *T. Job* 4.8; *2 Baruch* 85.15; Ep. Jer. 9.13; *LAB* 3.10; Liv. Pro. 10.5–6; 21.5; *Shemoneh 'Esreh* 2. The Jewish faith is clearly shared by other NT writers: see, e.g., Rom. 4.17; Col. 2.13; John 5.21.

[114] Burchard, 'Joseph and Aseneth,' *OTP*, II, 234; Hofius, 'Eine Altjüdische Parallele'.

[115] The reading συνεζωοποίησεν ἐν τῷ Χριστῷ is well attested in the earliest witnesses: see, e.g., P[46] B 33, et al. Metzger, *Textual Commentary*, reads v. 5a as συνεζωοποίησεν τῷ χριστῷ: 'The reading of ἐν τῷ χριστῷ seems to have arisen because of an accidental dittography of the previous verb συνεζωοποίησ[εν] or a deliberate assimilation to ἐν χριστῷ Ἰησου in verse 6' (602); so most commentators: see, e.g., Schnackenburg, *Ephesians*, 94–5; Pokorný, *Epheser*, 178, 180–91; Gnilka, *Epheserbrief*, 33; Kirby, *Pentecost*, 150–61; Wilson, 'We'; Schille, *Hymnen*, 102; Lincoln, 'Heavenlies', 472; NA[27]; UBSGNT[4], et al. There are, however, two weaknesses in Metzger's theory: (1) This alternative reading would break the triple parallel of 'in Christ', 'in Christ Jesus' in vv. 5–7, and more importantly (2) Metzger's theory is also weakened by the following examples which are excerpted from our epistle: (a) 1.20, in which the phenomenon of 'accidental dittography' is expected to occur, but does not: ἣν ἐνήργησεν ἐν τῷ Χριστῷ κτλ., and (b) 3.11: κατὰ πρόθεσιν τῶν αἰώνων ἣν ἐποίησεν ἐν τῷ Χριστῷ Ἰησοῦ τῷ κυρίῳ ἡμῶν.

love.[116] The most striking feature in v. 5a is that it is almost a word-by-word repetition of the essential content of v. 1a except that this time it alters the pronoun 'you' to an inclusive 'we' and 'sins' is omitted. This can be best explained by the hypothesis that the author is registering a statement of 'agreement' or admission/confession. However, this 'agreement' cannot be fully appreciated without taking into account the author's dialogic perspective, let alone his self-criticism in v. 3.[117] The force of his argument is clearly that what is true of the Gentiles (v. 1) is also true of 'all' (Jews, v. 3a): both were dead in their trespasses (violations of God's commands) and both were in need of God's mercy to overcome the power of death.[118]

The talk of Jews and Gentiles being enthroned in the 'heavenly places' (ἐν τοῖς ἐπουρανίοις) can be read in the same light: it reflects the common Jewish perception that there are many layers of heaven or the heavenly realm, which consists of a number of regions.[119] This understanding of the 'heavens' enables our author to speak in turn of the other 'powers' that populate 'the heavenly places', probably understood as the lower reaches of the highest height (v. 2; 6.12; cf. 4.10).[120]

The striking fact, however, is that the wide range of Jewish apocalyptic and mystical works shows unequivocally that there is no precedence for *Gentiles* having been seated in the heavenly places, and for both Jews and Gentiles to be honoured in the heavenly realms as companions in the heavens (i.e., *sunthronoi*!) is evidently unprecedented.[121] The idea of earthly

[116] There is no suggestion in Ephesians that the death from which Jews and Gentiles have been brought to life is their death with Christ, a theme which is characteristic in Paul's earlier letters: see, e.g., Rom. 6.8, 13; Col. 3.1. See also Bruce, *Ephesians*, 285.

[117] The conciliatory nature of the author's statement in v. 5 is often missed by modern commentators: see, e.g., Lincoln, *Ephesians*, 101 who contends that the connective καί in v. 5 is best explained on the basis of its repetition of v. 1, where its occurrence is in turn to be explained as being dependent on Col. 2:13; Best, *Ephesians*^{2}, 214, who argues that the initial καί in v. 5 is due to 'preformed material'; cf. Best, *Studies*, 69–85. The translation of NRSV is close to the mark; cf. Bruce, *Ephesians*, 279.

[118] Bruce, *Ephesians*, 285–6, notes that the author has departed from the distinctively Pauline usage in which 'you were raised with Christ' is always the sequel to 'you died with Christ': see, e.g., Rom. 6.8–13; Col. 2.20–3.1.

[119] See, e.g., Deut. 10.14; 1 Kgs. 8.27; 2 Chr. 2.6; 6.18; Neh. 9.6; 2 Cor. 12.2; *1 Enoch* 14.5; *2 Enoch* 8.1; 20.3; 21.6; 22.1; *T. Lev.* 3.8; 5.1; *Apoc. Abr.* 8.1; 9.19; Num. *R.* 14.12; Philo, *Leg.* 3.168; *Gig.* 62; *Virt.* 12. See further Gruenwald, *Merkavah Mysticism*, esp. 31; Lincoln, 'Heavenlies', 469. I therefore disagree with Käsemann, 'Epheserbrief', here 518, who suggests that the phrase ἐν τοῖς ἐπουρανίοις has links with Gnostic thought; cf. Conzelmann, 'Epheser', 57; Schlier, *Epheser*, 45–8.

[120] Cf. 1.20; 2.2; 6.12; cf. *Asc. Isa.* 11.23–33, where Beliar is said to have occupied 'the firmament', i.e., the region between the earth and the heaven.

[121] The language of 'sitting' here signifies, most probably, honour and privilege: see, e.g., Exod. 15.6; Ps. 20.6; 44.3; 80.18; 89.13; 118.5–6; Isa. 41.10; 48.13; Jer. 22.24; Mark

figures being exalted to the heavens and sitting on the throne is, though, repeatedly found in Jewish apocalyptic writings before and after the first century of the Common Era. The well-established axiom was always that only specific, privileged figures of distinctive pedigree (e.g., the righteous, the elect, or the pious ones) deserve that 'place'.[122] The exaltation of the Messiah Jesus to the heavenly place can certainly be understood in the same light (Eph. 1.20–2; 4.7–10). What could have prompted the author's daring if not provocative formulation?[123] Does he wish to express, as some assert, 'the believer's present eschatological situation'?[124] Should we read his statements here as presenting humankind with a challenge to existential decision, the transcendental dimension of human existence (e.g., Schlier's 'die Himmel Daseins')?[125] Was his use and selection

10.37; also Sir. 12.12; 2 Esd. 4.29. See also 4Q416 2.3.11–12 ('For out of poverty He has lifted up your head, and with nobles *He has seated you*, and in a glorious inheritance He has placed you in authority. Seek out His favour always'); cf. 1QH 3.19f.; 4Q521; Luke 22.27; Rev. 3.21–2. See further Hengel, 'Enthronement', here 166, 204; Grundmann, 'δεξιός'; Hay, *Glory*, 59–153; Segal, 'Ruler', esp. 218–20.

122 E.g., Enoch: *1 Enoch* 45.2–3; 51.3; 55.4; 61.8; 69.27–9, cf. Philo, *QG* 1.86; Heb. 11.5; Moses: *Exagoge* 74–5, 86; Philo, *Mos.* 1.158; Num. *R.* 12.11; *Deut. R.* 11.10 (240b); *midr.* Pss. 24.5 (102b); 68.11 (160a). See also 1QH. 3.19–23; 4Q491; *Asc. Isa.* 9.18. In Hellenistic Jewish thought, the heaven is the purest of all creation and is destined to be the most holy dwelling-place of manifest and visible 'gods': see, e.g., Philo, *Opif.* 27, 114; *Abr.* 272; *Spec.* 1.1; the heavenly region is where the citizenship of the wise lies, Philo, *Conf.* 78. Despite the fact that the idea of the heavenly enthronement is evident in the Jesus tradition (e.g., Matt. 19.28// Luke 22.28–30), it is always futuristic. The author of Ephesians has certainly gone farther than Col. 3.1–4, where the author claims that those who have been raised with Christ from death are exhorted to seek things above, but remains muted about their heavenly enthronement. See further Bauckham, 'Throne', 51–53, who argues that the role of the divine throne in the highest heaven symbolises the sole sovereignty of God over all things and that in most cases the throne of God is the only throne in heaven: even when on occasions several thrones are referred to in Jewish literature they are all thrones of God; Bockmuehl, *This Jesus*, esp. ch. 7; Bruce, *Ephesians*, 286–7; van der Horst, 'Throne Vision', here 71.

123 I have in mind the works of Halperin, 'Ascension', who contends that the unwelcomed ascent into the heavenly realm is considered by some Jews as a kind of invasion (47); Himmelfarb, 'Heavenly Ascent', 84–5; and Segal, *Two Powers*, esp. ch. 2. The suggestion that there is a second throne in heaven for the Messiah has given rise to no little controversy among the rabbis, cf. *b.* Hagigah 14a. Surprisingly, Bauckham, in his discussion of the throne of God in the highest height as a key symbol of monotheism representing one of the essential characteristics definitive of the divine identity ('Throne', 53–66, esp. 55–7), is muted about the Gentiles having been seated in the heavenly places. Could it be that the author of Ephesians is well aware that the throne of God symbolises the unique sovereignty which is intrinsic to God's unique identity, and places the Gentiles on it for the sake of a similitude: Gentiles will be in relation to the malignant 'powers' of the air as God (and Christ, cf. Eph. 1.20–2) is in relation to the cosmos?

124 See, e.g., Bruce, *Ephesians*, 287; Lincoln, 'Heavenlies', 469, 482–3; Lona, *Eschatologie*, 360–4; Arnold, *Ephesians*, 151–5, et al.

125 Schlier, *Epheser*, 45–8.

of eschatological terms prompted by a cosmic-anxiety (*Weltangst* – Lona)?[126]

One notoriously difficult problem in this connection is, of course, that the kind of imminent expectation discovered in Paul's earlier letters is alleged by some scholars to be absent in Ephesians.[127] So far as I can see, discussions of the realised aspect of the eschatology in Ephesians have come to a stalemate. Some progress, however, may be made towards the understanding of the selection and use of eschatological terms in v. 6 by the method here advocated and illustrated. The method in question is the simple one of enquiring about the factors that prompted the motif of heavenly enthronement. Two factors, in particular, need to be taken into account in any attempt to explain the vocabulary in v. 6. The first factor which may be looked to for some explanation of the heavenly enthronement may be described as the demand for constructing a new 'space' for the Gentiles. The point is that the heavenly enthronement in v. 6 is introduced in part to destigmatise the Gentiles' defective status: namely, the Jewish estimation that the Gentiles are 'sub-let' to the 'prince', whose residence is the 'air', can no longer be sustained. They have now crossed the boundary from the lower 'air' to the highest height. They no longer share the same space with the 'prince' but are enthroned in the heavenly places to which Christ is exalted, 'far above all rule and power and dominion' (1.20–1; 3.10; 6.12). The elevation of the Gentiles to the heavenly places can therefore be seen as a vindication of the Gentiles: they are 'relocated' in the place where Christ reigns, and should not be deemed 'out of place'.[128]

[126] Lona, *Eschatologie*, esp. 428–88, who argues that a crisis has affected the entire Hellenistic world under the Roman empire. Individuals felt estranged in spite of the unity brought by the Roman empire. The world has suffered from cosmic-anxiety (*Weltangst*) which was engendered by the realisation that the cosmos is unstable and is under the influence of malevolent, demonic powers capable of causing chaos (439). The eschatological statements in Ephesians thus reflect the way in which the author has responded to the cosmic-anxiety and the realised aspect of eschatology is to strengthen the recipients who faced the mounting threats of their environment (425–6, 442).

[127] See, e.g., Merklein, 'Rezeption', who suggests that the eschatological reservation recedes in Ephesians – 'Der eschatologische Vorbehalt fällt' (48). Lindemann, *Aufhebung*, goes so far as to suggest that futuristic eschatology is absent in Ephesians (129f.); cf. MacDonald, *Pauline Churches*, 143, 153.

[128] I therefore disagree with Knox, *St Paul*, who argues that Ephesians was written for Hellenistic readers who were not seriously concerned with the relation of Jews and Gentiles but wanted a mystery which would explain the Gospel and the practice of the Church in terms of ascent of the soul to heaven (190ff.); Conzelmann, 'Epheser', who links the concepts of Eph. 2.5–6 specifically with the Gnostic understanding of salvation, i.e., a liberation from the material world which involves the heavenly journey of the soul (66).

The second factor is that the heavenly enthronemant is a way of speaking of God's grace toward humankind and of the supreme demonstration of his power through Christ (vv. 4–6).[129] Based upon the conviction that the one God has raised Christ from death and enthroned him at his right hand (1.22; cf. Rom. 6.4), the author asserts that the glorious power of the same God is also at work in Jews and Gentiles, making them alive and transposing them from the power of death to the blessed heavenly places (1.3–4; cf. 1QH 3.19–23; 11.10–12). As a result this elevation appears to impart information about the new possibility which God has opened for Jews and Gentiles, namely that human life could transcend death by passing to the higher heavenly sphere 'now', an idea which is seen most often in Jewish apocalyptic writings.[130] By saying that Gentiles and Jews become fellow-σύνθρονοι in the heavenly realm,[131] the author was able to reinforce the idea of transition from the power of death (and the consequence of alienation from God) to close communion with God. Indeed the realm into which both Jews and Gentiles are translated is the dwelling-place of God (1.3; cf. Heb. 8.1; 12.2).

But God lavishes his mercy on Jews and Gentiles with a profound purpose: 'in order that he might show in the coming ages the immeasurable riches of his grace in kindness toward us in Christ Jesus'.[132] The juxtaposition of divine 'grace' and 'kindness' is not accidental, for it reminds the recipients of God's grace as the foundation upon which the forgiveness of their trespasses was based (v. 5; cf. 1.7).[133] Again, the author uses characteristically Jewish terms here to denote God's considerate generosity which is broadened out to both Jews and Gentiles (Ps. 24.7–8; 118.64–5; 144.7; P. Man. 7, 14; *Ps. Sol.* 5.13–14; 18.1; Philo, *Leg. All.* 3.73; Josephus, *A. J.* 11.144; cf. Rom. 2.4; 11.32),[134] with the accentuation that God's gracious attitude and act are now manifested 'in

129 Christ exercises a mediating function (ἐν Χριστῷ Ἰησοῦ) between God and humankind. Presumably the mediatorial role assigned to some angelic beings is now assigned to Christ. For the use of the preposition ἐν in the NT to express God's activity through Christ, see, e.g., Allan, 'In Christ'; Harris, 'Prepositions', 1192; Roberts, 'Instrumental ἐν'; cf. Rom. 3.24; 2 Cor. 3.14; Col. 1.16.

130 See esp. Collins, 'Apocalyptic Eschatology', here 36.

131 See further *PGL*, s.v.; LSJ, s.v.

132 The conjunction ἵνα with the subjunctive ἐνδείξηται introduces a final clause, indicating the end in view. The basic sense of the word ἐνδείκνυμαι (only in middle voice in the NT) is 'to show, to manifest, to reveal': see, e.g., Exod. 9.16; Wis. 12.17; Ep. Jer. 25; 2 Macc. 9.8; *T. Job* 50.2; *Arist.* 134; 2 Macc. Rom. 9.22.

133 Thus the arthrous χάρις which looks back to the same noun in v. 5b: 'By *grace* you have been saved'.

134 Although the word χρηστότης also occurred in non-biblical Greek, it was used only to characterise persons: see, e.g., Weiss, 'χρηστότης', 489. In the NT the term (10 times) occurs exclusively in Paul.

Christ'. If we may press further, it may well be that the author uses the term αἰώες to make a contemptuous pun with 'the Aion of this world'.[135] His somehow hyperbolic statement in v. 7 is meant to affirm the cosmic majesty of the one God over the foreign deity: the one God is the God of the 'ages' (οἱ αἰῶνες), and his immeasurable wealth of grace is not confined to 'the age (ὁ Αἰών) of this world' but is demonstrated in one 'age' supervening on another, as far into the future as thought can reach (cf. Tobit 13.10; Heb. 11.3; 2 Esd. 13.26; cf. *1 Clem.* 35.3; Justin, *Apol.* 1.41).[136] Once again, the thought world here is pre-eminently Jewish, where the term 'age' is regularly used to denote time as a sequence of 'ages' (1.21; 3.5, 9, 21; cf. Exod. 40.15; Isa. 51.9; Sir. 36.17; 3.9; Tobit 1.4; 14.5; 2 Esd. 13.26).

It takes our author only a small step, on the basis of God's gracious attitude and act toward both Jews and Gentiles, to remind his readers of God's gracious salvation. This he has done through the expression 'for by grace you are saved' (τῇ γὰρ χάριτί ἐστε σεσῳσμένοι διὰ πίστεως) in v. 8 which is almost a word-by-word repetition of the preceding clause in v. 5b. What was then thrown in as a kind of 'undercurrent' (*epitrechon*)[137] to God who 'made alive' the dead (v. 5a) now emerges as the main theme in vv. 8–10.[138] Suffice it to say that the repetition of the great truth in v. 8a is a fair reminder that God's gracious salvation is fundamentally a liberation from the power of death (vv. 1, 5; cf. 1QS 11.12–13). Salvation is the free grace of God and is dependent entirely upon him. The theme of heavenly enthronement can certainly be understood in the same light. The positive response (διὰ πίστεως) to the divinely bestowed grace suggests none other than the profound trust which the recipients of salvation placed in the one God who has the power to make alive the dead and to confer honour upon the undeserved in the heavenly places (cf. 1.13; 3.12, 17).[139]

[135] It is worth noting that there is also a word-play of χάρις, χρηστότης and χριστός in the same verse.

[136] *Contra* Lindemann, *Aufhebung*, 56–9, 129–33, who argues that v. 7 refers to personal Aions, the powers that rule over each age; cf. Conzelmann, *Epheser*, 97; Schlier, *Epheser*, 112–14; Pokorný, *Gnosis*, 114. Lindemann's rejection of the temporal/future reference is based entirely on his theory that Ephesians contains only a fully realised eschatology rather than on an actual reading of the text; cf. 3.5, 9, 21.

[137] Bullinger, *Figures*, 472–4; Wills, *Repetition*, 6. *Pace* Richardson, *Israel*, 150, who suggests that v. 5 is 'an interjection with significance in the situation addressed, and does not imply that only Gentiles need to be saved by grace'.

[138] This is confirmed by the use of the arthrous χάρις in v. 8 which looks back to v. 5b in which God's gracious salvation was mentioned. The same grace is mentioned in v. 7, although this includes God's having seated the believers in the heavenly realms.

[139] The prepositional phrase διὰ πίστεως occurs 8 times in the NT: Rom. 3.22; 2 Cor. 5.7; Gal. 2.16; Phil. 3.9; 2 Tim. 3.15; Heb. 6.12; 11.33; 1 Pet. 1.3. The more common phrase in the earlier letters of Paul is ἐκ πίστεως.

The meaning of the statement in v. 8b ('and this does not proceed from you, it is the gift of God') is somewhat ambiguous grammatically.[140] The question which arises immediately is whether τοῦτο refers to the preceding statement as a whole or only to the preceding word 'faith'.[141] If one accepts that the words 'and this does not proceed from yourselves, it is God's gift' are to be taken as parenthetical, then being inserted into the statement is the clause 'for you are saved by grace through faith'.[142] This reading necessarily results in an antithetical understanding of the relationship between 'faith' and 'works'. Unfortunately, much of the discussion along this line of argument suffers from trying to read our present passage through the lens of the entire Pauline corpus. Marshall, for example, reasons that the 'faith/work' dialectic or controversy is at work in our passage (cf. Gal. 2.16; Phil. 3.9), and, on this basis, the same Pauline theology must therefore emerge in Ephesians.[143] The dilemma of the foregoing interpretation is that it has failed to take into account the phenomenon of linguistic 'transcoding' (to use Bakhtin's word), which shows that the way in which language operates is much more sophisticated than some would have thought; and, on top of that, exegetes have often allowed themselves to be boxed into an 'either–or' condition in their interpretation of v. 8.[144] The dilemma, however, can be resolved when we read vv. 8b–9 as statements of refinement. While v. 8a provides a window into the author's own thought processes he had affirmed that faith is necessary as the positive response to God's saving grace. His position, however, subsequently changed to lay bare the fact that salvation-by-faith is none other than a 'gift' from God (τὸ δῶρον).[145] The paradox of this argument is that it categorically rules out its beneficiaries as the starting point of God's saving grace.[146] The statement in v. 9 (οὐκ ἐξ

140 Thus Bruce, *Ephesians*, who writes: 'If the Greek pronoun were feminine, agreeing in gender with "faith," then the reference to faith would be plain' (89); Ridderbos, *Paul*, 234 n. 57; Lincoln, *Ephesians*, 111; Schnackenburg, *Ephesians*, 98.

141 Cf. the discussion of the problem in Lincoln, *Ephesians*, 112; Schlier, *Epheser*, 151; Caird, *Letters*, 53.

142 E.g., Bruce, *Ephesians*, 289.

143 See, e.g., Marshall, 'Salvation', esp. 342–3. Marshall's essay is prompted by the 'New perspective on Paul' and its interpretation of 'works of the Law'.

144 So Lincoln, *Ephesians*, 111–12, who argues that the writer of Ephesians has taken up 'by grace' and 'by faith' as two inseparable companions which together provide the antithesis to any suggestion of human merit: v. 8b ('not from yourselves, it is the gift of God') is a further explanation of the 'grace aspect of salvation'; v. 9 ('it is not by works, lest anyone should boast') provides a further comment on the 'faith aspect' of salvation.

145 See also Matt. 2.11; Rev. 11.10. Perhaps the word is a clear reminder of a sacrifice which is offered at the altar: see, e.g., Matt 5.23–4; 8.4; 23.18–19; Heb. 5.1; 8.3–4; 9.9; 11.4. See further Schneider, 'δῶρον'.

146 The prepositional phrase ἐξ ὑμῶν excludes the Gentile readers as the source/origin of their salvation.

ἔργων), which is a partial reduplication of what was said earlier in v. 8b (οὐκ ἐξ ὑμῶν), can also be understood in the same light, amplifying the sense of negation which the author has hinted at in his earlier statement. The author's vigorous language is probably to prevent his Gentile readers from capitalising on the merit of 'faith' or/and 'works'. Before we return to the theme of 'works', a brief comment on v. 9b is now in order.

There can be little doubt that 'boasting' (καυχάομαι) is a favourite term in the earlier letters of Paul, which often refer to actual arrogance or even 'boasting' in a positive sense (e.g., Rom. 5.2–3).[147] No similar claim, however, is made by our present author. Instead the ἵνα-clause is inherently *notional*: it aids our author to visualise in a way that human 'boasting', with 'works' as the motivating force behind it, is still capable of awaiting realisation.[148] Suffice it to say that the indefiniteness of the author's statement (τις) serves, most probably, as a powerful weapon in preventing his readers from elevating themselves as the starting point of saving grace.[149]

In the history of interpretation the explanatory force of the author's statement in v. 10 is widely recognised by most commentators.[150] But it is more likely that v. 10 introduces a statement of 'correction', on the grounds that (a) the particle γάρ introduces an argument which is based on an opposition;[151] (b) vv. 9–10 consist of words whose meanings are close enough to be grouped within the same 'semantic domain' (e.g., ἔργοι, ποίημα, κτίζειν, ἔργοι ἀγαθοῖ, προετοιμάζω);[152] (c) the two words ποιήμα and ἔργος are interchangeable, denoting 'that which is brought into being' by God (e.g., Ps. 63.10; 91.5–6). In our present

[147] The term καυχάομαι occurs 37 times in the NT, 35 of which are found in Paul. The same term and its cognates occur most often in the nascent church at Corinth (21 times!): 1 Cor. 1.29; 1.31; 3.21; 4.7; 13.3; 2 Cor. 5.12; 7.14; 9.2; 10.8; 10.13; 10.15; 10.16; 10.17; 11.12; 11.16; 11.18; 11.30; 12.1; 12.5; 12.6; 12.9; cf. Rom. 2.17; 2.23; Gal. 6.13–14; Phil. 3.3; Jas. 1.9; 4.16; *T. Abr.* 19.4; *T. Jud.* 13.2–3; *T. Job* 15.6; 41.3; Josephus, *A. J.* 8.372. See further Zmijewski, 'καύχησις'.

[148] See in particular Gonda, *Moods*, 70; McKay, *Syntax*, 141–2. I therefore disagree with Barth, *Ephesians 1–3*, 244, who reads 2.8–9 as polemical words. He claims that v. 9 may refer to the same group of people mentioned in 4.14 and 5.6, namely those who in their ignorance of God as their creator have come to perceive the source of their salvation as 'without' the realm of divine grace.

[149] See further Du Toit, 'Vilification', here 406.

[150] See, e.g., Schlier, *Epheser*, 117; Schnackenburg, *Ephesians*, 98; Lincoln, *Ephesians*, 113, et al.

[151] Cf. 1 Cor. 9.17; 11.21; 15.53; 2 Cor. 5.1 (compare 4.18); 10.4; Gal. 1.12; 3.10, 26, 28; 5.5, 13; 6.9, 13; Phil. 3.3; Col. 3.25; 1 Thess. 4.7; 5.5; 1 Tim. 6.10; Jas. 3.7 (cf. 3.6); 4.14 (cf. 4.13). See further Zerwick, *BG*, no. 472–3; BAGD, s.v., 4.

[152] See further Jacques, *List*, 167–8; Louw and Nida, 4C and 42B.

context, ποιήμα denotes humankind as God's created 'work';[153] and (d) the author uses such words as God's 'work' (ποίημα, v. 10a) and 'good works' (ἔργοις ἀγαθοῖς, v. 10b) to make a playful 'pun' with human 'works' or labour (οὐκ ἐξ ἔργων, v. 9a).[154] The aim of this word-play is to eliminate all human factors by transcoding the human performers and their 'doings' into the accomplished 'work' of God,[155] leaving no scope therefore for boasting in themselves. The word-play reaches its climax when the author speaks of 'good works' in the sense of noble deeds: 'Rather, we are his work, created in Christ for good works, which God prepared beforehand, that we should walk in them.'[156] Although the idea of 'good works' is familiar enough to the Greeks,[157] the framework here is typically Jewish. The taken-for-granted axiom is that humankind owe their existence (and salvation) to God and that their 'good works' should reflect not their own effort/labour but God's gracious attitude and act toward them (3.9; 4.5–6; cf. Gen. 2.2–3; Isa. 29.15–16; 65.17; 66.22; Sir. 7.30; 4Q405 23.2.12; 4Q504 7.4; Philo, *Congr.* 61).[158] The very idea is well attested by Jewish writers, where 'good works' are simply virtuous deeds which serve the promotion of constructive social life or piety (e.g., 1QS 1.5–6, טוב מעשי; CD 4.6; Philo, *Sacr.* 53–4, 78; *Arist.* 18.4; *Apoc. Zeph.* 3.6; *Sib. Or.* 3.220–34; *2 Syr. Apoc. Bar.* 14.12; cf. Josephus, *A. J.* 9.182; 17.159). One of the effects of these noble deeds is certainly to glue or maintain decent and responsible social relationships (*T. Benj.* 5.1–3; *T. Asher* 3.2). Doing good is truly a test-case for those who considered themselves as belonging to God, i.e., the 'sons of God' (Deut. 13.8–14.1; cf. v. 2, 'sons of disobedience'; v. 3, 'children of wrath').[159] Our

[153] See also Jdg. 13.12, where τὰ ποιήματα in the Codex Alexandrinus (A) is translated as τὰ ἔργα in Codex Vaticanus (B); cf. Ps. 8.4–7; 77.7; 92.5–6; Job 10.3; 101.26; 138.8; 143.5; Isa. 45.11; Tobit 12.22; Wis. 13.1; Sir. 33.15, 39.16; *T. Abr.* 9.6; *T. Job* 49.2–3; *Ps. Sol.* 18.1; *1 Enoch* 2.2; 5.2; *2 Bar.* 14.17; 54.18; 2 Esd. 7.134; 8.13; Philo, *Leg.* 3.99; *Opif.* 171; *Cher.* 119; *Det.* 124, 155. The word ποιήμα occurs only once in the NT: ποιήματα, 'things that have been made', as that which mirrors the invisible qualities of God, his everlasting power and divinity (Rom. 1.20). See further Braun, 'ποιέω', 471; Radl, 'ποιέω'; Ringgren, 'עשה', 430; Bertram, 'ἔργον', here 637–9; Heiligenthal, 'ἔργον', 50; BAGD, s.v., 3; Louw and Nida, 42.30.

[154] It seems more natural to construe ἐξ as indicating not the basis or means ('by works') but the source or starting point ('from works'). See further Harris, 'Prepositions', 1188–90.

[155] The position of the pronoun αὐτοῦ is emphatic.

[156] For this usage of the preposition ἐπι, cf. Gal. 5.13; 1 Thess. 4.7. See further Moule, *Idiom*, 50; Zerwick, *BG*, no. 129.

[157] See, e.g., Hesiod, *Op.*, 307; Plato, *Pol.*, 352D–353E; Xenophon, *Cyr.* 1.5–8, et al.

[158] This is further confirmed by the use of the metaphor 'walk' denoting conduct in the walk of life. See my discussion of v. 2 above.

[159] Cf. *T. Ben.* 5.1–5; *T. Nap.* 8.4–6; *T. Aser.* 3.2.

present passage can be read in the same light: namely that the author continues to understand 'good works' in terms of a Jewish category (cf. 4.28; 5.11; 6.8).[160] That the thought world of our author is characteristically Jewish is also confirmed by his assertion that God has 'made ready' these 'good works' (προετοιμάζω). The note of divine predetermination is clear enough here (cf. Rom. 9.23; Wis. 9.8). Nevertheless, the concern here is not so much to predicate the pre-existence of 'good works' before the foundation of the world[161] as to affirm God's gracious act toward humankind, namely, so that humankind should be at a loss for none of the means to reflect in the end (ἐπί) God's kindness and grace (v. 7; cf. 1.7).[162]

It is clear that the 'deposit' of Pauline thought is found in vv. 8–10: faith, grace, works and boasting (2.8–9; cf. Rom. 2.22; 2 Cor. 5.7; Gal., 2.16; Phil. 3.9). But this is Pauline language retold, however. For it has undergone a perceptible development in Ephesians: the author no longer describes the nature of salvation in terms of a neat antithetical relationship between 'faith' and 'works', but asserts that God is in the truest sense the source or starting point of all things.[163] It is on this basis that the Gentile recipients are invited to gird their understanding of salvation, faith and works solely with the principle of God as the creator *par excellence* (see 1.3–4; 4.5–6).[164] The pragmatic effect of this method of reasoning is clearly that God should and will always be the starting point in any discussion of his gracious salvation. His gracious attitude and act toward humankind relativises thus all human factors. In short, the author of Ephesians has distanced himself from the dispute over 'faith' and 'works' among the earliest Christian Jews (e.g. Gal., 2), a controversy on which

[160] Cf. Rom. 13.3; 2 Cor. 9.8; Phil. 1.6; 2; Col. 1.10; 2 Thess. 2.17. The idea of 'good works' has become most developed in the Pastorals: see, e.g., 1 Tim. 2.10; 5.10, 25; 6.18; Titus 2.7, 14; 3.8, 14. See further Towner, *Goal*, 153–4; Knight, *Pastoral Epistles*, esp. 137.

[161] *Pace* Hamerton-Kelly, *Pre-existence*, who suggests that 'good works' had pre-existed in advance even before they were put into practice (184); Ernst, 'Epheser', 310; Houlden, *Letters*, 285; Barth, *Ephesians*, 227, 249; Lincoln, *Ephesians*, 115; Balz, 'προετοιμαζέιν'. NEB unaccountably alters the object of the verb προετοιμάζω from 'good works' to personal beings.

[162] A perfect parallel to our present passage can be found in Hellenistic Jewish thought: see, e.g., Philo, *Opif.* 77, where the same verb προετοιμάζειν is used to describe God's kindness and magnanimity toward humankind; cf. *Opif.* 69; *Spec. Leg.* 1.165, 262; 2.70; *Virt.* 145; *Deus* 96; 2 Esd. 8.52; *Asc. Mos.* 1.14.

[163] For a somewhat different exposition of vv. 8–9, see Dunn, 'Works of the Law', esp. 113–15.

[164] This sense is not altogether unparalleled in Hellenistic Jewish thought: see, e.g., Philo, *Mos.* 2.48: '[T]he father and Maker of the world was in the truest sense also its Lawgiver . . .'; cf. Add. Est. 13.11; Wis. 1.14; 6.7; Sir. 24.8; 36.1; 39.16; 2 Macc. 1.24; 3 Macc. 2.21; 4 Macc. 11.5.

modern scholars still lay a great deal of weight.[165] Indeed the controversy is unnecessary, for it is based upon a hermeneutical 'grid' which is quite alien to the author of Ephesians, a Jew who understands the one God as the source of all things.

2.4 Conclusion

It is time to pull the threads together. The bulk of evidence in Ephesians is quite enough to show that the author's language, terminology, thought and ideas can be best explained by the hypothesis that his conceptual background is sufficiently and characteristically Jewish. It has also become evident from the internal evidence of the letter itself that the author thinks and expresses himself in Jewish categories and images and suggests thus his strong Jewish background.

Within this context I have argued that the author represents the Gentiles from the perspective of a Jew. I suggested that the negative verdict on the former, however, is not the end of his argument. Instead, the dismal image of the Gentiles is but a preamble to a vigorous self-assessment of a (Christian) Jew, whose aim is to confess in reconciliatory terms, to mitigate the (social) distance between Jews and Gentiles, and more importantly to confront both human groups with God's gracious attitudes 'in Christ' and acts toward humankind who sin and his magnanimity which is now brought about by or through Christ.

We must add in passing that our conclusion by no means suggests that features which can be paralleled in literary works of non-Jewish

[165] E.g., Marshall, 'Salvation', who writes: 'Ephesians is attacking a view which sees human works of any kind as a basis for God's saving action and regards this view as standing in conflict with salvation by grace' (347); Nida and Taber, *Theory*, who could still write: 'You yourselves did not save yourselves. Rather, God gave you this salvation. You did not *earn* it by what you did. Therefore no one can boast about what he has done' (53–4); Lincoln, *Ephesians*, writes: 'Works now stand for human effort in general. Salvation is not achieved by human performance or any attempt to *earn* God's approval' (112); Bruce, *Ephesians*, refers to the works as a basis 'by which some credit could be claimed for it, human merit' (290); Caird, *Letters*, 53; Barth, *Ephesians*, 244–5 concedes that the 'works' refers to 'works of the law' to which *meritorious value* was attributed rather than human works in general. Kruse, *Paul*, claims that 'works' denote 'general moral achievements of Gentiles'. He argues, on the basis of the readers as predominantly Gentiles, that there is no hint in Ephesians that they were thought to have once relied upon the performance of Jewish works (whether these are understood as all that the Mosaic law demands or as Jewish identity markers) for their salvation (98). Kruse has failed, in my opinion, to recognise the Jewish perspective of our author, namely that what matters is the way in which the first-century Jew and Judaism would normally define 'works'. Thielman, *Paul*, is more cautious at this point, concluding that Eph. 2.4–9 is 'Paul's opposition of grace to human effort generally' (306 n. 54).

origin are simply not present in Ephesians.[166] As we shall see, the author of Ephesians clearly uses Greek political terminology of other contemporaneous traditions (see my discussion in chapters 3, 4 and 5, respectively). He may well have been aware of the idea of 'discord' which had plagued ancient city-states and extended the literary *topos* of ὁμόνοια or 'concord' to reinforce the notion of the oneness of his community (e.g., 4.1–16; 5.21–32). He is probably familiar with the Graeco-Roman ideas of οἰκονομία or 'household-management' (5.21–6.9), which shows that his concerns can be paralleled in the political theorists and ethicists in the Graeco-Roman world.[167] Other contemporaneous religious terms may well be borrowed to help sharpen his own thinking (see my exegesis of 2.2a in section 2.3.1 above). These features, however, cannot in any way rule out the fact that the author is at heart a (Christian) Jew, and that the overall impression given by Ephesians is (as we shall see more clearly later) of a Jewish perspective in which materials of non-Jewish origins have been taken over by a (Hellenistic) Jew, and domesticated and put to the service of his own christological convictions and purposes.

One cannot therefore deny that there are Christian features or a christological intensification of the various motifs and some 'dominical indicators' which show that the author of Ephesians might be thinking about Jesus and would be inclined to allude to his teaching (e.g., 4.20–1; 6.2–3).[168] Overall, Ephesians shows the distinctive contribution of a Christian Jew, who, like many other Jewish writers, was able to 'transcode' some of the meanings of the traditional material when necessary.[169]

[166] See esp. Furnish, 'Ephesians', here 538–9.

[167] See esp. Balch, *Wives*; cf. Balch, 'Household Codes'; Conzelmann, *Polemics*, 135–233.

[168] See in particular Thompson, *Clothed with Christ*, 34–5.

[169] See, e.g., Lincoln 'Use,' 45, who concludes that the author's 'exegetical techniques are subservient to a christological perspective whereby the OT texts are read in the light of the new situation which the writer believes God has brought about in Christ'; Dunn, 'Household Rules', 52–3; Schrage, 'Ethik', here 19–21.

3

'YOU WHO WERE CALLED THE UNCIRCUMCISION BY THE CIRCUMCISION': JEWS, GENTILES AND COVENANTAL ETHNOCENTRISM (EPHESIANS 2.11–13)

3.1 Introduction

In our epistle, the Gentiles are 'others' with a special position. The question for us is: what was it about them that prompted the author of this epistle to show such immense interest in them? Do the author's statements, which *say* much about the Gentiles, *tell* us also about the Jews, including some of their basic convictions? How should we then read the statements about the Gentiles or Israel? What questions should we ask?

This chapter will examine how Jews regarded the Gentiles in terms of their covenant status and indeed, also, how they perceived themselves. My thesis is that the estrangement between Jew and Gentile can be explained best by the hypothesis that the Gentiles were perceived by the Jews through the 'grid' of covenantal ethnocentrism in which identification between the Jewish ethnic group and the Jews' religious identity is far too close (thus covenantal ethnocentricity is understood as the functioning of a certain stream of Judaism as a 'closed-ethnic religion'); and this has made the Gentile inclusion impossible in a straightforward manner unless the notion of (God's) Israel is drastically redefined (see below my discussion of the 'holy ones' in ch. 5, section 5.2). I suggest that 'covenantal ethnocentrism' may therefore serve as a descriptive term for Ephesians' understanding of the functioning of a kind of Judaism. Ultimately, the formulation of Jewish attitudes toward the Gentiles, as outlined by the author in Ephesians 2.11–12, is animated by a kind of covenant theology which unveils the covenantal confidence in which God's gracious promise to ethnic 'Israel'/Jews is assured, even though it narrows the scope of the divine grace and so limits membership of what constitutes the 'body politic' ethnocentrically to include only ethnic 'Israel'/Jews or a much smaller group than the whole of humankind. It is 'covenantal' in the sense that its framework is based on the Jews' understanding of their privileged status in the covenant; and it is 'ethnocentrism' that it is a closed ethnic religion, referring to the Jewish evaluation of other human groups (and their cultures and practices), from the perspective of the Jews' own. It also includes the dismissive attitude of the faithful members of the covenant people towards non-Jews. In principle, such judgements may be in fact positive or negative but will entail misunderstanding, social barriers and even hostility.

The Jews who perceived themselves as *the* people of God have, in their attempt to preserve their ethnic and religious identity in distinction from the Gentiles, erected eventually ethnic and religious boundaries between themselves and the Gentiles. As we shall see, the author's representation or characterisation of his Gentile readers was a means of defining for his non-Jewish audience also the exclusivistic disposition of the Jews. The ultimate goal in his overall argument in Ephesians 2. 11–13 is to construct a new 'space' for the Christian Gentiles who had been marginalised by the Jews.

3.2 The Gentiles as the Jews saw them (v. 11)

R. L. Wilken argues well that in the search for identity the act of naming is an essential step, reverberating back on the thing itself to alter, expand, limit or in some other ways define the self-consciousness of those who bear it. Thus while it is significant that, according to Luke, the followers of Jesus of Nazareth were given the name of 'Christians' at Antioch (Acts 11.26), it is at least as significant that they did not name themselves. In Antioch they were first 'called' Christians, i.e., they were given the name by others: the name indicates how the Christian movement appeared to outsiders. How a group is understood by others, no matter how much this understanding is at variance with the group's self-understanding, is thus an essential part of the reality that makes the group what it is.[1] The phenomenon of external definition is an other-directed process, during which one set of persons defines the 'other'. From a consensual point of view, this may be a validation of the others' internal definition of themselves; while at the conflictual end of the spectrum of possibilities there is the imposition, by one set of actors upon another, of a putative name and characterisation which significantly affect the social experience of the categorised. How the Gentiles are perceived and therefore represented by others is an essential part of the reality that makes them what/who they are.[2] Does the author of Ephesians speak of the Gentiles from the

[1] Wilken, 'Christians', 100–25, here 100.

[2] For this sociological insight, see esp. Hartog, *Mirror*, xxiii; Vasaly, *Representations*, 131–55; Hall, *Barbarian*, 1–12; Haarhoff, *Stranger*, 51–9, 216–21; Balsdon, *Aliens*, 59–71, 214–59; Jenkins, *Ethnicity*, esp. 13–14, 52–63, 165.

perspective of a Jew revealing his own attitudes and convictions about non-believing Gentiles, and if so,[3] how and why?[4] Does he also set his statements about the Gentiles alongside the common perceptions shared by most typical Jews, and if so, why? Did he *re*-present Jewish ethnocentric perspective on the otherness of the Gentiles? These are salient questions that we would wish to examine in the course of our study.

3.2.1 Διὸ μνημονεύετε ὅτι ποτὲ ὑμεῖς τὰ ἔθνη ἐν σαρκί (v. 11a)

To begin with, it is worth noting that the designation 'You Gentiles in the flesh' (*not* 'You were Gentiles in the flesh') has been given a range of meaning in recent studies. Some have read our phrase as referring to the Gentiles' physical descent, i.e., Gentiles by birth.[5] Others insist on the dominance of the Gentiles by the fleshly nature, who within this realm are controlled by and live in accordance with their old or sinful nature, i.e., those 'in the flesh' take the side of the flesh in the Christ/Flesh conflict (Eph. 2.11 and 2.13).[6] Still others refer to the mode of existence of the Gentiles (i.e., they *were* in the (realm of the) flesh, but they are *now* in Christ or in the Spirit).[7] All these interpretations above share the common feature that 11a is thought to provide raw evidence for the author's *immediate* assessment of the Gentiles. However, it is most likely that the designation 'Gentiles in the flesh' is a way of referring to the perception of Gentiles typically shared by Jews – 'in the flesh' essential to covenant,

[3] The Jewish perspective in Eph. 2.11 is recognised by some scholars, although the full significance of the perspective for the author and the Gentile readers remains curiously unexplored: e.g., Moritz, *Mystery*, writes: 'The fact that [G]entiles are described in v11 as precisely that shows clearly that the discussion is presented from a Jewish perspective' (29). See also Caird, *Letters*, 55; Schlier, *Epheser*, 119; Mußner, *Epheser*, 70; Gnilka, *Epheserbrief*, 133; Best, *Ephesians*^{2}, 238; Lincoln, *Ephesians*, 135; Walter, 'ἔθνος,' here 382–3.

[4] See my earlier discussion of Eph. 2.1–2 in ch. 2, sections 2.3.1 and 2.3.2 and the reasons stated. See also the author's own attitudes and convictions about the Gentiles (now *Christians*) in Eph. 1.13–14; 3.5–6, 8–9; 4.17–19.

[5] So Patzia, *Ephesians*, 189–90; Best, *Studies*, 92; cf. Best, *Ephesians*^{2}, 238.

[6] As far back as 1840 Barnes already argued that our author refers to those under 'the dominion of the flesh, subject to the control of carnal appetites and pleasures' ('Ephesians', 44); Barth, *Ephesians 1–3*, 254; Lindemann, *Epheserbrief*, 43, et al. For the usage of the preposition ἐν in the NT, see especially Harris, 'Prepositions', here 1190–3, 1200; Porter, *Idioms*, 157, 159.

[7] So Percy, *Probleme*, who writes: 'ἐν σαρκί kann nämlich hier kaum nur limitativ gemeint sein, etwa: mit Rücksicht auf euer unbeschnittenes Fleisch, sondern muss wohl die Sphäre bezeichnen, wo der in dem Beschneidungsgebot begründete Unterschied zwischen Jude und Heide Gültigkeit hat im Gegensatz zu Christus, in dem dieser Unterschied aufgehoben ist . . . σάρξ bedeutet dann hier soviel wie der alte Äon' (262); Lona, *Eschatologie*, 259; Merklein, *Christus*, 17.

and covenant identity.[8] Indeed 'Gentiles in the flesh' is an ethnographic statement: it represents in our present context an epithet for the non-Jews who lacked the mark of circumcision.[9] The statement, in other words, situates 'another', and as such it reinforces an ethnic frontier at which the criterion of Jewishness lies in the 'flesh'.[10] It must be stressed at this point that the author is fleshing out the complex issue of the 'otherness' of Gentiles through this particular designation.

For us the question is, why does the author choose to describe the Gentiles as such? The most probable answer to this question is that the author intentionally evokes in his readers the awareness that the Gentile 'flesh' is important for Jewish self-definition.[11] His argument reveals the way in which Jews would normally apprehend the Gentiles and interpret the otherness of the Gentiles. Behind this designation lies the typical Jewish attitude towards the rest of the world, since the Gentile 'flesh' provides sufficiently a vivid illustration of the way in which Jews would develop their own correlational concepts by relating to a physical attribute/feature (cf. Rom. 2.28–9; Gal. 6.12–13; 3.3? Phil. 3.4–5; also Sir. 44.19–20; *Jub.* 15.26; Philo, *QG* 3.52; *Ps.-Philo* 9.13). Like most 'ideal' nicknames or stereotypifications, the Gentile 'flesh' is one of the most significant predicates that collect around the name of the non-Jews so as eventually to construct an image of the non-Jews *from a particular point*

[8] For the usage of 'Gentiles' as an *external* definition of the identity of non-Jews who do not belong to the chosen people of God, see esp. Gen. 49.10; Exod. 33.13; Deut. 4.19; Rom. 3.29; 9.30–1; 10.19; 11.11–12, 25; 15.8–12; Gal. 3.28; Eph. 3.1–10; 4.17; also Tobit 1.10–12; Judith 4.12; 1 Macc. 1.11–15; 5.63; 13.41; 2 Macc. 1.27; 8.9; 14.38; 3 Macc. 6.9; 2 Esd. 4.23; 9.7; also *T. Sim.* 7.2; *T. Jud.* 22.2; *T. Aser* 7.3; *T. Jos.* 19.9; *T. Benj.* 3.8; *Apoc. Sedr* 14.5. See further Tomson, 'Names', here 284–6, 287; Dunn, *TPA*, 504–8; Kok, *Truth*, 110–11; Bertram, 'ἔθνος', 364–9; Schmidt, 'ἔθνος', esp. 370. Stanley, 'Conflict', concludes that '[t]he use of the term "Gentiles" (ἀλλοφύλοι or ἔθνη) to designate all non-Jews represents a social construction of reality developed by a particular people-group (the Jews) in a concrete situation' (105).

[9] By 'ethnographic' I do not mean that the author gave a written description of what he had observed *directly* in his practical 'fieldwork' by studying the behaviour of the Gentiles; rather, the phrase denotes simply the description of the characteristics of an ethnic group from the perspective of another.

[10] *Contra* Rese, 'Church', 26. The weakness of Rese's thesis is, fundamentally, its failure to recognise that v. 11a contains ethnographic category and that the enumeration of 'the deficiencies of the gentiles' does not begin in v. 12 but in v. 11. Bruce, *Ephesians*, 291, n. 82 opts for an ambivalent reading of the term 'flesh'. See further Abbott, *Ephesians*, 56.

[11] I refer to the author – a Christian Jew – who appropriated the Jewish heuristic device of polar inversion for his Gentile addressees: what 'they' do and are, 'we' do not do and are not – and 'we' are who we are precisely because of that opposition. See further Hartog, *Odysseus*, ix.

of view.[12] It appears not simply as an extremely condensed symbol of the collective identification of the Gentiles by referring to *how* they may be distinguished from another social collectivity, it also reveals how the boundary between Jews and Gentiles can be sustained by that particular 'mark' on the flesh. So when the author of *Sirach* spoke of the covenant which God made with Israel he referred to the 'flesh': 'He [*sc.* God] has established the covenant in his [i.e., Abraham's] flesh' (44.20). Similarly, the author of Pseudo-Philo announced Israel's covenant relation with God as 'the covenant of *the flesh*' (9.13).[13] What is in view here is the notion of the *covenant milah* (ברית מילה). It should come as no surprise that the 'flesh' reminds these Jewish writers of their shared history and identity as the covenant people of God (Gen. 17; *Jub.* 15.25–34). The covenant 'flesh' has played an important role in fostering a deep sense of community between the Jews, whereby the difference between themselves and the non-Jews heightens their sense of belonging. The presence (or absence) of the 'flesh' as such serves to reinforce the latter as a boundary marker distinguishing the Jews from the non-Jews.[14]

It should by now be clear that the designation 'Gentiles in the flesh' is indeed value-expressive and self-justifying: the Gentiles *as Gentiles* are in the perception of most devout Jews simply lacking the mark of covenant and are, *ipso facto*, outside the sphere of the elect of God.[15] That is the point which the author had wished (and will continue) to evoke in the memory of the Gentiles (διό μνημονεύετε) in his representation of the Gentiles. We should be content with the fact that the statement about the Gentiles in v. 11a also concurs well with that of vv. 1–2 in terms of its function, i.e., it conjures up an image of the Gentiles which can only be explained and defined by reference to a distinctively Jewish evaluation. Just as vv. 1–2 focus upon a well-established motif in Jewish theology, the integration of the particularism of election with the universalism of monotheism, in order to underscore the outside status of the Gentiles with

[12] 'In societies where there are stigmas attached to belonging to a particular race or religious community ethnically revealing names begin to acquire an emotional or attitudinal load in proportion to stigma attached to the ethnicity' – Morgan, *Nicknames*, 5–6. See further Haarhoff, *Stranger*, here 51–9, 216–21; Balsdon, *Aliens*, 30–71, 214–59.

[13] Harrington, 'Pseudo-Philo', 316 concludes that in post-Biblical Hebrew, the term 'covenant' had become a technical term for circumcision.

[14] *Contra* Cohen, 'Jews'. Cohen argues that the Jews of antiquity cannot be *visually* distinguished from their neighbours (12–22). Cohen has failed to recognise the *social* aspect of the Jewish practices, and the 'cultural stuff' (to use F. Barth's word) out of which ethnic differentiation is socially constructed by the Jews.

[15] See also 1 Macc. 1.10–15, at which the idea of epispasm is hinted; *T. Mos.* 8.1–3; 1 Cor. 7.18. See further Garland, *Deformity*, passim.

respect to Israel's election, so also the designation of the Gentiles in v. 11a reveals from a Jewish perspective the 'have not' of the Gentiles in their 'flesh' in order that the ethnic boundary between the elect and the Gentiles who lay outside the sphere of the elect can be reinforced.

In summary: entering into ethnic identification is also a matter of categorisation, and the designation 'Gentiles in the flesh' serves well as a name given by the Jews to the non-Jews. Therefore the characteristically Jewish language of 'Gentiles in the flesh' denotes the non-Jews or 'the rest' who have not yet complied with circumcision, or the 'pre-conversion' state of the Gentiles according to the *Jewish* perspective rather than the pre-Christian situation of the Gentiles. The Gentile 'flesh' thus serves as an identity-marker for the Gentiles so that Jews and Gentiles can be marked out as distinct from each other (see also my discussion of v. 11b below). Even more striking is the designation of Gentiles as outside the covenant and therefore 'Gentiles in the flesh'. There is a strong *echo* of election-language embedded in this designation. As the author provides an ethnographic description for his Gentile readers, he translates them into the terms of the knowledge shared by typical Jews. His approach in turn opens up a complex question which revolves around the Gentiles' position in relation to Israel's election, a question which has become the preoccupation of the author as we advance further into his arguments in vv. 11b–12.

3.2.2 οἱ λεγόμενοι ἀκροβυστία ὑπό τῆς λεγομένης περιτομῆς ἐν σαρκὶ (v. 11b)

We have reached the conclusion in the foregoing that the author of Ephesians has set out to forge an 'external definition' of the identity of the Gentiles from the perspective of typical Jews. This conclusion raises a fundamental question concerning the boundary between Jews and Gentiles: where does the break dividing the 'same' from the 'other' occur? It is important that we can substantiate further the claim that 'Gentiles in the flesh' is truly a Jewish representation of the non-Jews. What we are mainly concerned with here are the following questions: how do the Jews conceptualise their social 'space' and the place of the Gentiles? Do they define themselves as they similarly defined others? How does the designation the 'uncircumcision' appear to the Jews?

What needs to be established at the very outset is that the appellation 'Gentiles in the flesh' does not simply introduce an ethnic 'other', it also indicates that the Gentiles' 'otherness' had affected their position before God. This becomes clear when the present designation is mapped onto another highly charged appellation which serves almost as an *epexegesis* of the previous statement about the Gentiles: 'the *uncircumcision*' (lit. the 'foreskin').[16] It is firmly established that the respective designations 'Gentiles in the flesh' and 'the uncircumcision' are inextricably linked, since the 'uncircumcision' (*not* the 'uncircumcised')[17] is unequivocally a Jewish way of designating Gentiles or 'outsiders' (e.g., Gen. 34.14(?); Acts 11.2–3; Rom. 2.26; 4.9; Gal. 2.7–9; cf. 1 Macc. 1.15; *Jub.* 15.25–34; 1QH 6.20–1), just as the 'circumcision' is a designation for the Jews (e.g., Rom. 3.1; 4.9; 4.12a; 15.8; Gal. 2.7, 8, 9; Col. 3.11).[18] But the 'uncircumcision' as a collective ethnic term is an *external* definition of the identity of Gentiles by the Jews, i.e., those who called themselves the 'circumcision'.[19] It presupposes a collective ethnic term shared by typical Jews, i.e., the 'circumcision'.[20] There is also little doubt that the Gentile 'flesh' is now seen in contrast to the Jewish 'flesh': 'Gentiles *in the flesh*' or 'the uncircumcision'/'the circumcision *in the flesh*'. The difference between Jews and Gentiles becomes acute simply because they both constitute part of a *singular* system – the symbolic world of the Jews – and because the distinction between two *ethnic* groups can be epitomised by the presence or absence of certain features in the 'flesh' which serve as a boundary marker. As simple as this may be, the differentiation enabled the Jews to make a complex social world orderly and predictable as they accentuated *intra*-category similarities and *inter*-category

[16] See also Meyer, *Ephesians*, 376; Schnackenburg, *Ephesians*, 108.

[17] *Pace* Bratcher and Nida, *Ephesians*, 50; Schlier, *Epheser*, 119; Merklein, *Christus*, 17, 26, 99; Lona, *Eschatologie*, 259; Patzia, *Ephesians*, 190; Wintle, 'Justification', here 53. See further Betz, 'ἀκροβυστία'. Walter, 'ἔθνος', fails to recognise that v. 11b consists of a Jewish representation of the ethnic 'other', and concludes that the author of Ephesians 'speaks disparagingly of non-Christians as "the Gentiles"' (383); similarly Meyer, *Ephesians*, 377.

[18] This self-perception of most Jews is reflected in the various comments on the topic of circumcision made by Graeco-Roman writers, who also took it for granted that it was a distinctively Jewish practice. See text in Stern, *GLAJJ*, 3 vols.

[19] *Contra* Conzelmann, *Epheser*, who overlooks entirely the ethnic dimension, arguing that v. 11 is about the fundamental, theological self-understanding of the former Gentiles: 'um das grundsätzliche, theologische *Sich-Verstehen* der ehemaligen Heiden' (99, italics mine). Against this view, it must be said that there is no Greek or Roman who would identify himself as the 'uncircumcision'. Some interpreters have read our phrase τῆς λεγομένης περιτομῆς in a derogatory sense, i.e., 'the so-called circumcision' (e.g., Meyer, *Ephesians*, 377; Ernst, 'Epheser', 312; Schlier, *Epheser*, 119; Abbott, *Ephesians*, 56; NJB, et al.).

[20] *Pace* Marcus, 'Circumcision', here 78. Marcus's main point is that circumcision or uncircumcision can be used as nicknames. But in our present context the point of central importance is not so much that the Gentiles *also* promulgated a nickname for the Jews. As significant as it is that the Gentiles were given the name of 'Gentiles in the flesh' or the 'uncircumcision' by the Jews in our epistle, it is equally, if not more, significant that the Gentiles did *not* name themselves.

differences. The 'outside' world appeared as though it were monolithic and homogeneous. In short, the circumcision/uncircumcision divide enabled the Jews to tell who belonged to the same ethnic group, and who did not.

It must also be said that the act of naming is only an initial step in the search for identity. For us the paradox is: why has the author of Ephesians chosen to pose a sharply defined antithesis between Jews and non-Jews? Why did he choose to identify Gentiles in this way rather than another? Why did he select one set of categories rather than another? Were there good reasons for him to echo how other Jews would perceive the ethnic 'other'? What is precisely the issue? One immediate answer naturally focuses on the act or practice of circumcision itself. The issue, in short, is in part bound up with the meaning and value of the rite of circumcision.

It is generally agreed that circumcision was by no means a Jewish monopoly, as other peoples also practised similar customs (e.g., Jer. 9.25–6; Herodotus, *Hist.* 2.36–7, 47, 104; Strabo, *Geog.* 17.2.5.824; Philo, *Spec.* 1.2; Josephus, *A. J.* 8.262; Josephus, *C. Ap.* 1.169–71; 2.141, et al.).[21] But circumcision became one of the most significant features considered by typical Jews as an emblem of difference between Jews and the rest of the world.[22] The practice was, alongside other features such as the observance of Sabbath and dietary laws, constitutive of what it meant to be a Jew.[23] It aided the Jews to mark out the ethnic boundary between themselves and non-Jews and, not least, to map out their own social space *vis-à-vis* the 'others'. Why was circumcision so important in the self-definition of the Jews? Why did circumcision become the chief point of differentiation between Jews and Gentiles? Why did the Jewish sense of distinctiveness come to focus on circumcision? To these questions we must now turn.

In our effort to understand the socio-religious significance of the circumcision/uncircumcision dichotomy, one must concede that it will be quite impossible to draw out a more complete picture without also taking account of its two close correlates, namely Israel's covenantal relationship with God, and the connections between circumcision and

[21] See in particular the collections of various primary sources in Stern, *GLAJJ*, II, 620; Hengel, *Judaism*, 137; Dunn, 'Circumcision', 303–5; Levine, 'Judaism', here 144.

[22] See also *m.* Eduyoth 5.2; *m.* Ned. 31b; *midr.* Tanhuma Mattot 3. See further Dunn, *Partings*, 29; Cohen, 'Boundary', 27.

[23] See in particular Dunn, 'New Perspective', 191; Barclay, *Jews*, 428–42; Sanders, *Law*, 102; Meeks, *Urban Christians*, 36–7, 97; Gager, 'Judaism,' esp. 109–10; Wilken, 'Christians', 104; Segal, *Rebecca's Children*, 34–5.

the Jewish Law.[24] The latter we shall return to in the course of this study (see my discussion on v. 11c, below). For the moment, the question for us is: what is the tie-in between circumcision and covenant in the perception of typical Jews?

There is little doubt that for typical Jews, circumcision is often understood as subsumed under the rubric of the covenant which God made with Israel.[25] It was first enjoined by God upon Abraham *and* his descendants (Gen. 17.9–14).[26] It seals the covenant consisting of God's promise to make Abraham the father of many nations. It became the sign that Israel belonged to the covenant with God and the guarantee of the blessing promised in the covenant (Sir. 44.20; Acts 7.8; *Ps.-Philo* 9.13, 15; *4 Ezra* 1.31; *b.* Menah 53b; *b.* Shabbat 135a (i.e., blood drawn at circumcision is covenant blood); *b.* Sanhedrin 99a).[27] The author of *Jubilees*, in his rewritten story of Genesis 17, clearly restated the same point, that 'everyone who is born, the *flesh* of whose foreskin is not circumcised on the eighth day, belongs not to the children of the covenant which the Lord made with Abraham, but to the children of destruction' (15.33–4). It was precisely Israel's sense of mutual belonging, bound tightly to the law of circumcision which affirmed her legitimate status, with which the author of *Jubilees* was preoccupied. One cannot therefore enter the world view of *Jubilees* without taking into account the importance of circumcision.

This importance reached its apogee in the Maccabean crisis during which circumcision sustained the Maccabeans in their belief that the one test of religious identity is 'resistance', i.e., when a certain religious tradition cannot be bent even when there is pressure to do so.[28] The crisis became acute when the Maccabeans regarded their religious

[24] The Law (and therefore the covenant) serves the function of an 'invisible grid' in the world-mapping of the Jews. It was through this grid that the author saw and it is that grid which, *implicitly*, allows the beholder to see what he saw. That the 'invisible grid' here in Eph. 2.11–12 is thoroughly Jewish in character is unequivocally confirmed in Rom. 9.4–5. See also Dunn, 'Circumcision', who concludes that '[c]ovenant, law, Jewish ethnic identity, circumcision were mutually interdependent categories, each inconceivable without the other' (305). See further Hartog, *Mirror*, 319–20.

[25] 'The root metaphor underlying Hebrew society is expressed in the word *covenant*': Segal, *Rebecca's Children*, 4; Preuss, *Theology*, 71–3, 92, 217; Nicholson, *Covenant*, esp. 191–217.

[26] Gen. 17 is 'the constitutional document of circumcision within covenant' – Dunn, 'Circumcision', 303. Barclay, *Truth*, writes: 'The explicit connection in the Genesis text between circumcision, Abraham and covenant ensured the frequent association of these themes in Jewish theology as can be seen in a wide range of Jewish literature, both from Palestine and Diaspora' (54 and n. 53); Mußner, *Epheser*, 70; Hahn, 'Circumcision', 308.

[27] See in particular Kaufmann, 'Circumcision'; Michel, *Römer*, 90.

[28] Wilken, 'Christians', 103.

self-definition as threatened by the general policy of Hellenisation, i.e., acculturating the non-Greek societies to the norms and accepted behaviour of Greek society, when some Jews 'removed the marks of circumcision, and abandoned the holy *covenant*. They joined with the Gentiles and sold themselves to do evil' (1 Macc. 1.15; cf. 1 Cor. 7.18; *T. Mos.* 8.1–3; *Tosefta Shabbat* 15.9).[29] So the Maccabeans responded, circumcising by force the children that were uncircumcised within the borders of their own land (1 Macc. 2.46; cf. Josephus, *A. J.* 13.257–8, 318).[30] Circumcision became of prime importance in this particular situation and appeared above all as a 'confessional sign', in harmony with the maintaining of the status of the covenant people of God. Its decisive value in the Jews' sight is understandable as it marked out ethnic identity and a defining boundary, and as the Maccabeans protected their external boundaries from outside intrusion they also protected themselves against the assimilation of foreign influences and customs into the Jewish way of life (4.7f.; 11.24; cf. *Jub.* 3.31; 7.20). Within this covenantal nomistic mindset it is not difficult to imagine why the Maccabeans had assumed that Israel must hold itself rigidly aloof and maintain its distinctiveness from the Gentile sinners: 'Eat not with them, and *do* not according to their works, and become not their associates' (cf. *Jub.* 22.16; *Arist.* 139, 142; Philo, *Mos.* 1.278; cf. Num. 23.9; Acts 11.3).

Circumcision is a *sine qua non* for Israel's self-definition as the people of God. The conversion of Achior the Ammonite, as described in *Judith*, confirms the point: for Achior to become a member of Israel, it was necessary for him to cross the boundary by carrying with him the mark of covenant identity in his *Gentile flesh*, i.e., to Judaise (Judith 14.10; cf. Sir. 44.20). The affirmation of Israel's social identity took place in *Judith* when Achior accepted circumcision as the most important symbol of belonging.[31]

More could be said on the subject.[32] It must suffice to say that the association between circumcision and the Abrahamic covenant 'remains unshaken', and this is taken for granted by Jews, both in Palestine and the diaspora (Theodotus *Fr.* 5; Philo, *QG* 3.49; also Rom. 2.28; Gal. 6.12–13; Phil. 3.3–5; *b.* Sanhedrin 99a; *b.* Yoma 85b; *b.* Shabbat 135a).

[29] This refers to some Jews who underwent a surgical replacement called epispasm in order to disguise their ethnic and religious identities. See further Rubin, 'Prepuce'; Cohen, 'Mishnah', here 200.

[30] See further Cohen, 'Boundary', here 27.

[31] Thus Christiansen, *Ritual Boundaries*, 67–103.

[32] See also Sanders, *Judaism*, 235.

In sum: circumcision as the sign of the election was (and still is) for the Jews the first act of full covenant membership and obligation.[33] In the self-understanding of Jews, circumcision entails the first commitment to live as a Jew, to 'Judaise' and to adopt the Jewish way of conduct as a whole (Esther 8.17, LXX; Sir. 44.20; Judith 14.10; Rom. 2.25; Acts 15.5; Gal. 5.2–3, 6.13; Josephus, *Vita* 113, 149; Josephus, *A. J.* 13.257; 20.39–46; *b.* Ned. 31b–32a; *b.* Yev. 47a–b, etc.).[34] Circumcision is a sure sign of Jewish identity and not least, a bond which holds the Jews together as the elect of God. As we shall see, it was the self-evident correlation between covenant and law as epitomised in circumcision that was at the heart of the problem for Jews and Gentiles.

There is however another factor which should not be ignored. How were the Jews understood by others? In our effort to understand how the Jews enhance self-definition *vis-à-vis* non-Jews, the perceptions of outsiders deserve as much consideration as the statements of the Jews themselves, since the statements of the 'others' can be used to enhance the sense of 'us' for purposes of identification.[35] Although this question cannot be discussed in detail here, it will suffice to say that circumcision as a sure sign of Jewish identity is well recognised by non-Jews, in particular non-Jewish intellectuals.[36] Undue emphasis was often given to circumcision by the latter. Sometimes circumcision was regarded as the Jews' sole identity-marker. Tacitus, among others, commented that the Jews 'adopted circumcision to distinguish themselves from other peoples by this difference' (*circumcire genitalia instituerunt, ut diversitate noscantur*, *Hist.* 5.5.2). It is clear that other *literati* had poked fun at circumcision and perceived the rite as a crucial mark of identification separating the Jews from other peoples and religions.[37] It is not necessary to

[33] Despite a few exceptions to the rule, circumcision was commonly regarded in early Judaism as an essential part of Jewish ethnic and religious identities. See in particular Dunn, 'Circumcision', 304 n. 19; McKnight, *Light*, 79–82, 145–6; Nolland, 'Uncircumcised Proselytes'; Sanders, *Judaism*, 214; Barclay, *Truth*, 57 n. 59; Schürer, *HJPAJC*, III, 169. Against McEleney, 'Conversion', who argues that a significant strand of Jewish thought, current in the first century, considered it possible for a convert to Judaism to be accepted as belonging to the Jewish side without the need of circumcision.

[34] See further Barclay, *Jews*, 411–12 who argues that the insistence on circumcised partners in Jewish marriage played a crucial role in keeping the Jewish nation 'pure'; cf. Barclay, *Truth*, 45–60; Dunn, *Partings*, 124–7; Betz, 'περιτέμνω', esp. 79.

[35] See in particular Barth, *Boundaries*, 14; Wallman, *Ethnicity*, 3; Wilken, 'Christians', esp. 100–4.

[36] See, e.g., Balsdon, *Aliens*, 231.

[37] See, e.g., Petronius, *Sat.* 102.14, fr. 37; Juvenal, *Sat.* 14.99; Persius, *Sat.* 5.176–84; Martial, *Epig.*, 7.82; 11.94. See further Stern, *GLAJJ*, nos 194, 195, 301; Schäfer, *Judeophobia*, 93; Gager, 'Judaism', here 109–10; Feldman, *Jew*, 158; Whittaker, *Graeco-Roman Views*, 80–5; Hengel, *Judentum*, 137.

document all the evidence for the attitudes of others here. It will suffice to say that circumcision, as a distinguishing mark for the Jews, continued to exert its force in subsequent centuries in the history of the Jewish people.[38]

In sum: (a) the author of Ephesians has introduced in Ephesians 2.11b a Jewish representation of the Gentiles. Stated simply, what we have here is an 'echoic utterance' or a 'straight reportage' of the opinion of typical Jews who would wish to amplify the significance of the fact and act of circumcision as playing an important role in shaping the identity of the Jews and, not least, of the Gentiles. Circumcision aids the Jews to provide an external definition of the identity of the Gentiles and, hence, marks out the boundary between the two ethnic groups. The chief effective significance of circumcision is that it so much embodied and expressed distinctively Jewish identity that it had indeed become a mark of *Jew* as distinct from *Gentile*. The report of Gentiles as the 'uncircumcision' therefore served to justify and strengthen the already deep-rooted tendency towards ethnocentrism which Jews exhibited in their dealings with the non-Jews. It should come as no surprise that ethnicity is an important dimension, *inter alia*, that needs close examination if we are to appreciate fully the dismissive attitude Jews expressed toward the Gentiles.

(b) Circumcision also helps the Jews to locate their own distinctive status as the legitimate heirs of God's gracious covenant. Thus, the formulation in v. 11b represents a combination of rationalisation and self-justification of the position of the Jews as the elect of God as they used circumcision as a means to carve out their identity as the chosen people of God as distinct from the Gentiles. The Gentiles, according to this ethnically based definition, are beyond the orbit of the covenant which God made with his chosen people.

[38] We may note, for example, the insurrection under the Hadrian rule. This event was occasioned by a general prohibition of circumcision (Spatian, *Hadrian* 14.2). Just how important circumcision was to the Jews as a marker of Jewish ethnic and religious identity can also be seen in their response to the emperor's sanction against which they chose to revolt, during the reign of Antoninus Pius (138–61 CE). The Jews eventually obtained permission to circumcise their own sons, but not the non-Jews – or they would face severe penalties: see especially Julius Capitol, *Ant. Pius* 5.4; Modestinus, *Digest* 48.8.11. See further Smallwood, *Jews*, who argues that Hadrian's ban on circumcision was based on the emperor's dislike of rite and his 'moral objection to the practice as a barbarous mutilation on a par with castration' (431); cf. Smallwood, 'Circumcision', here 340. Schäfer, *Judeophobia*, 103–5 argues, *contra* Smallwood, that Hadrian was guided *not* by 'moral objection' but by the ancient Greek ideal of beauty and perfection and considered circumcision 'a barbarous mutilation' and tried to prohibit it; cf. Schäfer, *Aufstand*, 43ff., 193ff.

(c) Given also the fact that non-Jews repeatedly commented on circumcision as one of the crucial elements of Jewish identity, we may say that the act and fact of circumcision were indeed integral to the identity of Jews. It shows that the perceptions of the 'outsiders' match those of the 'insiders' with respect to circumcision.

3.2.3 χειροποιήτου (v. 11c)

In the foregoing I have concluded that the 'uncircumcision' is a Jewish description of the ethnic 'other'. The external definition of the identity of the Gentiles presupposes a collective ethnic name shared by Jews. The author's informative intention is to remind his addressees that from the perspective of the Jews they *as Gentiles* lay outside the orbit of God's elect and the covenant which God made with Israel – after all, circumcision was (and still is) *the* sign of the covenant with Abraham and his descendants.

For us the relevant question is: has the author of Ephesians distanced himself from the perspective of other Jews, looking in from outside Israel? One immediate answer to this depends in part upon the way in which the laconic adjective χειροποίητος is interpreted. The older view that the author of Ephesians was breaking away from the Jewish matrix has dominated NT scholarship in recent decades. According to this assessment, the author of Ephesians is giving his own gloomy assessment of circumcision (and therefore, Judaism),[39] and the term χειροποίητος does not simply refer to circumcision 'which is performed on the flesh by hand' but also betrays a sharp contrast between external material aspects of the old order of Judaism and the spiritual efficacy of the new order inaugurated by Christ.[40] This reading of v. 11c in this sense has also led many to believe that 'the circumcision in the flesh made by hands' reflects the Pauline view that this is no longer the real (or ideal) circumcision. The

[39] So Meyer, *Ephesians*, 377; Lohse, 'χειροποίητος', 436; Lincoln, *Ephesians*, 136, et al.

[40] This same line of argument can be traced back to the Torah itself which speaks of a circumcision of the heart which God will perform (Deut. 30.6; 10.16) and thus a fully Jewish recognition that mere circumcision by human hands is of less value than God's circumcision of the heart. Hence, Lindemann, *Epheserbrief*, concludes that what is in view is the superficiality of the difference between Gentiles and Jews: 'Der zwischen Heiden und Juden bestehende Unterschied bezieht sich im Grunde nur auf Äußerliches' (44). Houlden, *Letters*, argues that the use of the term χειροποιήτος is 'to contrast the purely physical nature of the institutions of Judaism with the spiritual efficacy of their Christian equivalents' (289); Merklein, *Christus*, 17; Gnilka, *Epheserbrief*, 134; Schnackenburg, *Ephesians*, 108; Schlier, *Epheser*, 119; Lona, *Eschatologie*, 259; Thomson, *Chiasmus*, 95; Lincoln, *Ephesians*, 136.

direct corollary of this line of argument is predictable: the negative overtone is often invested in the term χειροποίητος *per se*.[41] Since fleshly circumcision is done by the hand of man, the reference is to the contrast with God's act and hence only relative validity attaches to the judgement that the circumcised pass on the Gentiles. However, this interpretation will not do in our present context, and a serious consequence is that it makes it more likely that we shall miss the whole point that the author is trying to establish in his argument – if not cause offence to devout Jews who cherish their first act of loyalty to the Torah. I shall indicate the basic reasons why I part company with this interpretation. They are twofold.

In the first place, and most importantly, this interpretation fails to appreciate the fact that the formulations in vv. 11b and 11c are quintessentially Jewish in character and must be read as 'echoic utterances'. That is, they echo the thought of other Jews.[42] Indeed, what vv. 11b–11c is talking about is a second-degree interpretation, an interpretation of the author's understanding of other Jews' thought. It represents the perspective of law-abiding Jews who hold a noble view about the act and fact of circumcision. The point which the author of Ephesians was trying to make is probably the importance of circumcision to Jews who wished to exhibit their allegiance to the law and covenant ('covenantal nomism'). Stated simply, the key to what the author of Ephesians was after is certainly to recognise that his formulation in v. 11 was *not* engendered in polemic heat,[43] and the expression 'the circumcision in the flesh made by hands' does not by itself constitute the author's evaluation of the Jews nor a euphemism for idolatrous action.[44] Less still does the author depict the act and fact of circumcision as 'artificial, as opposed to natural'.[45] Rather, the expression 'the circumcision in the flesh made by hands' should be read in its non-opprobrious sense, namely, to reinforce group identification, namely that members of the group will see themselves as similar. What is at stake is the collective identity of devout Jews. The author was

[41] So Gnilka, *Epheserbrief*, who writes: 'Die Wendung hat im NT immer *negativen* Klang . . . Die Beschneidung wa also vorläufig, ja belanglos' (134, italics mine); Pokorný, *Epheser*, writes: 'Die Beschneidung . . . ein mit (menschlichen) Händen . . . und nicht direkt durch Gott vollzogenes Zeichen' (113); Schlier, *Epheser*, 119 n. 3; Houlden, *Letters*, 289, et al.

[42] See esp. Sperber and Wilson, *Relevance*, 237–43.

[43] *Contra* Bruce, *Ephesians*, 293, who concludes that the author is depreciating the 'man-made external circumcision'.

[44] The following passages, therefore, are irrelevant to our present discussion: see, e.g., Mark 14.58; Acts 7.48; 17.24; Phil. 3.2–3; Col. 2.11; Heb. 9.11, 24.

[45] For this meaning, see, e.g., Herodotus, *Hist.* 2.149; Thucydides, *Hist.* 2.77; Philo, *Mos.* 2.51, 88, 168; Josephus, *A. J.* 4.55. See also LSJ, s.v.

trying to reveal how Jews would construct a sense of themselves and their fellows as belonging in a particular setting, and with each other. The significance of circumcision to create communal boundaries is therefore evident, namely that the Gentiles are the 'have nots' in their Gentile 'flesh'. The well-calculated expression of our author is therefore to represent the importance of 'circumcision made by hands' to Jews who wished to display their ethnic solidarity and their unswerving allegiance to the law and the covenant made between God and Israel.[46] From the perspective of the Jews circumcision 'made by hands' was entirely agreeable in God's eyes (e.g., Gen. 17.9–14; Lev. 12.3, etc.).[47] The Jews have responded faithfully to the divine promise given to their ancestors and their allegiance to the ancestral custom based on the Torah is not to be questioned. That is the kind of mood which the author of Ephesians wishes to transmit to his Gentile readers in vv. 11b, c. Having said that, we must also concede that the author has chosen to distance himself from those who polarised the human family from the Jewish side into the circumcision/uncircumcision divide. However, this distance is *not* suggested by the term χειροποίητος itself which has the same negative to neutral range as the 'flesh' (see above),[48] but by the wider context, in particular by temporal markers such as τῷ καιρῷ ἐκείνῳ χωρὶς Χριστοῦ or the ποτέ-νῦν schema within which the author has wittingly located the perspective of devout Jews.

In the second place, the traditional interpretation seeks too often to produce a single definition of the term in question and limit that definition to the realm or context of early *Christians'* anti-Jewish polemics.[49] While we must concede that the term χειροποίητος often carries negative overtones in certain contexts where extreme polemics are more likely to

[46] See, e.g., Judith 14.10; 1 Macc. 1.60–1; 2 Macc. 6.10, par. 4 Macc. 4.25; *Jub.* 15.25–34; cf. Acts 7.8; Rom. 2.25; Gal. 5.3; Phil. 3.5; *Gen. R.* 46.10; *Exod. R.* 30.12; Josephus, *A. J.* 20.38–45. See further Dunn, *Partings*, 28–9. For the construction of group similarity in sociological study, see esp. Jenkins, *Identity*, chs. 9 and 11, respectively.

[47] This particular perception probably enabled the Jews to regard the non-Jews as repulsive, see, e.g., 1 Macc. 1.15–16; *Jub.* 15.25–34; 1QH 4.20–1; and perhaps, Isa. 52.1. In the Mishnah, the uncircumcision was regarded as a blemish, and perfection was to be attained by its removal, e.g., *m.* Ned. 31b. Uncircumcision is almost understood as a synonym for death in *m.* Edu. 5.2: 'He that separates himself from his uncircumcision is as one that separates himself from the grave'; see also *ODJR*, 161. It must also be said that what is highly regarded in one culture may have an opposite value for 'another'. That said, the presence of the foreskin is for the Greek an ideal of beauty and perfection: see esp. Schäfer, *Judeophobia*, 105.

[48] *Pace* Bruce, *Ephesians*, 291–2; Lincoln, *Ephesians*, 136.

[49] So Lincoln, *Ephesians*, 136; also Bruce, *Ephesians*, 293; Lona, *Eschatologie*, 259.

be expected,[50] this cannot imply that the meaning of the term is already 'fixed' and that it denotes that the author of Ephesians has involved himself in disputation or confrontation with the Jews.[51] Another way of making the same point is that full weight must be given to the author's 'utterance meaning' (i.e., what does the author (a Jew) mean by this expression?) rather than 'sentence meaning' (i.e., what does this expression mean?), and the significance his utterance could have for typical Jews.

Be that as it may, the issue which the author recounts in vv. 11b, c is the way in which the *ethnic*-and-*religious* boundary between Jews and Gentiles could be underscored on the basis of an 'absence' model. This is so because the ritual of circumcision performed in the Jewish 'flesh' underscores precisely the 'have not' of the Gentiles in their 'flesh'. The more fervently the Jews insisted upon circumcision as denoting their distinctive ethnic and religious identities, the more likely they would be to create a 'hard' boundary which distinguished themselves from the Gentiles. The point is that the Gentiles who did not observe the ritual bore no distinctive 'mark' of covenant identity in their 'flesh' and stood outside the orbit of the covenant which God had made with Israel. If the practice of the Jewish ritual in question puts the practitioner *over* the boundary that separates Jews from the rest of the world, then the formulations in vv. 11b, c conjure up a picture of Jews and Gentiles being gathered *at* the boundary of identification and differentiation.

In view of what is said above, it is reasonable to suppose that what has been called into question is *not* the validity of circumcision as the God-given seal of the covenant as such; nor does our text indicate a disapproval of the commitment of the Jews to live according to the demand of the law. Less still is the physical circumcision itself attacked by the author as the most striking symbol (apart from the Jerusalem temple) of the old order as such.[52] Rather, the point of central importance is that the more zealously

[50] See in particular the polemical passages against idolatry and paganism in the Jewish scriptures and other Jewish writings: Lev. 26.1; Deut. 4.28; Ps. 115.4; Isa. 19.1; 46.6; Wis. 13.10; 14.8; 15.17; Judith 8.18; Ep. Jer. 51; *Sib. Or.* 3.606, 618, 722; 4.28a; Philo, *Mos.* 2.51, 88, 168; Josephus, *B. J.* 1.419; 1.420; 4.614; 7.176; 7.294; *A. J.* 4.55; 15.324.

[51] See, e.g., Herodotus, *Hist.* 2.149; Strabo, *Geog.* 13.4.7.7; 17.1.10.15; Diodorus Siculus, *Bib. hist.* 1.33.8.5; 13.82.5.3; 14.48.2.6; 15.93.4.6; 17.71.7.5; 19.97.1.7; Dioscorides Pedanius, 5.106.2.8; Josephus, *A. J.* 4.55; 15.324; cf. Acts 7.48; 17.24, et al. See further Simon, *Christianisme*, 163.

[52] *Contra* Best, *Studies*, who argues that '[s]o far as circumcision goes, the author does not wish to emphasize it as an important part of the distinction between Jews and Gentiles; it is only a physical (ἐν σαρκί) thing, made by human hands, χειροποιήτου' (92); Dahl, 'Gentiles', 36; Gnilka, *Epheserbrief*, 134; Pokorný, *Epheser*, 113; Lindemann, *Epheserbrief*, 44; Lincoln, *Ephesians*, 136; Lona, *Eschatologie*, 259; Patzia, *Ephesians*, 190; Bruce, *Ephesians*, 293; Thomson, *Chiasmus*, 95.

the Jews emphasised their loyalty and adherence to the law, the covenant and the ritual of circumcision, the more firmly the boundary was erected between themselves and the Gentiles. That is the issue (between Jews and Gentiles) which the author had wished to underscore in vv. 11b, c. Is it, then, still possible for the author to speak about the integration of the Gentiles into the people of God (Israel) when the boundary-issue remains untackled? To this question we shall return in the course of our exegesis.

To sum up. Undergirding the author's argument in v. 11c are two basic governing factors: (a) the aim of the author is to unveil a Jewish ethnocentric perception which tends to interpret humankind as being divided from one another. (b) For the author, the Gentiles were defined in relation to the Jews.[53] By labelling the Gentiles as the 'uncircumcision', the Jews also proclaimed their pre-eminence over 'the rest' with respect to their position in the covenant God made with Israel. Like a landmark in space, the Gentiles are allotted a position in a Jewish 'world' or system. Through the rule of attribution, the act and fact of circumcision identifies a 'place' for the 'uncircumcision' and confirms the belonging of the latter to a preordained class, i.e., the Gentiles *as Gentiles* stand outside the sphere of the covenant which God has established with his own choice of Israel.

3.3 Jews, Gentiles and ethnic ethnocentrism (vv. 12–13a)

If our analysis of v. 11 in the previous section is acceptable, namely that the issue at stake is that the ethnic and religious identity of the Jews is closely bound up with their distinctive position in God's gracious covenant(s), we cannot avoid asking what the consequence of this self-understanding would be for the Gentiles. To put the same point from a different angle, the author perceived the status of the Gentiles as still being defined in relation to Israel, no matter how 'unresolvable' this relation, *prima facie*, might turn out to be.[54] Also, the polarisation of Jews and Gentiles cannot be

[53] From a sociological perspective, the capacity to impose one's definition upon other people implies, most probably, that one possesses sufficient power and authority to do so; see esp. Jenkins, *Ethnicity*, 80; Hartog, *Mirror*, 242.

[54] See in particular Mußner, 'Geschichtstheologie', who argues that the epistle to the Ephesians has a historical theology in that 'the existence of the people of Israel guarantees the concrete historicity of the salvation history. For the salvation came from the Jews, the remnant people . . .' (59). However, he also concludes that the fundamental message (*Grundkerygma*) of Ephesians is that 'the Gentiles, in an unresolvable relation to Israel, had their own salvation made visible and understood against the backcloth of Israel'. What had led to the relationship between Israel and Gentiles being 'unresolvable' is not successfully tackled by Mußner.

understood simply as a matter of nominal difference, since expressions such as ‘Gentiles in the flesh’ or the ‘*un*circumcision’ are not simple designations, but carry subtle connotations. On the basis that the ‘seal of the covenant’ has been turned into an overt indicator of Gentiles’ ethnicity and hence their ‘otherness’, we can now set out to investigate whether our findings in v. 11 are associated with the statements about the Gentiles in the author’s subsequent arguments in vv. 12ff.

What I shall demonstrate below is that the author has set out to elaborate a self-confident Judaism which is bold enough to fence off the Gentiles on the basis of Jews’ distinctive identity in the covenant which God made with Israel.

3.3.1 ὅτι ἦτε τῷ καιρῷ ἐκείνῳ χωρὶς Χριστοῦ ἀπηλλοτριωμένοι τῆς πολιτείας τοῦ Ἰσραὴλ (v. 12a)

To begin our investigation, the following questions are most relevant. What does ‘the *politeia* of Israel’ denote? What do phrases such as ‘alienated from the *politeia* of Israel’ denote when they were used to describe the situation of the Gentiles (v. 12a)? Does the author wish to remind his Gentile addressees that they were separated from the ‘*theo*cratically constituted nation’ of Israel because God had restricted his electing purposes to the latter?[55] Or that the Gentiles were estranged from Israel with whom they had previously been in a relationship of some kind?[56] Was the author’s aim to underscore the notion that the Gentiles were somehow involved in at least some of this particular *politeia* and the other blessings of Israel, but not until the coming of the Messiah?[57] Was he suggesting that the Gentiles who were separated from Christ in the past have suffered from this alienation as their *major* deprivation, for to be without Christ himself is to be deprived of *any* of the blessings that he gives, including the ‘*politeia* of Israel’?[58] Is the author speaking of the various religious privileges which were inherited by the Jews but from which the Gentiles, for some reason, had been excluded? To these questions we must now turn.

55 So Lincoln, *Ephesians*, 137.

56 Bruce, *Ephesians*, argues that the term ἀπηλλοτριωμένοι, if translated as ‘alienated’, would suggest (wrongly) that the Gentiles had once been members of the commonwealth of Israel but had subsequently been separated from it (292 n. 84); Best, *Studies*, 94–5; Best, *Ephesians*^{2}, 241.

57 So Schreiner, ‘Völker’; Bruce, *Ephesians*, 293.

58 So Patzia, *Ephesians*, 190.

3.3.1.1 ἡ πολιτεία τοῦ Ἰσραήλ

The name 'Israel'[59] may denote the people or the nation in a general sense (e.g., Exod. 17.1; Judith 4.1; 9.14; Add. Est. E 10.13; 1 Esd. 1.32; 8.69; Philo, *Abr.* 54–7; Rom. 11.1–2). It can be used to denote the Jews as an ethnic group.[60] It is also used quite frequently in connection with the Jewish people's descent from their patriarch Jacob/Israel (e.g., Gen. 42.5; 45.21; 46.5; 50.25). As a collective term 'Israel' provides the Jews, as the backbone of the story of their descent, with their collective 'location' in a complex world. It explains the founding of the Jewish community and the rationale behind its existence.[61] This story, in particular, provided a persuasive answer for the Jews to questions of group identification, of similarity and belonging: because they are descended from the same ancestor (Jacob/Israel)[62] and belonged to the place (the land God promised), they belong together.[63] But most importantly, 'Israel' expresses the Jewish people's religious identity: that is, it denotes a self-understanding of the Jews in terms of election and covenant promise (e.g., Gen. 32.28; 35.10–12; *2 Bar.* 48.20; 2 Esd. 5.27; *Jub.* 15.31–2; *Pss. Sol.* 8.37f.; 9.8–9, 16–19; 14.3; 18.2; *Sib. Or.* 3.193f.; 218ff.; *Shemoneh 'Esreh* 14).[64] It is clearly evident that in our present context, the

[59] Mußner, *Tractate*, 52–108, 268–80; Dunn, *Partings*, 21–3, 140–62; cf. Dunn, *TPA*, 499–532; Harvey, *True Israel*, 148–266; van Buren, *Jewish-Christian Reality*, 116–93; Chilton and Neusner, *Judaism*, esp. ch. 4; Barth, *People*, passim; Gutbrod, ''Ισραήλ', 383.

[60] For the socio-religious significance of 'Israel' and 'Jew', see particularly Dunn, *TPA*, 504–6. See also Mußner, *Epheser*, 71 who suggests that the term 'Israel' is used as an honorary title for the Jews ('Der Verfasser spricht nie von den "Juden", sondern "von Israel", wenn auch nur in 2, 12. Er gebraucht also für die Juden ihren Ehrentitel "Israel"...'); Zeitlin, 'Names'; Kuhli, ''Ισραήλ', here 203.

[61] The name 'Israel' is the most fitted to carry the Jews' memories of their patriarch Jacob (e.g., Isa. 45.4; 48.1, 12, 20), of Moses and the exodus, of the law-giving at Sinai, and of David king of Israel. It is the name for the whole people, even during the division into the northern kingdom known as 'Israel' and the southern kingdom of Judah. Thus, when Ezekiel was sent to the Judaeans exiled in Babylonia, he addressed the latter not as Judaeans but as the 'children of Israel', e.g., Ezek. 2.3; see also Luke 1.16; Acts 5.21; 7.23, 37; 9.15; 10.36; Rom. 9.27; 2 Cor. 3.7; Heb. 11.22; Rev. 2.14; 7.4; 21.12; or, the 'house of Israel', e.g., Ezek. 3.4; cf. 8.1, 6, 7; also Matt. 10.6; 15.24; Acts 2.36; 7.42; Heb. 8.8. See further McCarter, 'Patriarchal Age', here 24–5.

[62] E.g., Rom. 9.6; Phil. 3.5; Sir. 45.5; Baruch 2.15; Judith 6.2.

[63] See, e.g., Matt. 2.20, 21; Luke 7.9; Tobit 1.4; Add. Est. 10.9; also Gen. 15.17–21; 17.1–8; Deut. 6.20–5; 26.5–10. See further Mußner, *Tractate*, 11–13; Smith, *Ethnic Origins*, 24.

[64] Dunn, *Partings*, 22, 145f., 286 n. 21; cf. Dunn, *Galatians*, 344; *TPA*, esp. 505–6; Kuhn, ''Ισραήλ'. Thus, Rom. 9.3–4; 11.1, reflecting most clearly Paul's burden over the destiny of 'his kinsmen by race'; also, in other NT writings, 2 Cor. 11.22; John 1.47; Acts 2.22; 3.12; 5.35; 13.16.

collocation of 'the uncircumcision', 'the circumcision', the 'covenants of the promise' and 'Israel' makes it impossible to define 'Israel' apart from her identity as the chosen people of God, to whom Israel is bound by a special contract or covenant.[65] Fundamental to the self-understanding of the Jews was the conviction that God had chosen Israel and set her apart for him and him alone: hence the idea of Israel as the 'holy people', or the 'holy ones' (cf. v. 19).[66] Whether or not 'Israel' must also be understood as synonymous with 'the circumcision' which is distinguished from 'the uncircumcision' or as being marked out from the 'Gentiles (in the flesh)'[67] we need not decide for the moment. The point of central importance is that here both 'circumcision' and 'the covenants of promise' serve as the most prominent indicators of Israel as God's choice and a covenanted people.[68] Neither expression can be fully appreciated without the other.

In his 1986 article on the usage of the designation 'Israel',[69] P. Tomson has argued that Jewish speech duality is found to operate in the NT writings as it does in Jewish sources: the designation 'Israel' is the inner-Jewish self designation and 'Jews' the appellation Jews use in outside communication in a non-Jewish context, with a non-Jewish perspective implied. Tomson also raises the question concerning the usage of 'Israel' in our epistle, arguing that the appellation 'Israel' in v. 12 is anomalous when compared with other Jewish writings which consistently stress the insider's perspective whenever the designation is employed.[70] He concludes that in the approach of the author the name Israel 'evokes a dynamic of identification which encompasses [G]entile Christians' and 'spiritually proselytizes [G]entile Christians and draws them into the circle of those called by the name of Israel (Isa. 48.1)'.[71]

[65] *Contra* Lincoln, *Ephesians*, 137 who has failed to relate Israel as God's choice to the notion of circumcision in v. 11. He also fails to see the way in which Israel is tightly associated with the covenants of the promise.

[66] See, e.g., Exod. 19.6; Wis. 4.15; 10.15; 12.7; 18.2, 5; Sir. 42.17; Pr. Azar. 12; 2 Macc. 15.24; 1 Esd. 8.70; 3 Macc. 2.6; *Jub.* 14.18; 33.20; *Sib. Or.* 4.130–6; Josphus, *B. J.* 6.425. See further my discussion of the meaning of 'the holy ones' in chapter 5, section 5.2.1 below.

[67] For the notion of the Israel/nations divide, see particularly Tobit 13.3; Add. Est. 14.5; 1 Macc. 1.11–15; 5.63; 13.41; 2 Macc. 8.9; 3 Macc. 6.9 (lawless Gentiles); 2 Esd. 3.32; 4.23; *T. Sim.* 7.2; *T. Jud.* 22.2; *T. Benj.* 3.8; *T. Asher* 7.3. See also *m.* Ned. 3.11; *m.* Shab. 16.6–8; 23.4; *m.* Avodah Zarah 2.1. During the Second Temple period, 'Israel' was often used as the wider, evocative, self-appellation of the Jews, while 'Jews' is their name in the non-Jewish world to highlight their sense of distinctiveness over against others (Dunn, *Romans 9–16*, 526; cf. Dunn, *Partings*, 143–4). See also Stern, *Jewish Identity*, esp. 32–7, 42–50; Harvey, *True Israel*, 258–60.

[68] Nicholson, *Covenant*, esp. ch. 10; Dunn, *Partings*, 23–31; Segal, *Rebecca's Children*, 4; Schürer, *HJPAJC*, II, 464–6, 492, 494–5, 580; III, 159, 199–200.

[69] Tomson, 'Names'. [70] Ibid., 285–6. [71] Ibid., 288.

Tomson's research into the issue of Jewish speech duality as a whole is generally persuasive and merits appreciation,[72] but his conclusion that 'not only are the "former [G]entiles" (2.11) begged not to stand aloof but to see themselves in the inner-Jewish perspective of God's cause with Israel' as spiritual proselytes or spiritual Israelites misses the point. Stated simply, Tomson has failed to recognise that 'Israel' is more likely to tell us more about the author (a Jew) who employed the term 'Israel' as an inner-Jewish self designation than about the Gentiles. We would therefore do better if the 'inner-Jewish speech' in v. 12a is understood as a reflection of the perspective of the author who perceived himself as *intra parietes*, within the walls of the Jewish people, rather than that of the Gentiles who 'were begged to see themselves also in the same perspective of God's cause with Israel'. The point of central significance is not so much that the author is hinting at what Israel would mean to the Gentiles as that the sense of looking out from an insider's perspective is still strong.

In short, there is no need to assume – at least *not* in our case – that the Gentile audience is perceived as 'insiders' when the name 'Israel' is used. The point is not so much that the author no longer wishes to speak of the Gentiles as being included in Israel, but is rather that the insular nature of Judaism (covenantal ethnocentricity) with which the author grapples has made this inclusion impossible unless the notion of (God's) Israel is redefined drastically. Given the fact that the Gentiles had been estranged from the 'body politic of Israel' by the 'circumcision'/Jews (see my discussion below), it is not at all likely that the Gentiles could become part of Israel without becoming proselytes. As will become clear in vv. 14–18, the author would need to transpose the meaning of an exclusive, ethnic-oriented body politic of Israel into an *inclusive* community-body before he could truly speak of the Gentiles and the 'holy ones'/Jews as being the fellow-members of a single citizen-body (v. 19).

In our present context the phrase ἡ πολιτεία τοῦ Ἰσραήλ (v. 12b), as it now stands, is more problematic, for the term πολιτεία has a wide range of meaning and resists any simple definition.[73] Despite the obscurities

[72] For an assessment of Tomson's theory of 'Jewish speech duality', see esp. Harvey, *True Israel*, 6–8.

[73] See in particular Plutarch who exemplifies the various shades of meaning of the term in his *Un. rep. dom.* 826B–827C. The various ancient sources excerpted below are by no means exhaustive, and should only be taken as examples. 'Way of life': 2 Macc. 4.11; 8.17; 4 Macc. 4.19; *CIJ*, no. 694 (Stobi); 'government': Aristotle, *Pol.* 2.1268 ᵃ40; Diodorus Siculus, 11.76.6; Thucydides, 1.18, 127; Polybius, 2.70.4; Plutarch, *Praec. ger. rei publ.* 783C; Josephus, *A. J.* 6.83; 'civil ordering' (i.e., πολιτεία ἀμίμητος): Plutarch, *Lycurgus* 31.3; 'state': Philodemus, *Piet.* 75.2165; Josephus, *A. J.* 5.186; 'affairs in the public realm': Plutarch, *An seni* 786B; 791C; 793A; *Sol. et Publ.* 3.3; 'constitution': Demosthenes,

of the meaning of the term,[74] it is almost certain that it was used widely in the ancient political philosophy of the city(-state).[75] Moreover, it will prove fruitful if we can take into account the way in which the present term is wedded to the notion of the organisation of the ancient city-state in works of ancient political theorists. What is proposed in this study is that the phrase in v. 12b has many analogues in ancient political literature in which 'the *politeia* of X' (= the designation of a larger political unit or citizen-body) was portrayed as a league/union of which different city-states or smaller political communities became members. The best-known political community of this kind was the 'Achaean league' (ἡ πολιτεία τῶν Ἀχαιῶν or ἡ Ἀχαϊκὴν πολιτεία, e.g., Polybius, *Hist.* 2.38.4; 2.43.3, 35; 2.44.5; 2.57.1; Plutarch, *Agesilaus* 23.7.5; *Aratus* 9.6.3; Philopoemen, 16.6.3),[76] which lies in a region on the north east of the Peloponnese.[77] This is a 'federal' organisation, a body politic developed by twelve Achaean cities united in the cult of Zeus Hamarios (Διος Ἁμαρίος, e.g.,

1–2 *Aristog.* 1.20; Strabo, *Geog.* 10.4.22; Polybius, *Hist.* 6.49.4; Plutarch, *Solon* 16.3.1; Josephus, *A. J.* 4.191; 'civic relations', Philodemus, *Piet.* 47.1334–6; 'citizenship': Dio, *Or.* 41.6.2; Josephus, *A. J.* 12.3; *C. Ap.* 2.38–41; Acts 22.28; 'citizen rights': Philo, *Legat.* 157; 'political system' or 'institution': Demosthenes, *Falsa Leg.* 184; Polybius, *Hist.* 2.38.4; 6.46.11; 'civil polity': Philo, 28–9; Plutarch, *Lyc.* 11.4; 'body politic' or 'corporate body': Philo, *Legat.* 193, 194; 'league': Polybius, *Hist.* 2.38.4; 2.44.5; 3 Macc. 3.21, 23. See also BAGD, s.v.; M-M, s.v.; Strathmann, 'πόλις', esp. 519, 526, 534.

[74] So Barclay, *Jews*, 62 comments: 'Πολιτεία (with its associate ἴση πολιτεία) is an exceptionally slippery term, since its meaning can range from "citizenship" through "constitution" and "civic rights" to simply "way of life".'

[75] See in particular Aristotle, *Pol.* 1268 ^{a}40; Demosthenes, 1–2 *Aristog.* 1.20; cf. Demosthenes, *Cor.* 222; Dio, *Or.* 6.43.5; Polybius, *Hist.* 6.47.9.4: the Karchedonian *politeia*; 2.38.4.3: the *politeia* of Achaians, cf. 2.44.5.1; 6.45.3.3: the Lacedaimonian *politeia*, cf. Aristotle, *Pol.* 1269 ^{a}29; Strabo, *Geog.* 6.4.2.88: the Roman *politeia*, cf. Plutarch, *Caesar* 4.9.5, Dio, *Or.* 41.6.2; Strabo, *Geog.* 8.5.4.5: the Laconian *politeia*; Strabo, *Geog.* 8.7.1.18: the Athenian *politeia*, cf. Polybius, 6.44.1.2; Strabo, *Geog.* 8.5.5.18: the Lycurgan *politeia*; Strabo, *Geog.* 10.44.22.6: the *politeia* of the Cretans, cf. Polybius, 6.46.11.3; Dio, *Or.* 6.46.11; Aristotle, *Pol.* 1271^{b}23, 24–5. See further Posidonius, *Testimonis et Fragmenta* 163B 33–4; 216.3; Dionysius Halicarnassus, *Ant. rom.* 2.8.1.11–12; 2.8.3.2; 3.49.6.6; 2.14.2.4–5; 2.14.2.3; 2.24.2.3; Sulla, 8.1.7; Philopomen, 16.6.3; Cato Maior, 3.3.4, par. 19.5; Plutarch, *Themistocles* 20.4.5; *Praec. ger. rei publ.* 802C.1–2; *Lucullus* 2.4.7; *Alex. fort.* 332C.1–2; Josephus, *A. J.* 6.83, et al. See further Jaeger, *Paideia*, who concludes that 'the polis is the social framework of the whole history of Greek culture' (I, 78); Fowler, *City-States*, 22–56; Meeks, *Christian Morality*, esp. 37–9; Mußner, *Epheser*, 71; Schlier, *Epheser*, 120; Pokorný, *Epheser*, 114; Lindemann, *Epheserbrief*, 45.

[76] See in particular Rhodes, *City States*, esp. §39.m-p; cf. §35 (On Hegemonic Leagues); Rhodes, 'Poleis', 175–7; Sakellariou, *Polis-State*, passim; O'Neil, 'Leagues', here 43; *OCD*, 4–5, 31–2, 391, 441–2.

[77] Various terms were used to describe the Achaean League. The following examples are excerpted from Polybius's *Hist.*: ὁ τῶν Ἀχαιῶν πολιτεύμα (2.46.4); δημοκρατία (2.44.6); σύνοδος (2.54.14), et al.

Polybius, 2.41.6–13, cf. 2.39.6; Herodotus, 1.145–6; Pausanias 7).[78] Constituent city-states were bound to the 'league' by συμπολιτεία (broadly conceived),[79] which involved basically civic rights, protection and potential citizenship.[80] Individual city-states of this league usually retained local autonomy, and had an active political life of their own. The Greek historian Polybius recounted that in his time (second century BCE) the whole Peloponnese united with the Achaean League, used the *same* laws, weights and measures, and coinage, elected *common* officers and had a *common* council and judges (*Hist.* 2.37.10–11).[81] The purpose of the Achaean πολιτεία was mainly to consolidate participating member-states within one larger body, to prevent each constituting member-state from disintegration (ἡ κοινὴ ὁμόνοια) and to take collective action against outside threats which contravened its terms when necessary (e.g., against the threats from the Persians or the Macedonians).[82] It should come as no surprise that such a league-body also provided the member-states (tribal units or city-state units) with a familiar *topos*: 'them' and 'us' (cf. Polybius, *Hist.* 2.37.11).[83] In short, the πολιτεία can be seen as 'a community of communities'.[84]

[78] The Achaean League broke up at the end of the fourth century BCE, but it was revived in 281/0 BCE and began to acquire members from outside the region of Achaea in 251/0 BCE, cf. Xenophon, *Hellenica* 4.6.1. See further Rhodes, 'Poleis', 175–6; Larsen and Rhodes, 'Federal States'.

[79] This best explains why the Achaean League was also known as ἡ Ἀχαιῶν συμπολιτεία: see, e.g., Polybius, *Hist.* 3.5.6.3; 20.6.7.4, par. Diodorus Siculus, *Bib. hist.* 29.18.1.7; cf. Polybius, *Hist.*, 2.41.13; 2.44.5; 3.5.6; 18.2.4; 18.2.6; 20.6.7. Cf. [Aristotle], *Rhet. Alex.* 2.1424 ᵇ28–40. The basic notion of συμπολιτεία is that two or more states are merged into one, and that an individual city-state did not bestow its citizenship on another, but took on a new citizenship belonging to a group. See also Plutarch, *Is. Os.* 370B.5 (ἕνα βίον καὶ μίαν πολιτείαν ἀνθρώπων καὶ ὁμογλώσσων ἁπάντων γενέ κτλ.); Dionysius Halicarnassus, *Ant. rom.* 4.58.3.7 (ἡ Ῥωμαίων ἰσοπολιτεία); Philo, *Spec.* 4.159.2–3.

[80] This is not to deny that individual city-states of the league-body had lost their local autonomy or political life of their own: see in particular Rhodes, 'Poleis', 176; Larsen, *Federal States*, xv, 203; Larsen and Rhodes, 'Sympoliteia', in *OCD* 1460–1.

[81] On the subject of the Achaean council and assembly, see in particular Wallbank, *Polybius*, esp. 406–14; Rhodes, 'Poleis', 176; cf. Rhodes, *City States*, §39.q–v.

[82] It is generally recognised that classical Greece was bedevilled by tension between impulses to unity and impulses to separation: see, e.g., Rhodes, 'Poleis', 161; Manville, *Citizenship*, 214–15. See further Polybius, *Hist.* 2.38.5–9; 2.40.5–6; 2.41.10–15; 2.42.3–7; 2.43.8.

[83] There are other less well-known political 'leagues' of a similar nature during the classical period: see, e.g., the Boeotian Confederacy (Thucydides, 4.76); the Aetolian League (Polybius, 18.2.6.5); the Arcadian League (Polybius, 18.2.6.5); and the Corinth League (Plutarch, *Phocion* 16.4.1). See further Larsen, *Federal States*, esp. 80–9, 215–40.

[84] See esp. Giovannini, 'Commonwealth', here 274.

Although it is beyond the scope of our present study to discuss the social or legal status of the Jews in the diaspora and elsewhere, it may be sufficient to note that the Jews in the Graeco-Roman diaspora did form their own 'body politic' or association.[85] Jewish writers during the Hellenistic period have also extended the common political metaphor of 'body politic' in ancient political philosophy to the Jewish community, much as did other Greek writers whom we mentioned earlier. Philo, for example, has perceived the *politeia* of the Jews as being based on an *ethnos*, or better known as the 'corporate body of the Jews' (ἡ πολιτεία Ἰουδαίων, *Legat.*, 193, 194; *Virt.* 8, 219).[86] Conversion to Judaism, according to Philo, entailed inherently three basic elements: the practice of Jewish laws; exclusive devotion to the (one) God of the Jews; and integration of proselytes into the Jewish community or *politeia* (*Virt.* 102–8, 212, 216, 219; *Spec.* 1.51–2; 4. 178; cf. Judith 14.10; Tacitus, *Hist.* 5.5.2).[87] We must also add that Philo may well have understood ἡ πολιτεία Ἰουδαίων – like other Greek writers – as referring not to a parochial (or local) body within a small city-unit but to a community-body in an 'inter-Judaic' sense, namely the Jewish *politeia* in its quality as specifically 'a community of (Jewish) communities' or a homogeneous body of the people of God. This ethnically based community-body is bound together by a network of ties of kinship and other moral obligations.[88] If we understand

[85] The consensus so far is that the Jews had organised themselves in some form of a society, association, league, fraternity or body politic: see, e.g., Lüderitz, 'Politeuma', esp. 187–9, 202–4 and 221–2. Lüderitz concludes that the term *politeuma* carries no fixed legal meaning that would distinguish it from other private associations or require civic approval for its existence or operation. See Zuckerman, 'Politeumata', 171–85. Zuckermann, who objects to an earlier theory of Kasher that the Jews in Egypt, and actually all over the Hellenistic diaspora, rejecting integration into Greek civic bodies, chose instead to fight for equal rights for their own 'independent political units', the *politeumata* (Kasher, *Struggle*), concludes, however: 'Thus when we insist upon the fact that the Jews of Alexandria were not *politai* of their own independent *politeuma*, it is not to deny the well known evidence concerning their communal institution and the limited autonomy they enjoyed' (172). Levine, *Caesarea*, concludes: 'As in other cities of the Roman Empire, the Jews of Caesarea were probably organized into a politeuma, a quasi-autonomous civic community similar to Greek municipal organizations' (23). Alexander, 'Galen', here 79–80, opines that the Jewish group had a semi-autonomous existence alongside the citizen-body of the community. Cf. Smallwood, *Jews*, esp. 356–88; Bickermann, *Jews*, 87–90; Rajak, 'Charter'; Rajak, 'Community'; Feldman, 'Groups'; Feldman, *Jew*, 63–5; Troiani, 'ΠΟΛΙΤΕΙΑ', here 12; Schürer, *HJPAJC*, III, 1.87–125, esp. 88–9, 126–37. Trebilco, *Communities*, provides a convenient summary of the evidence.

[86] We may also include Philo, *Spec.* 1.314, where Philo speaks of the Jewish community as a 'godly community': 'We who are born in a *godly community* and nurtured under the laws to incite every virtue . . .' (οἱ γεννηθέντες ἐν πολιτείᾳ φιλοθέῳ καὶ ἐντραφέντες νόμοις ἐπὶ πᾶσαν ἀρετὴν ἀλείφουσι κτλ., my own translation); cf. Philo, *Spec.* 1.51.

[87] This point is well argued in Cohen, 'Boundary', esp. 26–8.

[88] See further my discussion of v. 15 in chapter 4 below.

Philo correctly, this particular notion of the *politeia* has a significant bearing upon the way in which our passage in v. 12b is to be interpreted. But before we return to this subject, we may need to add at this point a final piece of evidence from 4 Maccabees, where the author speaks of the Jewish martyrs who died because of the attempt of the 'tyrant' Antiochus IV to destroy the '*politeia* of the Hebrews' (ἡ Ἑβραίων πολιτεία, 17.9). In a recent study, van Henten argued that 'the phrases and a related context of the abolition of a political system by a tyrant appear in pagan non-literary sources' and concludes that the 'epitaph' in 4 Maccabees is analogous to those of liberators of the *poleis* from tyranny.[89] However, it is more likely that the 'politeia of the Hebrews' refers not so much to a constitution as to a Jewish community now embodied in the Jewish martyrs (cf. 4 Macc. 3.20).[90] The Jewish martyrs, who regulated their way of life according to the Law (3.19, 23; 5.16; 8.7; 18.5; 2 Macc. 6.1, 11;11.25; 3 Macc. 3.4) and whose mood is more one of defiance and defensiveness than of cultural convergence,[91] had reacted against the 'tyrant' who attempted to destroy the distinctiveness of their community (καταλύω, cf. 4.11; 8.8, 9, 19; 11.4; 18.20). The archaic term 'Hebrews' is used here not simply to evoke the memory of the Jewish people of their remote past (cf. 4.11; 8.2; 9.6, 18), but also to emphasise the otherness of Jews in confrontation with the non-Jews embodied in the 'tyrant'.

In view of what was discussed above, it is safe to say that when the author of Ephesians employed the expression ἡ πολιτεία τοῦ Ἰσραήλ, he probably was extending a common political vocabulary in ancient political philosophy, by referring to Israel as a 'community of communities' which is formed on the basis of the self-understanding of the Jews as being chosen by God, as descendants of the patriarch (Jacob/Israel) through whom God's election and promise came.[92] This is a 'body politic' which is based on a particular *ethnos*. Members of the body politic were probably bound together by a 'network of ties of kinship' (i.e., the descendants of Abraham/Israel), covenants, the belief in the one God upon whom the Jews had laid their hope, and other moral obligations based on the 'law'.

[89] van Henten, '4 Macc 17: 8–10', here 64 and 66.

[90] *Pace* Hadas, *3–4 Maccabees*, 234–5, who translataes ἡ Ἑβραίων πολιτεία as 'the polity of the Hebrews'; also NRSV, 'the way of life of the Hebrews'; van Henten, '4 Macc 17: 8–10', here 64–5.

[91] Barclay, *Jews*, 369.

[92] *Pace* Gnilka, *Epheserbrief*, 135 who concludes that the author has spoken about the civic right of Israel ('. . . da bei πολιτεία nicht an das Israel verliehene Bürgerrecht oder an eine bestimmte Lebensführung, sondern an eine civitas zu denken ist'); also Lincoln, *Ephesians*, 137 who is of the opinion that 'Israel is being viewed as a theocratically constituted nation'.

These social relations were a particularity of the Jewish πολιτεία just as the relations of patron–client relationships were a particularity of the Graeco-Roman world.

To sum up. In our present context, the expression ἡ πολιτεία τοῦ Ἰσραήλ can be best understood as Israel in which the 'circumcision'/Jews have coalesced to develop into a kind of 'league' or 'alliance' on the basis of an *ethnos*.[93] This is a body politic which goes beyond any community in a specific locality (such as the Jewish synagogue). Indeed, it will be quite impossible to speak of the body politic of Israel or the community of God's choice in any parochial sense.[94]

3.3.1.2 Jews, Gentiles and ethnic estrangement

The conclusion we have reached in the foregoing gives rise to a pressing question: can the Gentiles be included in the 'body politic of Israel' whose connecting bond is the self-understanding of its members as *Israel*? To this question we must now turn.

The exegetical consensus portrait in the past has been that v. 12 is resumptive of v. 11 via ὅτι *recitativum*.[95] While there are good grounds

[93] Cf. Schlier, *Epheser*, 120; Robinson, *Ephesians*, 57; Dahl, *Auslegung*, 33–4; Mußner, *Epheser*, 77.

[94] This probably explains why the author has not chosen designations such as 'the body politic of the Jews', or 'the body politic of the Hebrews'. The designations above have very strong geographical connotations, whereas the 'body politic of Israel' underscores the electedness of the Jews. See further Cohen, 'ΙΟΥΔΑΙΟΣ', esp. 36. Cohen concludes that 'Jews' always has an ethnic-geographic meaning of 'Judaean by birth'; Dunn, *TPA*, 505–6. Hengel, *Judaism*, esp. 169 and nn. 99 and 102, suggests that the term 'Hebrew' would indicate the diaspora Jews who came from Palestine or who had special ties with their homeland. See also van der Horst, *Epitaphs*, esp. 68–71 and 87 who concludes that the word 'Hebrew' was used in combination with 'synagogue' (e.g., συναγωγὴ Ἑβραίων) to distinguish a *Jewish* community from other religious or ethnic groups; Smith, 'Fences', 19, concludes that the term 'Hebrew' indicates a Jew whose place of birth was in Syro-Palestine. See also van Henten, '4 Macc 17: 8–10', here 52–3, who suggests that the usage of the designation 'Hebrew' is connected with notions of the exclusiveness of the Jewish people, such as its long history, its own law and wisdom and its covenant with the Lord. Goodman, 'Jewish Proselytizing', concludes that the Jews, who were like the Romans and different from the Greeks, accepted the notion that their *politeia* was not fixed to any particular locality (61).

[95] Lincoln, *Ephesians*, 124, 136 argues rightly that the ὅτι in v. 12 takes up again the ὅτι in v. 11, but also suggests that 'the verb [*sc.* μνημονεύετε] from v. 11 has been *repeated* in line with the writer's resumption of the thought with which the pericope begins' (italics mine); cf. Lindemann, *Epheserbrief*, 44; Bruce, *Ephesians*, 292; Schnackenburg, *Ephesians*, 108; Bratcher and Nida, *Ephesians*, 50. Schlier, *Epheser*, writes: 'Mit Wiederaufnahme des ὅτι und Ersatz des ποτέ durch daß τῷ καιρῷ ἐκείνῳ heißt es V. 12: Bedenkt, daß ihr jener Zeit ohne Christus waret' (120). Modern translations such as NRSV, NEB also assume that the verb in v. 11 is to be 'repeated' in v. 12a. For the usage of the conjunction ὅτι, see esp. Moule, *Idiom*, 147; Zerwick, *BG*, no. 416–22; BDF, §456.

for this, the suggestion that here the train of thought interrupted by the lengthy way of describing the Gentile recipients should now be resumed by the insertion of the verb of v. 11 (i.e., [μνημονεύετε] ὅτι ἦτε τῷ καιρῷ ἐκείνῳ χωρὶς Χριστοῦ κτλ.) should not be pressed. It is also inappropriate to speak of vv. 11 and 12 as forming parallel structures in a strict sense, despite the fact that these verses are closely associated with one another. The figure of repetition (*gemination*) which is not so clear to commentators was clear enough to the author of Ephesians.[96] It is more likely that the author has made a substantial break halfway through his argument in v. 11c (οἱ λεγόμενοι ἀκροβυστία . . . χειροποιήτου) in order to particularise what is truly meant for his recipients to be categorised as 'Gentiles in the flesh', and therefore finds it necessary to resume as well as to elaborate his argument in v. 12 by introducing another statement about the Gentiles which is closely associated with the Jews.[97] The two ὅτι-clauses in vv. 11b and 12a are inextricably bound with each other, constituting the *content* of memory: that is, the Gentiles' unJewishness.

What, then, is the author's informative intention in v. 12? The old consensus was that the Messiah of Israel had no significance for the Gentiles who did not share the hope of Israel and did not know the God of Israel.[98] Lincoln has gone so far as to suggest that 'it would be a striking thought for Gentiles to have to entertain that having been apart from Christ can be set in parallel to having been separated from Israel'.[99]

The 'striking thought' mentioned above is due in part to the obscurities of the syntax of v. 12a, which most commentators have overlooked.[100]

[96] The suggestion that the main verb of v. 11a should be inserted in v. 12a is unnecessary: see, e.g., 4.11 (καὶ αὐτὸς ἔδωκεν τοὺς μὲν ἀποστόλους, τοὺς δὲ προφήτας, τοὺς δὲ εὐαγγελιστάς, τοὺς δὲ ποιμένας καὶ διδασκάλους κτλ.); cf. 6.11; 1 Cor. 8.4 (οἴδαμεν ὅτι . . . καὶ ὅτι κτλ.); 1 Cor. 10.19–20 (ὅτι . . . ἢ ὅτι . . . ἀλλ' ὅτι κτλ.); 1 Cor. 15.3–5 (ὅτι . . . καὶ ὅτι . . . καὶ ὅτι . . . καὶ ὅτι κτλ.); cf. Luke 4.10–11; Acts 19.25–6.

[97] *Pace* Barth, *Ephesians*, 255–6, who argues that the Greek conjunction ὅτι in v. 12 should be translated as 'because' and that v. 12 may not be a simple parallel or continuation of v. 11, but rather a parenthesis interrupting (though supporting) the thought expressed in vv. 11 and 13.

[98] So Mußner, *Tractate*, 25, writes: 'Israel possesses the hope of the Messiah'; cf. Mußner, *Epheser*, 70 ('Die Heiden waren "ohne Messias", ohne den verheißenen Heilsbringer . . .'); cf. Mußner, *Christus*, 77; Schlier, *Epheser*, 120; Rese, 'Church', 26; Gnilka, *Epheserbrief*, 135; Lona, *Eschatologie*, 260–1; Bruce, *Ephesians*, 294. Patzia, *Ephesians*, writes: 'In the past (at that time) the Gentiles were separated from Christ. In one sense, this was their major deprivation, for to be without Christ is to be deprived of any of the blessings that he gives' (190); cf. Best, *Ephesians*^{2}, 241.

[99] Lincoln, *Ephesians*, 136. Lincoln does not however see Eph. 2.11–12 as a discussion of the place of the Gentiles in the history of salvation (cf. Lincoln, 'Church', 608–9).

[100] Both UBSGNT and NA^{27} insert a comma after the genitive noun Χριστοῦ (ὅτι ἦτε τῷ καιρῷ ἐκείνῳ χωρὶς χριστοῦ, ἀπηλλοτριωμένοι κτλ.). This reading is followed by most

These obscurities have left several issues tantalisingly unclear. Does the author truly consider the Messiah as part of Israel's prerogatives? Is he speaking of the theology of history (*Geschichtstheologie*), or is Israel perceived simply as a foil to the Gentiles whenever it is mentioned? Can we still talk about the Gentiles *vis-à-vis* the Jews with respect to God's salvation plan at all, or have the latter simply faded to the remote past and hence are of no account at all? These questions show that a fresh look at these old issues is necessary.

My contention is that these obscurities can be mitigated if we adopt an alternative rendering of v. 12a, in which the auxiliary verb ἦτε is combined with the participial verb ἀπηλλοτριωμένοι to form an 'expressive' periphrasis.[101] The formulation of a periphrasis is dependent upon the syntactical relations between the auxiliary verb and the participial verb, but not upon the number of intervening, non-verbal elements between them.[102] Different from the non-periphrastic rendering is that the phrase 'at that time without/apart from Christ' (τῷ καιρῷ ἐκείνῳ χωρὶς Χριστοῦ) completes or modifies the perfect participle ἀπηλλοτριωμένοι rather than the auxiliary verb, and serves as a temporal-marker indicating *when* estrangement has actually taken place. The periphrastic rendering thus provides a *sense* which a simple (or 'monolectic') verb does not usually possess and changes inevitably the semantic landscape of vv. 12a, b: it helps to lay bare what had happened (to humankind) when the Gentiles had no positive connections with Christ ('without Christ').[103] Another way of saying the same point is that the author (a Christian Jew) does not specify the particular relationship between the Gentiles and Christ (e.g., 'You were without the hope of the Messiah' – Schlier, Mußner,

commentators: see, e.g., Schlier, *Epheser*, 118; Tachau, *Einst*, 137; Mußner, *Epheser*, 68; Lona, *Eschatologie*, 259–60; Lindemann, *Aufhebung*, 148; cf. Lindemann, *Epheserbrief*, 42, 44; Gnilka, *Epheserbrief*, 132; Bouttier, *Éphésiens*, 108, 112; Lincoln, *Ephesians*, 136; Schnackenburg, *Ephesians*, 108; Bruce, *Ephesians*, 292, 293–4; Patzia, *Ephesians*, 190; Pfammatter, *Epheserbrief*, 22; Best, *Ephesians*^{2}, 234, 240–1, et al. The one exception is Porter, *Verbal Aspect*, 470, who takes v. 12a to be a periphrastic construction: 'that in that time apart from Christ you were in a state of alienation from the citizenship of Israel'. Independently of Porter I have developed my own interpretation.

[101] See in particular Aerts, *Periphrastica*, 3; Porter, *Verbal Aspect*, 441–92, esp. 470; cf. Porter, *Idioms*, 45–9; Fanning, *Verbal Aspect*, 309–11, 318–22; McKay, *Syntax*, 8–12; Zerwick, *BG*, no. 360–2; Boyer, 'Participle', here 171–3; Moule, *Idiom*, 16–19; BDF §352.

[102] See, e.g., Luke 1.21; 2.8; 2 Cor. 5.19; also Mark 1.13; 10.22; Luke 2.8, 26; 15.1; 21.37; 23.8, 19; John 12.2, 16; Acts 8.16; 9.9, 28; 10.30; 11.5; 12.5; 16.9; 19.36; Rom. 13.6; 1 Cor. 1.10; 2 Cor. 2.17; Col. 2.10.

[103] With genitive of the person χωρίς means 'without, separate from': see, e.g., Rom. 10.14; 1 Cor. 4.8; 11.11; Heb. 11.40; John 1.3; 15.5; 1 Esd. 4.17; 5.41; *Arist.* 123. See further Louw and Nida, 89.120; BAGD, s.v., 2a; Bauer, 'χωρίς'; LSJ, s.v.; BDF §216.2.

Gnilka, Best, et al.) but only indicates the lack of relationship or involvement between the two: 'That you were in a state of being alienated from the body politic of Israel (at that time without Christ) and aliens to the covenants of the promise'. In favour of this rendering, it is no longer necessary for us to emphasise, as most commentators have done, the parallelism between the Gentiles' being 'apart from Christ' (or Israel's Messiah) and their being 'alienated from the body politic of Israel' or other God-given blessings.[104]

Of greater importance for us is the fact that the periphrastic rendering also enables us to ask a thorny question missed by most commentators: that is, if the Gentiles 'were estranged from the body politic of Israel at that time without Christ', who was the likeliest agent of alienation? Was it ethnic discord which has become the author's major concern? To these questions we must now turn our attention.

Part of our answer depends largely on the way in which the term ἀπηλλοτριωμένοι is understood in our present context. Used in its active sense the term ἀπηλλοτριόω normally carries overtones of dislike, denoting a hostile attitude, 'to cause to feel an aversion', 'to cause to become estranged', or 'to abandon or to dispose of'.[105] The negative overtones of the term should be retained in the passive form of the verb (e.g., Ps. 68.9; Ezek. 14.5, 7; 3 Macc. 1.3; Josephus, *A. J.* 11.148; 13.303; Polybius, *Hist.* 1.79.6; 1.82.7; Strabo, *Geog.* 5.3.11.38; Diodorus Siculus, *Bib. hist.* 11.48.6).[106] The perfect tense of the verb may well suggest the continuing effect of estrangement that had been inflicted on the Gentiles. Given the fact that ἀπηλλοτριωμένοι is also collocated with λεγόμενοι of v. 11b (both verbs in passive voice), we have good reason to suppose that the connection between these verbs is very close and that each has

[104] *Pace* Lincoln, *Ephesians*, 136–7; Tachau, *Einst*, 137 ('einst keine Juden – jetzt in Christus'); cf. Lindemann, *Epheserbrief*, 44. There are four other less feasible options which can be dismissed outright: (1) the Gentiles were 'without Christ' before their baptism (e.g., Pokorný, *Epheser*, 114); (2) for Gentiles to be 'without Christ' means that Christ was present with Israel in his pre-incarnate state (e.g., Schlier, *Epheser*, 120; Rese, 'Vorzüge', 219; Barth, *Ephesians 1–3*, 256); and (3) Christ was present with Israel in that he lived and died in historical Israel (e.g., Merklein, *Christus*, 18); (4) Christ was the Messiah for whom Israel hoped (e.g., Mußner, *Epheser*, 70–1; Gnilka, *Epheserbrief*, 134; Lona, *Eschatologie*, 260; Bruce, *Ephesians*, 293–4; Patzia, *Ephesians*, 190; Pfammatter, *Epheserbrief*, 22; Faust, *Pax*, 89, 110; Best, *Ephesians*^{2}, 240–1).

[105] See, e.g., Jer. 19.4; Sir. 11.34; 1 Macc. 11.12; Josephus, *A. J.* 4.3; also Aeschines, *Fals. leg.* 2.9, Aristotle, *Rhet.*, 1.5.1361 ^{a}22. See further Rengstorf, *Concordance*, s.v.; Büchsel, 'ἄλλος', 265–6.

[106] *Pace* Troiani, 'ΠΟΛΙΤΕΙΑ', who reads the verb ἀπηλλοτριωμένοι as having a reflexive significance, suggesting that it 'might preferably be used to indicate the abandoning of the precepts of the fathers' (19).

reference to the 'circumcision', i.e., the Jews who nicknamed the Gentiles the 'uncircumcision' were also the agent of estrangement (vv. 11b, 12a). Thus, the point at issue in v. 12a is *not* the Gentiles' existence as being separated from the 'theocratically constituted nation' prior to their conversion;[107] nor that the Gentiles as Gentiles did not know the Jewish tradition and therefore had no fellowship with the Jews.[108] Still less was the author referring to the Gentiles as being estranged from God.[109] Rather, it is human attitude and hostility, in particular it is the alienation between two ethnic groups prior to their reconciliation, that is in view: that is, the Gentiles were put in a position in which they had no share in the body politic of Israel by the 'circumcision'/Jews. The issue at stake is that the Israel (of God) had in the perception of the Jews become an exclusive, *ethnic* based 'body politic' or community from which the Gentiles *as Gentiles* are excluded. Israel as God's elect has been turned into an ethnic community according to their status as the 'circumcision'. Presumably the act and fact of circumcision has become one of the most important determining factors, if not the most important, of a man's status in the 'body politic of Israel'. In which case, certain (not all) Jews have shifted the focus of the covenant which God established with Israel by asserting that the seal of the covenant is a tool that sustains the ethnic and religious identity of the Jews as God's choice (= Israel).[110] It

[107] *Contra* Lincoln, *Ephesians*, 137. Best, *Ephesians*[1], 92. Best's gratuitous comment is that our letter contains no sign of tension between Jews and Gentiles, and it is unlikely that there were strains between these two groups; cf. Best, *Ephesians*[2], 241, where he argues that 'if Gentiles are in a state of exclusion from Israel . . . this does not imply that they were once included and then expelled or that they separated themselves; it was God who separated Jews and Gentiles through his choice of Abraham . . .' (241). Schnackenburg, *Ephesians*, 109, fails to take into account the ethnic factor that led to the alienation of Jew and Gentile.

[108] *Contra* Lindemann, *Epheserbrief*, 45: '. . . daß die Heiden die jüdische Tradition nicht kannten – kurz, daß sie keine Juden waren und Juden mit ihnen keine Gemeinschaft hatten'. See also Mußner, who writes: 'Wer das Bürgerrecht im Gemeinwesen Israel besitzt, gehört dem Verheißungsvolk, steht im Verheißungszusammenhang' (*Epheser*, 71).

[109] *Contra* Gnilka, *Epheserbrief*, 135. For the usage of the same verb in connection with human relationship to God, see, e.g., 4.18 and Col. 1.21.

[110] *Pace* Bruce, *Ephesians*, 292 n. 84. Bruce argues that the verb ἀπηλλοτριωμένοι, if it is translated as having the sense of 'alienated', might suggest (wrongly) that the Gentiles had once been members of the πολιτεία τοῦ Ἰσραήλ but had subsequently been separated from it; Best, *Studies*, 94–5. However, if we regard the alienation which is recounted in v. 12 as abnormal, a perversion of what God had originally planned for his people (see 1.3ff.), the verb may well have conveyed precisely the meaning intended by the author, namely that the Jews' judgement over Gentiles' eligibility on an ethnic basis has resulted in the Gentiles being alienated from God's *Israel* – this cannot be seen as God's original plan for his Israel. See my discussion of v. 19 in chapter 5, section 5.2.

is not difficult to imagine how the self-understanding of the Jews also sanctioned and rationalised their exclusive attitude towards the Gentiles. Since the notions of Israel, circumcision and covenant are inextricably linked, each being inconceivable without the other, it is reasonable to suppose that the self-definition of the Jews in a particularistic or ethnic sense would give rise, inevitably, to injurious *social* consequences such as ethnic discord. The question is: can the self-understanding of the Jews as mentioned above truly reflect what God had originally planned for his own people, *Israel* (cf. 1.4; 3.5–6, 8–9)?

Before we sum up our findings, we may add that the idea of Jesus as *the* Messiah (i.e., 'the anointed one') is not argued but taken for granted by the author. Probably the idea has already become a well-accepted norm among the readers and a key expression of faith by the time Ephesians was written.[111]

Our analysis of v. 12a can be summarised as follows.

(a) The 'body politic of Israel' denotes a corporate body of the Jews. It was not fixed to any particular locality – say, in the single *polis* or synagogue – but was 'a community of communities' which bound

[111] In our epistle, Christ is hailed as the (risen) Lord Jesus Christ (e.g., 1.2; 6.23); or, 'our Lord Jesus Christ' (1.3, 17; 5.20; 6.24; cf. 3.11). There is also little doubt that the author of Ephesians has conflated in a few phrases the proper name (i.e., a way of referring to Jesus) and the title of Jesus (i.e., *the* Christ) quite freely in his formulations (e.g., 2.13). Of course, the titular usage in the second half of v. 13 can also be understood as an anaphora, i.e., the (previously referred to) Christ (Jesus). In either case, Jesus (a Jew) is confirmed as the (Jewish) Messiah. The use of the Christ title is very common in our epistle: The full titular usage, i.e., '*the* Christ Jesus', is less common, occurring only twice (3.1, 11), but the more abbreviated designation '*the* Christ' is very common, especially in the paraenetic section of the epistle (where it occurs 21 times): 1.10, 12, 20; 2.5; 2.13; 3.1, 4, 8, 11, 17, 19; 4.7, 20; 5.2, 5, 14, 23, 24, 25, 29; 6.5. One may argue that some of these occurrences can be explained in terms of anaphoras, but closer examination shows that the following instances can almost certainly be seen as the title of Jesus: 2.5; 3.1, 8, 11, 17; 4.7, 20; 5.2, 5, 14; 6.5. Contextual exegesis may help us to decide to what degree the idea of the messiahship of Jesus is found in a particular passage in our epistle. For the usage of 'Christ Jesus' as a proper name, see esp. 1.1, 3; 2.6, 7, 10, 13; 3.6, 21; 5.32. In short, there is no need for us to enter into debates about the Christ title as reflecting early usage and the proper name as late, since a clear-cut distinction is not apparent – at least not in our epistle. Both the Christ title and the proper name of Jesus are simply taken for granted, not argued by the author. In passing, I have excluded instances such as those found in 4.12 and 4.13 from our discussion, since the syntactical structure of these passages can be explained otherwise (e.g., in terms of Apollonius's Canon, which states that two syntactically joined nouns are either both articular or both anarthrous). See further Dunn, *Colossians and Philemon*, who concludes that 'the fundamentally Jewish character of this Jesus (a Jew) and of the message about him (Jewish Messiah) was one of the most basic axioms and presuppositions of the new movement . . .' (45); cf. Dunn, *Unity*, 41–5. Juel, *Messianic Exegesis*, 175, 177 contends that the confession of Jesus as Messiah is the presupposition for NT christology but not its content; Dahl, *Christ*, esp. 17, 20–1, and n. 23; Best, *Ephesians*^{2}, 241.

together as an alliance/league the ethnic Jews (in western Asia Minor?) who perceived themselves as belonging to a common ancestor, i.e., Jacob/Israel. Given the fact that the author has wedded 'the circumcision' to the notion of this body politic of the elect, it is not unreasonable to conclude that members of this body politic probably had a very high view about circumcision, and that those involved in this community also kept up the practice according to the Law (cf. Eph. 2.15a). Indeed circumcision is necessary for membership in this body politic of the elect, and persistence in it indicates who were the real members *politai*. The notion of the 'body politic of Israel' must have created a profound sense of belonging among Jews who were alike in maintaining their 'ancestral traditions' (i.e., παράδοσις, see, e.g., Josephus, *A. J.* 13.297, 409; Philo, *Spec.* 4.150) and undergirding their solidarity and social self-definition.

(b) The 'body politic of Israel', however, was ethnocentric and exclusivistic: the Gentiles who lacked the 'mark' of the elect in their 'flesh' were by their origin of ethnicity excluded from it *by* the Jews, though this is mentioned by the author in no more than periphrastic terms (cf. vv. 11b, 12a). The possibility of receiving Gentiles into this ethnically based religion is closed. The Jews who made circumcision a *sine qua non* for their legitimation in this 'body politic' have also shifted the focus of the covenant which God established with Israel. They have made the seal of the covenant a tool which sustains their distinctive ethnically based corporate body. This identification in the Jewish attitude between the ethnic group and religious identity is so close that the reception into this religion of members not belonging to its ethnic group has become impossible. The informative intention of the author was to signify the social distance between Jews and Gentiles: the Gentiles *as Gentiles* stood outside the community of 'Israel' (= Jews). The discordance of different human groups has now been stressed by the Ephesians' author before he offers an alternative to the covenantal ethnocentrism. Our later discussion will show that the author looks forward to propose a non-ethnic religion, one with no ethnic ties whatsoever. Human groups of different ethnic backgrounds (i.e., Jews and Gentiles) could then gather around a common religious belief.[112]

[112] The 'non-ethnic religion' should not be confused with 'open-ethnic religion' in which the same identification is made between ethnicity and religion as the 'closed-ethnic religion'. In 'open-ethnic religion' conversion is possible, because there are ways for people who do not belong to the ethnic group to become members of the religion, albeit – through certain rites (e.g., circumcision). See esp. Runesson, 'Judaism', 62–3.

(c) What is much more difficult to determine from our present text is whether the alienation of Jews and Gentiles was also triggered by factors other than the desire of the Jews to exclude the Gentiles from the body politic of the elect. However, what our text has sufficiently revealed is that this alienation was closely related to the Jews' insistence on maintaining the identification between their ethnic and religious identity on one hand, and their attitudes toward the Gentiles on the basis of the above identification on the other. In either case, the consequence would be the same: the two ethnic groups alienated from one another.

(d) The author of Ephesians may well have perceived himself as *intra parietes*, one who is within the walls of Israel, as he described the body politic of Israel. But for him 'Israel' too has been turned into a powerfully *exclusive* expression understood by typical Jews as confined to ethnic Jews on the basis of their status as the elect of God.

3.3.2 καὶ ξένοι τῶν διαθηκῶν τῆς ἐπαγγελίας (v. 12b)

The argument in the first half of v. 12 is by no means complete. The connective καί probably serves to coordinate two closely associated ideas,[113] with our present phrase in v. 12b '*and* aliens to the covenants of the promise' functioning as a supplement to or a further determination of the earlier clause in v. 12a.[114] The difference between the 'uncircumcision' and the 'aliens' is extremely slight, as both can be taken as external designations of the identity of the 'outsiders' from the perspective of the Jews.[115] The 'otherness' of the Gentiles is reinforced in dismissive terms. The use of the plural 'covenants' is very unusual. Traditionally this has been taken to mean either a series of covenants which were made

[113] The collocations, πολιτεία and ξένοι, suggest that the two terms are unequivocally political terms: see, e.g., Aristotle, *Eth. nic.* 1123 a3; Aristotle, *Pol.*, 1275 b37; 1277 b39; 1300 b31; 1303 a38; 1324 a15; *Herodians*, 8.2.9; 1 Macc. 2.7; 3.36, 45; 1 Esd. 8.83; Wis. 19.14–15; Josephus, *A. J.* 11.159; *Vita* 372; Stählin, 'ξένος', 11–14. See also my discussion on Eph. 2.19 in chapter 5, below. The usage of the connective καί can either be epexegetical or consecutive; see esp. Merklein, *Christus*, 18.

[114] Thus Abbott, *Ephesians*, writes: 'A further specification of what is said by the preceding clause' (58); cf. Westcott, *Ephesians*, 35; Lindemann, *Epheserbrief*, 44; Pokorný, *Epheser*, 114; Bouttier, *Éphésiens*, 112–13.

[115] We may note, for example, the robust self-declaration of Esther who almost identified the status of the uncircumcised male with the alien: 'You [God] have knowledge of all things, and you know that I hate the splendour of the wicked and abhor the bed of *the uncircumcision* (ἀπερίτμητος) and of any *alien* (ἀλλοτρίος)' (Add. Est. 14.15, my translation); also Add. Est. 16.10; Ezek. 44.7, 9; 1 Macc. 1.38; 2.7; *Ps. Sol.* 17.15; Josephus, *A. J.* 3.214. In Philo, *QG* 3.61, the uncircumcised (i.e., Gentile) male was termed the 'alien seed' (ἀλλογενὲς σπέρμα). See also PGL, s.v. 2.

especially to the Jewish patriarchs,[116] or the several ratifications of the same 'promise' made to the Jewish patriarchs (e.g., Gen. 12.2–3; 18.18; 22.17–18; 26.3–5; 28.13–14; cf. Ps. 105.42–5).[117] The point is that the 'covenants of the promise', alongside other prerogatives of Israel, were the religious and cultural backbone of the Jews.[118] However, the nub of the issue here is *not* so much that the 'covenants of the promise' would one day come to the Gentiles when the Messiah arrived in the eschatological era, but rather that the author has used vigorous language to emphasise that the Gentiles who lay outside the orbit of the body politic of Israel were 'outsiders' to the *various* 'covenants' which God had promised the Jewish patriarchs. In insisting that the Gentiles were 'aliens to the covenants of the promise', the 'cultural stuff' (to use F. Barth's word) out of which the differentiation between Jews and Gentiles was constructed has also become a boundary marker which distinguishes the Jews from the Gentiles.[119] In our context, circumcision, Israel and the covenants of the promise are inextricably bound together; each is used to underscore the foreignness of the Gentiles, so that the difference between Jews and Gentiles enhances the Jews' sense of 'us' for purposes of group identification. Operating as an 'absent model', the position of the Jews in 'the covenants of promise' provides at the same time a means of apprehending the Gentiles as 'aliens' and of interpreting their *otherness*. 'Covenants of the promise' has become a symbol of Gentiles' 'otherness' which is now set alongside 'Gentiles in the flesh' and 'the uncircumcision' (vv. 11b, 11c). Who could have spoken so dismissively of the Gentiles and excluded the latter as such except those who were confident of their own belonging or prerogatives and of their pre-eminent position with respect to these privileges?

In sum: Gentiles as 'aliens', and their ineligibility and unsuitability in the covenants, had become a significant part in the theological thinking

[116] Bruce, *Ephesians*, 293, suggests that these are covenants which God made with Abraham (Gen. 15.18), with Israel (Exod. 24.8), and with David (Ps. 89.28–37); cf. Lincoln, *Ephesians*, 137; Gnilka, *Epheserbrief*, 136; Abbott, *Ephesians*, 58. This is preferable to the suggestion of Roetzel, 'Διαθῆκαι', here 386–7, that here διαθῆκαι refers to the 'oaths' which God gave to Israel, or 'tables' or 'instruments'.

[117] Thus Beare, 'Ephesians', 651; Dunn, *Romans 1–8*, 533–6; Moo, *Romans*, 563; Rese, 'Vorzüge'. See also Schreiner, 'Völker'.

[118] See, e.g., Wis. 12.21; 18.22; *Exagoge* 104–8, which interprets the covenant promises which were given to the Jewish patriarchs (Abraham, Isaac and Jacob) as God's δωρημάτα, i.e., 'gifts'. This is also confirmed in particular in the earlier Paul, cf. Rom. 9.4–5. See also Rese, 'Church', who contends that 'the direct enumeration of the Gentile Christians' former deficiencies is an indirect reference to Israel's privileges' (26).

[119] See in particular Barth, *Boundaries*, 15; Jenkins, *Ethnicity*, 106; Handelman, 'Ethnicity', here 200; Wallman, *Ethnicity*, 3.

of the Jews. What could hardly be expressed more clearly is the fact that, instead of being seen as inclusive, able to embrace non-Jews, the 'covenants of the promise' have become a boundary marker, distinguishing the Jews who lay within their orbit from the Gentiles.

3.3.3 ἐλπίδα μὴ ἔχοντες καὶ ἄθεοι ἐν τῷ κόσμῳ. (v. 12c)

We have argued that the thinking of the Jews was determined by the notion of covenantal ethnocentrism which can be best seen as the invisible grid that prompted their exclusive attitude toward the Gentiles. Can we then claim that v. 12c sums up, *in solidum*, the same exclusive attitude accentuated by the author in vv. 11b–12b? Can we say that the notion of the Jews as God's elect also provides them with a means of apprehending the Gentiles' 'hopeless' situation and of interpreting their state of being 'godless in the world'? We shall return to these questions in the course of our discussion. But there are a few preliminary observations to be made at this point.

It is worth noting that the author has collocated two statements of negation in reference to the Gentiles. The first denies any possible suggestion that the Gentiles possess any hope at all (ἐλπίδα μὴ ἔχοντες).[120] This is then followed by the appellation 'atheists' (Gk. with an α-privative), which normally denotes those who deny certain accepted 'virtues'[121] and were deemed impious, vicious, or even abandoned by the god(s) (cf. 4.17–24). The characterisation of the Gentiles as such sounds very much like a value-judgement[122] – and if so, what would be the best possible explanation for such value-expressive statements in our present context? Who is speaking, and to whom? Should we simply regard these statements of negation as *ad hoc* expressions which have no connection with the preceding clauses? What does the 'absence' of 'hope' and 'god' mean for

120 The position of the noun ἐλπίς is emphatic, cf. Jude 19. See further Louw and Nida, 69.3; Zerwick, *BG*, no. 440; McKay, *Syntax*, §7.5; Turner, *Syntax*, 284–5, §4; Porter, *Idioms*, 281; Perschbacher, *Syntax*, 97.

121 Similar designations are found in certain passages in the NT which employed the α-privative to underscore one's vices. The following examples show that a vilification and catalogue of vices are difficult to distinguish at times: Rom. 1.30b–31: 'disobedient of parents, foolish, faithless, heartless, ruthless'; 2 Tim. 3.2–3: 'disobedient, ungrateful, unholy, inhuman, implacable, profligates, fierce, haters of good'; Jude 3, 4, 6: 'ungodly, licentiousness'; 1 Tim. 1.9; 2 Pet 2.7, 13, 14. In Wis. 3.11–12a, the 'ungodly' served as the structural opposite in the author's polemics against the 'unjust' to the 'righteous ones', the 'elect' and the 'holy ones'.

122 This is recognised in Best, *Studies*, 97. Best, however, thinks that these phrases are not directly related to Israel.

the Gentiles?[123] Do these statements have reference to the world outside the *church* which the author now addresses as a Christian?[124] Last but not least, should we read these statements as directly reflecting the viewpoint of the Jews? To this cluster of questions we must now turn.

It must be said at the outset that neither 'hope' nor '(a-)theism', when considered separately, is a distinctively Jewish idea. Neither were these ideas something confined to Christians. For the Greeks atheism may denote 'not to recognise (νομίξειν) the gods' or to deny that the gods existed and hence 'to remove (ἀναιρεῖν) the gods'.[125] Drachmann has defined atheism in antiquity as 'the point of view which denies the existence of ancient gods'.[126] It is also evident that in the ancient world 'atheism' was seldom defined in a strict sense and its meaning depended largely on who was speaking, and to whom. Ancient philosophers such as Plato had spoken dismissively of the contemporary thinkers who held the view that the world is governed by nature or chance but not god as atheists (*Leg.* 10.889a–890a; 967A–B). Plutarch had likewise attacked the 'atheists' as those who displayed their 'ignorance and blindness in regard to [*sc.* Greek city] gods' (*Superst.* 164E; 165B; *Pompeius* 29.3.5; *Comm. not.* 1075A.7; cf. Strabo, *Geog.* 17.2.3.20). In the thought of Plutarch, the charge of atheism also implies that the latter is closely related to superstition: 'It occurs to me to wonder at those who say that atheism is impiety (ἀσέβεια) and do not say the same of superstition. The man who does not believe in the existence of the gods is unholy. And is not he who believes in such gods as the superstitious believe in them a partner to opinions far more unholy?' (*Superst.* 169–170A, 168B, 171B–F). The interpretation of atheism as impiety fits Graeco-Roman notions of piety which were defined by the public context of life within the cities:

[123] It is quite impossible to speak of the notion of godlessness in its absolute sense. See further Blank, 'Israel', who writes: 'Not that pagans had no religion or no god. On the contrary, their world was overfilled with them. However, precisely this pagan overabundance of gods and religions was and is the sign of a profound godlessless . . .' (136). See also Thrower, *Atheism*, 50.

[124] So Lindemann, *Epheserbrief*, who concludes: 'Denn Hoffnung ist für ihn ein christlicher Begriff; und Gott ist für ihn der Vater Jesu Christi, ja sogar "der Gott Jesu Christi", so daß Menschen "ohne Christus" selbstverständlich auch "gottlos" sind . . .' (46); cf. Mußner, *Epheser*, who writes: '. . . an die konkreten Erfahrungen mit der heidnischen Umwelt der christlichen Gemeinden denkt – den Heiden in dieser Umwelt waren ja vor ihrer Bekehrung die auf die Völkerwelt sich beziehenden Verheißungen der Propheten unbekannt, und so hatten sie auch keine wirkliche "Hoffnung", und darum hatten sie auch ein verkehrtes Zeitbewußtsein' (72); Tachau, *Einst*, 134–43.

[125] See, e.g., Parker, 'Atheism'.

[126] Drachmann, *Atheism*, 1; Stern, *GLAJJ*, II, 545, n. 43B; Stauffer, 'ἄθεος'. For a helpful survey of the notion of atheism in classical antiquity, see esp. Thrower, *Atheism*, 7–53.

atheism was not simply a private matter, but an extremely political matter, having to do with the cult of the ruler and state.[127] Plutarch probably has reference to those who had revolted against the major factor that constituted *Greek identity*.[128] The atheists who failed to participate in the traditional city cult, a sure sign of impiety, also failed to support the main means of social integration.[129] Similar charges of atheism have been used liberally in manifold polemics in antiquity.[130] So in Josephus's *C. Ap.*, Apollonius Molon of Alabanda had treacherously reviled the Jewish people as 'atheists and misanthropes' (ἀθέους καὶ μισανθρώπους, 2.148; cf. 1.239).[131] Similarly, Claudius Ptolemaeus could charge the Jews with being 'bold, *godless* and scheming' (θρασεῖς, ἀθεόυς καὶ ἐπιβουλευτικοί, *Apot.* 2.65–6). Indeed the Jews were 'a race remarkable for their contempt for the divine powers' from a Roman perspective ('*gens contumelia numinum insignis*', Pliny, *Nat. hist.* 13.9.46). The charge of atheism can also be motivated by reasons other than religious. The Jewish couple Flavia Clemens and his wife Flavia Domitilla (cousins of Domitian and the parents of his heirs), whom Domitian condemned and slandered alongside others when they drifted into the Jewish way of life, were atheists in the perception of the emperor (Cassius Dio, *Hist. rom.* 67.14.1–3).[132] The charge of atheism against other peoples is of a piece

[127] See esp. Conzelmann, *Polemics*, 143.

[128] See in particular Dihle, 'Response'. Dihle argues that the awareness of one's Greek identity was brought about through participation in the traditional cult of the Greek city; Sandvoss, 'Asebie'; Wilken, 'Christians', esp. 105–7.

[129] See also Cicero, *Nat. d.* 1.4. Cicero contends that wherever piety and religion disappeared, 'life soon becomes a welter of disorder and confusion; and in all probability the disappearance of piety towards the gods will entail the disappearance of loyalty and social union among men as well, and of justice itself, the queen of all the virtues'.

[130] Stauffer, 'ἄθεος', who concludes that 'charges of blasphemy, demonism and atheism are favourite weapons in the conflict between different faiths' (121); Drachmann, *Atheism*, 89–119; Conzelmann, *Polemics*, 46–9, 143.

[131] See in particular Schäfer, *Judeophobia*, who writes: 'In the eyes of the Greeks there could hardly be a verdict more devastating than this one' (36). Trebilco, *Communities*, 11–12, comments: 'Simple dislike of non-conformity was probably the basis of the problem with the strangeness of Jewish religious practices; Jewish monotheism and customs were distinctive and Jewish religion was not compatible with other religious options.' There can be little doubt that Apollonius was speaking from the perspective of a Greek, in particular, when he accused the Jews of being 'the most witless of *barbarians*', *apud* Josephus, *C. Ap.* 2.148. For other slanderous accusations laid against the Jews by Apollonius, see especially Josephus, *C. Ap.* 2.236, 255, 258 and 295. See also Feldman, *Jew*, 150–1, 426–7.

[132] Whether Domitian would have considered the Jewish couple as Christians we cannot tell. It is more likely that Domitian deliberately used the charge of atheism to eliminate those rivals and relatives he deemed dangerous; see esp. Schäfer, *Judeophobia*, 114. Barclay, *Jews*, 313, is of the opinion that the purge of the imperial family in question was probably motivated primarily by political rather than religious considerations: '[I]t appears that Domitian was

with the charge against the Jews.[133] The Jewish sibyl, despite prophesying in Gentile guise, promulgates forthrightly the essence of 'practical atheism': '*Godless ones* also call their images gods, abandoning the creator, thinking to have all *hope* and life from them. Trusting in dumb and speechless things with evil result, they are ignorant of God' (*Sib. Or.* 8.395; cf. 3.629).[134] Despite the fact of there being *various* deities venerated in the Gentiles' temples, in the perception of the sibyl these are 'godless temples' (ναοῖ ἄθέοι, *Sib. Or.* 3.32, 601–7); and the Gentiles who showed their fidelity to these heathen sovereigns were simply 'godless, unjust and lawless men' (*Sib. Or.* 5.309). Presumably the underlying assumption in the sibyl's statements is that there is only one temple for the one true God – were that defiled, as by the Gentiles, there would be no trace of veneration paid to the one true God at all (cf. Philo, *Spec.* 1.67; *Leg.* 347; Josephus, *C. Ap.* 2.193). The impression of the sibyl about the godless and their alien cult is also reflected in the *Wisdom of Solomon*: 'But miserable [*sc.* are the Gentiles], with their *hopes* set on dead things, they are those who gave the name gods to the works of human hands' (13.10; also 15.6); their hope 'is cheaper than dirt, and their lives are of less worth than clay, because *they failed to know the one* who formed them and inspired them with active souls' (*Wis.* 15.10).[135] It was the same for Philo, for whom the knowledge of the one true God is in fact a matter of life and death: 'The *law* tells us that all who cleave to God live [*sc.* Deut. 4.4], and herein it lays down a vital doctrine (δόγμα) fraught with much wisdom. For in very truth the *godless* (ἄθέοι) are dead in soul, but those who have taken service in the ranks of the God who only

able to seize on any Jewish "leanings" as a sign of disloyalty to the (Roman) Gods and an insult to his own divine status (*maiestas*)'. See also Smallwood, 'Domitian's Attitude'; Stern, *GLAJJ*, I, 380–1, n. 2; See also Whittaker, *Graeco-Roman Views*, 91. One vital effect, however, seems to stand out in the attitude of Domitian: that those who followed a monotheistic belief could be accused of atheism as much as those from another distinctive belief system.

133 Conzelmann, *Polemics*, 46; Gnilka, *Epheserbrief*, 136–7; Best, *Studies*, 98. See further Fascher, 'Gottlosigkeit'.

134 See further Collins, *Imagination*, 99–100, who argues that the third book of *Sibylline Oracles* is a highly propagandist document which presents Judaism to the Hellenistic world in terms that are primarily ethical, e.g., the avoidance of idolatry, superstition and sexual misconduct. Nickelsburg, *Jewish Literature*, 162–5, concludes that *Sibylline Oracles* Book 3 contains powerful polemics aimed against pagan idolatry and immorality.

135 See also Stern, *GLAJJ*, II, 157–8 (no. 333), who has noted that the phrase πιστὰ ἐλπίσματα, 'hopeful hopes', was used by Cleomedes, *Cir.* 2.1.91, in reference to 'Jewish vain beliefs'.

is are alive, and that life can never die' (*Spec.* 1.345; also *QE* 29.4; 30.1).[136]

More could be said about the *topos* of atheism/impiety which often appeared in ancient polemics and apologia.[137] It must suffice to note that for the Jews, the charge of atheism was made on their firm conviction of monolatrous belief, a belief that would lead them most likely to despise the alien, pluralistic and iconic cult;[138] for Gentiles who found their multiform religiosity categorically rejected, the counter charges of 'atheism' and 'impiety' are only what should be expected.[139]

It is reasonable, therefore, to suppose that the charge of atheism against the Gentiles is to be studied within the convention of 'the rhetoric of slander' outlined above.[140] The collocation of both ideas, 'hopeless' and 'godless', makes it all the more probable that these ideas should be interpreted according to the Jewish tradition which understood 'hope' as inextricably bound with the belief in the one true God (e.g., Deut. 6.4; Exod. 20.3; Acts 19.26; 1 Cor. 8.4–6; Gal. 4.8; 1 Pet. 1.21; *m.* Tamid; *Shemoneh 'Esreh* 1; also Josephus, *A. J.* 5.112).[141] 'Hope' always presupposes the notion of God (e.g., Ps. 64.6; 77.7; 145.5; Rom. 4.18; 5.4; 15.13;

[136] Philo does not speak of 'atheism' in a strict sense. In *Spec.* 1.344, he refers to those who ascribe divinity to their respective idols but deny the one true God as 'atheist' and 'the children of the harlot'.

[137] The early church, which adopted Jewish monotheism, also became heir to the same charge, e.g., *Martyrdom of Polycarp* 9.2, where Polycarp was coerced by the authority to 'swear by the genius of Caesar' to keep himself 'away from the atheists', and Polycarp waved his hand at the lawless mob and threw back the same charge: Αἶρε τοὺς ἀθέους. The charge of 'atheism' was harboured against Christians by Porphyry in late antiquity. Christians were deemed to be those who have apostastised from the gods by whom every nation and state is sustained: e.g., Eusebius, *Praep. ev.* 1.2.1–5; Athenagoras, *Leg.* 1–7, esp. 3–7. One imagines that Porphyry's accusations implied that the Christians neither stuck to the customs of the pagan gods nor followed the one God worshipped by the Jews. See further the convenient collections on the subject of atheism in Harnack, *Vorwurf*; Drachmann, *Atheism*, esp. 120–32; Stern, *GLAJJ*, II, 545 n. 43B; Schäfer, *Judeophobia*, 34–65; Lona, *Eschatologie*, 262 n. 25; Conzelmann, *Polemics*, 46; MacMullen and Lane, *Paganism*, esp. 175–8.

[138] Barclay, *Jews*, 428–34.

[139] See also Conzelmann, *Polemics*, who concludes that the charge of atheism against the Jews was in fact made on two grounds: 'the lack of images of God and the refusal of the Jews to participate in other cults' (46); Barclay, *Jews*, 432; Whittaker, 'Graeco-Roman Views', 114 n. 4. See also Rajak, 'Charter', here 107–23. Rajak argues that '[p]agansim is often said to have been tolerant and accommodating. But it was not so towards a monotheistic religion centred upon an invisible God, a religion which could not readily be assimilated, in the usual fashion, into the existing system' (122).

[140] See particularly Johnson, 'Slander'; Du Toit, 'Vilification'.

[141] See in particular Dunn, *Partings*, 19, who concludes that 'the first of the ten commandments was deeply ingrained in Jewish faith and praxis'. See also Schürer, *HJPAJC*, II, 454–63, 481–2; Str-B, Exckurs 9, 189; Bayer, 'ἐλπις', 439; BAGD, s.v.

1 Thess. 4.5; 2 Macc. 2.18; 7.20; Sir. 34.13; *Arist.* 261; 4 Macc. 11.7; 17.4; 2 Esd. 7.120; Philo, *Legat.* 196; *Det.* 138f.; *Abr.* 7–14; *Praem.* 11–14; also *Spec.* 1.310–11). In this tradition the idea of 'hope' is often understood as the 'trustful hope which is freed from anxiety', or the confidence one has in the one God who promises (cf. *Ps. Sol.* 9.8–11; Rom. 15.13). Such thought is rare among the Greeks whose hope is based upon the uncertainty of the future, and whose hope could mean merely 'expectation', with ἐλπίζω often used in the sense of fearing evil.[142]

Given the close connection between Israel's hope in the one God and the reference to the 'covenants of the promise' that engender 'hope', it is not so much that the Gentiles were godless or hopeless in the true sense (cf. 2.2);[143] rather, the two statements of negation in vv. 12b, c are a deliberate assessment of the situation of the Gentiles from the vantage point of the Jews. The informative intention of the author is to underscore the covenantal nomistic mindset of certain self-confident Jews (and therefore Judaism) who believed that the gracious God had chosen Israel as his own people and that their hope followed on his promise in the covenants to the patriarchs, but were bold enough to speak dismissively of the Gentiles.[144] In short, the Gentiles stood outside some of the major factors (God, Israel, covenant, hope, circumcision) that constitute the *Jewish* identity. There is hardly anything they have shared in common with the Jews. That is the Jewish perception which the author of Ephesians had wished to pass on to his Gentile readers.

To sum up. The identification of Gentiles as 'having no hope and godless in the world' carries heavily charged ethno-religious overtones. In the religious milieu of the Jewish world the Gentiles who 'have not' these blessings contrasted sharply with the privileged position of the Jews, indicating both their impiety and strangeness: that is, the *un*circumcision of the Gentiles, their *estrangement* from the Jewish body politic, their status as *aliens* to the covenants of promise, the 'absence' of *hope* and

[142] Thus Bultmann, 'ἐλπις', here 522–3, 529; Dunn, *Romans 1–8*, 218–19, 251–2; BAGD, s.v., 1; LSJ, s.v.

[143] So Mußner, *Epheser*, writes: 'Nicht daß die Heiden keine Religion und keine Götter gehabt hätten, im Gegenteil, ihre Welt war davon übervoll' (72); Lona, *Eschatologie*, 262.

[144] Thus Best, *Studies*, 97. Best is certainly correct in reading the statements of negation here as value-expressive, but he fails to recognise the fact that it was the confidence which the Jews had in their one God which led to the dismissal of the Gentiles as hopeless and godless, cf. Wis. 3.18; 15.10; *Sib. Or.* 8.395; *Ps. Sol.* 9.8–11. What the author of Ephesians wishes to pass on is not simply the value-judgement of the Jews but also the rationale behind such an analysis of the situation of the Gentile world: group identification is the cause of Jews' outright dismissal of the Gentile 'other' as godless; cf. my discussion of 2.2 in chapter 2, section 2.3.1.

their god*less*ness in the world – all these are best understood as Jewish categories; they are added together to indicate, cumulatively, the Gentiles' *otherness*. For the body politic of 'Israel', whose confident hope is firmly rooted in the one God who established the *covenants* with Israel, the Gentiles were simply irreligious and impious. Be that as it may, the author has elicited the Jewish attitude that Jews and Gentiles had shared nothing in common in their religion and had nothing that could bring them together into a common cause.

It will suffice to say that there existed a serious *distancing* of the Jews from the Gentiles which the author portrays in his representation of the Gentiles. His representation tells us much of the Jews. It unfolds how the Jews, confident of their identity as the chosen people of God, looked out on the Gentile world and displayed to it the 'sure hope' which they had procured from the one God who had promised and established a covenantal relationship with them.

3.4 'But now you who were far off are made near': the 'us-them' polarity deconstructed

We have suggested earlier that the author's statements about the Gentiles in vv. 1–2 allude to Jewish perceptions as he describes the Gentiles as being 'dead in their transgressions and sins' (v. 1a), walking in sins and being sub-let to an 'other' god of this world (vv. 1b, 2). He echoes the well-established motif in Jewish theology whereby the Jews could integrate the particularism of election with the universalism of monotheism: the Gentiles are sub-let to a 'power' other than God to govern them, while God has chosen Israel for himself.[145] Although I have made the suggestion that what is hinted at in vv. 1–2 is a Jewish perspective, the full picture of the framework behind such a covenantal mindset has yet to be unveiled, and the question of *who* would probably have propagated the particularism of election is less than clear at that point.

What is *implicitly* expressed about the otherness of the Gentiles is now spelt out explicitly in Ephesians 2.11–12, underscoring the dominant themes of Israel's election and covenant relation with God. The author not only addresses the Gentiles from the perspective of a Jew (e.g., 'Gentiles in the flesh', v. 11a), he also lays bare the way in which his Gentile readers appeared to the Jews (vv. 11b, 12a, 12b), who ascribed specific value to circumcision and exhibited thus their allegiance to the covenant

[145] Thus Dunn, *Galatians*, 192.

made between God and Israel, and to the Mosaic Law. Moreover, the Jews had formed a body politic from which the Gentiles were excluded (v. 12a). They had practised covenantal ethnocentrism by making judgements about the position of the Gentiles according to their own ethnic and religious assumptions. Another way of putting the same point is to say that covenantal ethnocentrism had become the governing principle or the 'invisible grid' best explaining the attitude of the Jews toward the Gentiles. It had become the principal reason for Gentiles being estranged from the ethnic-based body politic and Israel's blessings. In short, covenantal ethnocentrism interposed itself between Jews and Gentiles, creating as its net result a social distance between Jews and Gentiles.

If our findings above are sound, it means that the thesis which suggests that Ephesians 2. 11–13 does not consist of any sociological presentation but rather a Christian theological characterisation of the Gentiles or Judaism can no longer be held as accurate.[146] In his effort to represent the Gentiles' 'otherness' and the inclusion of the latter in Christ, the author who formulated his arguments from the perspective of an ethnographer also writes as a messianic believer. These two dimensions co-exist perfectly well in vv. 11–13 and should not be seen as mutually exclusive. The failure to appreciate the ethnographic discourse which appears in vv. 11–13 is a major deficiency in present scholarship.[147] Keeping all these findings in mind, we shall now proceed to interpret v. 13.

[146] *Contra* Best, *Studies*, here 91. The weakness of Best lies in his attempt to find a single (i.e., theological) dimension behind vv. 11–13. However, recent studies on the representation of ethnic 'others' enable us to read Eph. 2.11–13 from a different *perspective*; see esp. Hartog, *Mirror*; Vasaly, *Representations*; Hall, *Barbarian*; Hall, *Identity*; Garland, *Deformity*, passim; Hall, 'Other', 223–79.

[147] Conzelmann, for instance (*Polemics*, 254), contends that 'the letter to the Ephesians has no interest in either Israel or the law, but only in the present unity in Christ of those who were formerly Jews and Gentiles but are now together in the church created by breaking down the dividing wall that separated them, that is, the law (2.11ff.)'. This is an overstatement. So also Schnackenburg, *Ephesians*, who thinks that no direct conclusion can be drawn about the relationship of the continuing 'Israel' (i.e. Judaism at the time Eph. was composed) to the Christian Church (110). Merklein, *Christus*, 72–6, writes: 'Insofar as the "promise" (*sc*. 12b) moves towards the eschatological people of the Church grounded "in Christ", the "Community of Israel" is realized in the Church.' It is less than clear that the author 'appears to speak as the Jewish representative' and that 'the epistle may represent the voice of the Jewish Christian minority' (*pace* MacDonald, *Pauline Churches*, 94). The suggestion of Roetzel, *Conversations*, 141, 143, that 'the author of Ephesians argues for the inclusion of Jewish Christians *qua* Jewish Christians' is wide of the mark. It is difficult to tell (*contra* Käsemann, 'Ephesians', 291; Roetzel, *Conversations*, 143; MacDonald, *Pauline Churches*, 97, et al.) that the Gentile Christians had truly grown 'big' because of missionary activities or had become bossy in such a way that they despised the Jewish Christians. There are, however, clues that the Gentiles in 'Ephesians' were still weak and unstable in many aspects and needed reassurance: see, e.g., 1.16–20; 3.16; 4.14; 6.10.

3.4.1 νυνὶ δὲ ἐν Χριστῷ Ἰησοῦ ὑμεῖς οἵ ποτε ὄντες μακρὰν ἐγενήθητε ἐγγὺς ἐν τῷ αἵματι τοῦ Χριστοῦ (v. 13)

The author's argument has taken a new twist in v. 13. The sudden emphasis on the transference of Gentiles from one sphere (or category) to another as well as their participation in the new reality brought about by Christ demonstrates that the issue of Gentiles' status among the people of God is still at stake. But does this mean that the Gentiles can now enjoy the privileges that 'once' belonged to Israel, as some scholars have assumed?[148] Does he intend to link the Gentiles directly to Israel[149] or God?[150] or is this question simply unanswerable?[151] Gnilka, for example, is of the opinion that the 'far off/near' language is never meant to link the Gentiles to Israel but used to underscore (1) the Gentiles' admission to the Church at baptism[152] and (2) the Gentiles' regaining the blessings of which they had been deprived.[153] As far as we can tell, few have given sufficient attention to the issue of the social space of the Gentiles *as Gentiles*. For us the question is: how does the formulation in v. 13 relate to the exclusion of the Gentiles from the body politic of Israel, from the 'covenants of the promise', and so forth? Does the language in v. 13 intend to reflect such an exclusion and the Gentiles' position at the extremity or frontier? Another way of putting the same question is: does the author wish to unveil the social distance between Jews and Gentiles in the light of covenantal ethnocentrism? Before these questions can be answered, it is necessary to give a brief assessment of two major theories concerning the interpretation of v. 13.

[148] So Best, *Studies*, 99; Rese, 'Vorzüge'; Lincoln, *Ephesians*, 139.

[149] So Richardson, *Israel*, who argues that 'Gentiles must still be made near to Israel to become partakers of the covenants and to overcome their estrangement. Having done so, they have become fellow-citizens' (152, see also 156–7); cf. Barth, *Ephesians 1–3*, 277; Sanders, *Schismatics*, 200 argues that the 'near' in v. 13 is an epithet for the Jews.

[150] So Lindemann, *Aufhebung*, writes: 'Gemeint ist nicht, "Nahe" und "Ferne" seien miteinander vereinigt, die Heiden in ein zuvor bestehendes Gottesvolk "eingegliedert" worden, es geht vielmehr darum, daß diejenigen, die "einst" fern von Gott waren, ihm jetzt nahe sind' (155); cf. Lindemann, *Epheserbrief*, 46; Pfammatter, *Epheserbrief*, 22; Conzelmann, *Polemics*, 254; Patzia, *Ephesians*, 193; Schnackenburg, *Ephesians*, 111.

[151] So Gnilka, *Epheserbrief*, who writes: 'Die Frage, wem sie denn jetzt zu Nahen wurden, kann nicht mit der Alternative Gott oder Israel beantwortet werden' (137).

[152] Gnilka, *Epheserbrief*, writes: 'Hier ist ihren Eintritt in die Gemeinde gedacht, näherhin als die Taufe' (137); cf. Tachau, *Einst*, 133; Mußner, *Epheser*, 72–3. This view is rejected by Pfammatter, *Epheserbrief*, who writes in more cautious terms: 'Die Parallelen zur christlichen Taufe als dem sakramentalen zur Kirche-Kommen ist unübersehbar' (22).

[153] Gnilka, *Epheserbrief*, 137.

The first theory is found in the works of Stuhlmacher and Moritz who have both reached conclusions with primarily OT materials.[154] Stuhlmacher maintains that the author of Ephesians offers a christological exegesis of Isaiah 9.5–6, 52.7, and 57.19 in vv. 13–18: 'In the context of vv. 11–12 this exegesis serves to express the reconciliation of Gentiles and Jews through Christ with God and each other in such a way that the miracle of the reception precisely of the Gentiles in the church and the nature of this church as the new people of God also becomes visible.'[155] He concludes that the author's method of christological exegesis of scripture is inspired by the rabbis.[156] Moritz, who rightly rejects reconstructions of a Gnostic background in Ephesians, is of the opinion that the author's allusions to Isaiah enclose the very heart of vv. 13–17.[157]

This theory, however, is not entirely satisfactory on two counts.

(a) The language of 'far off' and 'near' which appears in v. 13a is very common in the Jewish scriptures (e.g., Deut. 30.11–14, cf. 13.8; 1 Kgs. 8.46; Esther 9.20; Ezek. 6.11–12; Dan [Theod.] 9.7; 1 Macc. 8.12; Isa. 33.13). Isaiah may be seen as part of the stream of this tradition in its use of the language which extends from the Jewish scripture, through our author (or other NT writers), and on to the later rabbinic texts; hence, the argument that the far off/near language in v. 13 constitutes a quotation of Isaiah 57.19 or an allusion to it is not compelling.

(b) This theory reads Isaiah 57.19 into our text too quickly, although the prophetic oracle is closely associated with v. 17.[158] It fails to address

[154] Stuhlmacher, 'Peace', 187; Moritz, *Mystery*, 23–55; Barth, *Ephesians 1–3*, 260, 276–9; Percy, *Probleme*, 283; Deichgräber, *Gotteshymhus*, 167 n. 1; Westcott, *Ephesians*, 36; Mußner, *Epheser*, 73; Mußner, *Christus*, 100ff.; Merklein, *Christus*, 25; Bruce, *Ephesians*, 295; Bouttier, *Éphésiens*, 114–15; Schnackenburg, *Ephesians*, 111; Conzelmann, *Epheser*, 99; Pfammatter, *Epheserbrief*, 22; Thomson, *Chiasmus*, 86; Patzia, *Ephesians*, 193.

[155] Stuhlmacher, 'Peace', 187; Barth, *Ephesians 1–3*, 260, 276. See also Mußner, *Epheser*, who writes: 'Die Lokative »nah« und »fern« stammen aus Jes 57, 19' (73); Pfammatter, *Epheserbrief*, 22; Schnackenburg, *Ephesians*, 111; Pokorný, *Epheser*, 116.

[156] Stuhlmacher, 'Peace', 187.

[157] Moritz, *Mystery*, 29. Earlier reconstructions of a Gnostic background by some scholars (e.g., Schlier; Käsemann, et al.) have been severely criticised: see in particular Mußner, *Christus*, 88–91; Percy, *Probleme*, 278–88.

[158] The 'far off/near' language in v. 13 should be read *adverbially* rather than *adjectivally* (the 'far off' or the 'near'). Even if one argues that v. 17 is an allusion to Isa. 57.19, it is worth noting that the meaning of the OT *Vorlage* in v. 17 is largely transposed by the author of Ephesians. For this, see my discussion of v. 17 in chapter 4, below. Suffice it to say that the author collocates both 'far off' and 'near' to convey the notion that Christ's proclamation of peace is an *all-embracing* ministry (v. 17). Isa. 57.19, which is re-applied in v. 17, is used by the author as a support to Christ's inclusive ministry.

the question whether the 'far off/near' language in v. 13 may have been prompted directly by the narrative in vv. 11–12. It does not go beyond the author's semantic representaton to appreciate the particular force of his statements about the Gentiles.

Against this first theory, some scholars suggest that the author of Ephesians is speaking of those 'far off' having come near, a notion not found in Isaiah 57.19, but common in Jewish discussion of proselytism (e.g., *Mek. Exod.* 18.5; Num. *R.* 8.4; *midr.* Sam. 28.6).[159] Dahl, for example, argued that Ephesians 2.13–18 is a kind of midrash on Isaiah 57.19, a passage which in Judaism was referred to those 'far off' Gentiles who had become proselytes and the Israelites, who were 'near'.[160] This theory has been revived recently by Lincoln, who asserts that the proselyte terminology has undergone a transformation, namely that the author applies to the Gentiles in the church what was valid among the Jews for proselytes: because of Christ's works, it can be used of Gentiles in general, not simply of proselytes to Judaism.[161]

The strong point of the theory outlined above is that the language of 'far off' and 'near' could become the author's own which he appropriates and adapts to his own purpose. However, this reasoning is not entirely satisfactory and I shall indicate the basic reasons why I part company with Lincoln and others at this point. They are twofold.

(a) The evidence adduced in favour of this theory is unconvincing. In the Qumran literature terms such as קרב are used in connection with the notion of 'entrance into the community', *intra muros*, within the walls of Judaism, and were *never* applied to the Gentiles (e.g., 1QH xiv.14; vi.16, 22; viii.9, 15, 16; cf. 4QFlor. 1–3.1.3–4).[162] The rabbinic sources (i.e., *Mek Exod.* 18.5; Num. *R.* 8.4; *midr.* Sam. 28.6) which are adduced as evidence are of very late date and are therefore not relevant in our present discussion.[163] In our present context, the Gentiles were said to have been 'brought near' by God who is the implied subject of the verb ἐγενήθητε.[164]

[159] So Gnilka, *Epheserbrief*, 137; Meuzelaar, *Leib*, 61–6, 75–86; Dahl, 'Creation', 437 n. 2; Barth, *Ephesians 1–3*, 260, 276, 278.

[160] Dahl, 'Creation', 437, n. 2. Dahl also concedes that in Judaism the 'far off' language in Isa. 57.19 was also referred to penitents other than the Gentile proselytes, e.g., *Tg. Isa.* 57.19; *b.* Ber. 34b; *b.* San. 99a.

[161] Lincoln, *Ephesians*, 139. Lincoln's view is dependent upon the earlier work of Meuzelaar, *Leib*, 75.

[162] *Contra* Lincoln, *Ephesians*, 139; Gnilka, *Epheserbrief*, 137 and n. 6.

[163] See in particular Stemberger, *Talmud*, esp. 259, 309–11, 357–8.

[164] The verb ἐγενήθητε in the passive voice (a 'divine passive').

(b) This theory fails to give sufficient weight to obvious ethnographic categories which situate the Gentile 'other' (vv. 11–12),[165] and to explain whether the exclusivistic tendency of Jews could have prompted the use of the 'far off' language in v. 13. One cannot rule out that the author's statement about the Gentiles in v. 13 is an inferrable interpretation against the backcloth of these categories.

In short, the theory that reads v. 13 in terms of Jewish proselytism is more likely to cause confusion than to add to our understanding of the text.

I am inclined to think that there is a simpler explanation, namely that the 'far off' language in v. 13 denotes, simply, the sequel to ethnic alienation which the Gentiles experienced (vv. 11b–12), and that the author's statement can be best accounted for against the backcloth of the self-understanding of the Jews. The Jewish tendency to divide via the circumcision/uncircumcision dichotomy must have had inevitable repercussions on the way in which the author articulated his statements about his Gentile recipients.

The suggestion that the language of 'far off' in v. 13a provides a glimpse of Gentiles at the outermost fringes implies that there is a need on the part of the author to recount to his Gentile readers how the non-Jewish world appeared to the Jews. His argument proceeds by *inference* (*a causis vocant*),[166] and the problem that faces the author is precisely that of *paraphrasis* or responsible translation.[167] He reasons on the basis of all the visible Jewish symbols he could accumulate and draws together what he has already outlined in vv. 11–12, and reflects to his Gentile recipients how the self-definition of the Jews had affected their position with respect to the various privileges of Israel. Paraphrasis functions more or less like a switching mechanism in order to make it possible to pass from the Jewish 'world' into the world where the Gentiles are addressed.[168] His 'far off'

[165] This is also recognised by some scholars – but, for different reasons: Mußner, 'Geschichtstheologie', 59; Patzia, *Ephesians*, 193; Moritz, *Mystery*, 53. Moritz, however, does not press further as to how the tension in v. 11f. would affect the author's subsequent formulations, but avers that v. 13 is a direct echo of Isa. 57.19. See also MacDonald, *Pauline Churches*, 94; Roetzel, *Conversations*, 141–2.

[166] See, e.g., Quintilian, who contends that this kind of argument 'consists in the inference of facts from their efficient causes or the reverse, a process known as argument from causes' (*Inst.* 5.10.80).

[167] See in particular Steiner, *Babel*, 28–9, 311–18, 415–17.

[168] The same procedure has already been employed by the author in v. 11a when he spoke of the non-Jews as 'Gentiles in the flesh'. The author does not speak simply as a Jew, he also 'translates' the Gentiles into the Jewish world, exhibiting the way in which Jews looked out on the non-Jewish world. See also my exegesis of Eph. 2.1–2 in chapter 2, above.

language resonates well with that of ancient ethnographers who described the way in which a certain ethnic group or nation perceived itself as occupying the position of central importance (e.g., the centre of the earth, or 'the navel of the world') and exercised its power to define the 'space' of others.[169] Those areas on the outermost fringes become the setting in which normal rules governing the 'central' community are suspended. Herodotus, for example, tacitly assumed that Greece was the centre by his theory of frontiers or 'extremities' (Gk. ἐσχατίαι, e.g., *Histories* 1.134, 191, 3 times; 3.115–16; 4.71; 6.127; 7.110).[170] Herodotus's world view was commonly entertained among other historians.[171] Ethnocentricity, however, could be reinforced in other ways.[172] While we can be sure that Jewish writers had not fully subscribed to the perspective of Greek

[169] The organisation of social distance in the ancient world is well attested in ancient historiography and ethnography. Herodotus, among other historians, recorded that the Persians interpreted their 'world' in terms of spatial distance, in which the Persians constituted themselves the centre of a concentric circle. In *Histories* 1.134 he writes: 'Of nations, they [*sc. the* Persians] honour most their *nearest* neighbours, whom they esteem next to themselves; those who live beyond these they honour in the second degree; and so with the remainder, the further they are removed, the less the esteem in which they hold them. The reason is, that they look upon themselves as very greatly superior in all respects to the rest of mankind, regarding others as approaching to excellence in proportion as they dwell *nearer* to them; whence it comes to pass that those who are the *farthest off* must be the most degraded of mankind' (tr. Rawlinson).

See further Tuan, *Topophilia*, esp. 30–44, 59–91; Romm, *Edges*, esp. 46–8, 54–5; Rykwert, *Town*, 163–87; Vasaly, *Representations*, 133–9; Dupont, *Life*, here 83–6.

[170] Herodotus's theory of extremities enables him to explain the 'otherness' of the rest of the world in spatial terms, e.g., 3.106: 'It seems as if the *extreme region* of the earth (αἱ δ' ἐσχατιαὶ κῶς τῆς οἰκεομένης κτλ.) were blessed by nature with the most excellent productions, just in the same way that *Greece* enjoys a climate more excellently tempered than any other country. In India, which, as I observed lately, is the *furthest region* of the inhabited world (τὴν ἠῶ ἐσχάτη τῶν οἰκεομένων κτλ.) towards the east . . .'; cf. 3.107: 'Arabia is the *last* of inhabited lands (ἐσχάτη Ἀραβίη) towards the south.' This probably explained why Delphi, the centre of Greece, could be called the 'navel of the earth' by the Greeks. See further Hartog, *Mirror*, 138–41; Thomson, *Geography*, here 44–93; Paassen, *Geography*, here 117–211; Romm, *Edges*, 9–44.

[171] See, e.g., Hesiod, *Theog*. 731; Demosthenes, *Ep*. 4.7; Xenophon *Vect*. 1.6; Strabo, *Geog*. 1.1.8.3; 3.3.8; 11.5.5; Polybius, *Hist*. 3.58.2.4; Diodorus Siculus, *Bib. hist*. 25.10.1.5 (of the world); Dio, *Or*. 13.9.8; 45.7.1; Theocritus, 15.8; Caesar, *Bell. Gal.*, 6.24; also 1.1, 36; 4.3; 4.14; Plautus, *Rudens* 1034. See further Hartog, *Mirror*, 232; Vasaly, *Representations*, 148.

[172] See, e.g., Cicero, *Resp*. 2.5–11 who considered Rome as 'the light of the world, the citadel of humanity'. For the Romans, Rome, which stood at the centre of the Italian peninsula, is the centre of the world, the frozen north is at one extreme, while the torrid south is at the other; see also Cicero, *Or. d.* 1.105; *Cat.* 3.1; 4.11; *Sull.* 33. The idea that Rome was situated in a latitude of *temperate* climate was incorporated into the mythology of Italy as the ideal Saturnian land, Pliny, *Hist. nat*. 37.201; Strabo *Geog*. 6.4.1. See further Balsdon, *Aliens*, 9–10, 59–70, esp. 59–64; Vasaly, *Representations*, 133–4.

(or Roman) ethnographers,[173] they were nevertheless acquainted with the similar idea of ethnocentricity and employed a notion of extremities analogous to that of the Greeks or Romans in order to make sense of their own symbolic world (e.g., Deut. 28.49; Isa. 48.20; 49.6; 62.11; Jer. 6.22; Ezek. 38.6; Matt. 28.19–20; Acts 2.39; 22.21; 1 Macc. 1.3, 3.9, 8.4, 12; Sir. 44.21, 47.15–16; cf. Judith 2.9; *Ps. Sol.* 8.15; Philo, *Mos.* 1.278; *Virt.* 223; *Praem.* 80; *Legat.* 144; Josephus, *A. J.* 8.348; *Vita* 318).[174] It should come as no surprise that the 'far off' language in v. 13a can be understood in the same light. It is formulated in such a way as to *echo* the world view which the Jews widely held.[175] It lays bare the thinking that viewed the periphery as a place of negative extremes and the Jews as central.[176] As far as its implication is concerned, the 'far off' language, like 'the uncircumcision' or 'aliens', is very close to an ethnic slur underscoring the defective status of the Gentiles. It reinforces the sense of the Gentiles as being spatially removed, and relegated to the utmost limit of the Jewish world. Closely associated with the Jews' belief that they occupied the position of centrality was probably their belief that the Gentiles belonged to a world disparate from that of the Jews; hence, the distant connection between the two ethnic groups.[177] Unlike the Greeks or the Romans, it

[173] See in particular Hall, *Barbarian*, esp. 102–13; Hartog, *Mirror*, 310–70; Balsdon, *Aliens*, 137–45.

[174] On Jerusalem as the centre of the world, see esp. Bauckham, 'James', who writes: 'Geography and religious meaning were deeply interconnected in the Jewish sense of the centrality of Jerusalem in the Diaspora and the world' (418). There can be little doubt that ethnocentricity was also practised by the Jewish sages, i.e., Israel is the centre of the world: see, e.g., *m.* Kel. 1.6–19.

[175] See, e.g., Deut. 13.8 (LXX); 28.49 (ἐπάξει κύριος ἐπι σὲ ἔθνος μάκρόθεν ἀπ᾿ ἐσχάτου τῆς γῆς ὡσεὶ ὅρμημα ἀετοῦ ἔθνος ὅ ούκ ἀκουσῃ τῆς φωνῆς αὐτοῦ); 29.22; 1 Kgs. 8.46; Ps. 64.6 (LXX); Isa. 33.13; 57.9; Jer. 4.16; Ezek. 6.12; 22.5; Mic. 4.3, par. Isa. 13.5 (ἔρχεσθαι ἐκ γῆς πόρρωθεν ἀπ᾿ ἄκρου θεμελίου τοῦ οὐρανοῦ); 43.6; Acts 2.39; 22.21. Philo, *Praem.* 80 employed both μακράν and ἐσχάτος to designate the notion of spatial extremity: 'For the commandments are not too huge and heavy for the strength of those to whom they will apply, nor is the good far away (μακράν) either beyond the sea or at the end of the earth . . . (ἐν ἐσχάτιαῖς γῆς κτλ.)'; 1 Macc. 8.4, 12.

[176] There can be little doubt that later rabbinic interpretations also practised (religious) ethnocentricity as they addressed the *Gentiles* (i.e., proselytes) as the 'far off': e.g., *no. R.* 8.4; *midr. Samuel* 28.6; see also Str-B, III, 585–7. See further LEH, s.v.; LSJ, s.v., 3; BAGD, s.v., 1.

[177] Similar ideas can also be seen in *Lev. R.* 16.116d. We are told that the lepers were forced by the law to keep *afar* from the community of the healthy (example cited in Str-B, IV, 751); cf. Luke 17.12. See also BAGD, s.v., 2. Roman writers such as Martial also used the 'far off'/'near' language to underscore the phenomenon of 'urban alienation' between residents in the *polis*, as he writes in *Epigrams* 1.86: *'tam longe est mihi* quam Terentianus, / qui nunc Niliacam regit Syenen. / non convivere, nec videre salten, / non audire licet, nec *urbe* tota / *quisquam est tam prope tam proculque nobis* (LCL).' See also Jos. 9.22; Sir. 27.20–2; Seneca, *Ben.* 5.19.3; Tacitus, *Ann.* 12.10. I therefore disagree with Schnackenburg,

was religious perception rather than politics, climate or geography that most powerfully reinforced the idea of Jewish centrality.[178] Given the Jewish perception that the Gentiles lacked the mark of covenant identity in their 'flesh', were alienated from 'the body politic of Israel', did not participate in 'the covenants of the promise' and had no hope and were godless, it would require simply a small step for the author to sum up in most succinct terms the attitude of the Jews toward the Gentiles as positioned at the outermost fringes.

In short, the author's depiction of the social distance between Jews and Gentiles has *not* been fully articulated until v. 13a. We must also add that the 'far off' and 'near' language operates at different levels: while the author's 'far off' language underscores the Gentiles' position at the extremity from the vantage point of the Jews, he also lays bare the reversal of that position. The Gentiles are brought near through the blood of Christ.

The death of Christ is in the perception of the author *the* solution to the problem of ethnic estrangement (v. 13b), although the full implications of Christ's death for both Jews and Gentiles have not been spelt out in full at this point.

In our present context, the expression 'the blood of Christ' refers to Jesus's death which has the *effect* of making the Gentiles 'near' (1.7; cf. Rom. 3.25; 5.9; 1 Cor. 10.16; 11.25; Col. 1.20). Here the 'blood' language is probably drawn from the understanding of Jesus's death in terms of cultic sacrifice,[179] that is, as a (sin)-offering which *represents* the

Ephesians, 111 who suggests that the Gentiles 'who were far (*from God*) have now in the blood of Christ become the "near"' (italics mine); Lincoln, *Ephesians*, 139, who speaks of the 'deficiencies of the Gentile readers' past as being "far off" *from Christ*' (italics mine). Both Schnackenburg and Lincoln have failed to take into account the process known as 'argument from causes' (*a causis vocant*), see esp. Quintilian, *Inst.* 5.10.80.

178 This notion is most obvious in *m*. Kel. 1.6–9, where a rabbinic model for organising *space* into a coherent pattern is portrayed. The model works from the outside in: Israel is contrasted with the rest of the world; Jerusalem is contrasted with the other cities of the land; the Temple is contrasted with Jerusalem; and the Holy of Holies is contrasted with the Temple. The Jews wedded a religious aspect to the notion of Jewish centrality. The intimate relationship between the space at the core and the distribution of honour is also well attested in ancient writings, see, e.g., Philo, *Post.* 109. See also Plato, *Theaet.* 209B; Dio, *Or.* 21.37; Diodorus Siculus, *Bib. hist.* 8.18; Cassius Dio, *Hist. rom.* 42.5.5.5; Appian, *Bell. civ.* 2.77; Lev. 21.2; Esther 1.14; Isa. 57.9. See further Helgeland, 'Space'; Holm, *Sacred Place*, 116; Urry, 'Space'; Sayer, 'Space'. If the pericope Eph. 2.11–22 in its context stands parallel to 2.1–10, there is good reason to suppose that the designations in vv. 1–2 and v. 13 have the same powerful effect as vv. 11–12: the Gentiles were *in the perception of the Jews* 'dead in trespasses and sins' (= Gentile sinners, cf. Gal. 2.15) and the 'sons of disobedience'.

179 See in particular Dunn, 'Death', here 133; Dunn, 'Sacrifice', here 43, 44; Barth, *Ephesians 1–3*, 299; Morris, 'Sacrifice'; Laubach, 'αἷμα', 222–4; Böcher, 'αἷμα'; and most recently, Carroll and Green, *Death*, 113–32, 256–79, esp. 269–72.

divided human family.[180] The point of central importance is not so much that the author perceives the death of Christ as a means of pacifying the displeasure of God. Nor is there any overt indication that Christ's death is a means of delivering Gentiles from inadvertent sins – despite the fact that this connotation cannot be dismissed outright (see 1.7). Rather, Christ's death is now – as distinct from other earlier Pauline passages (e.g., Col. 1.19–22) – applied to a different situation: it is the ethnic dimension that the author has singled out in his usage of the metaphor of sacrifice to draw out the significance of Christ, whose death has marked the end of human division and alienation. The use of the phrase 'the blood of *the* Christ' is also an acknowledgement that there is no way out for the human family in estrangement except through the sacrificial death of the Messiah Jesus.[181] But reconciliation as such is entirely the work of God, and humankind its object.[182]

If our analysis is correct, it is not necessary for us to sidetrack at this point into debates about the possible candidates to whom the Gentiles are brought near, since the author's aim is primarily to construct a new space for the Gentiles who were marginalised by the Jews who practised ethnocentricity. We must, however, concede that the full implication of Jesus's death for the social alienation between Jews and Gentiles is not yet unfolded at this point. But as we shall see, the author is about to draw out a particular implication which arises from Christ's death.[183]

To recap what we have discussed so far. The author's language in v. 13 is conciliatory, fulfilling two major functions which are inextricably linked. In the first place, it provides, *in solidum*, a summary of the net result or 'aftermath' of a self-confident Judaism which is bold enough to situate the Gentiles at the 'extremities' of its own 'world' – this point has been missed by most commentaries.[184] It introduces the notion of extremities

[180] *Contra* Sahlin, 'Beschneidung Christi'. Sahlin suggests that the 'blood' of Christ' in v. 13 is to be contrasted with the blood of circumcision. However, the main point in v. 13 is not the death of Christ as analogous to the Gentiles' making entrance into a Jewish community through proselyte sacrifice, it is *how* the social distance between two ethnic groups who were kept far apart from one another could be bridged by the death of Christ. There is also no good ground to believe McLean, 'Atoning Sacrifice', here 543 and 546, who plays down the significance of Christ's death as a sacrifice, saying that there is no textual reference to Christ's blood metaphorically to signify the blood of a sacrificial victim.

[181] The arthrous 'Christ' in v. 13b may be understood as 'the previously referred to Christ [Jesus]' (v. 13a).

[182] Bouttier, *Éphésiens*, 114 n. 242.

[183] See my exegesis of vv. 14–18 in chapter 4, section 4.4.8 below.

[184] So most recently Best, *Ephesians*^{2}, 245; cf. Best, *Studies*, 99, et al.

or frontiers (Gk. ἐσχατίαι) to intensify the Gentiles' otherness.[185] The implied premise of the author's argument is that on the basis of a closed ethnic religion (better known as covenantal ethnocentrism) the Gentiles were excluded from the Jewish body politic, aliens to the 'covenants of promise' and cut off from other God-given blessings.

In the second place, the high point of the author's argument, however, is in the second half of his statement (v. 13b) in which he provides a transition from the Gentiles' otherness to his own goal of assuring the latter that they are given a new 'space' through the death of Christ – although details about the way in which the Gentiles are brought 'near' are unfolded only ephemerally at this point.

Only when we take into account the Gentiles' otherness from the perspective of the Jews can we appreciate the full force of the author's argument in v. 13. While v. 13a sums up the estranged condition of the human family, with its different sections kept apart from one another, v. 13b is meant to obliterate the social distance between Jews and Gentiles. This is achieved by constructing a new space for the Gentiles who were at the periphery of the Jewish 'world'.

3.5 Concluding remarks

When one focuses on the rhetorical function of the statements in Ephesians 2.11b–12 put forth by the author of Ephesians, one must conclude that their preoccupation is to reinforce ethnocentric community-boundaries. One also cannot escape the fact that both religious practice (e.g., the importance of circumcision, the role of the 'body politic' understood as a Jewish social network in creating and maintaining ethnic and religious identity) and belief (e.g., monotheism and the covenants of the promise) are essential to reinforcing group distinction. Accordingly, the Gentiles are simply alienated and excluded as the 'uncircumcision' from the Jewish 'body politic' as a distinctively closed-ethnic community, and thereby the Jewish group is marked off from the Gentiles. In characterising the statements of 2.11ff. from the vantage point of the exclusivistic Jews, I therefore make an assumption when I claim that, from the context of both Ephesians and Judaism, such alienation of the Gentiles cannot be deemed normal. That is, the desire to live within the covenantal framework and to be marked off from the 'uncircumcision'/Gentiles cannot be what God had originally planned for humankind. To be precise, the

[185] This is precisely how the 'far off/near' language is understood in v. 17. See my discussion in chapter 4, below.

(Jewish covenant) God expressed in Ephesians 2.11–12 is not interested merely in Israel's own well being or Israel as God's portion or Israel being the people of a national God, but rather in having the Gentiles/nations as a whole come also to know the true God of Israel.[186] Indeed, the broader implication of what God does for Jews and Gentiles is already hinted at in the cosmic overtones of the *berakah* in Ephesians 1.3–14. The reason why ethnic alienation as stated in Ephesians 2.11ff. was abnormal was simply that Jews' behaviour and attitudes toward the Gentiles should be expected to symbolise the final outcome of God's plan for the entire humankind (a vision clearly expressed by the author who is also a Christian Jew, cf. 1.10, 13–14; 2.13; 3.5–6), but it did not. Therefore Ephesians 2.13, from the view of the overarching plan of God made known to the nation,[187] can be seen as a veiled criticism levelled against the Jews who ought to have played a role in a broader campaign. That said, we must also add that the continued existence of Israel as God's elect remained intact and unquestioned.

I suggested earlier that 'covenantal ethnocentrism' be used as a descriptive title for the Ephesians' understanding of the functioning of a certain stream of Judaism. Ultimately the formulation outlined in Ephesians 2.11–13 is animated by a kind of covenant theology which unveils the covenantal confidence in which God's gracious promise to ethnic 'Israel'/Jews is assured, even though it narrows the scope of the divine grace and so limits membership to what constitutes the 'body politic' ethnocentrically to include only ethnic 'Israel'/Jews or a much smaller group than the whole of humankind. While we claim to speak of the Judaism portrayed by the Ephesians' author in Ephesians 2.11–12 as representing one important stream of materials that witnesses to the kind of Judaism(s) of Paul's/NT days, we must avoid being accused of presenting an overly monolithic Judaism by not neglecting other kinds of Judaism, the religious systems worked out by others in the same period and geographical region

[186] The notion of God's reign over the whole world and the consequent international solidarity which that notion suggests has its origin not only in scripture but also in the extant literature of Second Temple Judaism: Gen. 12.1–3; Isa. 42.7; 49.1–6; 56; Sir. 13.15; 18.13; Wis. 18.4; *1 Enoch* 105.1; *Sib. Or.* 3.195; Philo, *Decal.* 41, 64, 99, 178; *Spec. 1.* 169, 308; *Praem.* 9; *Cher.* 109; *Abr.* 98; *Prov.* 2.6; Josephus, *C. Ap.* 2.291–5. By definition the effort to maintain the Jewish body politic or Jewish practice as something distinct and alienated from the Gentiles should now be abandoned.

[187] The formulation in Eph. 2.13–22 is more than an acknowledgement of Gentiles' right to be God's people. Rather it is a demonstration to the Gentile readers of the final outcome of God's plan in and through Christ for entire humankind, see my detailed discussion in the next chapter.

(e.g., Gal. 2.11–16; Col. 2.16, etc.). When speaking of the unfolding of the ideas in Ephesians 2, therefore, we stress that these ideas testify to the inner life and world view of only one Jewish group among the many.[188]

The Gentiles who lacked the ‘mark’ of the covenant in their Gentile ‘flesh’ were, *ipso facto*, excluded from the ‘league’ of Israel by the Jews who endorsed closed-ethnic religion. Indeed ‘the uncircumcision’ and other Jewish categories tell of a Jewish dismissive attitude towards the Gentiles who lay outside the orbit of the Jews/elect. The defective status of the Gentiles which the Jews evaluated in their own ethnocentric terms is a direct corollary of the Jews’ sense of their privileged position in the various God-given blessings. That is the issue which the author outlines forcefully in vv. 11–13a. However, the boundaries between Jews and Gentiles are *socially* innovated rather than inherent in the original plan of God (cf. 1.3–14).

We may also conclude that Ephesians 2.11–13 is by and large a *Jewish* discourse on the Gentile ‘other’. The author of Ephesians not only perceives the ‘Gentiles in the flesh’ from the perspective of a Jew (v. 11a), he is able to *re*-present the perspective of typical Jews by drawing the latter into the foreground as social actors in order to draw out some

[188] In this I am mindful of the contribution of Neusner. However, we may ask: how extensive was the problem of covenantal ethnocentrism in Second Temple Judaism and in the Judaism of the Roman period? In Second Temple Judaism a number of testimonies of covenantal ethnocentrism call for attention. These testimonies are contained not only in part of *Jubilees*, where the umbrella under which the statements in the document are typically subsumed is the idea of the covenant defined strictly in closed-ethnic terms. To be sure, the consistent feature of covenantal ethnocentrism in *Jubilees* is the interlocking ideas of election, circumcision and covenant that are found so central in *Jubilees* in which the solely ethnic Israel’s salvation is based on its elect status, purely an act of God’s good pleasure. This is in contrast to the status of Gentiles for whom there will be ‘no portion in the future world’ and who will be judged by Israel. The Gentiles will receive thorough condemnation, which is why Israel is repeatedly warned not to mingle with them. Moreover, Jubilees’ message to Jews is that if they deny the covenant – and thus the importance of obedience in maintaining that covenant status – they effectively become Gentiles. How then does one become Jewish? By election! Thus *Jubilees* discloses a religion that is completely closed to Gentiles and into which no conversions are possible. One must admit that an anti-Gentile mood based on covenantal ethnocentrism pervades the book of *Jubilees*. See further Endres, *Jubilees*, 236. Covenantal ethnocentrism is also evident among the Qumran covenanters, who redefined traditional covenantalism by narrowing the scope of divine grace and thereby limiting covenant membership to include only a ‘remnant’ (i.e., a much smaller group than the whole of ethnic Israel!). In this case the covenant with ‘Israel’ does not serve merely to maintain relationship with God, but the sectarian covenant is meant exclusively for the community (1QS 2.1–25). Suffice to say, the evidence of covenantal ethnocentrism shows that an overly monolithic Judaism must be avoided by recognising the level of diversity within Judaism(s). See further Carson, *Variegated Nomism*.

of their crucial beliefs or convictions (vv. 11b–12). The process of eliciting certain Jewish beliefs operates through the author's interventions in his narrative. For him, that which is most worthy of being reported is the way in which ethnic alienation has taken place. He acts as a conveyor and makes the alienation known to the Gentiles. He unfolds in his formulations the way in which the unfriendly attitude of certain (not all) Jews toward the Gentiles has triggered the cleavage between themselves and the non-Jewish world, so that he may in due course direct his recipients' attention to what Christ has accomplished to shorten the social distance between a divided humanity (vv. 13b–19). For us to make the above suggestions is not to claim that the author has overlooked the 'past' of the Gentiles in contrast to their Christian present. Rather, the author has set his statements about the Gentiles alongside the shared knowledge of the Jews: that is, vv. 11–12 contain elements which are thoroughly Jewish in character. He has put himself in the position of the Jews, and *re*-presents the exclusivistic attitudes of other Jews in the hope that he may also echo what the latter had thought about the Gentile 'other' (vv. 11b–13a). He has also taken significant steps to recapitulate in his argument the notion of extremities in which the Gentiles were relegated to the utmost limit of the Jewish 'world' (v. 13a). To say that the Gentiles were 'far off' is to translate them into this 'world' which is based on a particular *ethnos* and to reflect their position as beyond the orbit of the Jews. There are evidently *ethnic* factors which we should look into.

Finally, the intention of the author in bidding his Gentile recipients to 'remember' (μνημονεύετε) is not so much to resuscitate injurious memories of the past. Nor was his intention to preserve from decay the remembrance of how humankind has fostered division within itself. Rather, his modest aim is to evoke in his Gentile recipients the awareness that the estrangement which they experienced before they had any positive connections with Christ was an *ethnic* one. This in turn enables him to explain why ethnic reconciliation, the removing of that which stands in the way of a right relationship between Jews and Gentiles, is necessary.[189] Perhaps the author would also wish to put on record what could possibly return to haunt the community-body 'in Christ' in the present or

[189] Lincoln, however, comments: 'The writer does not spell out how it is that Israel too was alienated from God and needed reconciliation' ('Church', 617). The weakness of Lincoln's proposal is clearly his failure to give enough weight to the 'echoic utterances' of the author who underscores the 'circumcision' as having become the agent of ethnic alienation, and their exclusivistic attitudes toward the Gentiles.

future – and if that were the case, the 'memory' invoked is for the sake of prevention.

Our conclusion, as we shall see, has significant bearing upon our understanding of the author's subsequent formulations in vv. 14–22 in which the notion of ethnic reconciliation has become the focus of discussion.

4

'HE IS OUR PEACE': CHRIST AND ETHNIC RECONCILIATION (EPHESIANS 2.14–18)

4.1 Introduction

In the present chapter I shall argue that Ephesians 2.14–18 consists of an *amplification* (ἡ αὔξησις) which is in praise of the Messiah Jesus and his work in bringing reconciliation to the two estranged ethnic groups. Rather than a 'parenthesis' or 'digression' which is tangential to the primary design of the letter, as some scholars interpret it, I suggest that Ephesians 2.14–18 forms an integral part of the organisational and argumentative scheme of the author. It is to be seen as a 'purple' passage which comes directly after the author has underscored the defective status of Gentiles as Gentiles according to the exclusive attitude of the Jews. It reflects the author's utmost concern to redefine the identity of the people of God for the Gentiles for whom he wrote. It is my conviction that we cannot make full sense of the remarkably complex metaphors of the 'one new man' and 'one body' without giving the Jewish attitudes toward the Gentiles and the enmity between the two their due weight. These metaphors, as we shall see, are both society-creating and community-redefining metaphors; they are meant to reframe the notion of the people of God and to undercut the old ethnic forms of self-identification and allegiance as they replace them with a new community-identity in Christ. They lay bare the way in which Jew and Gentile could be correlated within one community-body, namely the body of Christ, and prepare for the Gentiles a place on which to stand within a *re*defined, inclusive community.[1]

The eulogistic approach of the author has also the effect of posing side by side two sharply contrasted sets of attitudes toward one's fellow human beings: it sets out to emphasise on the one hand the magnanimity of Christ who reaches out to all, including the spatially removed, and to lay bare on the other the 'little-mindedness' of the Jews (see above, my

[1] See my exegesis of vv. 19–22 in chapter 5 (section 5.2.1), where I lay out some of the implications of Christ's reconciling work for the Gentiles and for their redefined association with the 'holy ones'.

exegesis in chapter 3). The aim of this eulogistic approach, however, is not to vituperate but to reconstitute a healthy framework for Gentiles and Jews so that they too might emulate Christ's footsteps by developing an all-embracing attitude toward the ethnic 'other'. This chapter concludes with the assertion that the most natural context for a mention of Christ as the peace-bringer is the campaign on the part of the author, who sees himself as one who is inside Israel rather than looking in from outside, for the ending of the less-than-healthy estrangement between Jews and Gentiles and to restore both to (Israel's) God.

4.2 The literary structure of Ephesians 2.14–18

The mass of NT scholarly opinion today considers that Ephesians 2.14–16(17) consists of traditional material, probably a hymn which the author moulded for his own purposes.[2] Any discussion of vv. 14–18 needs therefore to deal with its literary structure, and more discussion has taken place over the decades over a possible 'basic document' (*Vorlage*) to this passage than for any other in our epistle. Before we can possibly advance to our own proposal, it is necessary to take a closer look at some of the major theories regarding the literary structure of Ephesians 2.14ff.

Haupt was among the first scholars in recent times to subject vv. 14–18 to form critical analysis. This led him to believe that the passage is parenthetical to the main thrust of 2.11–22.[3] Since Haupt's time a chorus of scholars who embraced his theory have endeavoured to 'discover' in these verses traditional material or a 'basic document' which they believe the author has incorporated in his letter. The arguments are as follows:

(a) The pattern of thought in vv. 14–18 is different from the preceding sections (e.g., vv. 1–2, 3–10, and 11–13) in that God has been the major actor, while Christ is the central actor in vv. 14f. The change of person from second plural to first at v. 14, and the reverse at v. 19, have led many to believe that the author of Ephesians steps aside from his previous subject by adding new

[2] See, e.g., Schille, *Hymnen*, 24–31; Dibelius and Greeven, *Epheser*, 69; Schlier, *Epheser*, 122–3, 216–18; Gnilka, *Epheserbrief*, 147–52; Richardson, *Israel*, 152–3; Fischer, *Tendenz*, 131–7, esp. 131–2; Sanders, 'Elements'; cf. Sanders, *Hymns*, here 88–92; Wengst, *Lieder*, 181–6, esp. 182–3; Wilhelmi, 'Versöhner-Hymnen'; Lincoln, *Ephesians*, 139–40; Lindemann, *Aufhebung*, 152–9, esp. 156–9; Burger, *Versöhnung*, 115–57, esp. 117–33; Martin, *Reconciliation*, 172. For a helpful bibliography on the subject, see Best, *Essays*, 63 n. 30. For a review on the debates concerning the literary form of Eph. 2.14–18, see in particular Merkel, 'Diskussion,' 3230–5; Merklein, 'Komposition'.

[3] Haupt, *Gefangenschaftsbriefe*.

materials beyond the scope of his main theme.[4] There is by no means a straightforward argument on the basis of the previous verses (vv. 11–13). These assumptions have, in varying forms and combinations, been guiding the perception and judgement of scholars from the beginnings of historical criticism to the present day.

(b) Vv. 14ff. contain a somewhat 'conflicting perspective' with that of the previous context,[5] namely that reconciliation of *both* Jews and Gentiles to God adds a new element into the discussion which does not fit quite as smoothly into the previous context (i.e., vv. 11–13). There Israel's election means that she is not alienated from God, but v. 16 speaks of *both* Jews and Gentiles being reconciled to God.

(c) Participial predications, as well as the opening predication on the pattern αὐτὸς ἐστιν, the heavy use of *parallelismus membrorum*, the piling up of a number of *hapax legomena*, the awkward syntax and the cosmic language all lend support to the conclusion that the passage uses traditional (e.g., hymnic) material.[6]

(d) The author, however, has made various redactional modifications to highlight his christological claims.[7]

In spite of the acceptance within certain circles of the reconstruction of the traditional material, the suggestion that vv. 14ff. are 'cast in poetic and rhythmic form' (in the words of Martin) is far from certain, and severe criticism can be levelled against this theory on the grounds that:

(1) Scholars who opt for an earlier (hymnic) form have faced enormous difficulty in setting the parameters of the original material.[8]

[4] See, e.g., Lincoln, *Ephesians*, 125, 127, who argues that the ποτὲ . . . νῦν contrast fades from view in vv. 14–18 but it is taken up again in v. 19. Lincoln has been constrained by the parameters of his own thesis, namely that vv. 14–16 consist of an *excursus* which has its focus on how the Gentile readers' change of situation was accomplished by Christ.

[5] So Lincoln, *Ephesians*, 145; cf. Fischer, *Tendenz*, 131, who contends that the argument in vv. 14f. moves constantly between two levels: a cosmic level, where it speaks of the annihilation of the sublime powers, and a historical level where it speaks of the reconciliation of Gentiles and Jewish Christians in the one Church.

[6] So Sanders, 'Elements', 217; Gnilka, *Epheserbrief*, 139, 148; Lincoln, *Ephesians*, 127, 145; Burger, *Versöhnung*, 132.

[7] So Sanders, 'Elements', who concludes that 'the hymn did not entirely serve the author's purpose, so that it was necessary for him to expand and interpret it somewhat' (218); cf. Roetzel, 'Relations', 82–4.

[8] Vv. 14–16: Sanders, Lindemann, Wilhelmi, Lincoln; vv. 14–17: Gnilka, Fischer, Burger, Pokorný; vv. 14–18: Schille; and vv. 12–19: Martin, who assumes a much longer underlying piece of tradition running from v. 12 to v. 19, the core being vv. 14–16, which was a 'hellenistic hymn of cosmic transformation' (*Reconciliation*, 171).

(2) There is also no sufficient evidence to make probable the hypothesis of the exact number of stanzas or strophes.[9] To create a neatly formed rhythmical balance of the alleged 'hymn', Wilhelmi, among others, has attempted to collocate v. 14c (τὸ μεσότοιχον τοῦ φραγμοῦ γύσας) and v. 15a (τὸν νόμον τῶν ἐντολῶν ἐν δόγμασιν καταργήσας) in the same stanza. This arrangement, however, is unlikely. As far as we can tell, v. 14c and v. 15a do not constitute *parallelismus membrorum* and they are not placed on a par (*vide infra*, my exegesis of v. 14).[10]

(3) Many alterations have been made to isolate an existing piece of traditional material which many believed the author of Ephesians has incorporated. These modifications, however, meddle too much with the given text.[11] To preserve the consistency of the alleged *Vorlage*, Gnilka, among others, has excluded from it all those elements which imply that human beings are reconciled to one another.[12] The only reconciliation left is that between heaven and earth. The reconciliation between God and the human sphere is only implicit and Gnilka has made the author of Ephesians responsible for this additional notion. Gnilka's reconstruction has enabled him to exacerbate the theses of a 'Gnostic' understanding of our text – once the (vertical) barrier/wall between humankind is removed. However, a more adequate explanation is possible other than the approach which requires to dislodge so many words and phrases in order to make way for the foregoing

[9] Schille, *Hymnen*, regards Αὐτὸς γάρ ἐστιν ἡ εἰρήνη ἡμῶν of v. 14a as the theme statement (*Themazeile*), and divides vv. 14–18 into three strophes: vv. 14b–15a; 15b–16a; 17–18. Wilhelmi, 'Versöhner-Hymnen', divides vv. 14–16 into two stanzas (148); Sanders, *Hymns*, 14.

[10] It will be sufficient to note that this observation by no means suggests that vv. 14–18 do not consist of parallel statements. Vv. 15b–16b, for example, are arranged in a form of 'couplet': (a) ἵνα τοὺς δύο κτίσῃ ἐν αὐτῷ εἰς ἕνα καινὸν ἄνθρωπον (v. 15b) // καὶ (ἵνα) ἀποκαταλλάξῃ τοὺς ἀμφοτέρους ἐν ἑνὶ σώματι τῷ θεῷ διὰ τοῦ σταυροῦ (v. 16a); and (b) ποιῶν εἰρήνην (v. 15c) // ἀποκτείνας τὴν ἔχθραν ἐν αὐτῷ (v. 16b); see also Wilhelmi, 'Versöhner-Hymnen', 148 (i.e., II, A and B).

[11] Schille, *Hymnen*, 17ff., regards the following words and phrases as the redaction of the author of Ephesians: τὴν ἔχθραν (v. 14d); ἀποκτείνας τὴν ἔχθραν ἐν αὐτῷ (v. 16b); ὑμῖν (v. 17a); οἱ ἀμφότεροι ἐν ἑνὶ πνεύματι (v. 18). For Gnilka, *Epheserbrief*, 149, 32 out of the total number of 84 words belong to the result of the redactional activity of the author of Ephesians. Wilhelmi, 'Versöhner-Hymnen', asserts that the redactional modifications in vv. 14–16, which include brief, mainly prepositional, additions to the underlying hymnic fragment, highlight the author's own christological claims (148). Lincoln, *Ephesians*, 128 is able to hair-split from the original material the following interpolations of the author: τοῦ φραγμοῦ (v. 14b); ἐν τῇ σαρκὶ αὐτοῦ (v. 14d), τὸν νόμον τῶν ἐντολῶν ἐν δόγμασιν (v. 15a); διὰ τοῦ σταυροῦ (v. 16a). Cf. Lindemann, *Aufhebung*, 157.

[12] Gnilka, *Epheserbrief*, 147–8; also Schlier, *Christus*, 83–5. Gnilka's approach has come under trenchant criticism by Stuhlmacher, 'Peace', esp. 184.

hypothesis to work properly, not to mention the consensus, still wanting, concerning the number of words that need to be categorised as the author's redactions.[13]

(4) In order to discover the the original *Vorlage*, some structural indices (e.g., γάρ, v. 14a; καὶ κτλ, v. 17a; ὅτι δι᾿ αὐτοῦ κτλ., v. 18a) in the primary text have also been dismissed as peripheral or attributed to the author's redactional activity.[14] When these indices are treated as later interpolations, it is possible for some to suggest that there was a specific context (e.g., of cosmic reconciliation) into which the alleged 'hymn' once fitted.[15] As we shall see, these indices are essential to the meaning of vv. 14–18.

(5) The attempt to read the neuter formulation in v. 14b (τὰ ἀμφότερα) as a particular criterion of traditional material cannot be seen as convincing. Schlier, among others, has argued that the neuter words have reference to 'a vestige of a myth of reconciliation of heaven and earth', being determined by the religious presuppositions which are visible in the Hellenistic myths.[16] Dahl concludes that the author has reflected with the neuter formulation the myth of a reunion of male and female.[17] Meeks, who regards Schlier's and Dahl's theories as not necessarily mutually exclusive, adds that the author of Ephesians '*historicizes* the mythical language of unification' (italics mine).[18] None of these scholars, however, has sought the antecedent of the neuter words in its own exegetical context,

[13] See also Mußner, *Christus*, who points out, and quite rightly so, that 'a defined methodology which makes it possible to distinguish tradition and redaction clearly needs to be developed' (96 and n. 96); Dunn, *Unity*, who concludes that there are no sufficient grounds for isolating an earlier form which the writer has incorporated (132–41, here 139).

[14] E.g., Lincoln, *Ephesians*, 128, even omits the connective particle γάρ in his reconstruction of the hymn, but see his later comments on v. 14 in 140; also Gnilka, *Epheserbrief*, 138. Schille, *Hymnen*, 24ff. reads the connecting particle as γάρ-*recitativum*, seeing it as not having any explanatory force. Schille's reading is revived more recently in Wilhelmi, 'Versöhner-Hymnus', 150 and n. 16 who further argues that the readers had the quotation already by heart: '[A]ber dennoch kann ein Zitat besonders für einen Hörer, der es bereits auswendig kenn, sehr gut causal werden: »Denn« = bekanntlich, vgl. Röm 10 13'.

[15] Gnilka, *Epheserbrief*, 147–52; Wilhelmi, 'Versöhner-Hymnus', 148; Lincoln, *Ephesians*, 128.

[16] Schlier, *Christus*, 18–26; Schlier, *Epheser*, 124. Schlier's theory is partially endorsed by Lincoln, *Ephesians*, 128, who argues that the writer of Ephesians may well have taken over traditional material which spoke of Christ as the one who brings cosmic peace and reconciliation; Lincoln, 'Use', 25–26.

[17] Dahl, 'Geheimnis', 74 n. 45.

[18] Meeks, 'Unity', combines the theories of Schlier and Dahl (see nn. 16 and 17); see also Smith, 'One,' 34–5, 41; Lincoln, *Ephesians*, 140.

which reveals that these scholars have been sidetracked into a peculiar theological slant and based their conclusions more on their ingenious theory than on an actual reading of the text. As we shall see, the neuter words in v. 14, which I believe hold some significant clues to the purpose of our epistle, can be sufficiently explained in the light of the discussion in vv. 11–13. These neuter words are closely associated with the Jewish conceptions about humanity and linked with the *two* categories of people which the author has referred to in v. 11b.[19] Thus, it is not necessary for us to have recourse to 'a remnant of the traditional material which originally referred to heaven and earth' for our explanation of the neuter formulation.

Other solutions to the difficulties of our present passage have been offered over the years.[20] It will suffice for our purposes to examine a theory which argues that the author of Ephesians provides a christological exegesis of Isaiah 9.5–6; 52.7; and 57.19.[21] In the context of vv. 11–22 this exegesis serves to express the miracle of the reception precisely of the Gentiles in the church and the nature of this church as the new people of God also becomes visible.[22] However, a number of objections tell against such a proposal.

(a) What is not in doubt is that the author alludes to the Jewish scripture which he moulds for his own purposes, but it is far from true that this endeavour must necessarily be read as a continuous

[19] See also Deichgräber, *Gotteshymnus*, 166 who points out that the 'both' and the 'two' language in vv. 14ff. is too much related to the context; also Stuhlmacher, 'Peace', 185, 186.

[20] Deichgräber, *Gotteshymnus*, 167. Merklein, 'Komposition,' esp. 95 concludes that vv. 14–18 are the author's own further refinement of the ecclesiological interpretation of the cosmic christological hymn preserved in Col. 1.15–20; see also Merkel, 'Diskussion', 3233–5. On studies positing a Jewish background, see, e.g., Wolter, *Rechtfertigung*, 62–73; Schnackenburg, *Ephesians*, 112; Smith, 'One'; Smith, 'Heresy'; Barth, *Ephesians 1–3*, 285–7; Percy, *Probleme*, 287–8; Stuhlmacher, 'Peace'; Faust, *Pax*, 111; Moritz, *Mystery*, 23–55; Best, *Ephesians*², 247–50, esp. 250. On studies which focus on the chiastic structure of Eph. 2, see, e.g., Thomson, *Chiasmus*, 84–115; Kirby, *Pentecost*, 156; Giavini, 'Structure'; Bailey, *Poet*, 63; Turner, *Style*, 98. Some scholars remain almost silent about the existence of an existing piece of traditional *Vorlage*, e.g., Bruce, *Ephesians*; Mitton, *Ephesians*; Caird, 'Ephesians'.

[21] So Stuhlmacher, 'Peace'; Wolter, *Rechtfertigung*, 62–73; Smith, 'One'; Schnackenburg, *Ephesians*, 112; Moritz, *Mystery*, 23–55.

[22] Stuhlmacher, 'Peace', here 187. Stuhlmacher's theory is followed by Schnackenburg, *Ephesians*, 112. Wolter, *Rechtfertigung*, 72 suggests that v. 14 is a quotation of Isa. 9.5–6. See also Moritz, *Mystery*, 46, 48. Moritz contends that Isa. 57.19 dominated the author's thought as early as v. 13, and this prepared the way for a more explicit use of Isaiah in v. 17.

exegesis of a single traditional *Vorlage* (e.g., of Isaiah).[23] Rather than introducing a Christian midrash on or exegesis of some Isaianic passages, I have argued earlier (above, chapter 4) that v. 13 does not consist of a citation of Isaiah, but of a *representation* of the Gentiles who were deemed people at the extremity according to Jewish ethnocentricity.[24] Although the use of Isaiah (52.19 and 57.19) in v. 17 is quite explicit (other Jewish scriptures are also present in v. 17!), the author has used the Jewish scripture as a tool so that he may turn the tables on the practice of Jewish ethnocentrism (see below, my exegesis of v. 17).

(b) While we cannot deny the fact that 'peace' is often understood as a soteriological term, denoting God's gracious salvation of mankind, we would constrict the meaning of the term if we *equate* it with the notion of salvation (i.e., 'salvation of God presented in Christ's atoning work', or 'the establishment of communion between God and humanity through Christ').[25] We will do better if information from the potential OT passages (i.e., Isa. 9.5–6; 52.7; 57.19) is not brought in until the epistolary 'situation' has been adequately clarified on the basis of internal evidence, or we shall prejudge the result of contextual exegesis. I am convinced that the parameters for understanding the 'peace' language in vv. 14, 16b and 18, respectively, can be safely set in the discussions of vv. 11–13. There are no good grounds for us to shy away from the fact that the author, who successfully outlined the exclusive attitude of the Jews (vv. 11b–12), has also implied in his formulations that there existed a less-than-healthy relation between the two human groups, and this in turn provides the most probable background for our understanding of the 'peace' language in vv. 14ff. To be sure, the author of Ephesians

[23] So Moritz, who argues that Eph. 2.13–17 forms a chiastic structure, and 'what appears to be deliberately chiastic is in fact the result of the deliberate use of the inclusio consisting of the allusions of Isaiah' (29). Moritz's thesis is primarily that vv. 14–16 are governed by Isaiah. Moritz is overconfident at this point. I disagree with Moritz on the following grounds. (a) The formulation in vv. 11–13 is framed within the 'then-now' schema, and v. 13 must be read in the light of vv. 11–12. (b) Moritz has watered down too many non-repetitive elements in vv. 13 and 17, and the exact wording in these verses is far too wide for the claim of a definite inclusio to be substantiated. For a more helpful discussion on the possible chiastic structure in Eph. 11.22, see esp. Giavini, 'Structure'; Thomson, *Chiasmus*, 234. None of these writers, however, have come to the same conclusion as to the parameters for the chiastic structure of vv. 11–22. See further Lincoln, *Ephesians*, 127; Bullinger, *Figures*, 245–9, on the figure of *inclusio*.

[24] See above, my discussion in chapter 4 *ad loc*.

[25] Stuhlmacher, 'Peace', 188.

was caught up in the reconciliation of Jews and Gentiles within God's total plan for his cosmos (cf. 1.9–10).[26] But his immense concern about the reconciliation of Jews and Gentiles has prompted him to invoke the 'peace' language and in part determined its meaning.

(c) The argument that there is a single basic document lying behind Ephesians 2.14–18 (or vv. 13–17) is greatly weakened by the fact that vv. 14–18 contain *also* traditions of different origin. We will do better if we allow our search for the background of vv. 14–18 to be broadened to include the possibility that the author has alluded not to one unified thought system but to helpful materials from different sources in order to express his specific concerns effectively.[27] The reflections on the notion of 'making peace' (v. 15c), for example, are an indication of points of contact with the realm of political rhetoric in the Graeco-Hellenistic world. The 'body' language can be similarly understood, and it probably belongs to the domain of political philosophy of the period. The notion of 'one new man' may well have been adopted from the Jewish tradition and Paul's earlier writings (2 Cor. 5.17).

My own inclination is that the 'hymn-like' passages in vv. 14–18 and vv. 11–13 are interwoven both linguistically and conceptually, and that the discussions of vv. 11–13 set the parameters for our understanding of vv. 14–18:[28]

(a) The language of ethnic estrangement and discord, as depicted in vv. 11b–13a, matches perfectly well with that of the integration of 'two' (groups) of people into 'one' in the narrow context of vv. 14–18. The author who underscored the deficiencies of the Gentiles has brought to light the way in which the marginalised Gentiles could become one with the Jews 'in Christ'.[29]

26 We would need to note that the idea of 'cosmic' reconciliation has already been adumbrated in 1.10, whereby the author asserts that *all things* – both heavenly and earthly – will be united in Christ: ἀνακεφαλαιώσασθαι τὰ πάντα ἐν τῷ Χριστῷ; cf. Col. 1.20.

27 Cf. Smith, 'One', passim.

28 See also Porter, *Καταλλάσσω*, 169–71, 185–9, esp. 185; Bruce, *Ephesians*, 295; Mußner, *Epheser*, 73ff.

29 This is perhaps the weakest point of Rese's thesis, 'Vorzüge'. He recognises the 'have not' of the Gentiles *vis-à-vis* Israel but fails to detect that the author of Ephesians has provided a characteristically *Jewish* representation of the Gentile 'other' when he speaks of the latter in vv. 11–12. Rese's thesis is undermined by his failure to detect the Jewish attitudes toward the Gentiles embedded in vv. 11–12 and his comments on the relationship between Israel and Church are gratuitous.

(b) Various images of corporate identity/representation are found, respectively, in vv. 11–13 and vv. 14–18: the 'body politic of Israel' (v. 12a), the 'one body' (v. 16a) and the 'one new man' (v. 15b). The 'one body' language, as we shall see, is being directed in a stark contrast to the exclusive, ethnically based 'body politic of Israel' (*not* Israel as a whole!).[30] As we have mentioned earlier (chapter 4), this peculiar 'body politic' is an 'umbrella' entity, denoting 'a community of communities' which would embrace the entire Jewish people of a particular region.[31] This conclusion has led me to believe that the thesis that '[Ephesians] 2.19 takes up where v. 12 left off with a straightforward reversal of the Gentiles' previous relationship to Israel' is unsafe, for the different imagery of corporate identities mentioned above provides a sufficient link between vv. 11–13 and vv. 14–18.

(c) There is also little doubt that the death of Christ, which is hinted at in v. 13 and elsewhere, continues to be a prominent theme in vv. 14–18.[32] The same theme is now expanded by the smooth transition from vv. 11–13 to vv. 14–18 via the reduplication of some key words/phrases which have their focus on Christ or his reconciling work: ἐν τῷ αἵματι τοῦ Χριστοῦ (v. 13b); ἐν τῇ σαρκὶ αὐτοῦ (v. 14c); διὰ τοῦ σταυροῦ (v. 16a); ἐν αὐτῷ (i.e., through the cross, v. 16b); and δι᾽ αὐτοῦ (v. 18).[33] These

[30] *Contra* Käsemann, *Perspectives*, 109–10 who argues that the body of Christ, i.e., a union of Christians, both Jews and Gentiles (= a union of two nations), and the people of God (= the Jewish Christian people of God) are two Pauline theologoumena which compete with one another. The only satisfactory explanation for this, according to Käsemann, is that at the time Ephesians was written, the Gentiles were pushing the Jewish Christians aside. The writer therefore reminds them of the Jewish Christians' priority in salvation history. Consequently the continuity with Israel as the people of God is energetically stressed. See below my exegesis of v. 16, and my critique of Käsemann's theory.

[31] It will be sufficient to note that both πολιτεία and σῶμα are used to denote political bodies, see, e.g., Plutarch's *Philopoemen* 8.1–2: 'The Achaeans who united themselves together to form the 'Achaean league' at a time when Greece was weak and easily drifted into individual city-states, had also proposed to form the Peloponnesus into a single political body and one power (τὰς δὲ ὁμονοία καὶ πολιτειά καταμιγνύντες εἴς ἑαυτούς, ἕν σῶμα καὶ μίαν δύναμιν κατασκευάσαι διενοοῦντο τὴν Πελοπόννησον)'; cf. Polybius, *Hist.* 2.38.4; 2.43.3, 35; 2.44.5; 2.57.1; Plutarch, *Agesilaus* 23.7.5; *Aratus* 9.6.3; *Philopoemen*, 16.6.3. See further Giovannini, 'Commonwealth'; Applebaum, 'Communities', esp. 475, 485, 491. See also my discussion of v. 12a in chapter 4, section 3.3.1.

[32] See especially Schnackenburg, *Ephesians*, 106–7, 111–12.

[33] *Contra* Fischer, *Tendenz*, 137, who argues that the notion of 'cross' in Ephesians has an essentially different meaning from that of Paul: the cross in Ephesians has a 'corrective function', but it is no longer the centre of the author's christology.

key words and phrases not only help to explain the Christ who brought 'near' the Gentiles by deconstructing the polarisation of Jew and Gentile, but also help to confirm the author's conviction that Christ is the antidote to the problem of *ethnic* estrangement. The 'far off/near' language in v. 13 which re-emerges in v. 17 can be understood in the same light. The claim that the author of Ephesians has stepped aside from his main theme in vv. 14ff. is weakened by both the linguistic and the conceptual links between the two units.

(d) Despite the Gnostic redemption saga which suggests that the 'flesh' in v. 14d denotes the Gnostic redeemer who breaks down the cosmic wall separating heaven and earth, this interpretation must be dismissed on the grounds that the author of Ephesians is probably employing a play on words (*paronomasia*): the 'flesh' by which the distinctive identity of the Jews as the chosen people of God is strengthened (v. 11c) is invalidated in Christ's own 'flesh' (i.e., on the cross, see below my exegesis of v. 14c). This explanation more closely fits the context.

(e) Do vv. 14–18 lend support to the view that these verses consist of 'a somewhat conflicting perspective', speaking of Israel as the elect of God on the one hand and of both Jews and Gentiles being reconciled to God? Probably not. To appreciate the precise nature of reconciliation as portrayed in vv. 14–18, it is necessary to decide at the outset whether Israel had been involved in alienating the Gentiles and whether the Gentiles had become the injured/antagonised parties (see below, my exegesis of vv. 15b–16b).[34] As mentioned in the previous chapter, the Gentiles had been estranged (and antagonised) from Israel and Israel's God-given privileges by the 'circumcision'/Jews. My contention is that there is an ethnic factor which can shed significant light on the notion of enmity/antagonism (vv. 14, 16), and this factor best explains the need of reconciliation of both Jews and Gentiles. Still more importantly, the reconciliation of the two human groups is integral to peace with God, although the vertical aspect of reconciliation, namely the reconciliation between God and Gentile or between God and Jew, is 'secondary' in the sense that God is not depicted in the context

[34] See in particular Porter, *Καταλλάσσω*, 16–17, on the usage of the term καταλλάσσω and its cognates in the extant Greek literature.

of Ephesians 2.11–18 as the antagonised or directly 'injured' party but as the ultimate goal of ethnic reconciliation (v. 18).[35] The alleged conflicting perspectives can only be sustained when the ethnic factor is ignored.[36]

4.3 Ephesians 2.14–18: an *amplification* of the laudable act of Christ

Instead of reading vv. 14–18 as an excursus consisting of an existing piece of traditional material or a Christian midrash on or exegesis of a single Jewish *Vorlage*, this study contends that Ephesians 2.14–18 is encomiastic: it is in praise of the extraordinary achievements of Christ as a peace-bringer to divided humanity via *amplification* (ἡ αὔξησις). The author who is caught up in the estrangement of Gentiles from Israel and Israel's God-given grace claims that Christ has resolved the hostility between Jew and Gentile. More than that, his articulation of the theme of reconciliation of Jews and Gentiles via *amplificatio* also serves to evoke thoughts of the magnanimity of Christ and his reconciling work.[37]

The praise of famous figures is a common practice in ancient epideictic rhetoric[38] which concerns questions regarding what is honourable (e.g., Aristotle, *Rhet.* 1367 ᵇ33). It is also in praise of these figures that the greatness of their virtue is set forth (e.g., Quintilian, *Inst.* 3.7.1–17, esp. 3.7.10–17 (on praise); [Cicero], *Ad Her.* 1.5.8).[39] Epideictic

[35] *Contra* Best, *Ephesians*², 264–5, 271; Lincoln, *Ephesians*, 146.

[36] *Contra* Lincoln, *Ephesians*, 145 who rightly observes that 'the Gentiles' alienation from Israel involved alienation from God'. Nevertheless, he has failed to recognise the fact that the Gentiles' alienation from God is also the upshot of the exclusive attitudes of the Jews. Percy, *Probleme*, 278–86, contends that Eph. 2.11–22 is not primarily concerned with the unity of Jews and Gentiles, but with the unity between individual members of the community without regard to their ethnic descent; the ethnic contrast between Jews and Gentiles belongs apparently for the author, as for the readers now, completely to the past; cf. Percy, 'Probleme', where Percy argues that the real theme of Eph. 2.11–22 is that Gentiles and Jews participate in salvation in equal manner and have equal standing before God, and the main stumbling block that prevents this equality is the Law (187–8).

[37] Cf. Aristotle, who writes: 'Magnanimity is a virtue productive of great benefits; the contrary is little-mindedness (μικροψυχία)' (*Rhet.* 1366 ᵇ11); cf. Aristotle, *Rhet.* 1366 ᵇ5–6.

[38] See, e.g., [Aristotle], *Rhet. Alex.* 1426 ᵃ4–7, who writes: 'When eulogising one must show in one's speech that one of these things [*sc.* just, lawful, expedient, noble, pleasant, etc.] belong to the person in question or to his actions, as directly effected by him or produced through his agency or incidentally resulting from his action or done as a means of it or involving it as an indispensable condition of its performance . . .'; cf. Quintilian, *Inst.* 3.4.12–13. See further Burgess, 'Epideictic Literature', esp. 105 n. 3.

[39] Rhetorical eulogy is common in the ancient world: see, e.g., Isocrates, *Evagoras*, *Helenae encomium*, *Busiris*, etc.

or encomiastic speech is often used in the amplification[40] of creditable purposes, actions and speeches and qualities attributed to persons eulogised (Aristotle, *Rhet.* 1368 ^{a}38–9; [Aristotle], *Rhet. Alex.* 1425 ^{b}36–7). This explains why ancient rhetorical 'handbooks' devoted enormous space to the *topos* of amplification, for this is the most appropriate device in epideictic rhetoric (e.g., Aristotle, *Rhet.* 1368 ^{a}40; 1391 ^{b}18; Quintilian, *Inst.* 3.7.6), and is often ranked as one form of encomium which expands and enriches arguments (e.g. Aristotle, *Rhet.* 1368 ^{a}39; [Cicero], *Ad Her.* 2.29.46). The elements out of which one ought to have composed rhetorical eulogy were already underscored in the works of Isocrates (e.g. *Helen* 11; *Busiris* 9; *Evagoras*, passim; cf. Philo, *Legat.*, 143–7, etc.), but it was Aristotle who set the trend for subsequent treatment by providing a catalogue of virtues and achievements (i.e., the 'signs of moral habit') that one should amplify in eulogistic oratory. The components of virtues which became 'the materials of amplification' include: justice, courage, self-control, magnificence, magnanimity, liberality, gentleness, practical wisdom, and so forth (Aristotle, *Rhet.* 1366 ^{b}3–19; 1393 ^{a}26; [Aristotle], *Rhet. Alex.* 1425 ^{b}40–1426 ^{a}3; 1440 ^{b}15–19, cf. 1421 ^{b}23–1423 ^{a}8; [Cicero], *Ad Her.* 3.2.3–3.4.7). The greatest virtues, according to these handbooks, must necessarily be those which are most beneficial to others (e.g., Aristotle, *Rhet.* 1366 ^{b}6; [Aristotle], *Rhet. Alex.* 1426 ^{a}1–19, et al.), and various methods of amplification were developed after Aristotle (Aristotle, *Rhet.* 1368 ^{a}38–40; [Aristotle], *Rhet. Alex.* 1426 ^{a}20–1426 ^{b}21; Quintilian, *Inst.* 8.4.1–27; [Cicero], *Ad Her.* 2.30.47–9, et al.).

In light of what is said in the foregoing, it is my conviction that Ephesians 2.14–18, which consists of an extended discussion of the reconciling work of Christ (v. 13), can be best explained in terms of amplification: after the author has made the assertion that the Gentiles were brought near in the blood of Christ (v. 13b), he eulogises Christ by

[40] See, e.g., Aristotle, *Rhet.* 1368 ^{a}38, who writes: 'We must also employ many of the means of amplification; for instance, if a man has done anything alone, or first, or with a few, or has been chiefly responsible for it; all these circumstances render an action noble . . .' For discussion of amplification as one of the most essential ingredients in ancient eulogistic species of oratory (τό ἐγκωμιαστικὸν), see esp. Aristotle, *Rhet.* 1368 ^{a}33, 39; 1391 ^{b}4; [Aristotle], *Rhet. Alex.* 1425 ^{b}34–1426 ^{b}20; Quintilian, *Inst.* 8.4.1–29. Amplification is also used in species of oratory other than encomium, see, e.g., [Aristotle], *Rhet. Alex.* 3.1426 ^{b}17–20. In this study I have followed the definition of 'amplification' given by Freese, who writes: 'Amplification is to be understood of the exaggeration of both great and small things. It is most suited to epideictic oratory, in which there is no doubt as to the facts; so that it is only necessary to accentuate their importance or non-importance' (*Rhetoric*, 264–5). See also Hellholm, 'Amplificatio', esp. 137; Bauer, 'Amplificatio'; Lausberg, *Elemente*, esp. 32, 58–63.

accentuating Christ's virtuous acts as a peace bringer who is putting to an end the hostility between Jew and Gentile.[41] His methods of amplification include:

(a) Reasoning (*ratiocinatio*, Quintilian, *Inst.* 8.4.15–26; [Cicero], *Ad Her*. 2.18.28). This form of amplification best explains the statement in v. 14a. It sets forth the causal basis for the statement which the author has made earlier, by intensifying the correctness of the proposition that Christ had truly brought the Gentiles 'near' (i.e., v. 13). Its (rhetorical) effect, however, is not found in the commencing statement (i.e., '*For* he [Christ] is our peace', v. 14a) itself. Rather, the function of the foregoing statement is to lead the readers on from the idea of 'peace' to Christ 'who made both one' (v. 14b) and who 'destroys the dividing wall/barrier' (v. 14c), and so forth. By lingering on the opening statement in v. 14a, the author is now inviting his audience/recipients, who are the beneficiaries of Christ's reconciling work, to estimate the content of 'peace' and to ponder upon what Christ was expected to accomplish in order to instil genuine peace/reconciliation.

(b) Augmentation (*incrementum*, Quintilian, *Inst.* 8.4.4–8; 9.3.28; [Cicero], *Ad Her.* 4.28.38). The distinctive feature of this form of amplification is its ability to strengthen the argument, e.g., 'He is our *peace* . . . , making *peace* . . . , he preached *peace* to you the far off and *peace* to the near' (vv. 14a, 15c, 17). The rhetorical effect of this form of amplification is that each clause is made more forcible than that which went before. Thus, the reduplication of 'peace' in v. 17 is to show not so much that Christ had preached to Gentiles and Jews *separately* but that Christ is magnanimous, and his inclusive approach praiseworthy.[42] He not only preached peace to the less significant, i.e., the marginalised or the 'far off' (17a), but also to the greater, i.e., the advantaged or the 'near' (v. 17b).

[41] For a discussion of the proper place where amplification should be introduced, see esp. Cicero, *Part. Or.* 8.27, who writes: 'Although amplification has its own proper place, often in the opening of a speech, and almost always at the end, yet it is to be used also in other parts of the discourse, especially when a point has been proved and refuted.' See also [Cicero], *Ad Her.* 2.30.47–9.

[42] See, e.g., Lincoln, *Ephesians*, 146–9, who reads v. 17 in its *literalness*, by analysing the meanings of words, phrases and sentences (i.e., 'sentence meaning'); Best, *Ephesians*^{2}, 269–73, and others. However, the same sentence in v. 17 could mean more than what the author says, see in particular Searle, *Expression*, 30; Levinson, *Pragmatics*, ch. 3 (on 'Conversational Implicature'), 97ff.; Barthes, *Challenge*, 173–8; Holmes, *Sociolinguistics*, 285–95; Thomas, *Interaction*, esp. 33–54, 55–86.

(c) Accumulation or 'piling up of words' (*congeries*, Quintilian, *Inst.* 8.4.26–7; [Cicero], *Ad Her.* 2.18.28). Although this form of amplification is closely associated with the foregoing (b), it refers to the accumulation of words and sentences which are almost synonymous or identical in meaning. We may take the *parallelismus membrorum* (i.e., an arrangement into couplets) in vv. 15b–16 for our example: 'in order that he might create . . . making peace; and [in order] that he might reconcile . . . killing the enmity . . .' (vv. 15b–c, v. 16); similarly, 'the dividing wall *of partition*' (v. 14b);[43] and, 'the law of commandments in ordinances' (15a).[44] What has often been deemed glossy, redundant, redactional or 'clarificatory stataments of the author' (as Wilhelmi says) are actually concrete displays of amplification![45] These accumulations *also* serve effectively as additional arguments which corroborate the briefly presented reason (*ratio*) indicated in v. 14a.

(d) Comparison (*comparatio*, Quintilian, *Inst.* 8.4.2, 9–14; see also Aristotle, *Rhet.* 1368 ^{a}38–9; [Aristotle], *Rhet. Alex.* 1426 ^{a}23–7; 1426 ^{a}28–1426 ^{b}12). Perhaps this is the subtlest, if not the most important, method of amplification in our passage. It is made most striking by displaying openly the magnanimity of Christ from cases of the opposite: if Christ's inclusive attitude/approach is praiseworthy and his magnanimity virtuous (vv. 17–18, see (b) above), what about that of the Jews (cf. vv. 11b–12)? By placing side by side two contrasting sets of attitudes/approaches,[46] the author, who has not lost sight of Jews/Judaism, has effectively evoked in his Gentile recipients thought of the virtuous qualities of Christ who embraces all and of the narrowly defined, inward-looking Jews/Judaism.

In sum, many recent studies have tried to 'discover' the hymnic nature of Ephesians 2.14ff., but the attempts to explore the (rhetorical) effect of the eulogistic speech in praise of Christ *vis-à-vis* Jewish attitudes toward

[43] It is generally agreed among scholars that the genitive phrase τοῦ φραγμοῦ is epexegetic, i.e., it elaborates the meaning of τὸ μεσότοιχον. See Sellin, 'Genitive', here 96–8.

[44] Thus Sellin, ibid., who writes: 'Die rhetorische Wirkung dieser dreifachen Synonymität ist zunächst eine Intensivierung und Steigerung' (90, also n. 23).

[45] *Contra* Gnilka; Lincoln; Sanders; Wilhelmi, et al.

[46] According to ancient rhetorical 'handbooks', one of the methods of amplification is to set in comparison with the thing (or person) one is describing the smallest of the things that fall into the same class, for thus one's case will appear magnified, see, e.g., Isocrates, *Evagoras* 49, 52–7; *Hel. enc.* 22.

the Gentiles are slight.[47] My analysis in the foregoing paragraphs has led me to conclude that Ephesians 2.14–18 reflects most probably the author's conscious compositional effort to eulogise Christ by accentuating his reconciliatory work and magnanimity.[48] The most striking effect of the author's *amplificatio* is that his encomiastic statements about Christ are set in comparison with those about the attitude of the Jews toward the Gentiles (vv. 11b–12). What becomes immediately clear in this ingenious composition is that in so doing he is able to set in comparison with the magnanimity of Christ the exclusive attitude of the Jews toward the Gentiles. We may say that the amplification, which comes immediately after the author has fleshed out the Jewish perception of the Gentiles, is prompted indeed by the latter, and has two major effects. In the *first* place, it could easily induce the Gentile recipients for whom he wrote to emulate the qualities of Christ which he accentuated (such as Christ's undisguised inclusivism, see below my exegesis of v. 18).[49] He maximises the expedient, noble act of Christ who brings peace to estranged humanity, whose death has in the author's perception provided a new framework (*pax Christi*) within which mutual acceptance or 'the oneness of spirit' between Jews and Gentiles may then be filled out (v. 18; also 4.1–6). In the *second* place, the author who praises Christ has, by implication, also repudiated the attitude of excluding or factionalising rather than of integrating. He presumably is denouncing the Jews who concerned themselves exclusively with the question of their own ethnic and religious identity but ignored the overall plan of God to include both Jews and Gentiles as his own people.

4.4 'He is our peace': Christ and ethnic reconciliation

We have shown in the preceding paragraphs that the discussion in vv. 11–13 should set the parameters for understanding vv. 14ff.[50] Our present task is to explore the way in which the author expands the reconciling work of Christ which he has already adumbrated in his earlier argument (v. 13b).

[47] Although Sellin, 'Genitive', esp. 90–1 and n. 23, recognises the rhetorical effect of *amplificatio* (*Steigerung*) in vv. 14–18, he does not however find any connections between the magnanimity of Christ and the Jewish attitudes toward the Gentiles.

[48] The death of Christ as a means of reconciliation also fits well in Hellenistic thought, and can easily evoke the thought that 'the works and sufferings of a good man are noble' (καλά, Aristotle, *Rhet.* 1366 ᵇ11, 14; [Aristotle], *Rhet. Alex.* 1425 ᵇ36–1426 ᵃ3).

[49] For a discussion of this particular purpose in eulogistic oratory, see esp. Isocrates, *Evagoras* 75, 77, 80; *Busiris* 47; [Cicero], *Ad Her.* 4.15.22; 4.39.51; cf. 3.13.24.

[50] See also Porter, *Καταλλάσσω*, 185.

4.4.1 Αὐτὸς γάρ ἐστιν ἡ εἰρήνη ἡμῶν, ὁ ποιήσας τὰ ἀμφότερα ἓν (v. 14a–b)[51]

The connections between our present passage in vv. 14–18 and the claims made by the author in his previous statements are now provided sufficiently as he *amplifies* these claims by explaining[52] why (and how) the hitherto defective status of Gentiles *as Gentiles* can now be redefined.[53] The distinctive feature of this form of amplification, however, is that its (rhetorical) effect is brought about at points other than where it is actually produced. So when the author argues that 'He (Christ) is *our peace*' (v. 14a),[54] the meaning of 'our peace' is not immediately clear in itself. But as he fleshes it out, enlarging it, the perplexing reference[55] to 'peace' in v. 14a is followed by a focus on the reconciling work of Christ in statements such as 'the one who made both one and destroyed the dividing wall . . .' (v. 14b; also 14c, 15a). The author's language here is downright *reconciliatory*, and this in turn sets the tone for his subsequent arguments.

[51] The articular participle (ὁ ποιήσας) is appositional to the masculine pronoun αὐτός which refers back to 'Christ' in v. 13.

[52] The usage of γάρ in our epistle is predominantly 'reason': see, e.g., Eph. 2.8, 10; 5.5, 9, 12, 14 (NA[27]), 29; 6.1; also 2 Cor. 11.14; also Matt. 1.21; Luke 20.42; John 2.25; Heb. 13.5. See also my discussion of 'ratiocinatio'.

[53] *Contra* Schille, *Hymnen*, 24 who reads vv. 14ff. as an *excursus* and concludes that the author has introduced in v. 14a a traditional *Vorlage* or hymnic fragment by an 'introductory' particle, i.e., γάρ-recitativum; also Schlier, *Epheser*, 122; Wilhelmi, 'Versöhner-Hymnen', 150 n. 16. Examples of γάρ-recitativum are clearly found in the NT writings, by which the Jewish scriptures are often quoted: see, e.g., Rom. 10.13; 13.9; 1 Cor. 10.26; 15.27; Heb. 10.15–16. However, none of these γάρ-*recitativa* can be isolated from its exegetical context, and made to lose its predominantly *explanatory* force. In addition to this, it is always possible for us to tell, with the help of other 'purple' indicators, whether traditional materials such as those from the Jewish scripture are incorporated: see, e.g., Rom. 2.24: 'For *it is written* . . .'; Rom. 9.17: 'For *the scripture says* to Pharaoh . . .'; Rom. 10.5: 'For *Moses writes that* . . .'; also Rom. 10.11, 16; 1 Cor. 1.19; Gal. 3.10; 1 Tim. 5.18, et al. Given that these indicators are not present in Schille's reading, his γάρ-recitativum must be deemed less than helpful in the sense that it is engendered not so much by any serious exegetical considerations as by the theological assertion that the alleged *Vorlage* – be it Gnostic or early christological hymn – is simply present and that its meaning can be determined by isolating it from the exegetical context of the given text. For a criticism of Schille's approach, see, e.g., Deichgräber, *Gotteshymnus*, who concludes: 'Das Wörtchen γάρ in V. 14 ist nicht "γάρ-recitativum", sondern ein ganz gewöhnliches, kausal verknüpfendes γάρ' (166); Merklein, 'Komposition', esp. 82–3, 88–95.

[54] The pronoun αὐτὸς which precedes the causal conjunction occupies a position of emphasis, BDF, §475(1).

[55] See, e.g., Lindemann, *Aufhebung*, who writes: 'In 2, 14 stellt sich die Frage, ob an den Frieden zwischen Gott und Mensch, an die Vereinigung von Juden und Heiden oder aber an beides zugleich gedacht ist; dabei ist jedoch unabhängig vom jetzigen Sinn der Stelle zunächst zu fragen, was εἰρήνη in der *Vorlage* konkret bedeutete' (160).

Since there is nothing in the previous verses (vv. 11–13) that corresponds with the ideas of 'both' (τὰ ἀμφότερα) other than the obvious polarisation (and alienation) of the 'circumcision' and the 'uncircumcision' – a point missed by most commentators (vv. 11b and 11c),[56] the neuter formulation here reflects most probably Jews and Gentiles who were estranged from one another by the act and fact of (un)circumcision.[57] To be sure, the formulation echoes the Jewish perspective that humanity can be divided into 'two' and that only one of the two is entitled to God's grace. Such 'us-them' division was far from healthy, and must have created considerable tensions between the 'haves' and the 'have nots'. This needs to be borne in mind before one can truly appreciate the reconciling work of Christ. There is, therefore, no compelling reason for us to accept the suggestion that the neuter words are determined by the religious presuppositions which are visible in the Hellenistic myths[58] or that the author of Ephesians is now historicising the mythical language of unification.[59] Rather, the author amplifies the reconciling activity of Christ in making/creating[60] the non-Jews, who were situated at the extremity of

[56] Mußner, *Epheser*, 75 has proposed an ambivalent character for the neuter words, suggesting that they should refer to the two realms, the two human groups and divisions of the two groups in religious realms.

[57] The neuter ἀμφότερα can be used to denote persons if it is not an individual but a general quality that is to be emphasised, see, e.g., Dionysius Halicarnassus, *Ant. rom.* 6.85.1, where the same neuter word is used with reference to two social groups in a state-body, i.e., those who formed the Senate and the multitudes or plebians. The term ἀμφότερα and its variants are also found in Dio's political speeches, denoting two rival groups of peoples, see, e.g., *Or.* 38.43, 45, 46. In Aristides, *Pan.* 41.3, the word is used to denote two distinguishable genders: 'Zeus had intercourse with Semele and when Semele conceived, Zeus wished to be both father and mother of Dionysius (ὁ Ζεὺς βουλόμενος ἀμφότερα αὐτὸς τῷ Διονύσῳ γενέσθαι πατήρ τε καὶ μήτηρ)'. See also Schlatter, *Briefe*, 184; Merklein, 'Komposition', 84; BDF, §138(1); LSJ, s.v.

[58] *Contra* Schlier, *Christus*, 18–26, who argues that the author of Ephesians is referring to 'a vestige of a myth of reconciliation of heaven and earth'; cf. Schlier, *Epheser*, 124. Schlier's theory is partially endorsed by Lincoln, *Ephesians*, 128, 140–1 who argues that the writer of Ephesians may well have taken over traditional material which spoke of Christ as the one who brings cosmic peace and reconciliation, but this material which lies behind vv. 14–16 need not be thought to have a Gnostic origin: cf. Lincoln, 'Use', 25–6; Dahl, 'Geheimnis', 74 n. 45, who contends that the phrase in vv. 14a–b reflects the myth of a reunion of male and female; Gnilka, *Epheserbrief*, 139; Martin, *Reconciliation*, 173; Lindemann, *Aufhebung*, 160; Lindemann, *Epheser*, 49, 51.

[59] *Contra* Meeks, 'Unity', who combines the theories of Schlier and Dahl (see n. 58), but adds that the author of Ephesians 'historicizes the mythical language of unification' (215); also Käsemann, *Versuche*, 280–3, here 280; Käsemann, 'Epheserbrief', 518.

[60] In the LXX the verb ποιέω is often used for ברא, denoting the activity of Yahweh in the creation of the world: see, e.g., Gen. 1.1; 2.2; Exod. 20.11; Prov. 14.31; Isa. 43.1; 44.2; Wis. 1.13; 9.9; Sir. 7.30; 32.13; Tobit 8.6; Judith 8.14; Baruch 3.35; 4.7; 2 Macc. 7.28; Philo, *Sacr.* 65; *Sib. Or.* 3.28. The NT writers have extended the LXX usage to express the notion of creation: Matt. 19.4; Mark 10.6, par. Gen. 1.27; Acts 4.24; 14.15; 17.24;

the Jewish world (v. 13a), *and* the Jews, who had turned Israel's privileges into ethnic and national assets, into one harmonious whole (cf. v. 10). He assumes that the two parts of humanity are kept apart because of Jewish ethnocentricity, and that Christ, the embodiment of 'peace', has come to bridge the gap between the two ethnic groups.[61] As we shall see below, this particular notion of the creative act of Christ is further exemplified as the author sets out to focus on Christ as making the divided humanity into 'one new man' (v. 15a).

To sum up: although 'peace' is often understood as a soteriological term elsewhere, its usage goes beyond this in our present context (cf. 4.3; 1 Cor. 14.33; Gal. 5.22),[62] and is best explained against the backcloth of a Jewish perspective in which a less-than-healthy attitude of the Jews has already been implied by the author.[63] The 'peace' language is prompted precisely by the author's concern about the Jewish attitude toward the Gentiles and the less-than-healthy relationships as implied in that attitude. When 'peace' in v. 14a (and later vv. 15c, 17) is understood in this sense, it best accounts for the need of reconciliation of Jews and Gentiles which involves inevitably the cessation of estrangement and antagonistic attitudes.

Christ is portrayed as the mediator of peace or the bearer of reconciliation. He effects peace by bringing to an end the estrangement between Jews and Gentiles. He 'made both one' not because the differences between Gentiles and Jews as two distinct ethnic groups are diminished but because Jewish identity had become so confused with Israel and Israel's God-given grace that this had been turned into a boundary marker by the Jews, separating and distinguishing Jews from the rest of humanity.

Rom. 9.20–1, et al. The verb ποιέω also fits very well the Hellenistic thought of creative activity (e.g., of Zeus): see, e.g., Hesiod, *Op.* 109f.; Epictetus, *Diatr.* 1.6.11; 1.9.7; 4.7.6; Aristides, *Or.* 43.7, et al. See further Braun, 'ποιέω', 459–60, 463; BAGD, 1β; Louw and Nida, §42.29, 30, 35.

[61] The genitive in ἡ εἰρήνη ἡμῶν denotes that both the 'circumcision' and the 'uncircumcision' are recipients of the advantage which Christ brought; see also Martin, *Reconciliation*, 187–8; Robinson, *Ephesians*, 160.

[62] *Pace* Stuhlmacher, 'Peace', 187ff.; Barth, *Ephesians 1–3*, 261 n. 36; Wolter, *Rechtfertigung*, 72. But see von Rad, 'εἰρήνη', 400–5, who concludes that peace can mean 'wholeness, not just in the sense of fullness for the individual but for the totality of human relationships within a community. A community characterised as a perfect harmony of free persons with their Lord and with one another is a political as well as a religious one'; Gaston, *Stone*, 335, who concludes that 'the redemption which the Messiah has come to bring to Israel will mean peace for all Israel and peace between Israel and the nations'.

[63] *Contra* Sanders, *Schismatics*, 200–2, who fails to acknowledge the exclusive attitude of the *Jews* as indicated in vv. 11–13. This failure leads Sanders to conclude that the '[law] observant *Jewish Christians* have become, for the author of Ephesians, relics hindering the effecting of the christological unity' (201, italics mine).

Our understanding of Christ as the embodiment of the 'peace' requires us to account for the *ethnic factor* which involves the estrangement of Gentiles from Israel by the Jews, and most importantly, the annulment of the social distance between the two by Christ. As we shall see, Christ who concludes peace has through his death on the cross become the terms of peace (vv. 15c, 16b). His death is the most decisive factor which determines the way in which a 'settlement' between the two estranged groups could be attained.

4.4.2 καὶ τὸ μεσότοιχον τοῦ φραγμοῦ (ὁ) λύσας (v. 14c)

The powerful image of a dividing wall is now grafted to the foregoing imagery, fleshing out the nature of Christ's peace-making ministry in more vivid terms. Here the need to break down the wall is presumably an indicator of the disharmony or the absence of 'peace' between the divided groups.

At least three *major* hypotheses have been proposed in recent decades as to what the author of Ephesians intended by the 'wall' metaphor. The first alternative is the previously much promoted view that the wall refers to the cosmic wall between the heavenly realms and the human sphere on earth,[64] and that a Gnostic redeemer has penetrated this wall, encountered enmity from heavenly powers and angelic powers, destroyed the wall and the enmity, and thus created peace.[65] As competent scholars in the field of history of religions have contested rather than confirmed the Gnostic influence upon our present passage on which theological interpreters had built their theories, this reading has now fallen by the wayside.[66]

The second alternative reads the 'law of the commandments with the statutes' as the dividing wall/fence.[67] The *law*, according to this view, is

[64] So Schlier, *Christus*, 18–26; Schlier, *Epheser*, 124; Dibelius, *Epheser*, 69; Fischer, *Tendenz*, 133; Pokorný, *Epheserbrief*, 117–24. Schneider, 'μεσότοιχον', 625, writes: 'The wall of partition which consists in the fence between God and man.' See also Lincoln, *Ephesians*, 141, who suggests a dual significance of the metaphor: '[O]riginally, the dividing wall had reference to a cosmic wall. The explanation that it is a fence is the writer's gloss in order to adapt to this new context.' It is probably better to look at our epistle individually, since otherwise its distinctive features might be lost.

[65] So Fischer, *Tendenz*, 132; Conzelmann, *Epheser*, 99–101; Lindemann, *Aufhebung*, 162–4; Wengst, *Lieder*, 181ff.

[66] For a recent review of this theory, see esp. Perkins, *Gnosticism*, esp. 91, 100; see also Barth, 'Traditions', esp. 20–1; Schnelle, *History*, 309. Newman, however, suggests that a similar Gnostic idea (without the Gnostic redeemer as such) is attested in Jewish mystical sources such as the Hekhalot texts, but also in earlier texts, see esp. his *Glory-Christology*, passim.

[67] So Mußner, *Epheser*, 76–7; Schnackenburg, *Ephesians*, 114; Lincoln, *Ephesians*, 141–2; Moritz, *Mystery*, 40–2, et al.

the stumbling block between Jew and Gentile.[68] To support this interpretation, reference has often been made to the Hellenistic-Jewish comparative materials such as the *Epistle of Aristeas* 139, 142 and other Jewish sources which claimed that the Torah itself provides an 'iron wall' and a 'fence' surrounding Israel (e.g., *m.* Abot. 1.1–2; 3.18).[69] 'The law', in Lincoln's words, 'in functioning as a fence to protect Israel from the impurity of the Gentiles, became such a sign of Jewish particularism that it also alienated Gentiles and became a cause of hostility.'[70] This interpretation, however, is not entirely satisfactory, and I would challenge it in three major ways.

(a) To scholars who place the function of the law in our passage and that of *Aristeas* on a par, it must be said that this misconstrues the point of focus in *Aristeas*, which aims, most probably, to synthesise Judaism and Hellenism by extending a famous Greek story to the situation of the Jews.[71] *Aristeas* 139–42 belonged to the Jewish story of self-aggrandisation: its author portrays the Jews as people held most dear to their own God. His idealised description of the Jews, and in particular his use of the 'wall' language, is reminiscent of the great legends about the Trojans in Greek literature. According to Homer's *Iliad*, Poseidon (the 'earth shaker') had 'built for the Trojans round about their city a wall, wide and exceeding fair, that the city might never be broken' (21.441–9, cf. 7.452–3). Concerning the city of the Trojans as Zeus's most honoured city on earth, Homer writes: 'For all cities beneath sun and starry heaven wherein men that dwell upon the face of the earth have their abodes, of these sacred Ilios [*sc.* city of the Trojans] was most honoured of my heart' (*Iliad* 4.43–9).[72] The Greek story is expanded at great length by Dio in one of his political speeches to the assembly of Tarsus.[73] Dio's emphasis

[68] So Dahl, 'Gentiles', who writes: 'The commandments of the Law are envisaged as a set of rules for common life and worship, a fence around Israel and a dividing wall that kept aliens outside and became a cause of hostility' (36); Moritz, *Mystery*, who concludes that '[t]he Law of commandments was a stumbling block to peace' (40); Stuhlmacher, 'Peace', 186, 194; Schnackenburg, *Ephesians*, 112–14; Lincoln, *Ephesians*, 141; Gnilka, *Epheserbrief*, 140; Caird, *Letters*, 58–9. Köster, *Introduction*, 270 overstates the twofold function of the 'wall', namely that 'the law is abolished not only as the dividing wall between Jews and Gentiles, *but also* as the cosmic wall between the heavenly realms and the human sphere on earth' (italics mine). Martin, *Reconciliation*, 174 argues that v. 15 portrays a 'more sinister understanding of the Torah'; also 185–7; Perkins, *Gnosticism*, 91. See also Radl, 'μεσότοιχον', who writes: 'The dividing wall formed by the barrier of the law, which separates Jews and Gentiles before Christ' (412); Paulsen, 'φραγμός', 437; BAGD, φραγμός s.v., 2.

[69] So Mußner, *Epheser*, 75–7, et al. [70] Lincoln, *Ephesians*, 141.

[71] For a helpful discussion of the various Greek elements alluded to in *Aristeas*, see esp. Nickelsburg, 'Stories', esp. 75–80.

[72] See further Kirk, *Iliad*; Richardson, *Iliad*.

[73] In *Or.* 33.21, Dio writes: 'And not only were the Trojans distinguished for wealth and richness of soil and number of inhabitants, but also human beings born at Troy were

on the Trojans' wall which fenced them about was to underscore the distinctiveness of the Trojans: they were the most blessed people of all and were different from the rest of the world.[74] It is highly possible, and perhaps probable, that both linguistically and conceptually the author of *Aristeas* stood in the Greek tradition and that his own version of the 'wall' language represents the perspective of a Hellenised Jew who wished to convey to his audience the idea that the Jews were marked out and separated from the rest of the world by their own God: just like the Trojans, the Jews were the people held most dear to God, and Moses, whose role is likened to that of Poseidon, has 'hedged' (περιφράσσειν) the beloved people of God on all sides with strict observances connected with meat and drink and touch and hearing and sight, after the manner of the law. We are informed of the fact that Eleazer's 'apologia' for the Jewish law is firmly established as his tenacious assertion is placed in the mouth of an *Egyptian* priest who 'confirmed' his claims that the Jews were the 'men of God' indeed (*Arist.* 140).

If our analysis in the foregoing is correct, the point of focus in *Aristeas* 139 and 142 is not so much to instil a sense of strangeness or alienation, nor to depict the law as being the cause of hostility, but to stir up the Gentiles' immense interest in, and admiration for, the Jews.[75] Indeed *Aristeas* 139–42 can be read as a confident 'apologia for the Jewish law' (to use Zuntz's word),[76] with its primary aim to advertise the Jews as the dearest people to their own God, just as the Trojans were to Zeus.[77] The point is clearly that in *Aristeas* the law serves as a bulwark[78] protecting the purity of the Jewish community and keeping them away from impurity (cf. Lev. 20,

very beautiful, both men and women, horses were very fleet, the people were held to be dear to the gods, and *they were fenced about with a circuit-wall most strong* – in fact that *wall* of theirs was the work of Poseidon and Apollo (καὶ θεοφιλεῖς ἐδολουν εἶναι, καὶ τείχει καρερωτάτῳ <u>περιπεφραγμένοι</u> ἦσαν. τὸ μέν τεῖχος αὐτοῖς Ποσειδῶνος ἔργον ἦν καὶ Ἀπόλλωνος). Moreover, Zeus declared that of all the cities beneath the sun he loved that city most.'

[74] But see *Or.* 33.22–3, in which the downfall of the Trojans is emphasised.

[75] See also a discussion of *Aristeas* in Barclay, *Jews*, 138–50, esp. 146–7, who refers to the Gentiles' admiration for the distinctive identity of the Jews, as expressed in their eating habits, moral and religious customs (147).

[76] See Zuntz, 'Aristeas', here 142.

[77] *Pace* Moritz, *Mystery*, who argues that 'the Jewish author [*sc.* of *Aristeas*] is very concerned with defending Judaism against challenges resulting from the influx of Hellenistic ideas' (30); but see Nickelsburg, *Jewish Literature*, 165 who concludes that *Aristeas* 'presents the most positive estimate of the Greeks and Greek culture and of the possibility for peaceful and productive co-existence between Jews and Greeks'.

[78] See also Plato, *Resp.* 2.365B, who also used the 'wall' language to underscore its protective purposes: 'Is it by justice or by crooked deceit that I the high wall shall scale and so live my life out in fenced and guarded security?' (ἐκεῖνο τὸ πότερον δίκᾳ τεῖχος ὕψιον ἢ σκολῖας ἀπάταις ἀναβὰς καὶ ἐμαυτὸν οὕτω περιφράξας διαβιῶ); Strabo, *Geog.* 4.5.2: 'For

esp. vv. 25–6). It would be far-fetched, therefore, to conclude that the law, in functioning as a fence to preserve Israel's purity (e.g., in matters of food, drink, touch) and therefore Israel's distinct identity, became 'a source of hostility'.[79] The law was never meant to engender hostility, if at all, in *Aristeas* (cf. 3 Macc. 3.4ff.; see below my exegesis of v. 14d).[80]

(b) Scholars who assert that the sole stumbling block between Jew and Gentile is the law *per se* have often been tempted to forge, on the basis of their particular theological presupposition, a strange interpretation of v. 15a, making the abolishing of the law into the author's sole meaning (e.g., '*having abolished* the hostility in his flesh, i.e., the law of commandments in ordinances'). This reading leaves behind the impression that Christ's making 'both one' (or destroying the wall of partition) depends on the prior abrogation of the 'law'.[81] A brief discussion of the syntactical possibilities of vv. 14–15 and the temporal reference of the participles in vv. 14–15 would show that this reading is gratuitous in linguistic terms: (i) the articular participle (ὁ ποιήσας) in v. 14b is placed in apposition with the pronoun αὐτὸς (v. 14a) and serves in our passage as a substantive: '*He* is our peace, *the one who made* both one'.[82] In addition to this, this participle is also linked with another participle, λύσας, in v. 14c in terms of syntactical possibility.[83] Had the author intended the third participial

the purpose of war they [*sc.* the Britons] use chariots for the most part, just as some of the Celtids. The forests are their cities; for they *fence* (περιφραξάντες) in a spacious circular enclosure with trees which they have felled, and in that enclosure make huts for themselves and also pen up their cattle – not, however, with the purpose of staying for a long time.' *M.* Aboth. 1.1–2 (or 3.18) can be read in the same light, namely the Law is such a precious 'asset' to the Jewish people that it should be strenuously safeguarded: 'Be deliberate in judgement, raise up many disciples, and make a fence around the Law.'

[79] Lincoln, *Ephesians*, 141; cf. Moritz, *Mystery*, 40–1; Gnilka, *Epheserbrief*, 140; Caird, *Letters*, 58–9; Martin, *Reconciliation*, 185–7. Dunn, 'Anti-Semitism', who recognises the boundary function of the law in *Aristeas*, is cautious at this point when he writes about the function of the Law 'as a palisade round Israel, marking Israel out among the surrounding nations by Jewish faithfulness to the Law, and marking Israel off from the rest as outsiders, outlaws' (158 and n. 36).

[80] A modern example would be the walls of Palos Verdes in Los Angeles, which protect some well-to-do communities from the presence of unauthorised outsiders. In the perception of those who lie outside the orbit they are not protective but exclusionary. See a helpful discussion by Marcuse, 'Walls', esp. 214–15.

[81] So Lincoln, *Ephesians*, 141, who argues that v. 14b ('having broken down the dividing wall') is paralleled by v. 15a ('having abolished . . . the hostility, the law'); cf. Wilhelmi, 'Versöhner-Hymnen', 148.

[82] See also Perschbacher, *Syntax*, 389.

[83] The article-participle-καί-participle construction is very common in the Pauline epistles and other NT documents: see, e.g., 1 Cor. 11.29; 2 Cor. 1.22; 2.21–2; Gal. 1.15; 2 Thess. 2.3–4, 16; also Matt. 27.40; John 3.29; 6.33; 11.2; 21.24; Acts 10.35; 15.38; Jas. 1.25; 3.6; Heb. 6.7; 7.1; 10.29; Rev. 22.8, et al. See also Wallace, *Grammar*, 274–5 who concludes that Eph. 2.14 well illustrates that even when there are several intervening words,

clause (καταργήσας κτλ., v. 15a) to be seen as parallel to the two participles of v. 14, we would expect a similar connecting particle (i.e., καί) to occur before καταργήσας.[84] Thus, the most that can be said is that the author reads v. 15a, *ad sensum*, as a circumstantial participial clause which underscores the circumstance under which the action denoted by the two preceding substantival participial clauses in vv. 14b and 14c takes place.[85] (ii) Given also that the temporal reference of a participle is normally established relative to its use in a specific context,[86] the third participle καταργήσας (aor.) which occurs *after* two other aorist verbs (ὁ ποιήσας . . . καί . . . λύσας) is more likely to denote either a concurrent or a subsequent action, but *not* an antecedent action.[87] That the law must be abolished as a prerequisite *before* peace between the two groups of people can be instilled is clearly a theological assertion which cannot stand up to serious linguistic analysis and should therefore be deemed an improbable reading.[88]

(c) The present theory also fails to give to the exegetical connections between vv. 14–18 and vv. 11–13 their due weight in understanding the function of the 'law'. It fails to account for the *oblique* references to the 'law' which the author has already adumbrated in vv. 11–12.[89] As we shall see, the immediate exegetical context reveals that the issue at stake is *not* the law *per se* but the way in which the 'circumcision'/Jews had expropriated the law to reinforce ethnocentrism, thereby fencing off the Gentiles from Israel and Israel's God-given grace (see below my exegesis of v. 15a).

The third alternative reads the 'wall' in its literalness: it alludes to the balustrade, the *soreg* in the (Jerusalem) temple courtyard which separated

the construction is not thereby invalidated. This syntactical construction also escapes the attention of Lincoln, *Ephesians*, 141, whose main interest is to argue that the law *per se* is the *sole* stumbling block between Jew and Gentile – in the face of linguistic evidence.

84 See, e.g., Phil. 3.6; also Matt. 4.24; Luke 6.47; Jas. 3.6, et al. The translation of v. 15 in NRSV is inaccurate, but see NIV.

85 The circumstantial clause in v. 15a relates not simply to the second substantival participle of v. 14, but to the entire article-participle-καί-participle construction. See also Healey and Healey, 'Participles', esp. 178–80, 253.

86 See, e.g., Porter, *Verbal Aspect*, esp. ch. 8.

87 See also Eph. 1.20. Another example will be v. 17, where the participle is placed right *before* the main verb, and may then be translated as follows: 'And having come, he preached (καὶ ἐλθὼν εὐηγγελίσατο) peace to you the far off and the near' (my translation). The preaching itself is the point of focus. See further the discussion of temporal reference of the participle in Porter, *Verbal Aspect*, 380–5; Porter, *Idioms*, 188.

88 *Contra* Gnilka, *Epheserbrief*, 147–52; Lincoln, *Ephesians*, 141; Wilhelmi, 'Versöhner-Hymnen', 184.

89 See my discussion of circumcision and its connections with the 'law' in chapter 3, where I posed the following question: is it possible to speak of the 'body politic of Israel' without referring to the 'law' which undoubtedly regulated the lifestyle of its members?

the court of the Gentiles from the more sacred precincts which only Jews might enter.[90] Proponents of this view argue that it is supported by the discovery of an inscription prohibiting the entrance of a foreigner under threat of the penalty of death.[91] If this is correct, possibly lying behind it is a particular understanding of the temple as a 'space' which is organised into a coherent pattern in terms of sacredness: Israel is contrasted with the rest of the world, Jerusalem is contrasted with the other cities of the land, the temple is contrasted with Jerusalem, and the Holy of Holies is contrasted with the temple.[92] As one moves inward from the temple mount the groups of people who are allowed to enter are progressively reduced. By implication, it is not that the Gentiles were refused access to the temple mount but that as a sacred place the temple has, in the perception of the Jews, allowed the latter to locate their relationships to the world, Israel, and Jerusalem in terms of the various degrees of holiness.[93] In this case our text and external sources tally. It implies that when the author spoke of the 'dividing wall' (i.e., the balustrade), he was alluding to the 'dislocated' position of the Gentiles or to the fact that Jews and Gentiles were divided by the barrier/'fence'; or else both are in view.

Although the 'wall' language permits this interpretation, it does not demand it.[94] It could well be that the author has had another kind of

[90] See esp. Josephus, *A. J.* 15.417; *B. J.* 5.193; 6.124f. Josephus has used two different words (μέσος + τοῖχος) to denote the wall in the temple building, but not the balustrade, e.g., *A. J.* 8.67, 71. Cf. *m.* Mid. 2.3. See further Robinson, *Ephesians*, 59–60, 158; Abbott, *Ephesians*, 51; Hanson, *Unity*, 143; McKelvey, *Temple*, 108; Dunn, 'Anti-Semitism', 158; cf. Dunn, 'Deutero-Pauline Letters', 139. See further Bickermann, 'Inscription'; Baumgarten, 'Exclusions'; Segal, 'Penalty'; Schürer, *HJPAJC*, II, 285 n. 57; Levine, 'Temple', esp. 244–5; Gaston, *Stone*, 191; Schwartz, 'Descent'; Barrett, *Paul*, 156; Madvig, 'μεσότοιχον'. See further Best, who writes: '[A]s an architectural term it was well known in Asia Minor, being found seven times in the instruction for the erection of the temple at Didyma' (*Ephesians*², 257 and n. 39). None, however, of these occurrences refers to the balustrade.

[91] See e.g., *OGIS*, no. 598: 'No foreigner may enter within the screen and the enclosure around the temple. Whoever shall be caught (doing so), shall be responsible for his own death which follows.' It is not possible that the Greek inscription includes proselytes as well as Gentiles (*contra* Schwartz, 'Descent').

[92] See in particular *m.* Kel. 1.6–19; Acts 17.27–30. See further Kunin, 'Judaism', here 116, 144 n. 4.

[93] The immediate context of *m.* Kelim 1.6–19 may well suggest that the question of purity/impurity has been the main concern of the rabbis.

[94] See in particular Schwartz, 'Descent', who concludes that 'it would be naive to suppose that Gentiles were the only group which was excluded from the temple precincts. There were increasing divisions between the sexes (for purity and other reasons), women had also suffered severe limitation to their access to the inner temple precincts and probably their participation in public ceremonies' (165–6). On the inclusion of (Gentile) proselytes in the Temple precincts, see, e.g., *m.* Bik. 1.4; *Mek. Exod* 12.49.

'dividing wall' in view, that is, one which is adumbrated not so much in the temple-balustrade but in the immediate exegetical context itself (vv. 11–13). The *topos* of 'wall' was a commonplace in the ancient world and writers in the Graeco-Roman world employed it to convey a wide range of ideas from exclusion[95] to sacrilege.[96] The same *topos* is employed in ancient political rhetoric to indicate an unstable condition between two communities, and thus the need to 'make peace'.[97] It is just as possible to argue that the Gentile readers may not have been familiar with the balustrade of the Jewish temple,[98] but they would find it less difficult to appreciate the idea of partition or exclusion denoted in the 'wall' *topos* which can be best understood against the background of ancient city(-state) politics, alongside other political metaphors (such as πολιτεία, ξένοι, v. 12; cf. v. 19).

[95] In the ancient world, the 'wall' denotes the partition between insiders and outsiders: see, e.g., Cicero, *Cat.* 1.5: 'Why, you see the general and commander of this enemy within the [*sc.* city] walls, and even within the Senate?'; cf. 1.13, 27. For Cicero, the temples, buildings, and walls of the city and the lives of its citizens are interwoven (1.12, 33; *Off.* 1.53–5). See Vasaly, *Representations* 45, 47, 52, 54–5. The 'wall' not only represents the safety of a city-state, it symbolises solidarity. Polybius noted that the inhabitants of a single city were 'enclosed by one wall' (*Histories*, 2.37.11).

[96] See, e.g., Quintilian, who alluded to the 'wall' language to denote the consequence of sacrilege: 'It is expressly stated in the law that for any foreigner who goes up to the wall the penalty is death' (*Inst.* 4.4.4). Quintilian is referring most probably to the *pomerium* (i.e., the line demarcating an augurally constituted city) which Remus had attempted to leap across, thus making the sacred wall traversible and profane. According to Plutarch, the Romans regarded 'all the city-wall as inviolable and sacred' (Δὶα πᾶν τεῖχος ἀσεβηλον καὶ ἱερον νομισουσι) and Romulus killed his brother because he was attempting to leap across the inviolable and sacred wall: *Quaest. rom.* 27, cf. *Romulus* 1.361; see also Varro, *Ling.* 5.143; *Digests* 1.8.1. For the Romans, the walls within the *pomerium* are the most sacred boundary of a new city: see, e.g., Tacitus, *Ann.* 12.24; Ovid, *Fasti* 4.821–5. See further Rykwert, *Town*, esp. 29, 126–7, 132–9, 163–87. Rykwert contends that 'the safeguards of the walls and the *pomerium* protect the well-being of the whole community directly' (134); Dyson, *Community*, 147–79, esp. 153–4. Dyson contends that 'the fortification wall marked the division between urbs and countryside, the city of the living and the dead. This division was codified in the concept of the *Pomerium*, the ritual boundary surrounding the city proper. However, the *murus* was more than a ritual boundary that defined urbanity. Communities had to be defended' (154).

[97] See, e.g., Andocides, *On the Peace with the Lacedaimonians*. When the Spartans defeated the Athenians, the latter demolished their walls, surrendered their fleet, and recalled their exiles as they 'made peace' (truce!) with the victors (11), cf. 14, 23, 36, 39. The episode is also recounted in Plutarch, *Lys.*, 14.4: 'This is what the Lacedaimonian authorities have decided: tear down the Piraeus and the *long walls*; quit all the cities and keep to your own land; if you do these things, and restore your exiles, you shall have *peace*, if you want it'; see also 14.5–6; 15.1–2. For the symbolic significance of Athenian 'walls' in Andocides' speeches, see esp. Missiou, *Andokides*, esp. 74–6, 175.

[98] Thus Dibelius, *Epheser*, here 69. Dibelius's view is revived more recently by Lincoln, *Ephesians*, 125.

In this maze of opinions that we have trodden so far, my own inclination is that the 'hedge/wall' language[99] in v. 14c can be best explained as the logical consequence of the representation provided by the author's argument in vv. 11–13a: that is, the purposeful and exclusive attitudes of the Jews have separated the Jews from the Gentiles and created a barrier that stood between two ethnic groups. The 'wall' refers to the *social* barrier which is closely associated with some of the boundary markers used by the Jews to separate themselves from the Gentiles (e.g., the mark of the covenant in the 'flesh', and the ethnically based 'body politic of Israel' and other indicators of Israel's God-given grace). According to this attitude, the acceptability of Jews to God and their standing before God depend on their physical descent from Abraham,[100] and on their identity as members of the narrowly defined 'body politic'. This exclusive inclination best explains the 'wall' as denoting the social distance between the 'circumcision'/Jew and the 'uncircumcision'/Gentile.[101] This barrier is the most immediate corollary of the Jews' reluctance to set God's grace on a broader canvas and constriction of it to a particular ethnic group.

To recap what we have discussed so far, Jewish ethnocentrism and the attitude to exclude – rather than a particular *locus*, be it the balustrade of the temple or the law *per se* – best explains the 'wall' that stands between Jew and Gentile, preventing one ethnic group from advancing to the 'other'. What we should look into is therefore the evocative power of the 'wall' imagery: its perspicuity must have caused the Gentiles to

[99] The term 'hedge' stands in apposition to 'partition', serving with epexegetic function: 'the partition, namely the hedge'. It was used often to denote the boundary/fence that separates, see, e.g., Num. 22.24; Ps. 79.12 LXX; Nahum 3.17; Mic. 4.14, LXX; Luke 14.23. The two terms, φραγμός and τοῖχος, are more or less synonymous: see, e.g., Isa. 5.5: 'And now I will tell you what I will do to my vineyard. I will remove its hedge (φραγμός), and it shall be devoured; I will break down its wall (τοῖχος), and it shall be trampled down.' See also Philo, *Det.* 105; *Agr.* 11, 14; *Conf.* 33; *Somn.* 2.262; *Mos.* 1.271. See also *Sib. Or.* 3.319–20: 'The earth will belong equally to all, undivided by walls or fences (οὐ τείχεσιν, οὐ περιφράγμος)'. The term φραγμός is understood as the palisade of a citadel in Herodotus's *Histories*: 'Certain of the old men were of opinion that the god meant to tell them the citadel would escape; for this was anciently defended by a palisade; and they supposed that *barrier* to be the "wooden *wall*" of the oracle' (οἱ κατὰ τὸν φραγμὸν συνεζάλλοντο τοῦτο τὸ ξύλινον τεῖχος εἶναι, 7.142, cf. 7.141; 8.52); Dioscrides, 1.120. See also Sellin, 'Genitive', here 96; LSJ, s.v., II; BAGD, s.v., 1.

[100] See my discussion of the connections between the observance of circumcision and Abraham in ch. 4.

[101] See also Bruce, who writes: 'The barrier . . . was both religious and sociological . . ., it consists of the Jewish law, more particularly of those features of it which marked Jews off from Gentiles – circumcision and the food restrictions . . .' (*Ephesians*, 296).

conjure up what was described with their 'eyes of the mind',[102] so that the verbally produced images might in turn stimulate corresponding *visiones* in their minds.[103]

4.4.3 τὴν ἔχθραν ἐν τῇ σαρκὶ αὐτοῦ . . . καταργήσας (v. 14d)

The 'wall' language, however, is *not* an end in itself but a means to an end: the Gentiles are invited to attach to that visualisation a stream of ideas associated with it – ideas concerning ethnic discord (vv. 11b–13a), enmity and, not least, the divisive force of 'the law of the commandments in ordinances' (v. 15a).

The question arises whether the term 'enmity' should be construed as the first object after the participial verb 'nullifying', in apposition with the 'law' of v. 15a, or as the second object of 'who destroyed the wall of partition' (v. 14b), in apposition with the 'wall' (v. 14c).[104] The balance of the clauses is better maintained by the first construction.[105] In our present context, the enmity can be best explained against a backcloth of the *Jewish* perspective that views the Gentiles, by definition, as outside the orbit of God-given grace to the 'circumcision'. This ethnically based perspective, alongside other imagery, lays bare the Jewish tendency to exclude or factionalise rather than to integrate (vv. 11b–12).[106] Indeed, what is revealed in this attitude is ethnic hostility or enmity understood

[102] For a discussion of the technique of vivid descriptions, i.e., *evidentia*, in ancient political rhetoric, see, e.g., Quintilian, *Inst.* 8.3.62, cf. 6.2.29–32; Plato, *Theaet.* 191C–D; Aristotle, *Mem. rem.* 450 ᵃ31; Theon, *Progymnasmata*, 2.118. See further Zanker, 'Enargeia'; Vasaly, *Representations*, esp. ch. 3 'Signa and Signifiers: A World Created', here 90–1 n. 4, 94, 102; Lausberg, *Handbuch*, I, 13–16.

[103] Vasaly, *Representations*, 95 and n. 12, 96–7. She concludes that the assumptions by ancient rhetoricians about the way vivid description worked in the minds of an audience suggests that ancient, non-literate society may well have possessed powers of pictorial visualisation much greater and more intense than our own (99).

[104] So Merklein, *Christus*, 31.

[105] Thus Bruce, *Ephesians*, 298; Beare, 'Ephesians', 655–6; Porter, *Καταλλάσσω*, 187. For a discussion of other syntactical possibilities, see esp. Abbott, *Ephesians*, 61f.; also Best, *Ephesians*^{2}, 257–9, who posits an ambivalent character for the phrase 'in his flesh': 'We have taken "in his flesh" as parenthetical, indicating where and how the action of the participles is achieved. It thus carries the same significance as blood in v. 13 and cross in v. 16' (259).

[106] That the source of hostility between Jew and Gentile can be found in the exclusive attitudes of the Jews toward the Gentiles and best explained against the backcloth of the Jewish perspective as it is depicted in vv. 11–12 is a point missed by most commentators, e.g., Lincoln, *Ephesians*, 141; Moritz, *Mystery*, 40–1; Gnilka, *Epheserbrief*, 140; Caird, *Letters*, 58–9; Martin, *Reconciliation*, 185–7; Best, *Ephesians*^{2}, who demurs: 'Yet is "enmity" not too strong a term to designate the difference between Gentile and Jew?'

in an inter-ethnic sense. It sums up the consequences of exclusion[107] and therefore the absence of amity or goodwill towards the ethnic 'other' and of a solidarity factor between two ethnic groups.[108]

The point of central importance, however, is presumably the belief that a wall-less community, or, better, a community without invidious walls within it, can only be erected when the enmity that signifies the social distance between Jew and Gentile is invalidated. I suggest that the author uses the expression 'nullifying the enmity by his flesh' to make a word-play (*paronomasia*) on 'flesh', which is closely associated with the source of enmity between Jew and Gentile: the 'flesh' (cf. 'Gentiles in the *flesh*', v. 11a; the 'foreskin', v. 11b; the 'circumcision in the *flesh*', v. 11c; cf. Gal. 6.12–13), which served as one of the most explicit boundary markers, marking off the Jews from the Gentiles, and the symbol of alienation between the two human groups, is now destroyed by Christ by his own 'flesh' (= body) on the cross.[109] One cannot rule out the

[107] See also Plutarch, who writes: 'A government which has not had to bear with envy or jealous rivalry or contention – emotions most productive of enmity (ἔχθρα) – has not hitherto existed' (*Inim. util.*, 86C). Enmity is often seen as the inevitable result of internecine conflict in ancient political philosophy. Plato, *Resp.* 1.351C–E, writes: 'For factions . . . are the outcome of injustice, and *hatreds* and internecine conflicts, but justice brings oneness of mind and love.' Dio writes: 'I consider it better for men in general, and not merely for you, both to refrain from entering lightly into an *enmity* which is not extremely necessary and so by every means possible to put to an end those *enmities* already existing, recognizing that the damage resulting from quarrelling with any people is greater than the loss incident to the *reconciliation*. For any *peace*, so they say, is better than war, and any friendship is far better than *enmity*, not only individually for our families, but also collectively for our cities. For *peace and concord* have never damaged at all these who have employed them, whereas it would be surprising if *enmity* and contentiousness were not very deadly, very mighty evils' (*Or.* 40.25–6). He concludes in *Or.* 40.34: 'For the fruit of enmity (ἔχθρας) is most bitter of all and most stinging, just as, in my view, its opposite, the fruit of goodwill (εὐνοίη), is most palatable and profitable.' Enmity and reconciliation are themes that belong to the same domain of discourse, see, e.g., Dio, who writes: 'That the reconciliation will be profitable for you two cities when it is achieved, and that the strife (στάσις) still going on has not been profitable for you down to the present moment, that so many blessings will be yours as a result of concord (ὁμόνοια), and that so many evils now are yours because of enmity (ἔχθρας)' (*Or.* 38.39). Dio deplored enmity/hostility as most baneful in his political speech to the Apameians (on concord): 'Any *enmity* towards any people is an irksome, grievous thing . . . But the works of hatred, indeed, of *enmity* are painful and grievous everywhere. The presence of an enemy is a grievous thing, whether in a serious business or in the midst of good cheer, a painful thing to behold and painful to recall, but beyond all things most baneful to experience' (*Or.* 41.11, 14).

[108] There is no compelling reason, *contra* Lincoln, *Ephesians*, 142, and others, for us to believe that the term 'enmity' would have referred in the traditional material to the enmity caused by the hostile 'powers' in the cosmos, and now refers to the hostility between Jews and Gentiles that is bound up with the law; see above, n. 106.

[109] *Contra* Käsemann, *Leib*, 139–42, who understands the 'flesh' here as the 'power of matter'. He concludes that the φραγμός originally referred to the 'flesh' in Gnosis, and

possibility that here the 'flesh' on the cross also makes a *contemptuous* pun with the 'flesh' that excludes.

To recap what we have said so far, it should by now be clear that the enmity which Christ abolished 'by his *flesh*' (i.e., on the cross) is closely associated with the 'flesh' by which Jews used to make a clear-cut ethnic and national division between Jews and Gentiles.[110] Christ's death has put to an end the *significance* which Jews had laid on the 'flesh' which accentuates the *inaccessibility* of one ethnic group to Israel and Israel's God-given blessings and becomes therefore the source of contention and antagonism/enmity between two human groups. To say that the enmity is abolished as part of Christ's peace-making mission means also that the old Jew/Gentile polarity based on the boundary-defining marker in the 'flesh' is now made ineffective.

4.4.4 τὸν νόμον τῶν ἐντολῶν ἐν δόγμασιν (vv. 14d–15a)

We have already mentioned that the phrase 'the enmity in his flesh' (v. 14d) is more closely linked with καταργήσας in terms of syntax than with the previous clause.[111] The collocation of the 'enmity' (understood as ethnic antagonism) with 'the law of commandments in ordinances' means that the author has placed the 'enmity' and the 'law' on a par. There is a kind of telescoping in the expression – the law is made ineffective by the nullifying of the enmity that is closely associated with it.

Much has been said in scholarly discussions about the 'law' as the object of destruction: how much of the 'law' is abolished? Over this issue scholarly opinions are widely divided. The maximalist interpretation claims that the author has issued a forthright statement of the abolition

that the 'flesh' is the cosmic wall that separates God and man. The immediate context of vv. 14ff., however, does not lend support to the ingenious interpretation of Käsemann, cf. vv. 11a, 11c. Equally unconvincing is the suggestion of Robinson, *Body*, 18 who argues that the 'flesh' refers to Christ who broke down the wall separating heaven and earth by his incarnation. Smith, 'Heresy', 86–93, writes that the 'flesh' denotes the circumcision of Christ. Smith's interpretation seems to be based more on his theory that Ephesians should be read in the light of Colossians (i.e., 1.22) than on an actual reading of the 'flesh' in our given text.

[110] See also Phil. 3.2–5; also Rom. 2.28; Gal. 6.12–13.

[111] *Pace* Schnackenburg, *Ephesians*, 114 who asserts that the dative phrase 'in his own flesh' must be taken to belong with v. 15a (i.e., 'abolishing the law . . . in his flesh'), while 'the enmity' must be left with what precedes it (i.e., 'and who destroyed the dividing wall, the enmity', v. 14c). Since there is agreement in the (accusative) case of the 'enmity' and the 'law', it is just possible that the whole phrase of v. 14d is to be seen together with v. 15a.

of the law *per se*: the law, with its various commandments and statutes, forms the dividing obstacle between Jew and Gentile and must therefore be nullified.[112] The minimalist interpretation, however, contends that the author does not speak of the law 'without reservation' as the object of destruction, but only a particular kind of law, one related to the dividing wall which separated Jews and Gentiles.[113] What is abolished, therefore, is that which is associated, but not identified, with the whole law. As the debate regarding the law as the object of destruction rumbles on, it also becomes apparent that a fundamental aspect of the 'law' remains curiously unexplored in recent studies: if there are no overt references

[112] So Lindemann, *Epheserbrief*, who writes: 'Der Verfasser des Epheserbriefes dagegen spricht ohne jede Einschränkung von der restlosen Beseitigung des Gesetzes durch Christus' (50). Lindemann's view is revived in Räisänen, *Law*, 205. See also Gnilka, *Epheserbrief*, who concludes that the law as the enmity has a double effect: 'Das Gesetz richtete aber auch Feindschaft mit Gott auf. Die Feindschaft in dieser doppelten Auswirkung, als Spaltung der Menschheit und als Loslösung der Menschen von Gott, hat Christus vernichtet' (141); Mußner, 'Modell', who writes: 'Nur in Eph 2,15 wird in einer aktivischen Konstruktion gesagt, daß *Christus* "das Gesetz vernichtet hat": eine äußerst radikale Formulierung, aber ganz gestaltet aus der Kenntnis paulinischer Rechtfertigungslehre heraus' (328). In *Epheser*, 77, Mußner recognises that the abolishing of the law through the death of Christ is a theme not reflected in earlier letters of Paul, but reads our present text as the 'consequence of Paul's theology of the law': '. . . daß Christus das Gesetz mit allen seinen Verordnungen »zunichte gemacht« habe, sagt Paulus nie. Aber diese radikalisierende Formulierung liegt letztlich doch in *der Konsequenz der paulinischen Gesetzestheologie*' (italics mine); cf. Mußner, *Epheser*, 82. Percy, *Probleme*, 279–80, concludes that the law is the means of salvation for the Jews, and as such was the obstacle that stood between Jews and Gentiles; cf. McKelvey, *Temple*, 118–120; Gärtner, *Temple*, 60–5; Wolter, *Rechtfertigung*, 62–73; Lincoln, *Ephesians*, 142; cf. Lincoln, 'Church', 611–12; Bruce, *Ephesians*, 294; Dahl, 'Gentiles', 36; Robinson, *Ephesians*, 161; Beare, 'Ephesians', 656; Best, *Ephesians*^{2}, 260; Mitton, *Ephesians*, 106; Smith, 'One', 41; Schlatter, *Briefe*, 185; Schnackenburg, *Ephesians*, 112, 115; Moritz, *Mystery*, 29–30; Pokorný, *Epheser*, 123; Sellin, 'Genitive', here 91; Köster, *Introduction*, 270; Martin, *Reconciliation*, 174, 176; Turner, 'Ephesians', 1231; Schweizer, 'Christianity', here 250; Roloff, *Kirche*, 242; Thielman, *Paul*, 226; Kruse, *Paul*, 262–4, esp. 264; Moo, 'Law', esp. 333, 367; Patzia, *Ephesians*, 193–4; Kittel, 'δόγμα', esp. 231; Walter, 'δόγμα', 340.

[113] See, e.g., Barth, *Ephesians 1–3*, 264, 290 who holds that only one specific sense of the Law is meant: the Law has created and demonstrated a separation of the Jews from the Gentiles. What is abolished, therefore, is the divisive function of the law but not the law itself: 'He has abolished the Law (that is, only) the commandments (expressed) in statutes' (264); cf. Porter, *Καταλλάσσω*, 186; Schlier, *Epheser*, 125–6 who holds that the primary reference in v. 15a is to the casuistic, legalistic interpretation of the 'law'. He argues that it is the *interpretation* of the law, not the law itself, which was synonymous with the 'dividing wall' and the 'enmity' it created. Roetzel, 'Relations', reads v. 15 in the light of Philonic speculation: 'What is advised and desired in Eph is not the abolition of Torah as Israel's story, but the abrogation of the principle of the Law seen in the commandments. The addresse[e]s who were conformed to a heavenly existence in Christ no longer needed the commandments. Living without the commandments would be seen as a sign of the heavenly existence' (87). Cf. also Grassi, 'Ephesians', 346; Patzia, *Ephesians*, 195.

to the 'law' elsewhere in our epistle except here in v. 15a (as Lincoln claims), can we then speak of the law in correlative terms, namely of the tie-in between the law and other fundamental and defining features of Jewish identity (such as circumcision, v. 11, etc.), and of covert or oblique references to it? Does our earlier discussion of Jewish ethnocentrism have any significant bearing upon the notion of the 'law'? Clearly however something of a fresh look at the old question is essential – especially a fresh look which sets the question about the law firmly against the backcloth of a Jewish perspective. But before we return to this, a brief comment on the phrase 'the law of commandments in the ordinances' is now in order.

That the 'law' and the 'commandments' are closely linked is widely acknowledged.[114] It is safe to say that the reference here is purely an echo of a typical Jewish expression for the Mosaic law (e.g., Exod. 24.12; Deut. 30.10; Jos. 22.5; 1 Kgs. 2.3; 2 Kgs. 17.13; 2 Chr. 14.3; Ps. 118, passim; Dan. 3.29, LXX; Sir. 45.5, 17; 1 Esd. 8.7; Baruch 4.12–13; *T. Dan* 5.1; *T. Benj.* 10.3; perhaps, *Jub.* 24.11; 1QSa[a] 1.11; CD 13.5[?]; 14.8).[115] As regards the term δόγματα,[116] it occurs in the Pauline letters only here and in Colossians 2.14.[117] In Colossians, the term echoes primarily Jewish concerns over purity: 'Do not handle, Do not taste, Do not touch' (2.14–22, esp. 21).[118] However, the term is used quite often in early Judaism, denoting the authoritative, ancestral law of the Jews.[119] It should come

[114] See, e.g., Schlier, *Epheser*, 125; Lincoln, *Ephesians*, 142; Best, *Ephesians*², 259–60; Sellin, 'Genitive', here 90–1; Chadwick, 'Ephesians', 859c; Schrenk, 'ἐντολή', here 546, 552; Limbeck, 'ἐντολή'.

[115] We have not found conjunctions of a similar kind between the two terms in the extant Greek literature, but see Matt. 22.36–40, where both our terms occur in a conversation between a Pharisee and Jesus. In Paul's earlier letters, both the 'commandment' and the 'law' are sometimes placed on the par, used interchangeably as virtual synonyms: see, e.g., Rom. 7.8–13; 13.9; see also Heb. 7.5; 9.19; 1 Esd. 8.7. The author of Ephesians may well have assumed that the 'commandments' were included in the 'law' as its hyponym, i.e., the 'commandments' *unilaterally* entail the 'law' and, by the same token, the 'law' is a superordinate of the 'commandments'; otherwise, our phrase may be read as a 'verbal genitive', i.e., the commanding law. See further Cruse, *Lexical Semantics*, esp. 88–9.

[116] It is possible to argue that the preposition ἐν is in part influenced by Semitic בּ; see further Zerwick, *BG*, no. 116.

[117] Elsewhere in the NT, the term occurs only in Acts 16.4, denoting the (apostolic) 'decrees' or the resolutions of the early church in Jerusalem. The noun is well attested in inscriptions and papyri, in its technical application to imperial edicts: cf. Luke 2.1; Acts 17.7; see esp. Horsley, 'δόγμα'.

[118] The verbal form of our term (δογματίζεσθε) occurs in Col. 2.20, denoting that the Gentile recipients at Colossae were either being lured by or attracted to the Jews who wished to impose their own 'teachings' on them. See further Dunn, 'Apologia', here 164–5; cf. Dunn, *Colossians and Philemon*, esp. 164–6, 188–90.

[119] See, e.g., 3 Macc. 1.3: 'Dositheneus . . . a Jew by birth who later changed his religion and apostatised from the ancestral *traditions*' (Δοσίθεος . . . τὸ γένος Ιουδαῖος,

as no surprise that the term δόγματα, which our author collocates with 'the law of commandments', is to be seen as closely associated with the (Mosaic) law.[120] The 'ordinances' denote the sub-set of the Mosaic law, i.e., 'the law of commandments *in the realm of ordinances*'. These 'ordinances' are the 'rules of the law' (or halakic rulings) which regulate and control the conduct of devout Jews (cf. 11QT 49.5–50.8, 17).[121]

A survey of the Jewish background of this expression in v. 15a has led me to believe that there is a likelihood that the author may well have been making his point by referring to the insiders' code for what was understood within Judaism as distinctive of Israel, and conceding from the Jewish perspective that the law of the Jews (himself included) was involved in the ethnic enmity.[122] The upshot of this reading is inevitably that the author's notion of the law must be understood as altogether conciliatory: it reflects the way in which a Jew is willing to acknowledge before his Gentile readers that the law has become indeed one of the constitutive elements in causing divisions and tensions between two ethnic groups and that its divisive function should therefore be removed. His estimate of the law contains shades of *admission*, understood in our present context as an acknowledgement of the fact that the law has played a substantial role in leading to the strains between two ethnic groups rather than as an overt attack on the law itself, although this point is missed by most commentators.[123]

ὕστερον δὲ μεταβαλὼν τὰ νόμιμα καὶ τῶν πατρίων δογμάτων ἀπηλλοτριωμένοι κτλ.). In 4 Macc. 10.2, the same term is used to denote simply 'the teachings [*sc.* from the Torah]'. See also Philo, *Leg.* 1.55: 'the holy precepts'; *Spec.* 1.269, the 'sacred *principles* of divine philosophy', i.e., the Torah. Josephus, *A. J.* 15.136: 'the noblest of our *doctrines* and the holiest of our laws from the messengers sent by God'; *C. Ap.* 1.42: 'the *decrees* [*sc.* the laws and the allied documents] of God'; *B. J.* 2.142: 'the doctrine of the Essenes'; *Sib. Or.* 3.656: '[The king] does not do all these things by his private plans but in obedience to the noble *teachings* of the great God'. See further BAGD, s.v., 1.

120 See also Schweizer, 'Christianity', here 250.

121 *Pace* Moo, 'Law', 367 who assumes that the 'law' in v. 15, by definition, demands meritorious works, concluding that 'a wider reference to the Law is certainly possible'.

122 *Contra* Schnackenburg, *Ephesians*, 114, who concludes: 'For Judaism the Torah was a divine protecting-fence of cosmic relevance, but *from a Christian point of view* it loses its importance and is in fact shattered as the "Law of the Commandments" by the event of the Cross' (italics mine); cf. Stuhlmacher, 'Peace', esp. 189; Lincoln, *Ephesians*, 141–2; cf. Lincoln, 'Theology', 106.

123 Martin, *Reconciliation*, is not alone in seeing v. 15 as the author's polemic against the law when he writes: '[The author] has a more sinister understanding of Torah as an alienating force driving Jews and Gentiles into mutual animosity' (174). Sellin, 'Genitive', writes: 'Die »Trennwand des Zaunes« (2, 14) zwischen den »Nahen« und den »Fernen« besteht gerade im *Gesetz* als ganzem (mit seinen Geboten und Vorschrifen) . . .' (91, italics his); cf. Schnackenburg, *Ephesians*, 114–15; Schlier, *Epheser*, 125–6; Stuhlmacher,

If the *Jewish* law has become an obstacle that stands between Jew and Gentile and should therefore be 'rendered powerless' (as Moo says), what more can we say about the precise nature of this obstacle and, therefore, about the law?[124] There are at least two salient factors that need to be considered.

(a) As has already been noted, some of the most obvious correlates of the law have already been adumbrated in vv. 11–12, such as (the observance of) circumcision and the 'covenants' (of promise). Covenant, law, Jewish ethnic identity, circumcision were mutually interdependent categories each inconceivable without the other.[125] Given that the tie-in between circumcision and the law is self-evident, i.e., bodily circumcision is understood by most devout Jews as the key expression of the law or the first act of Torah-observance,[126] it should come as no surprise that the Jews who had wished to maintain their distinctive status and loyalty by their Torah-observance could easily turn the God-given law into an ethnic-defining or boundary marker (cf. *Arist.* 139–42).[127] What is at stake, however, is not the law *per se* but the law as the Jews had used it to consolidate their Jewish identity. It had become a tool of estrangement in its too close identification with matters of the 'flesh' ('Gentile in the flesh', v. 11a; the 'uncircumcision' (lit. the 'foreskin'), v. 11b) and must therefore be abolished 'in his [Christ's] flesh' (v. 14d; see above my exegesis on v. 11).

(b) Consistent with our previous point is the way in which the 'law' is associated with the 'body politic of Israel'. For scholars who read vv. 14ff.

'Peace', 189; Lindemann, *Aufhebung*, 161; Gnilka, *Epheserbrief*, 141; Pokorný, *Epheser*, 123; Thomson, *Chiasmus*, 84–115; Kirby, *Pentecost*, 156; Giavini, 'Structure'; Bailey, *Poet*, 63; Turner, *Style*, 98. Much of the discussion of the law has suffered from taking our 'law' expression out of context by trying to read it in the light of the earlier letters of Paul: see, e.g., Lincoln, *Ephesians*, who writes: 'We can say that at this point Ephesians is in line with the clear stress on discontinuity in regard to the law's validity that can be found in Paul' (143); also Mußner, *Epheser*, 77. For a trenchant criticism of this approach, see esp. Porter, *Καταλλάσσω*, 186.

[124] That the 'law' has become an issue in Ephesians has been underplayed by Kitchen, 'Status'. Kitchen's assertion is that 'the law is not a great issue for the writer of Ephesians, even though his primary theological concern is with the relationship between Jews and Gentiles *in the church*' (italics mine, 145).

[125] Dunn, 'Circumcision', here 305; see also Mußner, *Epheser*, 75.

[126] Dunn, 'Circumcision', 297; Sanders, *Paul*, 544.

[127] See also Mußner, *Epheser*, who concludes that Jew and Gentile are divided in religious terms: 'die monotheistisch, gesetzlich eingestellten Juden – die polytheistisch, »gesetzlos« lebenden Heiden' (75). Schnackenburg, *Ephesians*, 109 reads Eph. 2.12 in the light of Rom. 9.4–5, and concludes that the *politeia* of Israel seems to combine four privileges: sonship, glory (the presence of God), the giving of the law, and the worship, i.e., privileges that are constituents of Israel's life as God's elected people; cf. Schnackenburg, 'Politeia', esp. 469–71; Rese, 'Church', here 26–7.

as an independent unit or 'excursus' (Tachau, Schlier, Conzelmann and others), it is not surprising to see that they have very little to say as regards the tie-in between the law and the 'body politic of Israel'. However, it will prove fruitful if we propose a different set of questions: is it possible to speak of the 'body politic of Israel' without taking into account the Jews who are within it as discharging their obligations in accordance with their own ancestral law(s)? Is it possible not to assume that the law which regulates the boundary-defining ritual such as bodily circumcision also acts on this *Jewish* 'body politic'? I suggest that the 'law' and the Jewish 'body politic of Israel' are mutually interdependent, each inconceivable without the other. The remaining question is: can our claims be substantitated by historical proof?

It must be said at the outset that the Jewish body politic sustained by the law which in turn *regulates* behaviours of its members is a notion well attested by Hellenistic Judaism. Philo, for example, has opined that the Jews 'were born in a godly body politic (ἐν πολιτείᾳ φιλοθέῳ) and nurtured under the *laws* which incite to every virtue' (*Spec.* 1.314; cf. *Virt.* 102–8, 212, 216, 219; *Spec.* 1.51–2; 4.178). Philo's statement suggests that the Jewish body politic and law-observance are inseparable. Indeed this is the shared 'body politic' of the Jews. It is a community of communities which cannot be confined to a narrowly parochial sense. It is safe to say that this is an ethnically based 'body politic' and the common religious observance by its members in accordance with the laws are essential expressions of the community's social cohesion.[128] To this we must also add that the correlation between the law and the πολιτεία came to the forefront during the Maccabean crisis, when the Jews were exhorted by their leader 'to fight bravely to the death for the laws, temple, city, country, and *commonwealth*' (ἀγωνίσασθαι μέχρι θανάτου περὶ νόμων, ἱεροῦ, πόλεως, πατρίδος, πολιτείας, 2 Macc. 13.14, NRSV;[129] cf. 4 Macc. 3.20). It may well be that the Maccabean crisis aided the devout Jews to cement the association between their laws and πολιτεία as expressing their distinctive Jewish identity and marking out the boundary between themselves and the intruders (including the renegades!).

One can assume that the light the foregoing documents throw on the notion of the law is invaluable. Suffice it to say that the key to

[128] See in particular Judge, *Pattern*, esp. ch. 2 ('Republican Institution: Politeia'), 18–29, here 25.

[129] A slightly different translation is found in Zeitlin, *2 Maccabees*, which reads: 'Judah handed over the onus of responsibility for the decision to the Creator of the world, and exhorting his men to fight nobly even unto death for the laws, temple, city, fatherland and *state* . . .' (italics mine).

understanding the meaning of the law in v. 15a is the recognition that the author of Ephesians may have conceived of the law and the Jewish body politic as being woven deep in the fabric of Jewish life.[130] It is possible, therefore, to argue that the law has indeed played a substantial role in consolidating the Jewish 'body politic' by preventing it from disintegration. When we add also to our foregoing analysis other correlates or constitutive bases of the Jewish body politic, such as circumcision and the covenants of the promise, hope and monotheism, we have evidence to be confident that the law and the 'body politic of Israel', alongside their correlates, are fundamentally defining features of Jewish identity, that each cannot be fully appreciated without taking account of the fact that both are perceived by the Jews as boundary/identity markers, reinforcing the Jewish sense of distinctiveness and marking them off from the Gentiles.[131] The consequences of this for our analysis of v. 15 have also become obvious: one can conclude firmly that the author of Ephesians does not single out the law (Torah) as the sole obstacle that stands between Jew and Gentile, nor does he speak of the law without reservation (*contra* Lindemann, Räisänen, Mußner and others). Rather, he speaks of the law in correlative terms, signalling to his Gentile readers that the law to which the Jews rallied has marked out the Jews (i.e., the 'circumcision') as the elect of God and united them in their ethnically based 'body politic', but has in turn become a boundary marker, aiding the Jews to distance themselves from the Gentiles.

In short, the author has spoken critically of the law, but this by no means amounts to a personal attack on the law. Rather, he is speaking from an insider's perspective on the law which Jews had deemed significant but used as an instrument of division in order to reinforce their distinctive identity (e.g., the 'circumcision' and the 'uncircumcision') and the 'body politic' as based on a particular *ethnos*. This, the enmity between Jew and Gentile, lies not with the the Torah *per se* but with the human attitude that

[130] See also Trebilco, *Communities*, esp. 13–19. The idea that a πολιτεία is sustained by the 'laws' is also found in the writings of the Graeco-Roman world, see, e.g., Demosthenes, who writes: 'For if any of you care to inquire what is the motive-power (τὸ αἴτιον) that calls together the Council, draws the people together into the Assembly, fills the law courts, makes the old officials resign readily to the new, and enables the whole life of the state (πόλις) to be carried on and preserved, he will find that it is the laws (τοὺς νόμους) and the obedience that all men yield to the laws; since, if once they were done away and every man were given licence to do as he liked, not only does the body-politic (πολιτεία) vanish, but our life would not differ from that of the beasts of the field' (*1–2 Aristog.*, 1.20, tr. slightly modified); cf. Polybius, *Hist.* 6.4.8.3; Plutarch, *Solon* 16.3.1ff.; cf. Plutarch, *Praec. ger. res publ.* 783B, 791C; *Un. rep. dom.*, 826B–F; Plutarch, *Gen. Socr.* 576E. See further Aalders, *Plutarch*, 37.

[131] See esp. Barth, 'Boundaries', esp. 15–16; also Dunn, *Romans 1–8*, lxix–lxx.

perverted the gifts of God into signs of separation and exclusiveness. He assumes that the law, and in particular 'the ordinances' which are closely associated with it, had ordered and regulated the *Jewish* life, enhancing the distinctiveness and separation of Jews from Gentiles. However, the law which has been expropriated to consolidate the ethnically based 'body politic of Israel' and other ethnic and religious boundaries on which Jewish identity as the people of God depended, and which therefore occasioned ethnic enmity, is now abolished through the death of Christ.

4.4.5 ἵνα τοὺς δύο κτίσῃ ἐν αὐτῷ εἰς ἕνα καινὸν ἄνθρωπον (v. 15b)

As noted earlier, the two ἵνα-clauses in vv. 15b–16b are arranged in the form of *parallelismus membrorum*.[132] They are meant to emphasise in a complementary manner the overriding purpose of the reconciliatory work of Christ. The way in which this projected purpose is arrived at is conveyed respectively via two (circumstantial) participle clauses: 'making peace' (ποιῶν εἰρήνην, v. 15c), and 'abolishing the enmity through it' (ἀποκτείνας τὴν ἔχθραν ἐν αὐτῷ, v. 16b). The motivating force behind these purpose-clauses, as we shall see, is the author's unequivocal emphasis on Christ who integrates (in principle) two ethnic groups into one unified whole (i.e., 'one new man', v. 15b; 'one body', v. 16a; 'in one spirit', v. 18).

Admittedly, our investigation of the meaning of 'one new man' means that we are opening up immediately the old tension that crops up from the designation itself. What does the 'one new man' language denote? Does it stand for both Jew and Gentile? Does it refer to Christ[133] or Christ as the 'corporate personality' into whom Jew and Gentile are incorporated?[134] Is the 'one new man' constituted by the abolition or denial of differences between Jew and Gentile? Is the author suggesting some sort of

[132] The ἵνα-subjunctive verb-καί-subjunctive verb construction occurs quite often in the Pauline corpus. Despite the fact that there are various intervening words, the construction is not invalidated: see, e.g., Eph. 6.22; Rom. 3.19; 15.31; 16.2; 1 Cor. 7.5; 2 Cor. 9.5; 2.10; 3.8–9; Phil. 2.10–11; 3.8–9; Col. 4.8; 2 Thess. 1.11; 4.17; Titus 1.5; also Matt. 19.13; 26.4.

[133] So Best, *Body*, 153 who concludes that 'the one new man is not a corporate personality but a genuine *individual*' (italics mine).

[134] So Conzelmann, *Epheser*, 101, who writes: 'Die beiden sind eines in dem – als Urmensch vorgestellten – Erlöser, ja, in ihm sind sie nicht nur eine*s*, sondern eine*r*, der neue Mensch' (101); cf. Lindemann, *Aufhebung*, 167; Fischer, *Tendenz*, 133–4; Schlatter, *Briefe*, 187; Percy, *Probleme*, 266 n. 16; Gnilka, *Epheserbrief*, 142; Schlier, *Epheser*, 135; Merklein, *Christus*, 42; Bruce, *Ephesians*, 299–300; Lincoln, *Ephesians*, 143–4; cf. Lincoln, 'Theology', 94; Allan, 'In Christ', esp. 60–1. The theory of 'corporate personality' has come under severe criticism in recent years: see esp. Rogerson, 'Personality'; cf. Rogerson, *Anthropology*, 46–65; Porter, 'Myths', here 294, 298.

mystical union between Christ and the 'new man',[135] or that the 'new man' is created 'in/by him', being shaped and governed *by* Christ and his actions?[136] Are we to regard the 'one new man' as denoting a new type of character, neither Jewish nor Gentile but a Christian 'third race' which transcends the old divisions?[137] Does the author wish to speak of the notion of restitution, i.e., the recovery (including the glory) of God's first creation?[138] Different answers have been offered to these questions over the years.[139] My own inclination is that the notion of '*one* new man' can be best understood against the backcloth of ethnic enmity: it is a society-redefining metaphor which stands in stark contrast to the *Jewish* conception about mankind and the social ramifications that follow from it. According to this notion, circumcision and lack of circumcision summed up the difference between Jew and Gentile, so that mankind could be readily split into two separate categories (τοὺς δύο).[140] Indeed, one cannot truly appreciate the thrust of the notion of 'one new man' without reference to this perspective.[141] The *Jewish* perspective, and its *social*

[135] So Mußner, *Epheser*, 81 who suggests that the union of the new man is created *at baptism*; Mußner, *Christus*, 94ff.; Pokorný, *Epheser*, 123.

[136] The preposition ἐν can be taken as having an instrumental usage which anwers to our 'by' or 'by means of'. See further Houlden, 'Christ', who concludes that v. 15f. is far from supporting an idea of incorporation and that it 'sets Christ in distinction from the people whom he brought into being' (269); Allan, 'In Christ', 60–1; Moule, *Idiom*, 80; Porter, *Idioms*, 157; Roberts, 'Instrumental ἐν'. The tension in the meaning of v. 15b is highlighted by Dunn in his essay, 'Body', 152.

[137] So Chadwick, 'Absicht', 147; Gnilka, *Epheserbrief*, 139; Houlden, 'Christ', 272; Lincoln, *Ephesians*, 144; cf. Lincoln, 'Church', 616; Lincoln, 'Theology', 94.

[138] So Dahl, *Christ*, 422–43.

[139] For a brief history of the interpretation, see Rader, *Hostility*, esp. 222ff.

[140] The interpretation of the 'two' (τοὺς δύο) in the sense of two categories of people, i.e., Jews and Gentiles, fits perfectly well in our present context. See also Schlier, *Epheser*, 123 n. 1; Abbott, *Ephesians*, 65; Merklein, 'Komposition', 85. Lincoln, *Ephesians*, 128–9 suggests that the passage has a cosmic context in the 'original' material, and that the two entities (i.e., τὰ ἀμφότερα, v. 14a; τοὺς δύο, v. 15a; τοὺς ἀμφοτέρους, v. 16a) refer to the two parts of the cosmos, heaven and earth. Nothing, however, has made the acceptance of Lincoln's hypothesis mandatory. The suggestion of Lindemann, *Aufhebung*, 166, that it is perhaps possible that a neuter τὰ δύο stands in the original traditional material instead of the masculine τοὺς δύο, which the author now changes at v. 16a–18 for the sake of adjusting his own argument, is not convincing; cf. Lindemann, *Epheserbrief*, 50–3, in which Lindemann reaches for an agnostic conclusion: 'Möglicherweise ist die Frage, wen oder was der Verfasser mit den »Zwei«, den »beiden«, den »Fernen und Nahen« im einzelnen gemeint hat, gar nicht beantwortbar' (53).

[141] *Contra* Merklein, *Christus*, esp. 23, 76, 99 who concedes that vv. 11–12 set Jew and Gentile in contrast but concludes that 'the antithesis is established from the perspective of the Church and is substantiated also in the Church' (23); Best, 'Judaism'; Schnackenburg, 'Politeia', 482 ('. . . der Verfasser vom christlichen Standpunkt aus für belanglos hält . . .'); Schnackenburg, 'Exegese'; Schnackenburg, *Ephesians*, 115–16; Lindemann, *Aufhebung*,

implications, can be summed up as follow: the Jews were *the* 'circumcision' – despite the fact that there were other peoples who also practised circumcision (cf. Herodotus, *Hist.* 2.104.2–3; Strabo, *Geog.* 17.2.5, etc.);[142] only the 'circumcision'/Jews belonged to the 'body politic *of Israel*' (v. 12a); only the Jews were the legitimate heirs of the 'covenants of the promise' (v. 12b); and only the Jews 'have' hope, and (one) God (v. 12, cf. v. 2).

The consequence that follows from the attitude mentioned above is that the Gentiles,[143] by definition, are marginalised as regards Israel's various privileges and can be slandered on this basis as being the 'have nots' – in terms of hope and of the one God who has chosen Israel as his people (v. 12c; cf. vv. 1–2; 4.4, 6). I believe this Jewish perspective and the attitude embedded in it provide the best explanation for the inherent imbalance of ethnic and religious privileges and for the social distance between Jews and Gentiles (vv. 14b–15a). *That* is the issue which the

147; cf. Lindemann, 'Bemerkungen', here 249–50; Rese, 'Vorzüge'; cf. Rese, 'Church'; Lincoln, 'Church', 608–10; Lincoln, 'Theology', 93–4, 106, 132–3. Although Lincoln is fully aware of the Gentiles' pre-Christian past in terms of their status as Gentiles in relation to Israel's privileged position in God's purposes for salvation, he has failed to account for the Gentiles' defective status as being closely associated with the Jews' practice of estranging ethnocentrism.

[142] We should point out that Jews were not the only people who demarcated their own world from others: see, e.g., Plato, who underscored the *Greek* perspective in his attack on those who would separate mankind into two separate categories, namely Greeks and barbarians (*Pol.* 262C–E). Plato discusses whether Greeks and non-Greeks must be seen as parts (μέρος) of the genus (γένος) men or quantitative parts of the aggregate mankind (*Pol.* 262E). Strabo, *Geog.* 1.4.9, writes: 'Now, towards the end of his [*sc.* Erathosthenes'] treatise – after withholding praise from those who divide the whole multitude of mankind into *two* groups, *Greeks and barbarians* (τούς δίχα διαιρροῦντες ἅπαν τό τῶν ἀνθρωπων πλῆθος εἴς τε Ἕλληνας καὶ βαρβάρους κτλ.), and also from those who advised Alexander to treat the Greeks as friends and the barbarians as enemies – he goes on to say that it would be better to make such divisions according to good qualities and bad qualities; for not only are many of the Greeks bad, but many of the barbarians are refined . . .'. See also Plutarch, *Alex. fort.* 329A–D. See further Avi-Yonah, *Hellenism*, 136: 'The Egyptians, the Jews, and the Greeks are the only three nations of antiquity who, to our knowledge, drew a dividing line between themselves and all other people.' Smith, 'One', 39, argues that 'deeply imbedded within Greek philosophy of the classical and hellenistic periods are traditions which concern unity, duality, opposites, harmony, the δέσμος, etc . . . These traditions . . . have been taken up by hellenistic Judaism and early Christianity.' See also Haarhoff, *Stranger*, 51–9; Baldry, *Unity*, 82; Balsdon, *Aliens*, 67; Hall, *Barbarian*, 3–13; Thompson, *Blacks*, 57–85.

[143] It is not necessary for us to assume that the term 'Gentile' denotes the Greeks or Romans. What is important is the *unjewishness* of other ethnic groups from the Jewish perspective. See also Stanley, 'Conflict', who writes: 'The use of the term "Gentiles" (ἀλλοφύλοι or ἔθνη) to designate all non-Jews represents a "social construction of reality" developed by a particular people-group (the Jews) in a concrete historical situation' (105); BAGD, s.v. ἔθνος, 2.

author of Ephesians wished to address in employing the language of 'one new man'. The Jewish tendency to divide or factionalise, rather than to integrate, needed to be faced down before one could possibly speak of the Gentiles' legitimate place in the people of God (see below my exegesis of vv. 19–22).[144] Thus, the nub of the issue is not so much that Jew and Gentile no longer exist as two ethnic groups of distinct background – the 'one new man' is not constituted by the abolition or denial of the differences between the two.[145] Still less is the author's interest in a Gnostic *Urmensch*.[146] Rather, at stake are the *social* implications embedded in the Jewish conception of humanity: the *Jews* had reinforced their identity as the people of God on the basis of the division between 'us'/the 'circumcision' and 'them'/the 'uncircumcision' and prevented the Gentiles from being part of the people of God. Surely a redefinition of the corporate identity of God's people against the self-understanding of the Jews was necessary, and the author introduced precisely the imagery of '*one* new man' to subvert the social implications embedded in the Jewish notion of humanity.[147] The '*one* new man' imagery – like other

[144] Barth is correct (in principle) when he argues that there is only one people of God and that Eph. 2.11–22 presents Israel as having continuing significance for the church. However, he has failed to account for the *ethnic* factor that prevents 'the naturalisation of the Gentiles' in the people of God: see his *Wall*, 115–27; Barth, *People*, 45–9; cf. Barth, *Ephesians 1–3*, 130–3.

[145] See also Campbell, *Gospel*, 110–14, here 114. *Contra* Best, *Body*, 154 who overstates his case: 'There are Jews and there are Gentiles; but the Jews that become Christians *lose their Jewishness* and are not Jewish Christians, and the Gentiles that become Christians *lose their Gentile-ness* and are not Gentile Christians; both are simply Christians – a third and new type of man distinct from the old twofold classification of Jew and Gentile. There are now three races of men, Jews, Gentiles, and Christians' (italics mine); cf. Chadwick, 'Absicht', 147; Lincoln, *Ephesians*, 143–4, et al. One must admit that the proponents of the theory of substitution have in the end denied inevitably the distinctive identity of the Jews.

[146] *Contra* Conzelmann, *Epheser*, who writes: 'daß Erlöser und Erlöste in den Substanz identisch sind' (100); cf. Fischer, *Tendenz*, 131–7; Lindemann, *Aufhebung*, 167.

[147] Although our author employed a different society-enhancing imagery in his argument, his language of oneness is not entirely novel. It occurs quite often in Greek literature, which reflects the notorious fact that Greek communities were bedevilled by tension between impulses to unity and impulses to separation. Plato, for example, had already spoken of a revised version of humanity, i.e., a 'single human flock' (ἀγέλης) – in a distant golden era when God became the shepherd of mankind – who are no longer divided into city-states and who do not possess wives and children among them (*Pol.* 274E, cf. Plato, *Leg.*, 680E). There can be little doubt that Plato did envisage the oneness of mankind at some point, although the possibility of its realisation in his own time was deemed highly unlikely. The same line of thought is probably echoed in Aristophanes, *Lys.*, 568–84, esp. 578–84, who writes: '[A]ll in one basket of love and of unity, citizens, visitors, strangers, and sojourners, all the entire, undivided community' – perhaps this is the earliest record of the Greek woman's perspective on the unity of 'humankind' (i.e., the Greeks). Plutarch, *Alex. fort.*, recounts that the Stoic founder Zeno has dreamt of a philosophic well-ordered society and told the Athenians that

imagery that enhances the oneness of Jew and Gentile (e.g., 'in one body', v. 16; 'in one spirit', v. 18) – shows the author's attempt to overcome the perspective which lays stress on the distinctiveness and separation of Jews from the rest of the world, and is never anything other than his own revised estimate of the 'us' – 'them' polarisation on the basis of a particular *ethnos*. He claims from a christological perspective (i.e., 'in Christ')[148] that the Jewish Messiah has opened up the possibility of a new beginning for humanity in his creation. Here the theme of creation is Jewish in character, echoing the story of the first humans in the Jewish scriptures (cf. vv. 9–10; 4.24),[149] a prominent theme in Paul's earlier letters (e.g., 1 Cor. 15.44–9; 2 Cor. 5.17; Gal. 6.14–15; Col. 3.9–10).

they should not live split up into city-states and demes: '[T]hat our life should not be based on cities or *peoples* each with its own view of right and wrong [i.e. polis-centrism], but we should regard *all humans* as our fellow-countrymen and fellow-citizens (πάντας ἀνθρώπους ἡγώμεθα δημότας καὶ πολίτας), and that there should be *one life* and *one order* (εἷς δὲ ἦ καὶ κόσμος), like that of a single flock on a *common* pasture feeding together under a *common* law' (329A–B); cf. 330D: 'But Alexander desired to render all upon the earth subject to *one* law of reason and *one* form of government and to reveal all humans as *one* people' (ἕνα δῆμον ἀνθρώπους ἅπαντας ἀποφῆναι βουλόμενος). We also encounter on numerous occasions the language of oneness as a society-enhancing metaphor in ancient political rhetoric, which endeavoured to overcome civil or interstatal discords. See, e.g., Dio, *Or.* 41.10, who spoke of the two strife-driven city-states of Prusa and Apameia as being almost '*one* community, *one* city' (εἷς ἐστε δῆμος καὶ μία πόλις) when he urged concord between the two; cf. Dio, *Or.* 39.5 (= *On Concord in Nicaea upon the Cessation of Civil Strife*). Philo, *Conf.* 170 also used the language of oneness to describe the entire human race before it divided into several groups, cf. *Conf.* 192. Baldry has summed up the ideal of the ancient Greek philosophers thus: 'The belief that φιλία, avoidance of στάσις, is the key to the lasting happiness of the communities, is implicit in nearly every Greek thinker and a commonplace in Plato (e.g. *Leg.* 628) and Aristotle (e.g. *Eth. nic.* 1155 ᵃ22)': see his 'State', esp. 12–15. In the NT, Paul's language of oneness in his earlier letters can certainly be placed on a par with the Greek writers, except that he *Christianises* the notion of oneness in a significant way, making it serve a different kind of community structure: see, e.g., Gal. 3.28; 1 Cor. 10.17; 12.13; Col. 3.11.

[148] The pleonastic 'in him' formula in v. 15b is probably another indication of typical Christian habit (v. 13a). Scholars who opt for an unaspirated form (ἐν αὑτῷ, 'in himself', e.g., UBS[2], but see UBS[4]!) often take the prepositional phrase as conveying a reflexive meaning; the variant ἐν ἑαυτῷ ('in himself') is also found in **D G**, et al. to strengthen the case for the latter sense, but see UBS[4]; NA[27]; Metzger, Textual *Commentary*, 602, 616. However, it is more likely that the 'in him' formula has a back reference to 'in Christ' (ἐν Χριστῷ Ἰησοῦ, v. 13a), and is set against other phrases such as τῷ καιρῷ ἐκείνῳ χωρὶς Χριστοῦ (v. 12) and νυνὶ δὲ . . . ἐν χριστῷ (v. 13a). Whether the usage of 'in him/Christ' is to be regarded as subjective, i.e., the believers as being in Christ (e.g., 3.17, cf. v. 12, τῷ καιρῷ ἐκείνῳ χωρὶς Χριστοῦ) or objective, i.e., the redemptive act which happens 'in' Christ (e.g., 2.13) is sometimes difficult to decide. In our present context, it probably denotes that both Jews and Gentiles have acquired a new corporate identity in the light of the (objective) reconciling work of Christ who inaugurated the eschatological era. See further Dunn, *TPA*, esp. 399–401; Fitzmyer, *Theology*, 90.

[149] The idea of a new creation has a classic place in Jewish literature: see, e.g., Ps. 89.47; 102.26; Isa. 43.19; 65.17ff.; 66.22; Sir. 17.1; *1* [Ethiop.] *Enoch* 72.1; 91.16; 1QS 4.22ff.; 1QH 13.11–12; *Jub.* 1.29; *Gen. R.* 39.14; *Targ. Jer.* 23.23; 2 Cor. 5.17; Gal. 6.14–15; 2 Pet.

In short, the belief that the cessation of ethnic enmity is the key to a harmonious (and healthy) community has prompted the author of Ephesians to introduce the idea of 'one new man', reinforcing a broad view of humanity which is undivided by artificial barriers or divisive (boundary) markers.[150] The 'one new man' denotes the new corporate identity or image of both Jew and Gentile. It focuses on the way in which both Jew and Gentile are to perceive themselves and to be presented to and perceived by others. Whereas the old paradigm used to define humanity by divisions, the author's '*one* new man' lays stress on the new way in which Jew and Gentile ought to relate to one another, claiming that the ethnic enmity between the two human groups is overcome (in principle!) as they are held together as a unified whole in Christ. The author's endeavour ought not to be read as a levelling and abolishing of all ethnic differences – Jews still remain Jews, and Gentiles – but as a repudiation of the ethnocentric perspective which perceives the differences as grounds for estrangement and discrimination.

We also have reason to believe, on the basis of our analysis, that the vivid imagery of the 'one new man' is not of Christian Jews and Christian Gentiles who had constituted the new humanity in the sense that the church had replaced Israel as the people of God. Indeed, it would be difficult to conceive of the 'one new man' without a close connection to Israel:[151] the author does not conceive of the 'one new man' without a connection to the 'circumcision' or the 'body politic of Israel', but argues

3.12f.; Rev. 21.1, 5. See further Black, 'Creation', here 14 n. 3. Black argues that Isa. 65.17ff. is the Hebrew *locus classicus* for the idea of new creation, and might well be held to warrant most of the later tradition in the Apocrypha, Pseudepigrapha and rabbinical sources. See further Str-B, III, 840–7; Groß, 'Geschöpf', esp. 101, 104, 108–9; Fitzmyer, *Theology*, 70; Baumbach, 'Schöpfung'; Sjöberg, 'Wiedergeburt', here 53f.; cf. Sjöberg, 'Neuschöpfung'; Barbour, 'Creation', here 35; Foerster, 'κτίζω'; Tobin, *Creation*, passim. Mußner, *Christus*, 94 suggests that the notion of new creation is adopted from proselyte terminology; cf. Dahl, 'Christ,' 425, 436–7. Nevertheless, the concern of our present passage is concord 'in Christ' rather than conversion. There are also no good grounds for us to speak of the influence of Gnostic ideas (*contra* Lindemann, Fischer and others) linking the primordial (heavenly) Man – sometimes identified with the Saviour – and the first created man.

[150] It is beyond the scope of this study to explore the ethical implications of the motif of 'new man' in our epistle (e.g., 4.24), but we may note that the 'new man' stands in contrast not merely to the 'old man' which is morally corrupt, but also to the *divisiveness* of the latter; cf. Col. 3.9–11.

[151] See in particular Richardson, *Israel*, 22–32, who suggests that it was not until after the New Testament period that the Christian Church came to be recognised explicitly as a 'third race', neither Jewish nor Gentile but Christian; cf. Fischer, *Tendenz*, 80–1; Moule, *Birth*, 51 n. 2; Markus, *Christianity*, esp. ch. 2 (on 'The Third Race'), here 24–47. For the idea of Christians as *tertium genus*, see esp. Clem. Alex., *Strom.* 6.5.41; *Diogn.* 1; Tertullian, *Scorpiace*, 10.

that the new humanity no longer defined itself on the basis of an *ethnos* and by separation of the 'circumcision'/Jew from the 'uncircumcision'/ Gentile, but embraced both 'in Christ'.

4.4.6 ποιῶν εἰρήνην (v. 15c)

The author has marked the creation of the 'one new man' as the turning point for both Jew and Gentile in terms of their new identity and, by implication, their relationship with one another. But he argues that this turning point can be achieved only by the attainment of peace by Christ.[152] For us the important question is, why 'making peace'? In what context did this formulation normally arise and what motives could have prompted its use here? Is he speaking of making peace as the end of human enmity and hostilities? It is possible to detect at least two influencing factors.

(a) The concept of making peace is a commonplace in ancient political rhetoric, in which the state of hostility or tension that existed between different people groups is always presupposed.[153] To make peace is to urge

[152] Despite Lincoln, *Ephesians*, 143, and others, who claim that the 'original' hymn ends in v. 16 and that the present participial clause 'making peace' concludes by stating the end result of Christ's creative act ('thus, making peace', e.g., NRSV), it is more likely that the author stresses here the circumstance under which the 'one new man' can come into being. Lincoln's claim would also make a nonsense of v. 17 where the author clearly elaborates the way in which peace is instilled by Christ. The most that can be said is that v. 15c answers only part of the question, namely *how* the 'one new man' is created, and that the activity that leads to the emergence of the 'one new man' is not unveiled until vv. 17–18. Scholars who are of the opinion that vv. 14–16 is an excursus or a *Vorlage* are often inclined to read v. 15c as one of the concluding statements which is paralleled by v. 16b ('thus putting to death that hostility through it', e.g., NRSV). That the author's argument has already reached its climax in v. 16 (or v. 17) should not be pressed.

[153] See, e.g., Polybius, *Hist.* 5.29.1: 'The Aetolians were on the one hand anxious to make peace (ποιήσασθαι τὴν εἰρηνην), since the *war* told heavily on them and things were turning out far otherwise than they had expected.' It is beyond the scope of this study to explore the various reasons for internecine strifes in ancient city-states; it may be sufficient to cite the following important works: e.g., Andocides, *On the Peace with the Lacedaimonians*; Isocrates, *De pace*. The political speeches of Dio to the various city-states of Bithynia (e.g., Nicomedia, Nicaea, Prusa and Apamea, see his *Or.* 38–41) focus without exception on the topic of concord or the overcoming of civil or interstatal discords and hostilities. Dio also preached reconciliation of disputes between various cities (e.g., between Prusa and the Roman colony of Apamea; between the leading cities of Bithynia, Nicomedia and Nicaea; and between Tarsus and its neighbouring cities, Aegae, Mallus and Adana: see, e.g., *Or.* 32, 34, 38, 39, 40, 41). He also includes in *Or.* 34.19 the following as the main causes of internal and internecine strife: envy, rival ambitions, self-seeking and neglect of the public interest. Cf. *Or.* 38.24–6, 30, 40. For a discussion of internal strife in the Greek city-states under the Roman rulership, see, e.g., Plutarch, *Praec. ger. rei publ.*,

for reconciliation or to attain a condition of non-war. It is mainly in this connection that we encounter the theme of 'making peace' in the political orators.[154] Fundamental to ancient political philosophy is the conviction that 'making peace', a virtual synonym for reconciling, is the best means to avoid the evils of strife[155] and the preservation of territorial or national solidarity (i.e., secure from dangers and threats from outside).[156] This precisely explains why the instilling of peace (and concord) between two rival city-states or citizen-bodies is often considered in the ancient period as the noblest activity of a statesman.[157] Peace, i.e., the ending of civil

esp. 824A. Cf. Aristides, *Or.* 7 (= *On Behalf of Making Peace with the Lacedaimonians*); In his *Or.* 23.12, 66 (= *To the Cities on Concord*), Aristides mentions the quarrels between Ephesus and Smyrna over 'primacy' or 'presidency' (τό πρωτεῖον), cf. Dio, *Or.* 38.24–6, 30, 40; Thucydides, *Hist.* 8.93.3; Andocides, *Lac.* 1.73; Lysias, *Or.* 18.17f. For the (ethnic) conflicts between Jews and Greeks at Alexandria, see Josephus, *B. J.* 7.47; Philo, *Flacc.*, 135–45. See further Aalders, *Plutarch*, passim; Jones, *Dio*, esp. ch. 10 (on 'Concord'), 83–94.

154 Examples in ancient literature are extensive. Andocides, who devoted himself to a vigorous campaign for the ending of war between Athens and Sparta, has turned the clause 'make peace' into a catch-phrase in his *On the Peace with the Lacedaimonians* (ποιεῖν + εἰρήνη, 16 times: 1, 2, 6, 8, 11, 12, 13, 19, 20, 21, 23, 25, 27, 28, 30, 41). Cf. Isocrates, *De Pace* (= *Or.* 8) 16.1–2; Isocrates, *Philippus* (= *Or.* 5) 7.7; *Archidamus* (= *Or.* 6) 11.2, 13.8–9, 29.41, 33.2–3, 34.2, 55.7; *Panathenicus* (= *Or.* 12) 105; *Panegyricus*, 116; Xenophon, *Hell.* 2.2.20, 22; Demosthenes, *Or.* 11.1; *Phil.* 2.28; Dionysius Halicarnassus, *Ant. rom.* 19.9.4; 10.21.8.4; Thucydides, *Hist.* 5.17.2.7; Polybius, *Hist.* 2.18.9.3–19.1.1; Diodorus Siculus, 14.15.1, 14.110.3; Plutarch, *Pyrrhus* 6.8; 12.8; *Pericles* 10.4; *Timoleon* 34.2; *Agesilaus* 23.1; *Nicias* 9.8; Aristides, *Or.* 11.151; *Pan.* 154.3; 158.4–5, etc. Although the notion of 'making peace' is also found in the Jewish scriptures, the expression is extremely infrequent. In the LXX of Isa. 27.5 (twice), it occurs in a context in which the Israelites were estranged from Yahweh and were urged to 'make peace' with their God; the other occurrence in Isa. 45.7 is of no relevance. The same idea is clearly present in the Apocrypha, and it does not go beyond the Greek usage: 1 Macc. 6.49; 11.51; cf. 6.58, 13.37. Elsewhere in the NT the same expression 'make peace' occurs only in Jas. 3.18–4.3 in which the author of the epistle deals with internal strife between members of the same community; cf. Col. 1.20. For the idea of 'making peace' (עשה שלום) in the Mishnah, see esp. Foerster, 'εἰρήνη', 419; see also Beck & Brown, 'εἰρήνη', 782–83.

155 See Dio, *Or.* 39.3–7, who told the Nicaeans that concord made it possible to make good use of the other advantages of city life; Aristides, 24.12ff., equates concord with good sense and its absence with madness. Sheppard, 'Homonoia', concludes that 'the quest for concord in city life had two aspects: the avoidance of factional strife between public bodies or aristocratic cliques, and the prevention of disorder among the mass of the people or the community at large' (242).

156 See, e.g., Andocides, *Myst.*, 107–8; Isocrates, *De pace*, 18–20; Aristides, *Pan.*, 1.277ff.; 298–301, 318–30. This thesis is expounded at considerable length by Sheppard, 'Homonoia', esp. 239.

157 See in particular Plutarch, *Praec. ger. rei publ.* 808C, 824D. Plutarch argued that it remained for every ideal statesman to involve himself in noble activities which instil concord and friendship and remove strifes, discords and all enmity (825E). See also Jones, *Dio*, 94.

strife or inter-state disputes, and concord[158] have always been lauded as political virtues,[159] while strife, war and enmity are always despised as evils and belong to the same side of the taxonomy.[160]

Given that the author of Ephesians is familiar with the ideas of 'making peace' in the political sphere,[161] he may well have used this *terminus technicus* of contemporary politics like the others. Recognising that the tensions which often afflicted the ancient state-bodies could be (potentially) present between Jews and Gentiles, he was attracted to the use of the language of 'making peace'.[162] Thus, the principle of Christ's 'making peace' which the author invokes in order to put to an end to the

158 The coupling of 'peace and concord' in ancient political rhetoric can be easily documented: e.g., Dio, *Or.* 39.2; Plutarch, *Praec. ger. rei publ.* 824C; *Aem.* 4; *SIG*^{3}, nos 685.14; 742.1, 1f., 10f.; Josephus, *B. J.* 2.340f., et al.

159 See, e.g., Aristophanes, *Pax* 290–309; Dio, *Or.* 38.10; 40.26; 41.13, et al. The expediency of 'peace' (τὸ συμφέρον) was made abundantly clear in ancient rhetorical handbooks and political rhetoric, see, e.g., [Aristotle?], *Rhet. Alex.* 1422 ^{a}5–15: 'What is *expedient* is the preservation of existing virtues, or the acquisition of goods that we do not possess, or the rejection of existing evils, or the prevention of harmful things expected to occur . . . Expedient for a state are such things as *concord*, military strength, property and a plentiful revenue, good and numerous allies. And briefly, we consider all things that resemble these expedient, and the things opposite to these inexpedient.' Cf. also 1422 ^{b}34–5: 'As it is expedient for people in health to be on their guard against contracting disease, so also it is expedient for states enjoying a period of concord to take precautions against the rise of faction (στασιάσωσις)'. Isocrates openly declared in his political oratory that the role of a king is to act as a benefactor in promoting concord: 'And yet, if kings are to rule well, they must try to preserve harmony, not only in the states over which they hold dominion, but also in their own households and in their places of abode' (*Nic.* 41); also *Phil.* 16, 30, 83; Isocrates, *De pace* 16: 'I [*sc.* Isocrates] maintain, then, that we should *make peace* (ποιεῖσθαι τὴν εἰρήνην) . . . For we shall not find terms of *peace* more just than these nor more *expedient* for our city'; Aristides, *Or.* 7.28, 31.

160 See, e.g., Isocrates, *Philippus* 7; Aristophanes, *Pax* 310, who eulogised (the deity) Peace, but despised war as a 'demon'; Thucydides, 8.93.3; Dio, *Or.* 40.26; Aristides, *On Behalf of Making Peace with the Lacedaimonians* (= *Or.* 7), 24. A comparison with the parallels in the Jesus tradition may lead us to the same conclusion. According to Matt. 5.9, those who disinterestedly come between two contending parties in order to establish peace are highly lauded as the 'sons of God' (υἱοὶ θεοῦ); cf. Jas. 3.18. See also Foerster, 'εἰρήνη', 417. See further Baldry, 'State', esp. 12–15.

161 It is most striking to see that our present expression, and in particular its underlying assumption of ethnic 'discord' or *stasis*, has been overlooked by almost all interpreters over the years: see, e.g., Gnilka, *Epheserbrief*, 141–2; Lindemann, *Aufhebung*, 167–74; Schnackenburg, *Ephesians*, 116; Bruce, *Ephesians*, 298–300; Lincoln, *Ephesians*, 143–4, et al. I can also see no real progress in the suggestion of Swartley, 'War', esp. 2385 that we draw a clear-cut division between religion and politics.

162 We would need to note, however, that in Greek literature the phrase 'make peace' may denote (a) a peace settlement between two people groups/city-states that were in rivalry (e.g., Andocides, *Lac.*, 12ff.; 1 Macc. 11.50–1), or (b) a truce (σπονδὰς), understood in the sense of the vanquished being 'imperialised' by the victor (e.g., Isocrates, *Panegyricus*, 116, or the 'Peace' of Antalcidas in Isocrates, *Pan.* 105). The difference between 'peace' and 'truce' is well defined by Andocides, *Lac.* 11: 'A peace is made by men on equal terms, having reached agreement with one another over their differences; a truce is made by

estrangement between Jews and Gentiles[163] is that which aided ancient political writers to counter the evils of strife in their own communities.

(b) The second factor, perhaps the more important, is that the author of Ephesians is wrestling with the corporate unity of Jew and Gentile: how could the Gentiles who did not derive from Abraham (i.e., the 'uncircumcision') relate to those who already did?[164] Given the fact that the Gentiles had been estranged from the 'body politic' based on a particular *ethnos*, is it possible to speak of a rapprochement of Jew and Gentile? If so, *how*? For our author, the estranged human groups can become a harmonious whole by Christ's peace-making ministry perceived as an act which holds together the two estranged groups as one.[165]

In short, the author's skill consisted of his ability to draw into use the technical language of ancient political rhetoric in such a way that he could speak of Christ as a fervent campaigner whose ultimate aim is to create a mankind which is in concord by bringing to an end human enmity and estrangement.

injunction by the victors, after winning the war, over the vanquished, just as the Spartans, after defeating us in the war, enjoined us to demolish our walls, surrender our fleet and recall our exiles.' See also Polybius, *Hist.* 21.4.12: 'But when, upon the Aetolians inquiring on what conditions they should make peace (ποιεῖσθαι τὴν εἰρήνην), Lucius Scipio informed them that there were two alternatives open to them, either to submit entirely to Rome or to pay a thousand talents at once and make a defensive and offensive alliance, the Aetolians present were exceedingly distressed to find that this decision was not at all conformable to their previous conversation. They, however, said they would submit the conditions to the people of Aetolia.' Cf. 5.107.6.5–7.1; 18.1.11.3–12.1; 21.4.12.1. See also 1 Macc. 6.49: we are told that Antiochus Epiphanes IV 'made peace' (ἐποίησεν εἰρήνην) with the people of Beth-Zur, but the latter evacuated the town because they had no provisions there to withstand a siege, cf. 6.58; *T. Jud.* 7.7–8.

163 *Contra* Lindemann, *Epheserbrief*, 50–1, who argues that Colossians has exerted an influence upon Ephesians in the usage of the term. Whereas the author of Colossians uses a slightly different term (εἰρηνοποιέω, 1.20) to express the broad sweep of Christ's reconciling work ('through him . . . to reconcile *all things*, whether on earth or in heaven, making peace by the blood of his cross'), the peace that is effected by Christ between Jew and Gentile is 'earthly' in our present passage.

164 This includes those who did not believe but belonged to 'Israel' (cf. v. 11b, the 'circumcision') and those who have already believed in Christ, i.e., the Christian Jews (cf. 1.12).

165 Although the author of Ephesians for some reason avoids using the term ὁμόνοια in his formulations, the urge to maintain concord between members in the 'one body' of Christ is clearly evident in his paraenesis: 'I therefore, a prisoner for the Lord, beg you to lead a life worthy of the calling to which you have been called . . . eager *to maintain the unity of the spirit by the bond of peace*' (σπουδάζοντες τηρεῖν τὴν ἑνότητα τοῦ πνεύματος ἐν τῷ συνδέσμῳ τῆς εἰρήνης, 4.3). The difference between ὁμόνοια ('oneness of mind') and 'oneness of the spirit' is very thin. Our author may well have been aware of the idea of 'oneness of mind' and Christianised it.

4.4.7 καὶ (ἵνα) ἀποκαταλλάξῃ τοὺς ἀμφοτέρους ἐν ἑνὶ σώματι τῷ θεῷ διὰ τοῦ σταυροῦ, ἀποκτείνας τὴν ἔχθραν ἐν αὐτῷ (v. 16)

The reconciliation of 'both in one body' is a thought which is parallel to that of the creation of the two ethnic groups into 'one new man'.[166] Indeed, the second ἵνα-clause fleshes out what is said in the first. The act of reconciliation is now described by the unique doubly compounded verb ἀποκαταλλάσσω, a term which is used elsewhere in the NT only in Colossians (1.20, 22), but not in any other extant Greek literature.[167] It is not impossible that the term was coined by either Paul or his associate/disciple. Like its simpler form καταλλάσσω,[168] the compound verb also occurs in contexts where relationships had turned hostile or unfriendly.[169]

So far as we can tell from our present context, the author is referring to the reconciliation of the two different categories of peoples, as suggested by the phrase τοὺς ἀμφοτέρους, reminding us of the 'circumcision'/Jew and the 'uncircumcision'/Gentile.[170] Thus, the key to understanding

[166] This is shown by the fact that v. 16 is still governed by the ἵνα of v. 15b, describing the purpose of Christ's reconciliatory work from a different angle.

[167] See in particular Porter, *Καταλλάσσω*, 189; Büchsel, 'ἀποκαταλλάσσω', 258; Merkel, 'καταλλάσσω', 261.

[168] See, e.g., Rom. 5.11; 11.15; 2 Cor. 5.18–19, etc. See further Porter, *Καταλλάσσω*, 39–50 for a helpful discussion of the usage of καταλλάσσω among Hellenistic writers. On the Biblical understanding of reconciliation, see Vorländer and Brown, 'καταλλάσσω,' 172; Büchsel, 'ἀποκαταλλάσσω'.

[169] See Col. 1.15–20 (esp. vv. 20, 22), where the concern is primarily with the cosmic reconciliation between the various constituents of the cosmos to God. However, the suggestion that our author is influenced by Colossians, which had taken the compound verb from the alleged 'hymn' about the overcoming of cosmic hostility and restoration of harmony between heaven and earth, must be deemed highly speculative (e.g., Lincoln, *Ephesians*, 145; Lindemann, *Epheserbrief*, 50–1). So far as we can tell, the usage of the compound verb in our present context differs from Colossians in that it lays stress on the reconciliation effected by Christ between two estranged human groups. Best, *Ephesians*^{2}, 264, suggests that the word ἀποκαταλλάσσω may have been in used in the 'Pauline school'. For a convenient bibliography on the theme of reconciliation in the NT, see Lincoln, *Ephesians*, 145.

[170] I therefore disagree with Lindemann, *Aufhebung*, 175 n. 159, who argues that our present term refers to 'all' ('Alle') in the Hellenistic usage; cf. Lindemann, *Epheserbrief*, 53. Lindemann is constrained by the parameters of his own theory of Gnosticism. We have enough evidence to show that the original sense of 'both' should be maintained in Ephesians: see, e.g., Plato, *Gorg.* 498B (i.e., the coward and the brave); Pindar, *Pyth.* 2.76 – 'to both sides', i.e., the slanderers and the slandered; 10.2 (Lacedaimon and Thessaly); Isaeus, *On the Estate of Philoctemon* (= *Or.* 6) 63 (both classes of children, i.e., children of one's own and adopted); Xenophon, *Hell.* 7.4.35 – 'both parties', i.e., the Arcadians and the Eleans; Dio, *Or.* 38.43 – 'both peoples', i.e., the Nicomedians and the Nicaeans who were in discord, cf. 38.45, 46; see also LSJ, s.v.

the notion of reconciliation is the recognition that the author sees the condition from which both Jews and Gentiles are delivered as one of ethnic antagonism which is closely associated with the exclusive attitude of the Jews.[171] It is in this connection that Christ is depicted as effecting reconciliation of the two ethnic groups by exchanging ethnic alienation and enmity for peace and fellowship through his death on the cross (διὰ τοῦ σταυροῦ; cf. Col. 2.14). The death of Christ here could easily evoke the idea of the noble death of a peace-maker, an idea which is evidently present in the Graeco-Roman world.[172] This by no means plays down the vertical aspect of reconciliation, i.e., between God and Gentile (or between God and Jew). In our present passage, God is not portrayed as the antagonised or 'injured' party in a direct sense (cf. Rom. 5.10; 1 Cor. 7.11; 2 Cor. 5.19), and the vertical aspect of reconciliation is not what the author will argue *for* at this point. The point is that the author sees reconciliation as being closely associated with two interrelated factors, namely the *Jewish view* that the Gentiles, by definition, are cut off from Israel's God-given grace and presumably from their God (thus, the derogatory name-calling 'atheists', v. 12; see also vv. 1–2; 4.17–18), *and* the ethnic enmity which came as one of the outcomes of that view.[173] Reconciliation must therefore include, primarily, the cessation of ethnic enmity and, subsequently, the termination of the hitherto defective status of the Gentiles in the eyes of the Jews. The author argues that 'both' the Gentiles who were estranged from Israel's blessings by the Jews on ethnic considerations *and* the Jews who had played a substantial role in excluding

[171] *Contra* Lincoln, *Ephesians*, 146 who fails to take into account the way in which the Jews perceived the Gentiles and their exclusive tendency toward them, and therefore fails to give adequate reason why both need to be reconciled to God; also Schnackenburg, *Ephesians*, 116. Best's conclusion that Ephesians 'contains no sign of tension between Jew and Gentile' must be deemed erroneous (*Ephesians*^{1}, 92); cf. Best, *Ephesians*^{2}, 264–5, 271. Merklein, who overlooks the exclusive attitude of the Jews, has come to the conclusion that the author of Ephesians has set Jew and Gentile in contrast in vv. 11f., in which the antithesis itself is produced from the viewpoint of the Church and also exemplified in the Church (*Christus*, 22–3).

[172] Plutarch, for example, provided a good account of the associations between death and the attainment of peace/reconciliation. In the last speech before Otho committed suicide in order to end the civil strife, he made it known to his people that he wanted to sacrifice himself for the sake of 'peace and concord': 'For I do not see how my victory can be of so great advantage to the Romans as my offering up my life to secure peace and concord (εἰρήνης καὶ ὁμονοίας), and to prevent Italy from beholding such a day again' (*Otho* 15.6).

[173] I therefore disagree with Lindemann, *Epheserbrief*, 50–1 who concludes that our present passage speaks of cosmic rather than ethnic reconciliation; also with Fischer, *Tendenz*, 134.

(and antagonising) them need to be reconciled and restored to God (cf. v. 18).[174] That the two ethnic groups need to be restored to God implies that the author (a Jew) has denounced the claim that the Gentiles were 'atheists' by removing the Gentiles' label of 'otherness' and, most importantly, eradicating the boundary between Jew and Gentile (v. 12c). The reconciliation of the 'have nots', i.e., '*a*theists', and the Jews who already placed their hope in the one God also shows that the author embraced a unversalistic approach by assuming that reconciliation of the two human groups cannot be deemed complete unless both are also restored to the one God of Israel as its ultimate goal (τῷ θεῷ).

For us, the most important question is: what does the author mean by the 'one body' in which Jews and Gentiles are reconciled? Does it denote an ecclesial body, namely the 'Church', which is to be reckoned with alongside Israel?[175] Has Israel found her genuine prolongation exclusively in the church of Jewish and Gentile Christians, and has the election of Israel passed over to Christians? Is it true that the fate of the Israel of God and its existence, an issue which had greatly disturbed Paul (see esp. Romans), was no longer an issue for the author of Ephesians?[176] Different possibilities have been offered over the years as regards the author's 'one body' imagery; several, however, are little to the point.[177]

Käsemann suggested that at the time when Ephesians was written, the two Pauline theologoumena, 'the people of God' and 'the body of Christ', compete with one another.[178] He argued that the normal development from the theme of the people of God to the body of Christ which we

[174] Lincoln, *Ephesians*, 145 is correct in saying that 'the Gentiles' alienation from Israel involved alienation from God', but he has failed to explain whether there is an ethnic factor which is now embedded in this alienation; also Schnackenburg, *Ephesians*, 117. It is more likely that the author assumes that ethnic enmity is subsequently enmity of humanity against God: see esp. Barth, *Ephesians 1–3*, 291.

[175] See, e.g., Käsemann, 'Ephesians', 288ff., who argues that the church in Ephesians has become 'a force in history'; Martin, *Reconciliation*, 'The separation of Christianity and Judaism is recognised . . . , the threat was that Gentile Christians should want to cast off all association with the Old Testament faith and disown their origins in Israel's salvation history' (160); Stuhlmacher, 'Peace', who concludes that the church is the 'true Israel' (188); Merklein, *Christus*, 45–53, 98; Houlden, 'Christ', here 272; Best, *Body*, 153; Schnackenburg, *Ephesians*, 117, et al.

[176] This is the main contention of Rese, 'Vorzüge', 222; cf. Rese, 'Church', esp. 28–9.

[177] Dunn, 'Body', esp. 157–8, is an exception. Dunn finds an intimate connection between the usage of the 'body' language and Paul's wrestling with the problem of Israel in his epistle to the Romans. He concludes that the 'body' language is introduced to solve the problem of how Jew and Gentile could be correlated within the one community, and that this problem is one of the major factors that determine the usage of the 'body' imagery in Paul; cf. Dunn, *TPA*, esp. 533–52.

[178] Käsemann, *Perspectives*, 109–10; cf. Käsemann, *Versuche*, 281.

usually find in Paul is reversed in Ephesians 2.11ff.:[179] the conversion of the Gentile Christians is depicted as incorporation in the Jewish Christian people of God, and the body of Christ is correspondingly interpreted as a union of Christians, both Jews and Gentiles, i.e., a union of two nations. He therefore concludes that there is only one satisfactory explanation for this phenomenon: what Paul considered in Romans 11.17ff. as a threatening possibility had already happened, namely that the Gentile Christians were pushing the Jewish Christians aside. The author of Ephesians therefore reminds them of the Jewish Christians' priority in salvation history. Consequently the continuity with Israel as the people of God is energetically stressed.[180] It is dubious, however, whether the two Pauline theologoumena in question are competing with one another. As has already been noted (above, chapter 3), what is pressed to the fore and challenged by the author is *not* Israel's status as the people of God, but Jewish ethnocentrism, in which the Gentiles were estranged from the constricted 'body politic of Israel'. Käsemann is confusing Israel as the people of God with the 'body politic' which is based on a particular *ethnos*, with the result that he misses the whole point of the author's argument in vv. 11ff. His comments that the Gentiles had displayed haughtiness over the Jews,[181] and therefore needed to be reminded of their *Jewish* roots, must be deemed gratuitous. Equally unconvincing is the suggestion that the author of Ephesians 'knows only about the particularity of Israel when looking back to the time before Christ came; after Christ has come the election of Israel has passed over to the Christian Church'.[182] According to this view, the description in Ephesians (esp. 2.12) of how Israel's privileges make up the past deficiencies of the Gentiles serves the purpose of emphasising the salvation-historical difference between Jews and Gentiles that was in force *before* the coming of Christ. It is arguable that the author still has the 'salvation-historical difference between Jew and Gentile' in view (see above my exegesis of v. 12 in chapter 4),[183] but this can hardly rule out a

179 See also Käsemann, 'Ephesians', who writes: 'Paul's pupil . . . does so when he emphatically juxtaposes the expression the body of Christ with that of the people of God, the holy remnant, and thereby in effect modifies the Pauline ecclesiology' (296).

180 Ibid., esp. 291, 297. Käsemann's theory is revived in Roetzel, 'Relations'; Roetzel, *Conversations*, 140–4.

181 Martin, *Reconciliation*, 193 who comes to the same conclusion as Käsemann.

182 Rese, 'Vorzüge', 222; cf. Rese, 'Church', 28; Schlier, *Epheser*, 120; Lincoln, 'Church'.

183 The salvation-historical approach has come under heavy criticism in Lindemann, *Aufhebung*, esp. 146, 191–2, who concludes that the interest of the author is not in the history of the church nor its historical character: 'Das Interesse des Verfassers richtet sich aber nicht auf eine Geschichte der Kirche, ihr Wachsen ist ein strukturelles, kein geschichtliches Merkmal' (191); Tachau, *Einst*, 142.

reference to the fact that the two ethnic groups were estranged from one another on the basis of *ethnos*.[184] Merklein, who argues that the author has set the Jew and Gentile in contrast only from the standpoint of the Church, the eschatological people of God (*den ekklesiologischen Blickwinkel*), has opted for an ambivalent character for 'Israel': Israel refers to the community of Israel (*Gemeinde Israels*) in the OT sense and at the same time to the Church as the eschatological people of God.[185] The most salient question for us is: who is Israel? Clearly Merklein has not been aware of the fact that 'Israel' has become an exclusive, ethnocentric entity in Ephesians (see above my exegesis of v. 12a in chapter 4). Although Merklein has raised an important question in his study, namely, *how can Jew and Gentile be the eschatological people of God?*, and sees this as 'the theological basic-structure of the letter to the Ephesians',[186] the more fundamental question, *why couldn't (or didn't) Jew and Gentile become the one people of God (before the conversion of the Gentiles)?*, is not adequately dealt with.

A significant deficiency of recent NT scholarship consists of its failure to account for the problem (and definition) of 'Israel' from a proper perspective, and to include vv. 11–13 (esp. v. 12a) as the *crux interpretum* providing the most important clues for understanding the 'one body' language in this passage.[187] The present study hopes to fill that gap. My own contention is that the 'one body' is not meant to be a substitute for Israel, as the new people of God (*contra* Stuhlmacher, Merklein, Schnackenburg and others), nor should we read the church-body and Israel as being two separate entities overlapping each other only in the Jewish Χριστιανοί (*contra* Rese). Still less should we say that 'Israel as God's privileged people seems to be only an entity of the past; in the present it has been replaced by the church, and this church

[184] Rese, 'Church', here 27, who fails to see the confusion of Jewish identity and the ethnically based '*politeia* of Israel', reaches the following conclusion: although the Gentiles were excluded from the *politeia* of Israel in their pre-Christian time, now as Gentile Christians they have become members of the *politeia* of Israel, as Eph. 2.19 indicates. Rese evidently assumes that the Gentiles' 'naturalisation' is straightforward.

[185] Merklein, *Christus*, 23, 28, 74, 99, concludes: 'Die Einzelexegese von Eph. 2,11–18 zeigte den *ekklesiologischen Blickwinkel* des Verfassers. Nur von diesem Standpunkt aus läßt sich der Inhalt der für diesen Abschnitt konstitutiven Begriffe voll erfassen.' Merklein, however, does not consider the possibility that the author's perspective is that of a Jew who perceives the Gentiles from inside Israel and that he is trying to hold Jew and Gentile in a community-body, a para-Israel that is not tainted with exclusivism.

[186] Ibid., 28.

[187] I have in mind in particular scholars who read vv. 14–18 as an excursus or 'insertion' (e.g., Gnilka, Schlier, Conzelmann, Lincoln, Roetzel and others), thereby isolating the passage in vv. 14–18 from its most immediate context of vv. 11–13; cf. my discussion in section 4.2 above.

has lost sight of the unbelieving Israel'.[188] Rather, the 'one body' is to be read as community-redefining imagery: it is prompted precisely by an alternative community-body imagery, namely the exclusive, inward-looking 'body politic of Israel' which the Jews had constricted as an ethnically based and closed-ethnic community (v. 12a). The 'one body' is not directed to stand in a stark contrast to God's Israel but to an 'Israel' which is so confused in Jewish identity. It supplants 'a community of communities' which is based on the ethnic form of identification and allegiance with an inclusive 'body' identity in Christ. This means that our 'one body' language must be read against the backcloth of the *Jewish* perspective. The author is wrestling with the problem and definition of the people of God: who is the people of God? Can God's people be constricted as the 'body politic of Israel' from which the Gentiles *as Gentiles* are excluded? The issue, in other words, is not whether the church(-body) has parted company with the Israel of God or Israel has found her genuine prolongation exclusively in the church ('the true Israel', as Stuhlmacher claims). Rather, the 'one body' language has grown out of the author's recognition that there were tensions afflicting the relationship of Jews and Gentiles, and that the Gentiles were excluded from 'Israel' by the Jews. The author's ideal is to transpose the exclusive 'body politic of Israel' into an inclusive (and non-ethnic) community-body in which the 'holy ones'/Israel and Gentiles who believe in the Messiah could be together as a harmonious whole (hence, 'in *one* body'). However, there was a real need for the author to provide a corrective to the narrowly defined 'Israel' before he could possibly speak of the 'holy ones' and Gentiles being related to one another in 'one body'. I shall return to this in section 5.2.

It must be said that the 'one body' language in our passage is not novel, for ancient writers had made their appeal to the same *topos* for unity or combating factionalism. This is illustrated by no small number of ancient political texts in which the 'body' is often used as a central metaphor for political and social order, denoting the coherence and unity of a state(-body).[189] For example, the much celebrated fable of Menenius

[188] *Contra* Rese, 'Church', 27.

[189] The 'body' imagery was used with the state as early as Aristotle, *Pol.* 1302 ^{b}35–1303 ^{a}3: 'For just as the body (σῶμα) is composed of parts . . . so also a (city-)state is composed of parts . . . ; cf. Epictetus, *Diatr.* 2.4.24–6, who argues that man is part of a state, cf. 2.10.4; Dio, who employed 'the body of disease' to denote civil or external strife at work in communities and nations (*Or.* 39.5; 41.9, cf. 33.16); Plutarch, *Cor.* 6.3–4.

Agrippa employed the 'body' to contemplate the ruptured relationships between the *boule*, i.e., the senate, and its plebs (Livy, *Ab urbe condita libri* 2.32.12–33.1). What is not in doubt is that the chief aim of the fable is to urge concord or the oneness-despite-diversity principle within a state-body which consists of *different* constituents, and the emphasis on the 'body' as the medium of oneness is indeed a way of dealing with differences and internecine strains. The *topos* is also used by other writers to flesh out the importance of oneness in a political organism and argue for its stability.[190] It will be sufficient to say that fundamental to ancient political philosophy is the conviction that a state-body can be likened to a body (hence the modern parlance of 'body politic').

[190] See, e.g., Dionysius Halicarnassus, *Rom. Ant.* 6.86.1–5. Dionysius employed the 'body' imagery to inculcate the sense of mutual belonging and responsibility of the different constituents within the city-state: 'A city-state resembles in some measure a human body . . . For a city-state is composed of many classes of peoples not at all resembling one another, every one of which contributes some particular service to the common good, just as its members do to the body' (tr. slightly modified). Plutarch, *Solon* 18.6, likened the citizens of a city-state to the 'members of the body' (τοὺς πολίτας ὥσπερ ἑνος μέρη [*sc.* σώματος]); Plutarch, *Praec. ger. rei publ.* 815B: 'For when physicians cannot entirely eradicate diseases, they turn them outwards to the surface of the *body* (σῶμα); but the statesman, if he cannot keep the *state* entirely free from troubles, will at any rate try to cure and control whatever disturbs it and causes sedition, keeping it meanwhile hidden within the State, so that it may have as little need as possible of physicians and medicine drawn from outside [*sc.* Roman interventions]'; cf. 824A. Aristides, *Or.* 24.39, also used the same 'body' language to emphasise the oneness of the strife-torn state of the Rhodians: 'And how shall you differ from the women who tore Pentheus apart, when you yourselves have torn apart with your own hands *the body of the city* (τὸ κοινὸν σῶμα τῆς πόλεως) which you all share?' (39); cf. pars 5, 16, 18, 38; *Or.* 23.66. See also Marcus Aurelius Antoninus, 2.1, who argues that the various parts of the body have come into being for co-operation, and to thwart one another by showing resentment and aversion is against nature; cf. Xenophon, *Mem.* 2.3.18. In the *Oration of* Maximus of Tyre (2nd century CE) the 'body' imagery was used to encourage active participation of its members in the city-state: *Oration* 15.4–5 (example cited in Malherbe, *Exhortation*, 149, no. 63); Seneca, *Ira* 2.31.7; Cicero, *Off.* 3.5.22. See also *SEG* 44, no. 949.ii.26 (Teos, Ionia: 'Decree Concerning Measures to be taken for the Payment of the Ransom to Pirates' (*c.* 250–200 BCE)), which speaks of 'the bodies of the freedmen' (ἐλευθερα σώματα). These 'bodies' may denote either the congregations of citizen-lenders or the resident aliens; cf. *SEG* 14, no. 479, *SEG* 38, no. 644. In the NT, the 'body' imagery is found exclusively in the Pauline letters. It aided the apostle to explain how internal discords could cause much harm to the fledging community (e.g., at Corinth), and the importance of the interdependence of the various parts of a Christian assembly: see, e.g., 1 Cor. 1.13; 6.15; 12.12–26; Col. 2.19. See further Lietzmann, *Korinther* II, 62 (on 1 Cor. 12.12); Mitchell, *Reconciliation*, 99–105, 157–64; *OCD*, s.v. 'body'. Despite Arnold, 'Head', who claims that the head–body imagery used by Paul in Colossians and Ephesians draws on the current physiological understandings of the head in relationship to the body as exhibited in the medical writers to enrich his notion of the church as a corporate body (366), the head–body language is often used by ancient politicians to denote the political body.

Given that the author of Ephesians is familiar with the ancient political idea of the state-body, it should come as no surprise that he has reached for the 'body' language as a means to reinforce the *oneness* of Jew and Gentile.[191] To be more precise, he is stretching the 'one body' language in the same way as other ancient political philosophers to assert his own theology of oneness of the community-body.

Perhaps the most important factor of all is that '*one* body' is here a community-enhancing metaphor.[192] Thus, the author perceives that the tensions which afflicted the ancient state-bodies were also present between Jews and Gentiles, and the awareness of this prompts him to use the 'one body' language to reinforce the fact that the oneness to which a stable or healthy community must aspire depends on the oneness of mutual recognition between Jew and Gentile rather than on an exclusivism based upon the opposition of the 'circumcision' and the 'uncircumcision' (vv. 11–12; cf. vv. 1–2).

Although the author of Ephesians has taken his 'body' language from the wider usage of the Graeco-Roman world, for him it is the 'body of Christ' (1.22–3; 4.4, 12, 16; 5.23, 30), through whom a new possibility is now opened up for peoples of different ethnic background to become fellow-members of the same corporate body (εἶναι τὰ ἔθνη συγκληρονόμα καὶ σύσσωμα καὶ συμμέτοχα τῆς ἐπαγγελίας ἐν Χριστῷ Ἰησοῦ διὰ τοῦ εὐαγγελίου, 3.6). He assumes that this is made possible when ethnic enmity is put to an end by Christ on the cross, i.e., Christ has become the terms on which the enmity can be ended. The participial clause, 'putting to death the enmity by/through it' (ἀποκτείνας τὴν ἔχθραν ἐν αὐτῷ),[193] as it now stands, is parallel to 'making

[191] This *topos* is found also in Paul's earlier letters, esp. Rom. 12.5; 1 Cor. 10.17. The usage of 'one' both here and in v. 15 ('one new man') is the same: the author is referring to the reconciliation of Jew and Gentile rather than seeing them as a numerical collective.

[192] See again Plutarch, *Philopoemen* 8.1–2, in which both πολιτεία and ἕν σῶμα are used to describe the same inter-state league of Achaeans: 'The Achaeans who united themselves together to form the Achaean league/confederacy at a time when Greece was weak and easily drifted into individual city-states, had also proposed to form the Peloponnesus into a single political body and one power' (τὰς δὲ ὁμονοία καὶ πολιτειά καταμιγνύντες εἶς ἑαυτούς, ἕν σῶμα καὶ μίαν δύναμιν κατασκευάσαι διενοοῦντο τὴν Πελοπόννησον). I therefore disagree with Percy, *Probleme*, 280ff., who concludes that the 'one body' refers to the body of Christ on the cross; Percy, 'Probleme', 191ff.; Schweizer, 'σῶμα', 1080; Benoit, *Jesus*, II, 67.

[193] The pronoun in the prepositional phrase ἐν αὐτῷ may denote the cross as the means by which the enmity between Jew and Gentile is put to an end. The author's method of argument is extremely close to that of Gal. 6.14: 'But far be it from me to glory except in *the cross* of our Lord Jesus Christ, *by which* (δι' οὗ) the world has been crucified to me, and I to the world.' (Otherwise, the dative phrase may refer to Christ who is the agent of reconciliation.)

peace' in the previous verse,[194] speaking of the reconciliatory work of Christ from a different angle. The point is clearly that reconciliation must include the removal of the ethnic enmity,[195] the outcome of Jews and Gentiles being held apart from one another. The ironical fact, however, is that peace is achieved through the death of Christ on the cross which is understood by our author as the means of peace. As we shall see, the peace-making procedure of Christ (*pax Christi*) has prepared a brand new framework within which mutual acceptance between members of the 'one body' might in turn be filled out (vv. 18, 19–22; 4.1–6). This framework, to be sure, is constructed not by brutality or bloodshed (like the *pax Romana*), but by Christ's own sacrifical death on the cross (cf. vv. 14d, 16).[196]

To sum up: the notion of reconciliation in our passage is best understood against the backcloth of ethnic enmity. The image of 'one body' is introduced as a community-enhancing metaphor, in order to face down the human factor that tended to prevent the harmonious unity of Jew and Gentile as the one people of God. The author undercuts the exclusive Jewish 'body politic' which was constricted as an ethnic or national community. By transposing the exclusive body politic to a *unified* church-body, as opposed to that from which the dissimilar (i.e., the '*un*circumcision') were excluded, the author of Ephesians solves the

[194] *Pace* Schlier, *Epheser*, 135 who suggests that the phrase 'making peace' is to be understood simultaneously with the first part of the second purpose clause in v. 16a; Lincoln, *Ephesians*, 146, who suggests that the participial clause in v. 16 is parallel to 'having abolished the hostility in his flesh' in v. 14d.

[195] *Pace* Stuhlmacher, 'Peace', 190, who concludes that the author is referring to the removal of 'double hostility' – between God and sinners (the guilt of Gentiles and Jews) and between Jew and Gentile. The graphic picture of a violent termination of the enmity between Jew and Gentile, as indicated in the term itself, should be retained here. See further Frankemölle, 'ἀποκτείνω'; BAGD, s.v., 2.

[196] *Pace* Faust, *Pax*, who suggests that the author of Ephesians was making an implicit comparison of Christ with the Roman emperor, who was regarded as the creator and maintainer of peace (esp. 226, 324, 378f.). But there is an essential difference between *pax Christi* and *pax Romana* (for the *pax Augusta*, see esp. Augustus, *Res* 12; Tacitus, *Ann.* 1.4.1). The latter, to be sure, was a pseudo-peace or a 'truce' in a strict sense: it was hegemonic and was made by injunction by the victors, after winning the war, over the vanquished: see, e.g., *SIG*[3] 684. From a Roman perspective, peace was the framework appointed by the Romans which had to be filled out with mutual concord by those who had been pacified by force and bloodshed. This best explains why the author has avoided the term 'concord' in his arguments (cf. 4.1–6), for in the Roman world concord always presupposes the 'peace' (*pax Romana*) which is established by the Roman authority. For the connections between *pax Romana* and mutual concord in the Roman society, see, e.g., *IBM*, IV, 894. For the imposition of orderly government and concord between the cities by the Roman authority, see esp. *SIG*[3], no. 684. See further Wengst, *Pax*, esp. 11–26, 105–18, 181 nn. 101 and 102.

problem of estrangement between Jews and Gentiles, but poses no challenge to the status of Jews/Israel as the people of God.

4.4.8 καὶ ἐλθὼν εὐηγγελίσατο εἰρήνην ὑμῖν τοῖς μακρὰν καὶ εἰρήνην τοῖς ἐγγύς (v. 17)

It should be clear by now that the author of Ephesians has made 'peace' the core principle of his thought as he speaks of the reconciling work of Christ (vv. 14, 15c; cf. 4.1–6; 6.15). What matters now is the way in which this peace-making ministry can be summed up, and the question whether the peace of Christ is that between God and Gentile *and* between God and Jew.[197] To the latter question we shall return in due course. For the moment, it is enough to point out that the language here is categorically (re)conciliatory,[198] depicting the way in which reconciliation is promoted.

It is generally agreed that the author's language here is typically Jewish,[199] echoing a number of prophetic passages in the Jewish scriptures (e.g., Isa. 52.7; Nahum 2.1, LXX), and in particular Isaiah 57.19 which refers to peace being preached to two different groups of people.[200] In our present context, the 'far off' is certainly an overt nickname for the Gentiles: 'You, the far off' (*not*: 'you who *were* far off'; cf.

197 So Best, *Ephesians*^{2}, 271, who is not alone in reading v. 17 in its *literalness*: see, e.g., Lincoln, *Ephesians*, 145–6, who concludes that Christ has come to preach peace, separately, to Gentiles *and* to Jews; Mußner, *Christus*, 101–2; Mußner, *Epheser*, 84–5; Merklein, *Christus*, 59–60; Lindemann, *Epheserbrief*, 51, et al.

198 Despite the omission of the second reference to peace in ψ^{m} sy^{h} Mcion^{T}, its presence is strongly attested by good witnesses: P^{46} A B D F G P it$^{d.g}$ vg cop$^{sa.bo}$ et al.; see especially Metzger, *Textual Commentary*, 602. Two further observations may be added to our claim that the second εἰρήνη should be retained. (a) There are five words altogether which begin with the same letter (ε). It is likely that the author employs a word-play here (i.e., paronomasia; cf. 3.14–15). (b) The reduplicatio of εἰρήνη in the second half of the expression is probably for the purpose of amplification: while the first εἰρήνη states what is proclaimed by Christ, the second intensifies it. On the discussion of the figure of *reduplicatio* in ancient rhetorical handbooks, see esp. [Cicero], *Ad Her.* 4.28.38; Quintilian, *Inst.* 9.3.28.

199 In the [ἐλθὼν + indicative verb] construction, the participle always assumes the role of introducing the main theme which is expressed by the main verb. In the NT, this construction occurs most often in Matthew, one of the most Jewish writings in the NT: see, e.g., Matt. 2.23; 4.13; 8.7, et al. One cannot rule out that what we have here is another typical example of Semitism in terms of its syntax; cf. Mark 9.12; John 16.8; 2 Cor. 11.4; 1 Thess. 3.6. See further Porter, *Idioms*, 188.

200 Thus Moritz, *Mystery*, who concludes that the 'cross-ethnic thrust must not be played down in favour of a purely geographical notion restricted to Jews at home and in the diaspora' (32); also Schlier, *Epheser*, 123; Gnilka, *Epheserbrief*, 147–52; Lincoln, 'Use', here 25–30. Others have argued that Isaiah refers only to Jews in the homeland and in exile, e.g., Barth,

v. 11a: 'You, the Gentiles').[201] The Gentiles, in other words, are as much the 'far off' as they ever were, i.e., from the Jewish perspective. We can see no way to avoid the conclusion that this designation is a reminder of the author's delineation of the Jewish perspective in which the Gentiles were referred to as spatially removed from the Jewish social world or beyond the pale of the 'body politic of Israel' (v. 13a).[202] Although the referent of the 'near' is not explicit at this juncture, its immediate context suggests that this is an epithet of a people-group other than the Gentiles, i.e., the 'circumcision'/Jews (note that it is not: 'to those who *were* near', *but* 'to *the near*', cf. vv. 16a, 18, οἱ ἀμφότεροι).[203] The Jews are as much the 'near' as they ever were, i.e., according to their own self-perception. It is safe to say that here the author is using the language of the Jews, echoing the previous 'us-them' divisions (cf. vv. 13; 14a–b; 15b–c). However, what concerns him is the breaking down of the boundary between the two ethnic groups through Christ's reconciling effort, though this point is missed by most interpreters.[204] His choice of language here is to

Ephesians 1–3, 266–7; Lindemann, *Epheserbrief*, 51. Nevertheless, the notions of 'far off' and 'near' have already been hinted at in Isaiah's earlier passages, e.g., Isa. 33.12–14 (LXX), where the language was used to denote, respectively, the 'sinners in Zion' and the 'godless', cf. Isa. 13.4–5; Mic. 4.3.

[201] *Pace* Richardson, *Israel*, 152; Schnackenburg, *Ephesians*, 105; Bruce, *Ephesians*, 294; Martin, *Reconciliation*, 168; Lincoln, *Ephesians*, 146; but see Merklein, *Christus*, 14, 57; Barth, *Ephesians 1–3*, 267.

[202] *Contra* Stuhlmacher; Moritz. The suggestion that v. 17 is a 'fulfilment' of the prophetic oracle of Isaiah should not be pressed here, *contra* Beale, 'Reconciliation', here 578–9 who claims that the new creation and the reconciliation are the inaugurated fulfilment of the prophetic promise of a new creation (Isa. 40–66) in which Israel will be restored into a peaceful relationship with God, and that the death and resurrection of Christ mark the beginning of the fulfilment of OT promises of Israel's restoration. It is dubious, given the fact that 'Israel' has been defined so narrowly in ethnic terms (see my discussion of v. 12), whether the 'fulfilment of OT promises of Israel's restoration' can be understood in a straightforward manner without first considering a revised estimate of the definition of 'Israel'. See further Lincoln, 'Use', 29, who concludes, and quite rightly so, that '[t]he citation of the OT does not stand in its own right as a prediction or prophecy that is then said to be fulfilled, but rather the OT wording is used in address to the readers'. See further Hinkle, *Peace*. Hinkle's thesis is that the OT is always read in light of the author's conviction that the believers are one in Christ.

[203] The translation of NRSV is inaccurate; also NIV. There is also no good ground for us to surmise that the spatial imagery in v. 17 denotes cosmological powers (*contra* Köster, *Introduction*, 269), and that the conceptual background for v. 17 is to be sought in Gnostic thought.

[204] See, e.g., the gratuitous comments of Lindemann: 'Wurde sich τοῖς ἐγγύς auf die Juden beziehen, so müßte man zumindest erwarten, daß die Ablehnung der Heilstat Christi durch die Juden in irgendeiner Weise mitbedacht wird' (*Aufhebung*, 178, n. 174); Lindemann, *Epheserbrief*, 51, in which he concludes that the proclamation of peace to the Jews suggests that their priority is negated.

emphasise the *undisguised inclusivism* of Christ, who came to promulgate peace to Jews and Gentiles in order to eradicate the social distance between the two. His inclusivistic approach undercuts the ancient polarisation of the 'near'/Jew and the 'far off'/Gentile.[205] The underlying assumption is probably that the enmity between the two must be deemed abolished or conquered as Christ has come (more or less like a 'messenger', Heb. מבשר : see, e.g., 1 Sam. 31.9; 2 Sam. 1.20; 18.19, 26, 31).[206] His peace-making ministry is to include both Jew and Gentile as one. To suggest anything less than that would be to distort the true nature of Christ's reconciliatory work, making his peace-making 'mission' sound parochial and inward-looking.[207]

If this analysis is correct, it means that conjectures such as that ἐλθὼν κτλ. denotes the life of Christ on earth or Christ acting by his Spirit in his messengers are not necessary.[208] Nor is the concern here with peace between humankind and God as such. Instead, the point is that Christ assumed a laudable role in reconciling estranged humanity to God; he has come disinterestedly between Jew and Gentile, and his inclusivistic approach is a sign of his magnanimity.[209] His peace-making ministry is a concrete display of the way in which divided peoples can become reconciled.[210]

205 Thus Bauder and Link, 'ἐγγύς', who write: 'The pair of words "the near and the far" is a description of totality, meaning and embracing all' (53). The inclusivistic view is also expressed by Luke in Acts 2.39: 'For the promise is for you, for your children, and for *all* who are *far away*, everyone whom the Lord our God calls to him'; see also Preisker, 'μακράν', here 374.

206 See also Friedrich, 'εὐαγγελίζομαι', 707–8. Caird, *Letters*, 60, opines that Christ has uttered a 'royal proclamation' that hostilities are at an end; Moritz, *Mystery*, 51; BAGD 2a, δ.

207 *Contra* Mußner, *Christus*, 101, who suggests that v. 17 is to be read in the light of the ministry of Christ as depicted in the gospel, e.g. Matt. 10.5, 23, 15.24. Mußner, however, has changed his position from that in *Christus* over the years: see his *Epheser*, 84–5.

208 For a summary of the various interpretations of ἐλθὼν κτλ., see Merklein, *Christus*, 57–9. See also Schlier, *Epheser*, 136–7, who concludes that v. 17 relates to the descent of the crucified redeemer who broke through the horizontal wall separating heaven and earth; Best, *Ephesians*^{2}, 271–3; Abbott, *Ephesians*, 66. For other views, see, e.g., Schlatter, *Briefe*, 187 who suggests that v. 17 is a fulfilment of the prophetic word; similarly, Moritz, *Mystery*, 44. Pokorný, *Epheser*, 128, who thinks in Gnostic terms, argues that the risen Lord meets the earth in the confession of the Church and in their spiritual offering, because Christ comes to abolish the barrier between the above and the below.

209 See, e.g., Aristotle, who writes: 'And those things are noble which it is possible for a man to possess after death rather than during his lifetime . . . ; all acts done for the sake of others, for they are more disinterested; the successes gained, not for oneself, but for others; and for one's benefactors, for that is justice; in a word, all acts of kindness, for they are disinterested' (*Rhet.* 1367 ^{a}18–20); Dio, *Or.* 41.10.

210 *Contra* Merklein, *Christus*, 62–8, in which he argues that the Church is first created as the realm of salvation through the death of Christ on the cross, and reconciliation is given through the Church. He concludes that this 'primacy of ecclesiology over soteriology' is characteristic of the author of Ephesians.

To sum up: the author has displayed in his argument the undisguised inclusivism of Christ who instilled peace. He lays bare the magnitude of the blessings which Christ in his peace-making work has extended to estranged humanity, designated as Gentile and Jew. This stress upon the inclusivistic approach of Christ can be seen as the author's earnest campaign for the ending of ethnic enmity and of *Jewish* ethnocentrism. He assumes that Christ is the unifying force that brings the two ethnic groups together. Most importantly, Christ's reconciling ministry as such truly opens up the real potential of a universal inclusion of the nations, no matter how far apart they are socially, as the people of God in the 'one body'.

Christ's all-embracing approach would pose a sharp challenge to those who practised ethnocentrism and excluded the Gentiles from the fold of Israel. By inaugurating an all-embracing ministry, Christ provided an alternative framework which could easily galvanise the Gentiles (and Jews as well) into re-estimating their attitudes toward the ethnic 'other' and, most importantly, to *emulate* his footsteps as messengers of peace/reconciliation (cf. 6.15; Isa. 52.7; Nahum 2.1, LXX).[211]

4.4.9 ὅτι δι᾽ αὐτοῦ ἔχομεν τὴν προσαγωγὴν οἱ ἀμφότεροι ἐν ἑνὶ πνεύματι πρὸς τὸν πατέρα (v. 18)

The author's argument in v. 18 lays bare the reason[212] why Christ has adopted an inclusive approach in his reconciling ministry. As we shall see, the full resonance of 'Christ is our peace' is achieved as the attitude of mutual acceptance is being embraced by Jews and Gentiles within the framework of *pax Christi*.

The author of Ephesians probably assumes from an insider's perspective that the one God of Israel is the common Father to both Jews and

[211] This point is missed by all commentators. It is possible that the 'gospel of peace' in Eph. 6.15 can be defined as the gospel which brings reconciliation to the not-yet harmonised cosmos (cf. 6.10–12).

[212] *Pace* Mußner, *Epheser*, 85 who opts for an ambivalent character for the particle ὅτι, namely that it has both causal and declarative ('therefore') functions. See also Best, *Ephesians*², 273 who argues that 'it is difficult to see v. 18 as providing the reason for something in the preceding verses; rather it summarises and explains what has gone before: the Gospel of peace is the joint access of Jew and Gentile to the Father'. However, Best's conclusion would make a nonsense of vv. 19ff. (ἄρα οὖν κτλ.) which sum up the implications of the reconciling work of Christ for the Gentiles in connection with the 'holy ones'. For the usage of ὅτι as denoting a causal clause, see, e.g., Zerwick, *BG*, no. 416, 420; BDF §456 (1); Louw and Nida, 89.33; Schlier, *Epheser*, 139; Lincoln, *Ephesians* 149; NRSV, etc. For a discussion on the figure of ætiologia (Lat.: 'cause shown'), see in particular Bullinger, *Figures*, 963.

Gentiles (cf. v. 19; 3.14–15; 4.6),[213] and that they could gain unhindered access through Christ, *the* passage of access.[214] The term προσαγωγή may be used in an intransitive sense, denoting simply 'access' (e.g., 3.12; also Rom. 5.2): Christ is the one who creates access for 'both' Jews and Gentiles;[215] or transitively as denoting 'introduction to' a person, especially to a kingly presence: Christ may then be seen as one who introduces Gentiles and Jews to God.[216] Either way, the essential meaning is the same, namely that both Gentiles and Jews, on the basis of Christ who disinterestedly came between them as a mediator (and thus, between mankind and God), have become co-partners in their access to God's presence.[217]

If the author of Ephesians, as most interpreters have assumed, lays stress on the 'one Spirit', i.e., the divine Spirit,[218] as the medium of access to the presence of God (cf. 2.22; 3.5; 5.18; 6.18), he may easily evoke thought that such access no longer requires a concrete temple to symbolise or facilitate it.[219] This reading, however, is by no means conclusive. Our author may be accentuating here the unity of Gentiles and Jews

[213] See my discussion of the theme in chapter 2, section 2.2. See further Bruce, *Ephesians*, 301 who concludes that the term 'father' is a family name by which God's family members address him ('Abba, Father'); Chilton, 'Father' 151–69. Chilton's thesis is that the designation 'father' in the NT is hardly unprecedented in Jewish convention. See also Fitzmyer, *Paul*, 47–63; Schrenk, 'πατήρ', here 956–8, 978–82, 984–96, 1006–11; Quell, 'πατήρ', 972–4.

[214] The prepositional phrase δι' αὐτοῦ is placed at the position of emphasis in the sentence. Christ has assumed the mediatorial role which is elsewhere attributed to the archangels in Judaism: e.g., Tobit 12.12, 15; *1 Enoch* 9.3; 99.3; 104.1; *T. Levi* 13.5; 5.6–7; *T. Dan* 6.2. NT writers attributed this role to Christ: see, e.g., 1.5; also Rom. 1.8; 2.16; 5.21; 7.25; 16.27; 2 Cor. 5.18; Phil. 1.11; 1 Tim. 2.5; Titus 3.6; Acts 10.36; Heb. 13.21; Jude 25. See further Dunn, *Romans 1–8*, esp. 28.

[215] See, e.g., Polybius, *Hist.* 9.41; Plutarch, *Luc.* 15.4; Arrian, *Anab.* 1.20.8; LSJ, s.v., II.2; BAGD, s.v.

[216] See, e.g., Xenophon, *Cyr.* 7.5.45; Demosthenes, *Or.* 23.174.2; BAGD, s.v. See further Caird, *Letters*, 60 who concludes that the author has used a political rather than a cultic term; Grassi, 'Ephesians', 346. For a contrary view, see, e.g., Schnackenburg, *Ephesians*, 118; Lincoln, *Ephesians*, 149.

[217] It is not impossible that the word 'access' implies also a welcoming note, cf. Dio, *Or.* 41.11.

[218] So Mußner, 'Epheserbrief', 746; Merklein, *Christus*, 60; Chadwick, 'Absicht', 147; Barth, *Ephesians 1–3*, 267–8; Sampley, *One Flesh*, 162; Adai, *Geist*, 161–78, here 170–1. Martin, *Reconciliation*, 188 argues that the author is referring to the unifying Spirit of Eph. 4.4. Bruce, 301 opines that the author is speaking of 'the Spirit of God's Son'; cf. Schlier, *Epheser*, 139; Lindemann, *Aufhebung*, 179; Lincoln, *Ephesians*, 149. Schnackenburg, *Ephesians*, 118 writes: 'Christ's ministry as Mediator is thus carried on and made effective in the ever-present Spirit which fills the Church and all her members.'

[219] See, e.g., Mußner, *Epheser*, 87, who writes: 'Das Pneuma öffnet den »Raum« Gottes; »der Zugang zum Vater« ist geistlich »geortet«, nicht mehr geographisch-lokal wie im Tempel zu Jerusalem oder wie im gnostischen Mythus'; cf. Mußner, 'Modell', here 328. See also Dunn, *TPA*, 545–6, commenting on Rom. 5.2.

(ἔχομεν . . . οἱ ἀμφότεροι ἐν ἑνὶ πνεύματι).[220] Rather than stressing the work and agency of the Spirit (cf. 1.13; 1 Cor. 12.8–9)[221] or the effect of the (Holy) Spirit joining together Jew and Gentile (e.g., in unveiling the realm of God), the author uses the 'one spirit' language as a society-consolidating metaphor. Harmonious attitudes, to be sure, are his main concern here: 'both' Jews and Gentiles,[222] on the basis of and through Christ's reconciling work (δι' αὐτοῦ), gain unhindered access to Israel's God *in a common spirit* (cf. 4.3; Phil. 1.27).[223] His language of oneness is extremely close to that of ancient writers who urged reconciliation or concord in their communities plagued by strifes and divisions.[224] The implication of this is clearly that the barrier that stands between the two ethnic groups has now been broken. Rather than curtailing or reducing

[220] *Contra* Lindemann, *Epheserbrief*, 53 who has an agnostic conclusion concerning the meaning of 'both'.

[221] So Pokorný, *Epheser*, who writes: 'Der Geist ist nicht Mittler des Heils wie Jesus, er ist schon ein »Unterpfand des Erbes«, ein Teil des Heils, in ihm ist das Oben den Menschen nahe geworden' (129); cf. Chadwick, 'Absicht', 147. If the reference in v. 18 is to the 'one Spirit' denoting the Spirit as the medium of access to God, this would make the transitive sense ('introduction') of προσαγωγή an awkward rendering. This difficulty, however, disappears if we take the 'one spirit' as denoting human attitude. This reading also has the advantage of providing a smooth transition from v. 18 to vv. 19ff., in which the oneness of Gentiles and the 'holy ones' is still the author's main concern.

[222] *Contra* Lindemann, *Aufhebung*, 179 who reads 'both' as 'all' (*Alle*). The designation οἱ ἀμφότεροι is a fair reminder of 'both' sides of the divided human family, see vv. 14a, 16a. See further Homer, *Il.* 3.416 (The Trojans and the Danaans); 13.303 (the Ephyri and the Phleyes); Pindar, *Pyth.* 2.76, 'both sides' (i.e., the slanderers and the slandered); 10.2 (Lacedaimon and Thessaly); Herodotus, *Hist.* 1.76.4 (two contending powers, i.e., the Persians and the Ionians); 4.201.1; Polybius, *Hist.* 3.25.3 (the Carthaginians and Pyrrhusians), 6.24.8 (of two groups of centurions), et al.

[223] *Contra* Schlier, *Epheser*, 140, who argues that the author is speaking of the Spirit in a 'trinitarian' sense; Gnilka, *Epheserbrief*, gives an ambivalent character to the spirit: 'Unbeschadet der Tatsache, daß der eine Geist von ihnen erfahren wird und erfahren werden soll, ist jener Geist gemeint, der den einen Leib, die Kirche, durchwaltet' (146); Grassi, 'Ephesians', 346, who writes: 'A trinitarian formula expressing that through Jesus' humanity, the source of the Spirit, men can approach God the Father'; Schlatter, *Epheser*, 187, who speaks of 'Jesus's spirit in us'; Abbott, *Ephesians*, 68. It is more likely that the author has employed a play on words (*paronomasia*) here and in his later argument. In 4.3–4, he says two *different*, but closely related, things about the 's/Spirit'. Admittedly, the phrase 'eager to maintain the unity/oneness of the *s*pirit in the bond of peace' in 4.3 denotes a Christianised notion of 'mutual concord': he lays stress on the human effort to live 'in one mind' in accordance with the 'calling' (4.1). However, he also speaks of the 'one *S*pirit' a few words later in 4.4.

[224] See, e.g., Dio, *Or.* 41.10, who uses the language of oneness to stress the peculiarly intimate nature of the ties existing between Prusa and Apemeia: 'You [*sc.* peoples of Prusa and Apameia] are *one* demos and *one* citizen-body (εἷς ἐστε δῆμος και μία πόλις)'; Dio, *Or.* 39.5; Aristides, *Or.* 24.39). See also Philo, *Virt.* 35; *Spec.* 1.67; Josephus, *C. Ap.* 2.193; *Num. R.* 18.8, cf. Aristotle, *Pol.* 5.2.10; etc. It is indicative of the author's thorough-going argument for unity that the term 'one' occurs so often in the epistle (e.g., εἷς, ἕν, μία, see 4.3–6). See further Mitchell, *Reconciliation*, esp. 90–1, n. 141.

either side to one's own dimensions or measuring it with regard to one's small or servile spirit (cf. vv. 11b–12), the author lays stress on the way in which Christ's all-embracing attitude/approach bears on the attitudes of Jews and Gentiles toward the ethnic 'other'.[225] We can argue firmly that the author is striving to hint to his recipients that their attitude toward the ethnic other must always reflect the 'spirit' of Christ, i.e., his undisguised inclusivism (v. 17).[226] He not only perceives Christ as an antidote to the social distance between Gentiles and Jews, he also envisages the way in which a community-body of ethnic diversity could be healthily sustained (cf. 4.1–16). Rather than focusing on some 'trinitarian' formulations, we may say firmly that the author's thought is still hanging on Christ's peace-making ministry, which provides a fresh framework within which mutual concord – understood in our present context as mutual acceptance – is to be expressed by Jews and Gentiles. What matters, therefore, is the *new* attitude expected of both Jews and Gentiles who are reconciled in the one body of Christ (cf. vv. 11b–12).

To sum up: the author's formulation in v. 18 is fundamentally christological: it conjures up a picture of Jew and Gentile, who, on the basis of *pax Christi*, have gained access (or been introduced) to the one God of Israel, and faced down the old ethnic divisions by cultivating an inclusive attitude toward the ethnic 'other'. The author is obsessed with the oneness of Jews and Gentiles to the point that the Jews' access to God cannot be considered as complete without the Gentiles, and vice versa. If covenantal ethnocentrism is the major factor which results in Gentiles being marginalised and held outside the orbit of Israel and Israel's God-given grace (cf. vv. 11b–13a; cf. vv. 2, 6), the main aim of the author's argument here is to reverse the hitherto disadvantaged status of Gentiles *as Gentiles* by accentuating the fact that both Jew and Gentile have gained access to God on the basis of the reconciling work of the Messiah, and most importantly to make known to the Gentiles (and Jews alike) that a new paradigm is opened up for them, that through Christ 'both' could

[225] I therefore disagree with Lindemann, *Aufhebung*, 179, who argues that the phrase 'in one Spirit' has the same significance as 'in one body' in v. 16, and is 'the determination of the Christian self in the "body of Christ"'; Pokorný, *Epheser*, who writes: 'Als der Geist des einen Gottes wirkt er unter den Menschen zur Einheit hin' (129). It is very unlikely (*contra* Mußner and others) that the author is thinking of the baptismal experience of his readers. The same phrase, ἐν ἑνὶ πνεύματι, also occurs in 1 Cor. 12.13, denoting the initial condition of Christian life. This, however, is *not* the point of Eph. 2.18.

[226] *Pace* Percy, who argues that the 'inequality' between Jew and Gentile is caused by the Law, and concludes that the factual centre of Eph. 2.11–22 is the proclamation of the equal standing of Gentiles with Jews: 'daß die Heiden in gleicher Weise wie die Juden am Heil teilnehmen' (*Probleme*, 278–86; Percy, 'Probleme', esp. 187–8).

(and should) embrace the ethnic 'other' as partners in their access to God (cf. vv. 19–22; 3.6).

4.5 Conclusion

One of the most unfortunate features in the Christian history of interpretation is that Ephesians 2.14–18 has often been taken as a pretext for the view that Israel and the church have parted company from one another and that the 'Church' has stepped in to become the 'true Israel'. I have rejected this line of argument on the grounds that this theory has failed to account for the nub of the issue, i.e., the meaning and problem of 'Israel' in Ephesians from a proper perspective. My own inclination is that the church has not superseded Israel, and that the relationship between Israel and the church cannot be fully appreciated unless we take into consideration the ethnic factor which best explains the Jewish attitudes toward the Gentiles. I also argued in the present chapter that the discussion in vv. 11–13 should set the parameters for understanding vv. 14–18, which conjure up a picture of covenantal ethnocentrism and of Christ as *the* antidote to ethnic estrangement (and enmity) between Jews and Gentiles. The author has amplified the reconciling work of Christ, who came between Jews and Gentiles and concluded peace and reconciliation among the human groups. What is put in question, therefore, is not Israel as God's choice, but Israel which has become so entangled with ethnic identity that it would be quite impossible to speak of the inclusion of the Gentiles in an ethnically based Israel. The ethnic factor, if we may press further, will probably accelerate the 'partings' unless it is sufficiently dealt with.

It would also be wrong to suggest that different community-consolidating metaphors are used by the author to reinforce or to accelerate the separation of Israel and the church. Rather than to set the church over against the two parts of humankind from which it derives its members, we have argued at some length that the author's main concern is the oneness of (Christian) Jew/'holy one' and Gentile in an inclusive community. Metaphors such as 'one new man' and the 'one body' are *not* meant to imply a replacement of Israel but to replace, respectively, the Jewish notion of humanity which is based on the 'circumcision'/'uncircumcision' divisions, and the 'body politic of Israel' which is so confused in Jewish identity. They are used to counter a Jewish ethnocentrism in which Jewish identity was so confused among the Jews that it constricted Israel as an ethnically based body politic, encompassing only the Jews. This self-understanding of the Jews had serious social implications: it underscored inevitably the defective status of Gentiles *as Gentiles*. The self-assertive attitude which intensifies the privileges of one ethnic group while marginalising the 'other' as inferior can no longer be deemed significant 'in Christ', and the author of Ephesians has undercut this narrowly defined notion of 'Israel', in the hope that this exclusivistic 'body politic of Israel' can be transposed into 'one body' in which both Jews and Gentiles, or the 'near' and the 'far off', can be held together as the one people of God through the Messiah Jesus who died on the cross, while Israel's status as the people of God remains intact and uncontested. The 'one new man' language can be seen in the same way. It denotes the *new* corporate identity of an eschatological humankind consisting of Jew and Gentile as opposed to a humankind defined by the opposition of the 'circumcision'/'near' and the 'uncircumcision'/'far off'. The unity of Jew and Gentile as 'one new man' marks the turning point of humankind and, inevitably, the beginning of the transformation of the whole cosmos (cf. 1.10).

Many recent studies have tried to 'discover' the hymnic nature of Ephesians 2.14–18 but the attempts to explore the (rhetorical) effect of the eulogistic speech in praise of Christ *vis-à-vis* Jewish attitudes toward the Gentiles are slight. My analysis in the foregoing paragraphs has shown that our passage reflects most probably the author's conscious compositional effort to eulogise Christ by accentuating his reconciliatory work and magnanimity. The most striking effect of the author's *amplificatio* is that his encomiastic statements about Christ are set in comparison with those about the Jewish attitudes toward the Gentiles (cf. vv. 11b–12). What becomes immediately clear in this ingenious composition is that in so doing the author of Ephesians is able to set in comparison with the magnanimity of Christ the exclusivistic attitude of the Jews. The amplification, which comes immediately after the author has fleshed out the Jewish perception of the Gentiles, is prompted indeed by the latter and it has two major effects. In the *first* place, it could easily induce the Gentile readers for whom the author wrote to emulate the expedient and noble act of Christ, namely his undisguised inclusivism toward humankind (v. 17). Christ's death has in the author's perception provided a new framework (*pax Christi*) within which mutual acceptance or 'the oneness of spirit' between Jews and Gentiles may then be filled out (v. 18; also 4.1–6) and through which access to the one God of Israel in a *common* spirit is made possible. This also implies that the old ethnic forms of identification and allegiance are (and should be) faced down as an inclusive attitude is cultivated toward the ethnic 'other' on the basis of *pax Christi*. Finally and in the *second* place, the author who praises Christ has, by implication, also repudiated the attitude of excluding or factionalising rather than of integrating. He presumably is denouncing the disposition of the Jews who concerned themselves exclusively with the question of their own ethnic and religious identity but ignored the overall plan of God to include both Jews and Gentiles as his own people (cf. 1.3–14).

5

ISRAEL AND THE NEW TEMPLE (EPHESIANS 2.19–22)

5.1 Introduction

As mentioned in the foregoing chapter, the theme of ethnic reconciliation has been given a prominent position in the author's argument in Ephesians 2.14–18. Jews and Gentiles are reconciled through the peace-making ministry of Christ. The social distance between Jews and Gentiles has been rendered redundant because of Christ's undisguised inclusivism. The two human groups can both have access (in principle) to the Father God in/with a common spirit, i.e., on the basis of *pax Christi*.

5.2 Israel redefined: the Gentiles are fellow-citizens with the 'holy ones'

We want to examine in the present chapter some of the vital implications of the reconciling work of Christ for the Gentiles and, not least, for their relation to the 'holy ones'. My contention is that the implications above can be best explained by the hypothesis that the author of Ephesians conceives of the new identity of the Gentiles as having a close connection to the people of God, just as he consistently conceives of the Gentiles' past in relation to Israel and Israel's God-given grace. I shall be arguing that the author's aim is to articulate a particular vision of an *inclusive* community in which the Gentiles who previously had no place among the people of God could be located within the same domain. I shall be arguing that this ideal community, which is marked by its undisguised inclusivism, underscores the author's arduous effort to surmount a humankind that has hitherto been marked by divisions.

5.2.1 ἄρα οὖν οὐκέτι ἐστὲ ξένοι καὶ πάροικοι ἀλλὰ ἐστὲ συμπολῖται τῶν ἁγίων (v. 19a)

The author provides a logical connection between the present status of the Gentiles and the peace-making ministry of Christ in reconciling the two ethnic groups together. This is evident when he uses an 'emphatically inferential connective' (ἄρα οὖν) indicating that a conclusion is now drawn from what preceded.[1] That his argument in v. 19 is replete with the terminology of politics is clear enough. We are informed not only that the Gentiles are no longer 'aliens' (ξένοι) and 'resident aliens' (πάροικοι), but also that they are 'fellow-citizens (συμπολίται) with the holy ones' and 'members of the household (οἰκεῖοι) of God'. It is not irrelevant for us to ask: what does the author intend to achieve through the language of 'politics'? Before any answer to this question is suggested, it is necessary to take note of the way in which these terms have been traditionally understood.

The term ξένοι conveys, quite often, the conventional sense of being or living as aliens in a *foreign* territory other than one's homeland (e.g., Acts 7.6/Gen. 15.3; Acts 7.29/Exod. 2.15; Acts 13.16; 1 Pet. 1.17; 2.11, etc.).[2] It signifies one who is in an 'other' space in a geographical sense. In the Graeco-Roman world where one's culture is primarily associated with an emphasis on citizenship or membership in the *polis*, the term 'citizen' is often coupled with our present term and takes on considerable importance in defining a common in-group identity and creating the concept of 'aliens' in contrast.[3] Aliens, in other words, are people at the periphery as opposed to those at the centre (of the *polis*). The marginal character of the 'aliens' is made all the more apparent when it is coupled with πάροικοι,[4] the foreigners or resident aliens,[5] reinforcing the inferior or

[1] The combination of both particles, ἄρα and οὖν, is peculiar to the Pauline epistles, see esp. Thrall, *Greek Particles*, here 10–11. In our present context, the two particles provide an emphatically inferential connective to the entire preceding paragraph (i.e., vv. 11–18) rather than the immediately preceding sentence. I therefore disagree with Lincoln, *Ephesians*, who concludes that the author of Ephesians resumes his thought in v. 19 from v. 12 (126, 131, 150).

[2] *Pace* Friedrich, 'ξένος', who argues that the term ξένος in v. 19 can mean 'house guests'. There can be little doubt that the term ξένος may allude to the notion of 'hospitality' in ancient literature. But in a context where there is a stark contrast between 'citizens' and 'aliens' or 'resident aliens', it is extremely unlikely that ξένος has reference to 'house guests'. A helpful analysis of ξένοι as having the sense of 'friends who met through hospitality' or 'guest-friendship' (ξένια) in the Graeco-Roman world can now be seen in Konstan, *Friendship*, 33–7.

[3] ξένοι is often coupled with πολῖται (or ἄστοι) so that a clear distinction in their social status can be drawn: see, e.g., Pindar, *Isthm.* 1.51; Plutarch, *Alcib.* 4; Herodian 8.2.9; also Josephus, *Vita* 372; Philo, *Congr.* 22–3; *Post.* 109; *Ios.* 47; *Spec.* 4.142, et al.

[4] See, e.g., Diodorus Siculus, *Bib. hist.* 20.84.2; *SIG.*[3] 398.37; 742.45f. A more common term to use was μέτοικός ('metic'), which is often coupled with ξένος: see, e.g., Thucydides, *Hist.*, 4.90; Demosthenes, *Symm.* 163C; Plutarch, *Exil.* 607A; Diodorus Siculus, *Bib. hist.* 4.27.3; *Syll.*[3] 799; Philo, *Mos.* 1.34; *Abr.* 231. See further Schafer, 'Paroikos'.

[5] See, e.g., Gen. 23.4; Exod. 12.45; 18.3; Lev. 22.10; 25.23; Philo, *Cher.* 108, 119–20, 268; *Congr.* 22–3; *Somn.* 1.45; cf. Isocrates, *Nic.* 22; Diog. Laertius 1.82. See further Whitehead, *Metic.*

adjunct status of those who lie outside the orbit of the normal civic body or body politic.[6] A similar notion is also found in the Jewish scripture:[7] the 'resident aliens' were those who resided beside the Israelites, who could enjoy certain rights of legal protection and social acceptance, but who were restricted from participation in certain cultic rights and duties (e.g., 1 Chr. 29.15; Ps. 38.12; 118.19, 54; 119.5; Jer. 14.8; Acts 13.17; also Judith 5.9; 3 Macc. 7.19; Wis. 19.10; Sir. 16.8; 41.5; *Ps. Sol.* 17.17).[8] The basic notions of 'aliens' or 'resident aliens' above make it possible to pose the question of 'otherness', this time not in a geographical but in a cultural sense: embedded in the expression 'aliens' and 'resident aliens' is the way in which social groups define those at the periphery, in contrast to those who are at the centre of their social world-mapping. The author of our epistle has found this basic notion appropriate in order to produce his own representations of the Gentiles, reinforcing the fact that they are no longer at the marginal position as a result of the reconciling work of Christ on the cross: 'So then you are no longer aliens, *not even* resident aliens' (tr. mine).[9]

The observation above has led me to believe that the language in v. 19 is best understood as the author's 'political' vision to which our attention should be directed. But what does this vision truly entail? Why is such a vision necessary in our present context? These are important questions to which we shall turn as we advance our present exegesis.

As far as we can tell, the cohesiveness of a community or social group can often be asserted by making the differences between themselves and 'outsiders' clear. This is precisely what writers in the ancient world had been doing, in order that the distinctions between 'us' who were at the centre stage (e.g., in the city-states) and 'them' at the periphery could be forcibly established. There can be little doubt that when 'citizens' and 'aliens' are coupled together, they constitute unequivocally one of the most significant features in the ancient world serving as *signals and emblems of difference*. This can be easily attested in both Greek and

[6] See further Davies, 'Citizenship'.

[7] See also Barth, *Ephesians 1–3*, 269, who notes that 'the various Hebrew terms that denote different degrees of strangership were confused rather than clarified by the LXX'.

[8] Schmidt, 'πάροικος', concludes that a 'resident alien was often used in the Jewish tradition for one in relation to whom certain legal and social rights developed in Israel, but who as such is to be distinguished as a non-Israelite from the member of God's people or the resident' (844–6). Schürer, *HJPAJC*, III, 177ff., has also pointed out that Gentiles were regarded in the Jewish environment as a kind of client. See also Gnilka, *Epheserbrief*, 153.

[9] The conjunction καί may therefore be understood as having an emphatic force.

Roman writers.[10] We also have ample evidence from various inscriptions which indicate unequivocally that the terms 'citizens' and 'aliens' are often coupled together as emblems of difference in one's status in an ancient society, based on the customary structure of a city-state.[11] The status of 'strangership' is also well attested in the Jewish scriptures. Jewish writers such as Philo and Josephus were fully aware of these distinctions, not to mention their concerns about the 'struggle' of the Jews as foreigners *vis-à-vis* the native citizens, and vice versa (Philo, *Post.* 109; *Spec.* 4.70; *Mos.* 1.34–5; *Flac.* 44–8; *Cher.* 120f.; Josephus, *Vita* 372; *A. J.* 9.291; 14.21; *C. Ap.* 1.314; 2.257–9; 1 Macc. 1.10ff.; *CPJ*, nos 150–6).[12] Struggles between citizens and aliens were often described using closely related designations such as citizens/'Greeks' and aliens/'barbarians'. Suffice it to say that prejudice against foreigners has stamped its inextinguishable mark on ancient history.[13] In addition, we also have ample evidence which shows that various measures had been introduced in ancient city-states in order to exclude 'outsiders' and curb the assimilation of 'outsiders' into the proper body politic, thus consolidating the boundaries between citizens and non-citizens.[14] Certain oaths of loyalty to the city-state were imposed, especially upon new citizens, and these normally consisted of expressions that would promote firm allegiance to their own city-state and unity (ὁμόνοια) against threats

[10] The primary sources are extensive and the following must only be seen as examples: Plato, *Leg.* 8.850; cf. Plato, *Gorg.* 473D; Aristotle, *Eth. nic.*, 4. 1123 ^{a}3; cf. Aristotle, *Pol.* 3.1275 ^{b}37, 1277 ^{b}34–9; 4.1300^{b}31; Isocrates, *De pace* 48; cf. Isocrates, *Panegy.* 4.50; *Ep.* 3.5; Aristophanes, *Pax* 297; *Lys.* 580; Polybius, *Hist.* 4.72.3–4; cf. 1.36.3; 4.54.5; 13.8.3; Diodorus Siculus, *Bib. hist.* 11.76.6; Plutarch, *Cimon* 10.1.4; cf. [cons. Apoll.] 120A.10; *Sept. sap. conv.* 151A.2; Diog. Laertius, 6.63, 93. For Roman writers: see, e.g., Cicero, *Officiis* 1.124–5, 3.47; Ennius, *Seneca* 6; Pliny, *Persa* 753; Livy, *Ab urbe* 22.38; Q. Curtius Rufus, *Hist. Alex.* 8.14.46. See further Fowler, *City-States*, esp. 1–22; Murray, 'Polis'; Davies, 'Citizenship'; Crawford, 'Citizenship'; McKechnie, *Outsiders*.

[11] For example, see *SIG*^{3} 398.37 (Cos, 278 BCE). All the three terms, 'citizens', 'resident aliens' and 'aliens', appear in the same sentence; also *SIG*^{3} 495; 708; 729; *OGIS*, 693; cf. *SIG*^{3} 55.29.

[12] In rabbinic Judaism proselyte, godfearer and resident alien are classified under the same category as aliens who stand in a certain religious and social relation to 'Israel' but are not full members. See further Str-B, II, 715–23; Meyer, 'πάροικος'.

[13] Hostile attitudes toward 'outsiders' are expressly described by ancient writers: see, e.g., Juvenal, *Sat.* 3.58–65, 69–78, 81–7, 100–6; Cicero, *Flac.* 15, 16; Martial, *Epig.* 10.76; Petronius, *Sat.* 26.9; 32.1; 37.1–6, 8, 9; 38.6–7; 46.3, 5–8; 71.1–4; 75.8–11; 76.1–9; 77.4, 6). See also Hecataeus Abdera, *Aegyptiaca* (*apud.* Diodorus Siculus, *Bib. hist.* 40.3.1–2); Philo, *Ios.* 29–31; *Opif.* 19. Echoes of the same prejudice reverberate loud and clear in Aristides (117–81 CE), who writes: 'No one is a foreigner who is worthy' (ξένος οὐδεὶς ὅστις ἄξιος, *Or.* 26.60). See further Finley, *Politics*, 122–41, esp. 125; Aalders, *Plutarch*, 26–44; Grant, *Greeks and Romans*, 123–32; Sherwin-White, *Roman Citizenship*, 258–9.

[14] See esp. the discussion of the subject in Manville, *Citizenship*, esp. 217; Sinclair, *Democracy*, 105f.; Sherwin-White, *Roman Citizenship*, 259; Davies, 'Citizenship'.

from without. So according to Xenophon, 'everywhere in Greece, it is customary for the citizens to swear to preserve concord and everywhere they swear that oath' (*Mem.* 4.4.16).[15] It will suffice, therefore, to say that it was a normal practice for ancient authors to speak of the citizen/alien polarity so that the 'insiders' could be marked off from the aliens and that the cohesiveness among the 'insiders' might be firmly reinforced. Just as in the case of the well-known linkage in classical Greek literature of the words 'Greek' and 'barbarian',[16] indicating the entire human race from a particular perspective, or other conventional stratifications in ancient society,[17] the polarisation of 'citizen' and 'alien' is one of the customary distinctions which most ancient writers in the Graeco-Roman world would have accepted as a premise or axiom in strengthening the differences and boundaries between 'insiders' and 'outsiders'.[18] Such formulations, however, tend also to turn the citizen-body into a closed, enfranchised, privileged body politic,[19] outside which lay the inferior or adjunct strata such as aliens and foreigners.

In view of what we have discussed above, it should come as no surprise that our author's 'political' language is no more than a permutation of a classical *topos* found among ancient writers.[20] He was familiar with the

[15] See also *Syll.*^{3} 526, where it records that an oath of loyalty was imposed upon the new citizens of Itanos (Crete), who thus pledged unswerving loyalty to the city-state: text cited in Austin, *Hellenistic World*, no. 90. Similar oaths were required when two city-states decided to fuse together politically as homopoliteia or 'isopoliteia' (i.e., equal citizenship): see, e.g., Polybius, *Hist.* 4.3.6; 28.14.3; *Staatsv.* III.545 (Homopoliteia of Cos and Calymnus, *c.* 205–200 BCE); *SIG*^{3} 647 (Sympoliteia of Stiris and Medeon in Phocis, 2nd cent. BCE), cited in Austin, *Hellenistic World*, nos 133 and 134. See further Linderski and Rhodes, 'Isopoliteia'; cf. Linderski and Rhodes, 'Sympoliteia'.

[16] See, e.g., Herodotus, *Hist.* 9.11.2; 9.55.2, where the barbarians were also known as *xeinoi*; Aristotle, *Pol.* 1.1252 ^{b}8; Euripides, *Iph.*, 1379 and 1400; Xenophon, *Ages.* 1.12; cf. Xenophon, *Mem.* 8.67; 18.253 and 270; Isocrates, *Ep.* 2.10; Strabo, *Geog.* 14.2.28ff.; Plutarch, *Alex. fort.* 328C–329C; Philo, *Prob.* 48, 138; Cicero, *Resp.* 1.37, 58; Ovid, *Tristia* 5.10.37; *SIG*^{3} 643, et al. See further Aalders, *Plutarch*, 13; Hall, *Barbarian*, esp. 5; Goldenberg, 'Scythian-Barbarian'; Wright, 'Barbarians'.

[17] (a) Rich and poor: Xenophon, *Symp.* 4.35; Strabo, *Geog.* 14.2.5.652–3; Livy, 42.29–30.7; Diog. Laertius, 6.11; 50; 72; 104. (b) Freedman and slave: Aristotle, *Pol.*, 1.1253 ^{b}20; Diog. Laertius, 6.4; 29; 30, 74. Paul is fully aware of these distinctions: Gal. 3.28; 4.7; 1 Cor. 12.13; Philem. 16. See further Sabine and Smith, *Commonwealth*, esp. 18.

[18] See also Davies, 'Polis'; Sealey, *History*.

[19] For the inferior position of the aliens and foreigners, compare Cicero, *Off.* 3.47 and *CPJ* 153, where foreigners are clearly classified as those who resided in 'cities not their own'. Finley, *Politics*, 125 concludes that 'the good life was possible only in the *polis* and that the good man was more or less synonymous with the good citizen, that slaves, women and barbarians [*sc.* in the perception of the Greek citizens], were by nature inferior and so fell without the pale of the *polis*.' See also Gnilka, *Epheserbrief*, 153; Aalders, *Plutarch*, 26–44.

[20] See, e.g., McKechnie, *Outsiders*, 16–33; de Ste Croix, *Class Struggle*, 9–10.

way in which humankind had been structurally classified in the ancient world and employed similar 'citizen'/'alien' polarity to aid him in consolidating the identity of the Gentiles. His 'political' agenda, however, is *essentially* different from that of most contemporary writers in the ancient world.[21] His aim is to eliminate at a stroke the 'us-them' polarity that had long dominated the ancient world and to deconstruct the antinomies by which one ethnic group demarcated its world from the 'other'. That is the issue with which the author has been fully preoccupied. That is his 'political' vision when he comes to *re*define the identity of his Gentile recipients.

However, the total picture of the author's vision cannot be fully appreciated without taking into account the following factors. Who else – if anyone – would he have in mind when he set out to strengthen the 'inside' status of his Gentile recipients? Why is he using *inclusive* language to speak of the status of the Gentiles *vis-à-vis* the 'holy ones'? Are his formulations in v. 19 *ad hoc* expressions, or do they reveal our author's more subtle concerns? How does his 'political' vision fit into the reconciling work of Christ expounded in vv. 14–18?

Part of the answer to our questions above lies in the designation the 'holy ones'. The way in which the 'holy ones' should be interpreted in this reference is a matter of scholarly dispute. There are three main interpretations. (1) Some interpreters contend that the 'holy ones' refers to the angels or heavenly beings.[22] It has been argued that this reference is found elsewhere in the OT[23] and the Pauline corpus (e.g., 1 Thess. 3.13; 2 Thess. 1.7, 10). The covenanters at Qumran had also attributed special importance to the position occupied by the 'holy ones', i.e., the heavenly angels to whom the elect community on earth is joined.[24] However, we have had occasion to reject this reading on the grounds that the emphasis from v. 19 onward is basically *not* the union of earthly beings and heavenly beings but an earthly one. As mentioned in the foregoing chapter, the 'barrier' that is removed is not a horizontal one (i.e., one between heavenly

[21] I have intentionally punctuated the various political terms with inverted commas, for I think the author's main intention is not political, despite the fact that he is fully aware of the politics of his day (see, e.g., the notion of 'household-management' in Eph. 5.22–6.9; cf. 2.12). He uses the familiar political terminology mainly to impart to his Gentile recipients the conception of oneness between two ethnic groups whose relationships were tainted with disharmonious, hostile attitudes.

[22] Lindemann, *Aufhebung*, 183; Gärtner, *Temple*, 322; Gnilka, *Epheserbrief*, 154; Mußner, 'Contributions', 166, who changed his view in his commentary from that in *Christus*, 105–6, see below n. 25.

[23] See, e.g., Job 5.1; Ps. 89.6–7; Zech. 14.5; cf. *1 Enoch* 1.9.

[24] See, e.g., 1QS 2.8–9; 8.11; 11.7–8; CD 20.8; 1QM 12.1, 4, 7; 1QH 6.13; 1QSb; 4QEnoch^{c} 1.1.15; 4Q181 1.4. See further Davidson, *Angels*, 165–6, 272.

beings and earthly beings) but a vertical one, i.e., between two human groups.[25]

(2) Others who have rejected the above interpretation contend that Ephesians 2.11–22 describes the pre-Christian past of the Gentiles as a stark contrast to their Christian present and that the 'holy ones' must therefore refer to *all believers*.[26] In favour of a reference to 'all believers' are the facts that in the writer's view they now constitute the people of God as Israel *did* in the past, that elsewhere in the letter ἅγιοι is used of Christians in general, and that the συν-compounds in vv. 21, 22 and 3.6 have in view the rest of the church.[27] One must admit that there is some truth in this interpretation. However, while the author's language permits such an understanding of the 'holy ones', it does not demand it. This interpretation also overstates the discontinuity between Israel and the church. As we have mentioned in our previous chapters, the Jews and the Gentiles were designated as structural opposites: the 'circumcision'/the 'uncircumcision' (v. 12); the 'near'/the 'far off' (v. 17). The 'otherness' of the Gentiles was expressed in characteristically Jewish terms: 'Gentiles in the flesh', 'aliens to the covenants of the promise', 'having no hope and godless in this world' (v. 11b, 12). There is therefore no sufficient ground to rule out the Gentiles and the 'holy ones' as constituting another pair of structural opposites which is similar to those mentioned above. The context of vv. 11–22 requires thus a narrow interpretation of the designation in question, pointing *not* to 'the rest of the church'.

(3) For some scholars, the Gentiles are still closely related to *historical* Israel. Barth, for example, argues that 'through his *incorporation into Israel* a Gentile finds communion with God' (italics mine).[28] The question for us is: which 'Israel'? Does it refer to the 'body politic of Israel' from which Gentiles were excluded? Does the author mean that the Gentiles started out with a disadvantage and had to be drawn near to participate in the ancient privileges which Israel offered?[29] It appears that the 'incorporation' is by no means straightforward, as so often assumed.

[25] *Pace* Lindemann, *Aufhebung*, 183; also Gnilka, *Epheserbrief*, 154; Mußner, 'Contributions', 166.

[26] So Lincoln, *Ephesians*, 151; Abbott, *Ephesians*, 69; Robinson, *Ephesians*, 67; Hanson, *Unity*, 147; Pfammatter, *Bau*, 76–7; Merklein, *Amt*, 132; Schnackenburg, 'Politeia', 471; Mußner, *Christus*, 105–6.

[27] Lincoln, *Ephesians*, 151.

[28] Barth, *Ephesians 1–3*, 169–70; Meuzelaar, *Leib*, 63. Sanders, *Law*, 172, contends that 'the Gentiles were adopted into Israel according to the flesh'.

[29] Richardson, *Israel*, 156–7.

We have mentioned earlier that the rationale behind the argument of the author in v. 19 is based consistently upon his conviction that the boundaries between 'insiders' and 'outsiders' have been torn down through the peace-making work of Christ and that the same rationale should determine our understanding of the status of the Gentiles vis-à-vis the 'holy ones'. What is proposed below is that the union that is in view is a *social* one. I shall argue that the concern in v. 19 is the implications of Christ's reconciling work for two ethnic groups that had kept apart from one another (vv. 11–12, 14–18). There can be little doubt that the designation 'holy ones' is often used as a reference to the self-understanding of Israel as the elect of God who are singled out and consecrated for God (e.g., Exod. 19.6; 22.30; Lev. 20.26; Num. 15.40; Deut. 7.6; 14.2, 21; 26.19; 28.9; Ps. 16.3; 106.6; Isa. 62.12; Jer. 2.2; Dan. 7.27; 12.7; Wis. 3.9; 4.14; 10.15, 17; 18.9; 3 Macc. 2.6; 1QM 10.10; 12.8; 11QT 48.7, 10; 4Q400 1.17; 4Q504 4.10; 4Q511 2.7; 4QFlor. 1.4; 1Q34 3.2.5–7; 4Q160 3–5; 4Q511 2; *T. Abr.* 20.14; *T. Levi* 5.4; *T. Job* 43.15).

For us, however, the most important question is, why does the author refrain from saying that the Gentiles are fellow-citizens with Israel, the elect of God? The most probable reason for this avoidance is the fact that 'Israel' understood as the people of God has become too narrowly defined by the Jews (2.12). Indeed, it will be quite impossible to speak of the inclusion of the Gentiles into an Israel which is inward-looking.[30] With the 'holy ones', however, it is possible for our author to redefine the people of God afresh. The close connection between the Gentiles and the Israel of God is firmly established. Thus said, the 'holy ones' can certainly include the Jews who perceived the world as divided into two distinct categories (the 'circumcision' and the 'uncircumcision'). The point is that the author's language here denotes his undisguised inclusivism.[31] The implication is that the 'us' and 'them' dichotomy is disintegrative and characterises the old era – 'the time without Christ' (vv. 11b–12) – and should now be left behind. To assert that the 'us'-'them' boundary is no longer significant is just another way of saying that an inclusive community should no longer place its emphasis upon the factors that would effect disintegration *but* upon those that would encourage integration of Jews and Gentiles who come from different ethnic backgrounds. That is precisely what the author wishes to achieve by his language of conciliation which we now find in v. 19. A new image of the Gentiles emerges:

[30] See my discussion in 3.3.1.1 and 3.3.1.2, respectively.

[31] We cannot, however, tell whether the author's inclusivistic perspective is embraced by those Jews who estranged the Gentiles (cf. vv. 12).

they are fellow-citizens with the 'holy ones' (cf. 3.6).[32] Their status as the 'other' (i.e., 'aliens', 'alien residents') has been done away with. They and the Jews now share the same 'socio-political' space.

To sum up our discussion thus far, the author's 'political' vision is marked by its undisguised inclusivism. His aim is to assure the Gentile readers what the reconciling work of Christ meant for them, and more importantly for their new relations with the people of God. His language of conciliation reinforces his conviction that the 'us'-'them' boundary which had hitherto divided the 'circumcision' from the 'uncircumcision' has been broken down on the basis of *pax Christi*. The Gentiles are on the same side with the 'holy ones'/Israel. His language is that which advances concord: the Gentiles and Jews are now one, without any inward-looking dispositions and *ethnic* factors interposing between them to mark them off as distinct from each other (cf. vv. 11–13a).

5.3 The Gentiles are God's own and the holy dwelling of God

We are informed that the Gentiles are not simply 'fellow-citizens with the 'holy ones' but also 'members of the household of God'.[33] The author's language here thus enables us to see more accurately the double-movement of his argument concerning the Gentiles' new identity.

5.3.1 καὶ οἰκεῖοι τοῦ θεοῦ, ἐποικοδομηθέντες ἐπὶ τῷ θεμελίῳ τῶν ἀποστόλων καὶ προφητῶν (vv. 19b–20a)

Some scholars have suggested that our attention should be drawn to the *cultic* associations of οἶκος τοῦ Θεοῦ as the reference to the spiritual temple already present here.[34] Others have opined that there is a shift here from the political imagery of the state or commonwealth to the more intimate picture of a family.[35] It is more likely that the term οἰκεῖοι, which appears *collocatively* with such political terms as ξένοι or πάροικοι, is one of the constituting elements of the author's 'political' vision. This

[32] The term συμπολῖται is rarely found in classical Greek, but see Aeschylus, *Sept*. 605, ξὺμ πολίταις; Euripides, *Heracl.* 826; Theophrastus, *Piet.*, 2.25; Josephus, *A. J.* 19.175; BAGD, s.v. Cf. *SIG*³ 633.33, where the idea of συμπολιτεία is well expressed: 'The Melesians will be fellow citizens of the Heracleans, and the Heracleans of the Milesians'. See further Rhodes, 'Poleis', here 175, 181; Larsen & Rhodes, 'Sympoliteia'. See also my discussion in 3.3.1.1, n. 75.

[33] The evidence for the second ἐστε is strong: P⁴⁶ᵛⁱᵈ ℵ A B C D* F G 33, et al. The repetition is probably for the sake of emphasis. Elsewhere in the NT, the second auxiliary can always be elided: see, e.g., Gal. 4.7: 'So *you are* no longer a slave but a child'; Mark 10.8: 'So *they are* no longer two but one flesh.'

[34] Thus Mußner, *Epheser*, 92; Merklein, *Amt*, 133–4.

[35] So Lincoln, *Ephesians* 1–3, 152; Barth, *Ephesians 1–3*, 270.

is clear as we refer to evidence from literary authorities which indicates that the term οἰκεῖοι when coupled with ξένοι[36] or ἀλλότριοι[37] always helps to enhance the 'us' and 'them' distinctions in ancient society (i.e., *polis*).[38] But the most striking analogy is to be found in Plato's work, *Protagoras*. The wording in v. 19 is extremely close to the speech of Hippias the sophist, a younger contemporary of Protagoras, who rebuked his audience (including Prodicus) in a dispute over the difference between 'nature' and 'law': 'I regard you all as kinsmen and intimates and fellow-citizens by nature, not by law; *for like is akin to like* by nature, whereas the law, despot of mankind, often constrains us against nature' (ἡγοῦμαι ἐγὼ ὑμας συγγενεῖας τε καὶ οἰκείους καὶ πολίτας ἅπαντας εἶναι φύσει, οὐ νόμῳ· τὸ γὰρ ὅμοιον τῷ ὁμοιῳ φύσει συγγενές ἐστίν κτλ., 337C; cf. Plato, *Pol.*, 6.494B; Plutarch, *Alex. fort.* 329 A–B; *Sul.* 9.7.3; *Lyc.* 3.5.3). Here the rhetoric of 'sameness' is clear enough: like is akin to like. In view of what we have discussed above, we have reason to believe that the author of Ephesians is making the same point as Hippias and other writers by using some of the most common terminology of politics to reinforce the idea of intimate relations among humankind when he speaks of the new status of his Gentile recipients.[39] The author is making

[36] See, e.g., Philo, *Mos.* 1.34; *Spec.* 4.70, et al.

[37] See, e.g., Plato, *Leg.* 2.666C; cf. Plato, *Theaet.* 126B; *Pol.*, 5.463B; Philo, *Post.*. 109; *Spec.* 4.70; *Virt.* 173; *Legat.* 294; Josephus, *B. J.* 4.275. Both ξένοι and ἀλλότριοι are always categorised under the same rubric as structural opposites to 'relations, citizens, friends' (οἰκεῖοι, πολίται, φιλοι): see, e.g., Philo, *Post. Cain.* 109; Plato, *Gorg.* 509B; *Prot.* 313A; *Pol.* 1.328D.

[38] See, e.g., Aristophanes, *Vesp.* 1022 (οὐκ ἀλλότριων, ἀλλ' οἰκεῖων Μουσῶν στομαθ' ἡνιοχνσας); Josephus, *A. J.* 2.27 (οὐκ ἀλλότριων ὀντων, ἀλλ' οἰκεῖων); cf. Josephus, *A. J.*. 4.275; 20.210; *Vita* 31. See also Thucydides, 3.13; 2.39; Plutarch, *Symm.* 7.668C, 708C; *Nicias* 9.7.3; *Curios.* 519E.1; *Ages. et Pomp.* 4.9.3–5.1; *Sol. et Publ.* 1.6.2; Herodian, 6.9.8.

[39] It would be less accurate to suggest that 'there is a move from the political imagery of the state of commonwealth to the more intimate picture of a family' (*pace* Lincoln, *Ephesians*, 150, 152), since both the family and citizenship can be seen as belonging to the *topos* of politics in the Graeco-Roman world: see, e.g., the phrase οἰκεια χώρα used by Aristotle to denote the 'city-community' when he referred to the *citizens* of the city-state, as opposed to those who were outside the orbit of the *polis*, see his *Pol.* 2.1265 ^{a}24 and 2.1273 ^{b}31; cf. *Politics* 1.1253 ^{b}1, where Aristotle considered 'household' the 'component part of the city-state'. Seneca, *Ben.* 1.53, spoke not only of the citizens of a city-state as 'members of the same city' sharing their common facilities such as the town square, temples, covered walkways, roads, law and constitution, law-courts and election, customs and associations and the dealings and agreements that bind people to others, but also of the 'household' (*familia*) as the means by which *a closer bond between human relations could be built* as this is 'the element from which a city is made, so to speak, the seed-bed of the state' (1.53–4); cf. Cicero, *Off.* 1.53–4, 3.69; Thucydides, 2.40, 3.65; Isocrates, *Plat.* 51; Andocides, *Lac.* 4.15; Philo, *Fug.* 36; cf. Philo, *Mut.* 148–50; *Ios.* 38; *Post.* 109; *Mos.* 1.34–6; *Spec.* 4.70.

known to his Gentile recipients that they are actually 'God's own',[40] they belong to God's household and should no longer be perceived as foreigners. It would not be rash to conclude that the author is using some of the political terminology to 'institute' a single community in which the citizens/aliens boundary had been breached and left behind.

To recapitulate what we have said so far, the formulation in v. 19b denotes the author's arduous effort to overcome the handicapped position of the Gentiles by relocating them as firmly as possible among the 'holy ones', *intensifying* thus the intimacy between his recipients and their Jewish counterparts on the one hand, and their 'householder' (*sc.* God) on the other. He asserts that the Gentiles are *familia Dei* (cf. Gal. 6.10), while saying nothing about the status of the Jews – probably because their status in the 'house of God' is never put in question or denied.[41] His language shows that there is now a complete shift of the Gentiles from a position at the periphery to a close bond with God. They are no longer 'home-changers' (to use Whitehead's word for 'resident alien'), but 'God's own'.

5.3.2 ἐποικοδομηθέντες ἐπὶ τῷ θεμελίῳ τῶν ἀποστόλων καὶ προφητῶν (v. 20a)

Despite the fact that the 'us'-'them' dichotomy has been made redundant as a result of Christ's reconciling work, the reshaping of the new identity of the Gentiles is far from complete. To be sure, the conclusions we have reached in the preceding paragraphs have a significant bearing upon the way in which vv. 20–2 should be interpreted in at least two ways. In the first place, the author has unveiled by his use of various political images the blueprint of an ideal community which is marked by its undisguised inclusivism. In the second place, what is left for our author is to lay bare the distinctive features of this community. We must not lose sight of the inclusivistic perspective mentioned above as we advance our exegesis.

The use of such architectonic images as 'building', 'cornerstone', 'foundation', 'temple' and 'dwelling place' has attracted much scholarly attention in recent decades.[42] However, what has not been sufficiently

[40] Cf. 1 Tim. 5.8; Aristotle, *Rhet.* 1.1361 ^{a}21; Pindar, *Nem.* 12.19; Herodians, 6.9.8; Philo, *Ios.* 46; *P. Lille* (3 BCE) 1.7.5; *P. Magd.* (217 BCE) 13.2; *P. Grenf.* (103 BCE) 2.28.5, examples cited in M-M.

[41] See, e.g., Jer. 31.31; Judith 4.15; 6.17; Baruch 2.26; Matt. 10.6; Acts 2.36.

[42] See esp. Schnackenburg, 'Bau', 258–72; Pfammatter, *Bau*, 78–97; cf. Pfammatter, *Epheserbrief*, 22, 24. For a brief bibliography, see Barth, *Ephesians 1–3*, 270 n.73; Lincoln, *Ephesians*, 154.

appreciated is the way in which these terms relate to the new 'location' acquired by the Gentiles in the light of ethnic reconciliation and of the Gentiles' defective status in the perception of the Jews. I shall argue in what follows that the various architectonic images are meant (a) to consolidate the 'new identity of the Gentiles' by reinforcing their interconnectedness with other members who belong to the same community and (b) to (tacitly) substantiate the *set-apartness* of Gentiles for God, by implying that the Gentiles who are built into the temple are indeed holy.

The author uses various οἶκος words to reinforce the Gentiles' sense of belonging. Such οἶκος words as ἐποικοδομηθέντες, οἰκοδομή, συνοικοδομεῖσθε and κατοικητήριον are prompted, most probably, by his earlier statement in which οἰκεῖοι (τοῦ Θεοῦ) serves almost certainly as a paronym for these words (vv. 20a, 21a and 22).[43] It is fair to say that the author describes the new 'location' of the Gentiles in a strikingly pictorial way. The purpose of this 'vivid description' (ἐνάργεια) is probably to induce his readers to envisage the scene of a 'building' or 'house' in their 'mind's eye', thereby rendering it immediate and affective.[44] To understand what the author is trying to do with the various οἶκο-images and 'stone' metaphors we need look no further than the quite common practice of ancient political theorists who made use of the 'stone' and 'building' *topoi* to consolidate group or corporate identity.[45] Thus, when Dio Chrysostom spoke of the people of his ideal community, he defined their identity in terms of 'a *polis* on the rock' (*Or.* 36.13, 20; cf. Clement of Alexandria, *Strom.* 4.26; Eusebius, *Praep. ev.* 15.15).[46] Seneca, who uses similar *topoi* to describe community life, writes: 'Our relations with one another (*societas nostra*) are like a stone arch, which would collapse if the stones did not support each other, and which is upheld in this very way' (*Ep.* 53).[47] No different are the settlers at Qumran, who made use of similar *topoi* to strengthen and legitimate their own identity as the eschatological community. The 'architects' or initial nucleus of the covenanted community were the three Zadokite priests and twelve laymen who not only laid the *foundations* of the Council of the Community but also became the components of that foundation themselves (1QS 5.5;

43 See further Shanor, 'Master Builder'. See further Banks, *Community*, esp. ch. 3.

44 See esp. Zanker, 'Enargeia'; Vasaly, *Representations*, 19–25; Lausberg, *Handbuch*, I, 399–407. The same technique of *evidentia* is probably employed by the author of 11QT, where the 'Temple' is described in great detail; cf. Ezek. chs. 40–8.

45 See, e.g., Malherbe, *Exhortation*, 149.

46 See further Schofield, *Stoic Idea*, esp. 59, 73.

47 See esp. Mitchell, *Reconciliation*, 100.

8.1–11; 9.3ff.; cf. 1QH 6.25–7; 7.8f.; 4QpIsa).[48] There can be little doubt that NT writers also introduced similar *topoi* to underscore the corporate identity of their own communities (e.g., 1 Cor. 3.9–17; 6.19; Matt. 16.18). It should occasion no surprise that the author of Ephesians is making use of the 'stone' and 'building' images to legitimise the 'inside' status of his Gentile recipients. Suffice it to say that the author's endeavour must have provided the Gentile readers with a deep sense of identity and security.

That the author uses the 'foundation' (θεμελίος) to denote the apostles and prophets as a category of people who possess a status of central importance to a community is clear enough (cf. 1QS 8.7–8; 4QpIsa^{d} 1.3, par. Isa. 54.11–12; Philo, *Praem.* 150; Rom. 15.20; 1 Cor. 3.10–12; also Matt. 16.17–18; Rev. 21.14).[49] The point is that the apostles and prophets are 'the beginning which precedes all else' (to use Philo's words).[50] The author probably had in mind the distinctively inclusive character of the two orders of ministry when he spoke of the foundational role of the apostles and prophets. To be sure, they are agents who received the divine 'mystery' and lay bare the 'mystery' which is marked by its undisguised inclusivism: it has now been revealed to his holy apostles and prophets in the Spirit that the Gentiles have become fellow-heirs, members of the same body, and partakers in the promise in Christ through the gospel (3.1–13; cf. Rom.11.13ff.; 15.15; 1 Cor. 4.9; also 1 Cor 15.7–9).[51] The Gentile recipients' sense of identity through an awareness of their connection to the foundation of the community is now enhanced.

It should be clear by now that the 'foundation' upon which the Gentiles are built is both 'apostolic' and 'prophetic'.[52] What made 'apostles and prophets' notable was, most probably, that the ministry in which

[48] See also Bruce, *Ephesians*, 305.

[49] Cf. Rev. 3.12; 21.14; *Joseph & Aseneth* 17.6. It is mentioned in *midr.* Yalkut Shimeoni 1.766 on no.23.9 that Abraham is the 'foundation' upon which other stones (i.e., Israel) would be constructed into a living community of faith. See further Horgan, *Pesharim*, 125–6; Aune, *Revelation 1–5*, esp. 241–2.

[50] In Hellenistic Jewish thought, the role of foundation is attributed to 'nature' (φύσις), which is also understood as the 'original, the earliest and the real cause': see, e.g., Philo, *Her.* 115–16.

[51] *Pace* Pfammatter, *Epheserbrief*, 25, who argues that the author's aim is to define a form of church government, e.g., that of 'a holy catholic and apostolic church'.

[52] *Pace* Pfammatter, ibid., 24–5, who overstates the importance of the 'apostolic church': 'Kirche ist deshalb immer "apostolische" Kirche – oder *sie ist nicht die Kirche Christi*!' (italics mine); cf. Merklein, *Amt*, 147–9. Closer to the mark is Schnackenburg, *Ephesians*, who writes: 'If the apostolicity of the Church is considered as an element of ecclesiology, we must not overlook the fact that for Eph. the prophetic-pneumatic is also part of the foundation of the Church' (123).

they engaged was distinctively inclusive in character.[53] The divine revelation they received has shaped, presumably, the entire nature of their ministry: this would involve, by implication, the demolition of the old 'us'/'them' dichotomy (e.g., the 'circumcision'/'uncircumcision' polarity) which symbolised the old era (6.18–20; cf. Isa. 58.12). The importance of the apostles and prophets in the 'building' upon which the Gentiles are built can therefore be assessed by the fact that they have become symbols of inclusiveness in the eschatological era and their only 'authority' is to safeguard and preserve the inclusive nature of the gospel and to foster its expression in sustaining what is the body of Christ (3.10–13; 4.11–16).[54]

Despite the fact that both apostles and prophets received revelation from above (3.5), we must concede that the distinction between the two different kinds of establishing ministry remains discernible. This is evident when the 'apostles' who received divine revelation are called the '*holy* apostles' (3.5). The language suggests the set-apartness of the 'apostles', perhaps in the sense of commissioning, in order to perform the ministry of proclaiming the gospel of reconciliation (cf. 6.19–20). The prophets who *also* received revelation from the one God are probably pneumatic or 'charismatic': they are 'prophets in the Spirit', that is, the 'Spirit' has become the new criterion by which their ministry as prophets is to be judged.[55]

[53] Many contemporary discussions – especially among Pentecostal communities – about the role of 'apostles' or 'prophets' have failed to recognise that the main thrust of the author's argument is not about the different orders of ministry that should be available in an organisational sense but about the spiritually gifted persons whom God expects to deliver the important message that the Gentiles are forming part of the new and inclusivistic community.

[54] Grudem, *Prophecy*, 42, confines himself to the 'infallible authority' of the 'apostles who are also prophets'. He has given too little attention to the way in which the notion of 'authority' is understood in our present passage, namely that the authority of the apostles or prophets is to impart to their audience the gospel of *inclusiveness*, namely the gospel that considers ethnic boundaries or an 'us'/'them' dichotomy as utterly insignificant.

[55] *Pace* Lincoln, 180 who takes ἐν πνεύματι in 3.5 as qualifying the verb 'revealed', so that the revelation to the apostles and prophets is said to have taken place 'through' or 'by' the Spirit; cf. Abbott, *Ephesians*, 83; Bruce, *Ephesians*, 315; Robinson, *Ephesians*, 78; Gnilka, *Epheserbrief*, 167; Mußner, *Epheser*, 102. However, the reference here is neither to the Spirit as the agent/instrument of revelation nor to the prophets who '*speak* in the Spirit', but rather to prophets who are controlled by the Spirit and are aware of the fact that genuine revelation is never self-prompted: see esp. Eph. 5.18–19; 1 Cor. 12.19; Col. 3.16; 1 Thess. 5.19–20; also Matt. 22.45. The suggestion of Käsemann, 'Ephesians', that Ephesians was written when charismatic ministers had begun to give way to more regulated functionaries is inaccurate; cf. Käsemann, *Questions*, 236–51; cf. MacDonald, *Pauline Churches*, who has ignored the importance of the Spirit in 'Ephesians' in shaping the symbolic world of the Gentile recipients (passim). There can be little doubt that the Spirit still plays a very

5.3.3 ὄντος ἀκρογωνιαίου αὐτοῦ Χριστοῦ Ἰησοῦ (v. 20b)

As the author sets out to consolidate the Gentile recipients' new identity in relation to the apostles and prophets, he also appends to his argument a fresh element which, if taken at face value, seems to demarcate the Messiah Jesus both from 'the foundation of the apostles and prophets' and from the Gentiles who were built upon that foundation.[56] Does the author use the 'stone' *topos* here (like the 'foundation' in the immediate statement) to reinforce the oneness of the community to which the Gentiles belong? Before we return to this question, a brief comment on the meaning of ἀκρογωνιαίος is in order.

The term ἀκρογωνιαίος (like that in 1 Pet. 2.6), which is unknown in non-Biblical Greek, appears originally in the Greek version of the Jewish scriptures (Isa. 28.16), denoting the 'stone' at Zion, i.e., the Temple Mount. Traditionally the term is used of the 'stone' that is located at the foot of the building.[57] But this interpretation was challenged by J. Jeremias, who argued that ἀκρογωνιαῖος refers to the 'keystone' (*Abschlußtein*) crowning the building, and probably installed over the entrance of the temple.[58] Jeremias's theory thus underscored the prominent and exalted position of Jesus in the building laid on its θεμέλιος, and has won many followers.[59]

Against Jeremias's interpretation a number of objections can be made, however. In the first place, the evidence which was introduced to support his contention is problematic, since none of the passages cited by Jeremias can be safely placed in the first century with any degree of

important role in shaping the identity of the Christian Gentiles: see, e.g., 5.19; cf. 1.13, 17; 4.23, 30; 5.18f.; 6.17f; 4.3, 7, 12. See further, Dunn, *Jesus*, 289, 346–7.

56 Thus Gaston, *Stone*, who writes: 'It seems that Jesus has been added to an image in which originally he had no place as is shown not only by his introduction in a subordinate genitive absolute, but even more by the fact that his place in the image is not really appropriate' (193, 222, 223); Lincoln, *Ephesians*, 154. The participle ὄντος, which stands as an independent verb in a genitive absolute construction, may function in a similar way to a finite verb expressing the secondary determination of the main sentence in a syntactically independent manner. The phrase in v. 20b may then be interpreted in at least two possible ways: (a) '[while] the Messiah Jesus is its [sc. 'foundation'] cornerstone'; and (b) 'the Messiah Jesus himself being the cornerstone'. See further Zerwick, *BG*, no. 48; Moule, *Idiom*, 43; Porter, *Idioms*, 183–4.

57 See, e.g., McKelvey, *Temple*, 195–204; Mußner, *Christus*, 108–11; Schnackenburg, *Ephesians*, 124–5; Krämer, 'γωνία', 268.

58 Jeremias, 'Eckstein'; cf. Jeremias, 'Eckstein-Schlussstein'; 'ἀκρογωνιαῖος'.

59 See, e.g., Barth, *Ephesians 1–3*, 271; Best, *Body*, 165–6; Conzelmann, *Epheser*, 101; J. Gnilka, *Epheserbrief*, 158; Lindemann, *Aufhebung*, 185–6; Schlier, *Epheser*, 142. Lincoln, *Ephesians*, 157–8 has modified Jeremias's theory slightly, but his conclusion is the same as that of Jeremias: ἀκρογωνιαῖος is the crowning stone.

certainty and do not therefore have compelling force.[60] That is true of Symmachus's Greek recension, a very late source.[61] Although the 'chief cornerstone' (ראש פנה, κεφαλὴ γωνίας, Ps. 118 [117].22) was translated as ἀκρογωνιαῖος by Symmachus,[62] it is less than certain that the author of the Psalm itself had the uppermost part of the building in mind.[63] The most we can say is that during the second or third century CE, there was a tendency among ancient writers to equate ἀκρογωνιαῖος with κεφαλὴ γωνίας.[64] Consequently, the texts above provide no sure indication that the interpretation of ἀκρογωνιαῖος as a 'keystone' was current in the first century. In the second place, the evidence which Jeremias adduces as of the first importance comes from *Testament of Solomon*. Nevertheless, the *Testament* is more likely to represent one of the ways in which Jewish scriptures could be 'misread', with the meaning of ἀκρογωνιαῖος being extended in a brand new direction. The most we can say is that the *Testament* provides evidence of a trajectory of interpretation extending from the first century to this later text.[65] And finally, in Ephesians 2.20 the building to which this 'stone' already belongs – if we follow the sense of the text – is not yet complete![66]

Our discussion above is not to abjure the exalted position of Christ in the community. There is little doubt that Christ is, for the author, the 'head of the body' (1.22; 4.15). My hesitation with regard to the 'keystone' theory is partly due to the fact that the way in which the 'stone' in v. 20 is associated with the Gentiles' defective status in the past has not been adequately appreciated by Jeremias and those who adopt his view. Given that the 'stone' (or 'building') images and other political terms in vv. 18–22 did not emerge until the author had sufficiently outlined the work of Christ in reconciling Jews and Gentiles and in breaking down the barriers and alienation between Jews and Gentiles, we have good reason to ask whether the introduction of the metaphor of a 'cornerstone' for Christ

[60] Jeremias's theory has been heavily criticised by various scholars: see, e.g., Schäfer, 'ἀκρογωνιαῖος'; McKelvey, *Temple*, 195–200; Vielhauer, *Oikodome*, 118; Merklein, *Amt*, 144–52; Percy, *Probleme*, esp. 328–35, 485–8; Pfammatter, *Bau*, 143–51; Lona, *Eschatologie*, 350 and n. 132; Krämer, 'γωνία'.

[61] See esp. O'Connell, 'Greek Versions'; Evans, *Noncanonical Writings*, 74–5.

[62] See Jeremias, 'Eckstein', 67.

[63] McKelvey, *Temple*, 199. See also BAGD, ἀκρογωνιαῖος, s.v., 2b.

[64] The Peshitta (Syriac) version of Isa. 28.16 is probably dependent upon the various Targumim and the LXX. See further McKelvey, *Temple*, 188–92.

[65] Jeremias's theory has been criticised by Mußner, 'Contributions', 172 n. 59, who argues that the discovery of the *Community Rule* at Qumran (esp. 1QS 8.7) has made Jeremias's intepretation of ἀκρογωνιαῖος as the 'lintel' dubious. See also 1 Pet. 2.6.

[66] See further Schäfer, 'ἀκρογωνιαῖος', esp. 220–1; Krämer, 'γωνία', 268.

(like the 'foundation' for the 'apostles and prophets') here suggests no more than the author's arduous effort to consolidate the Gentiles who were previously alienated from the ethnically based 'body politic'. His 'stone' language can then be explained against the backdrop of ethnic alienation and reconciliation (vv. 14–18). The nub of the issue, then, is not so much that the 'foundation' can be distinguished from the 'cornerstone' as that the author's primary aim is to lay bare the fact that the Gentiles' new status cannot be fully understood 'without' Christ and that one cannot speak of the 'foundation' of a community without Christ (see also section 5.3.4 below).

In recent years we have also seen the interpretation of v. 20a in terms of 'stone' *testimonia*.[67] According to this theory, the phenomenon of scriptural quotation in the New Testament may be accounted for by the hypothesis that a collection of 'messianic proof-texts' was compiled at a very early date, and used by NT writers for some particular (e.g., apologetic) purposes.[68] Lincoln, for example, has forcibly argued that the use of ἀκρογωνιαῖος in v. 20 is probably not a direct allusion to Isaiah 28.16 but an appropriation of the 'stone' *testimonia*.[69]

While one must concede that there is evidence for 'stone' *testimonia* in NT documents, it is less than clear that our present text should be read in the same light. Since both ἀκρογωνιαῖος and θεμέλιος in v. 20 are clearly present in the single text of Isaiah 28.16, there is nothing to strongly suggest that the author of Ephesians is dependent on the *testimonia* rather than directly echoing the Jewish scriptures.[70] To be sure, the same OT passage had also become a precursor to the interpretative technique displayed by the other Jewish writers and it is also cited on a number of occasions in the NT, with a distinctively christological slant (e.g., Rom. 9.33; 10.11; 1 Pet. 2.6). It is also clear that the same passage (esp. Isaiah 28.16b) was often conflated with other OT passages for apologetic purposes in the early church.[71] That said, there is no indication that the 'cornerstone' of Isaiah 28.16a was applied in the NT in the same

67 See in particular Bouttier, *Éphésiens*, 129–30; Lincoln, *Ephesians*, 155.

68 The research on the subject has been considerable. The standard analysis remains that of Harris, *Testimonies*. See further Dodd, *Scriptures*, 23; Hatch, *Essays*, 203; Fitzmyer, '4QTestimonia'; Ellis, *Use*, 98–107; Lindars, *Apologetic*, 177–9; Snodgrass, *Stone Testimonia*.

69 Lincoln, *Ephesians*, 155–6.

70 See also McKelvey, *Temple*, 195–204; cf. McKelvey, 'Cornerstone'; Percy, *Probleme*, 330–2, 485–8; Schäfer, 'ἀκρογωνιαῖος', 220–1; Bruce, *Ephesians*, 304–5; Hübner, *Vetus Testamentum*, 442–3.

71 See, e.g., Rom. 9.33, where Paul conflates Ps. 118.22 and Isa. 8.14. The author of 1 Peter cited three separate passages in 1 Pet. 2.6–8: Isa. 28.16, Ps. 118.22 and Isa. 8.14.

fashion. If we consider the extant literature which quotes or alludes to Isaiah 28.16a, the most striking feature is that the 'stone' is often used in consolidating the identity of a community. Thus, when the Isaianic text is quoted explicitly in 1 Peter 2.6, Christ is referred to as one of the most important 'stones' of the 'building', the 'living stone' which holds other stones together as they constitute the 'spiritual house'. There is also little doubt that the metaphor of a 'cornerstone' for Christ belongs firmly to the realm of temple symbolism as it is closely associated with other cultic terms such as 'living stones', 'holy priesthood', 'spiritual sacrifice acceptable to God' and 'spiritual house' (vv. 4–5).[72] In Qumran literature, the author of the *Community Rule* also alluded to the same Isaianic text.[73] Suffice it to say that the same 'stone' *topos* was used as a metaphor and refers to the covenanters as 'the tested rampart, the cornerstone' (יקר פנת, 1QS 8.7). It should come as no surprise that our author has recourse to the Jewish scriptures, using the same 'stone' language to enhance the Gentiles' sense of security and identity. He proceeds, however, to invoke a fresh metaphor, Christ as the 'cornerstone' of the 'foundation' consisting of the apostles and prophets, and so to reframe the meaning of both 'cornerstone' and 'foundation' in the earlier text.[74] The point is that Christ has occupied a status of central importance, like the apostles and prophets, in the 'household' to which the Gentiles belong. As we shall see, Christ is the unshakeable 'bedrock', the 'precondition' (*Voraussetzung*)[75] 'in whom' the whole community is being bonded together and grows into the temple.

To sum up: the author brings to life his descriptions of the Gentiles' present status in the household of God by alluding to the 'stone' language in the Jewish scriptures (Isa. 28.16). The metaphor of a 'cornerstone' (at Zion) for Christ, as we shall see, also paves the way for the author to speak of Christ as the cornerstone of the new Temple. To this theme we must now turn.

[72] It is worth noting that when the same author assumed a hostile stance against the unbelievers, he used a different set of 'stone' metaphors: see, e.g., v. 7, par. Ps. 117.22; v. 8, par. Isa. 8.14.

[73] Gaster, *Scriptures*, 60–1; Knibb, *Qumran Community*, 131–2; Bruce, *Ephesians*, 306 n. 153; Gärtner, *Temple*, 16–122. Mußner, 'Contributions', 168 suggests that the change from 'stone' to 'rampart' in 1QS was influenced by Isa. 30.13. However, it is more likely that the influence comes from Isa. 58.12. Despite the presence of a lacuna at the end of 1QS 8.7, the general sense of ll. 7 and 8 is clear.

[74] Bruce, *Development*, suggests that the 'stone' in Isa. 28.16 refers to 'the remnant of the people of God, the hope of the future, which in other oracles of Isaiah is embodied in the promised prince of the house of David' (65).

[75] Lona, *Eschatologie*, 351.

5.3.4 ἐν ᾧ πᾶσα οἰκοδομὴ συναρμολογουμένη αὔξει εἰς ναὸν ἅγιον ἐν κυρίῳ, ἐν ᾧ καὶ ὑμεῖς συνοικοδομεῖσθε εἰς κατοικητήριον τοῦ θεοῦ ἐν πνεύματι (vv. 21–2)

The author's argument is brought to a climax by stressing the oneness of the building-community and thus the interrelatedness of the components of the structure (cf. 4.16). The structural parallel between v. 21 and v. 22 is clear enough.[76] The author probably uses the figure of repetition in his argument.[77] To be sure, the formulation in v. 22 can be seen as a gemination of v. 21 (by instances of anaphora and mesodiplosis), allowing these verses to form an interlocking pattern (ABCA'B'C') which is marked by the paralleling of key motifs:

A	ἐν ᾧ πᾶσα οἰκοδομὴ συναρμολογουμένη	(v. 21a)
B	αὔξει εἰς ναὸν ἅγιον	(v. 21b)
C	ἐν κυρίῳ	(v. 21c)
A'	ἐν ᾧ καὶ ὑμεῖς συνοικοδομεῖσθε	(v. 22a)
B'	(-) εἰς κατοικητήριον τοῦ θεοῦ	(v. 22b)
C'	ἐν πνεύματι	(v. 22c)

The emphasis is that the 'building' is made into a unity by means of Christ who is perceived presumably as the bonding factor that holds the various parts in mutual harmony and oneness.[78] The whole 'building' is understood metaphorically as a community (cf. 1 Cor. 3.9, θεοῦ οἰκοδομή).[79] It is 'in' or 'through' Christ (ἐν ᾧ) that members of the building-community firmly adhere together.[80] The underlying assumption is probably that the interconnectedness of the various members is and should be a characteristic of an inclusive community which constitutes a unity (cf. Philo, *Migr.* 180–1). The sense of a communality is

[76] See also ibid. [77] See further Wills, *Repetition*, 43–264, esp. 173–86.

[78] In Hellenistic Jewish thought, the same role is attributed to the 'Word (of God)' which is the bond of all existence: see, e.g., Philo, *Fug.* 112; cf. Philo, *Plant.* 9–10; *Her.* 188; cf. Cicero, *Nat. deorumii* 115.

[79] The same word is used not infrequently in the OT (Heb. מבנה) as the 'house of God': see, e.g., 1 Chr. 26.27; 1 Esd. 5.62–3, 73; cf. Matt. 24.1 par. Mark 13.1–2. The present reading πᾶσα οἰκοδομή is supported by א* B D F G Ψ with the majority of cursives. There is no good reason to read our present phrase as 'every building' that grows together to form a grand complex edifice. See further Middleton, *Greek Article*, 158, who concluded that the syntax here (πᾶς + substantive) points towards a meaning which is equivalent to ὅλος; Zerwick, *GA* 582; Bruce, *Ephesians*, 307; Schnackenburg, 124; Lincoln, *Ephesians*, 124, 156; Comfort, 'Temple', here 925.

[80] McKelvey, *Temple*, 115 understands the phrase ἐν ᾧ as conveying more than an instrumental sense: it has organic overtones and approximates in sense to the expression 'in Christ' (2.13). I therefore diasgree with Schlier, *Christus*, 57f., who contends that there is a direct link between the thought and vocabulary of our letter and those of Gnostic ideas, namely the σῶμα of a redeemer and a *heavenly* οἰκοδομή; cf. Michel, 'οἰκοδομή', here 145.

made abundantly clear by the term συναρμολογουμένη, denoting that the various parts of the building-community are 'fitted' or joined together.[81] The same metaphor of 'fitting together' is used in 4.16. There it is transferred to the 'body of Christ', where the verb is understood as having a physiological sense.

The building-community is conceived dynamically, since it 'grows into a holy temple' (αὔξει εἰς ναὸν ἅγιον).[82] The importation of the biological language into the architectonic terms prevents one from treating the image as in any sense static and concrete but is analogous with images like the body and the flock.[83] In our present passage, the underlying assumption of the animate nature of the 'building' or 'holy temple' is probably that 'in the (exalted) Lord' (ἐν κυρίῳ) there cannot be dead material, and, as we shall see, the 'dwelling place' of the *living* God cannot be lifeless.[84] There can be little doubt that the author is employing one of the most prominent motifs in Jewish tradition: the 'holy temple' is a place of high pathos for most devout Jews (1 Sam. 1.9; 3.3; 2 Sam. 22.7; Dan [Theod.] 3.53; Judith 4.2; Sir. 49.12; Tobit 1.4; Pr. Azar. 31; cf. Matt. 23.16–21; Mark 15.38, par. Luke 23.45; Luke 1.9, 21–2; 2 Thess. 2.3; Josephus, *A. J.* 15.391; *B. J.* 5.207, 209).[85] This would be true not only when the temple still stood, but also when the temple was no longer there (cf. 2 Esd.; *T. Sol.* 1.1–2; *2 Bar.* 7.1–8.5; *m.* Aboth 6.1–10, etc).[86] For the devout Jews the Temple is the focus of the holy land of covenant promise and the place which God had appointed as the primary expression of his presence on

[81] The passive voice of our verb probably suggests that the implied subject is God himself. See further Dunn, *TPA*, 402–3; Kellermann, 'συναρμολογουμένη'; Whitaker, 'συναρμολογούμενον'; BAGD, s.v.

[82] The verb is used quite often in a biological sense in the NT: see, e.g., 1 Cor. 3.6–7; Col. 1.6; Matt. 13.32; Mark. 4.8; Luke 12.27, 13.19; Sir. 39.13. If we were to take into account the logical relations between the passive participle συναρμολογουμένη which occurs before the finite verb αὔξει, the participle would refer to an antecedent action, as the following translation shows: 'In whom the whole structure, having been fitted together, (then) grows into the holy temple'. This is better than interpretations which involve inserting a conjunction (e.g., NRSV). See further Zerwick, *BG*, no. 363, 371; Porter, *Verbal Aspect*, here 381–9; cf. Porter, *Idioms*, 187–9.

[83] McKelvey, *Temple*, 119; Bruce, *Ephesians*, 306–7; Mußner, *Epheserbrief*, 95, Lona, *Eschatologie*, 350–1, et al.

[84] Perhaps the closest parallel to our present passage is that of 1 Pet. 2.4–5, where God's temple is made up of 'living stones' (vv. 4–5). Allison, '4Q403', has noted that the inanimate objects in God's heavenly temple are living creatures.

[85] The distinction between ἱερόν and ναός in either meaning or range is very thin.

[86] Despite the fact that there were 'other' temples that rivalled that in Jerusalem, the Temple in Jerusalem was regarded as the one legitimate sanctuary where the name of God chose to dwell: see, e.g., Deut. 12.5; 16.2; 26.2; Josephus, *A. J.* 11.306–12, 321–4; 12.254–8. For the significance of the Jerusalem Temple as the one legitimate sanctuary for the vast majority of Jews in the land of Israel and in the diaspora, see esp. the discussion of Hayward, *Jewish Temple*, passim; Schürer, *HJPAJC*, II, 237–313; Dunn, *Partings*, 57–74.

earth. The idea of a building-community that 'grows into a holy Temple' means that the centre of the Jews' symbolic universe is now redefined in dynamic terms.[87] The author may well have thus signalled a gloomy assessment of those who had kept a very high view about the 'earthly' (Jerusalem) temple – be it in the past or future – as the fundamental expression of God's presence (e.g., 2 Sam. 22.7; Ezek. 40–8; Tobit 1.4; Add. Est. 14.9; Baruch 1.8, 14; Pr. Azar. 31; 2 Macc. 15.32; 1 Esd. 1.55; 5.70; 2 Esd. 1.33).

The high point of the author's argument, however, is to underscore the interrelatedness of the Gentiles with other members who constitute the Temple. This is made most evident when he argues that the Gentiles are also built into the 'dwelling-place of God'. The phrase εἰς κατοικητήριον τοῦ θεοῦ takes up the image of the holy temple (εἰς ναὸν ἅγιον), conveying the sense of 'entrance' (*eisodus*).[88] The framework here is, again, Jewish. For the bulk of devout Jews, the 'dwelling-place of God' (κατοικητήριον τοῦ θεοῦ) often means the habitation of God either in the Jerusalem temple (e.g., Exod. 15.17; 1 Kgs. 8.13; Ps. 75.3; 1 Esd. 1.50; 2.5; Philo, *Plant.* 47) or in heaven (e.g., 1 Kgs. 8.39, 43, 49; 2 Chr. 30.27; Ps. 32.13–14; 3 Macc. 2.15). The Gentiles are allotted the proper 'space' in the holy dwelling (= 'house') of God.[89] An exposition like that has evidently made irrelevant topographical, ethnic and social distinctions, that is, in the temple-community that is now perceived as God's 'living temple-house' (cf. 1 Cor. 3.16; 6.19; 2 Cor. 6.16–18).[90] Indeed, this exposition is well calculated to impress the Gentile recipients with a profound sense of the nobility of the honour into which they now enter.[91] It also means that the traditional Jewish meaning of the 'holy' temple is 'transcoded' and given a new twist as the non-Jews are also allotted a proper place in the temple, that is, 'by the Spirit' (ἐν πνεύματι). The author probably

[87] The emphasis on the building-community as the 'temple' is characteristically Pauline: see, e.g., 1 Cor. 3.16–17; 6.19; 2 Cor. 6.16. A possible parallel to the 'dynamic terms' of the temple being built may be apparent in *4 Ezra* 10, in which the heavenly temple is described as one which is in the process of 'being built'. 4QShirShab provides evidence for the notion that parts of the heavenly temple could be conceived as animate beings. I am very grateful to Dr. Stuckenbruck for this particular insight.

[88] See also Lincoln, *Ephesians*, 158, who concludes that the preposition εἰς in v. 22 should be read in a telic sense with the adjacent κατοικητήριον τοῦ θεοῦ, indicating 'the goal of the building process'.

[89] Gnilka, *Epheserbrief*, 158–9; Lincoln, *Ephesians*, 158; Lona, *Eschatologie*, 351; Schnackenburg, *Ephesians*, 124–5; Mußner, *Epheser*, 95; Lindemann, *Epheserbrief*, 54–5; Schlier, *Epheser*, 144.

[90] Cf. 4QFlor. 1–4, where the Gentiles, alongside the 'deformed', were excluded from the 'holy ones', i.e., the covenanted community; 1QS 8.4–12.

[91] In Hellenistic Jewish thought, the idea of the 'soul' as God's house is common: see, e.g., Philo, *Somn.* 1.149; *Sobr.* 62; *Cher.* 98, 106.

refers to the Spirit as the *new* criterion by which the Gentiles' position in the temple-community is to be judged, in contrast to the 'flesh' (ἐν σαρκί, v.11). It is safe to say that the Spirit has become the *new* identity-consolidating and redefining marker for the Gentiles: whereas the 'flesh' conjures up a picture of a divided humankind, i.e., of 'Gentiles in the flesh' and the 'circumcision in the flesh', the 'Spirit' language here is meant to lay bare the inclusiveness of the new Temple in which Gentiles are integral components. In short, the usefulness of temple symbolism is that it enables the author to transpose the Gentiles from the periphery to the centre of the Jewish symbolic world while sustaining the traditional notion that the 'temple' is still the holy space of God's presence.[92]

5.4 Concluding remarks

We may conclude this chapter of our study by observing some significant characteristics of vv. 19–22. The author rounds off his argument in vv. 19–22 by encapsulating some vital implications of Christ's reconciling work for the Gentile readers *vis-à-vis* other members who constitute a community, and for their relation to the 'holy ones'/Israel of God.

The Gentiles and the 'holy ones' are now on the same side – be it in a community or in a new 'body politic' (a *sympoliteia*?). The language of 'politics' which our author employed in v. 19 not only takes up some aspects of vv. 11–12 in which the Gentiles were deemed 'aliens of the covenants of the promise' and were estranged from the Jewish 'body politic', it is also akin to that of the political theorists in the classical world, where city-state life was to most Greeks and Romans the normative pattern of human existence. No Greeks or Romans could miss what the author was trying to do with the 'political' language. His was the language of inclusion. His aim is to assure the Gentiles that the community or 'body politic' to which they belong transcends the old division of 'us'/citizens and 'them'/aliens. His vision of an ideal community, however, can be understood only if his arduous effort to overcome the polarisation of humankind is fully appreciated. What is in view is therefore the idea of the surmounting of polarity, which is occasioned by the divisions of humankind: the divisions of 'citizens' and 'aliens', the 'circumcision' and the 'uncircumcision', and, not least, the 'far off' and the 'near'.[93] The new community is marked by undisguised inclusivism and is based

[92] See, e.g., Tobit 14.4–5; Judith 9.1; Add. Est. E 14.9; Sir. 47.13; Baruch 3.24; 1 Macc. 7.37; 2 Macc. 15.32; 1 Esd. 1.55; 2.4; 5.56–7; 6.2, 19–20, 26; 8.55, 79; 3 Macc. 2.18.

[93] The idea is readily taken up by Gnostic writers in a later period, but in itself the concept of the overcoming of divisions is not Gnostic.

on the assumption that Christ's reconciling work has reconciled Jews and Gentiles.

The use of the various architectonic terms to describe the inter-relatedness of the members who constitute a building-community is prompted by the author's effort to promote a community that overcomes 'us-them' divisions. To consolidate the Gentiles' position in the holy temple/dwelling of God and to emphasise their togetherness with other members who constitute the community amount to the same thing: these are simply ways of reinforcing the normality of a community and of implying the insignificance of those factors that engender distinctions and disintegration – be it in a 'body politic' or in a 'household' (cf. vv. 12, 19). The same motif and concern are clearly echoed elsewhere in the letter (e.g., 4.3, 15–16; cf. Col. 2.19).

What gives the Gentiles' corporate identity its distinctiveness is that humankind (rather than the static Temple) has become God's living temple-house and the 'realm' of God's real presence that is determined by the criterion of the 'Spirit', in contrast to the 'flesh' (see v. 11). It may fairly be claimed that the author's attitude to the Temple implies that he has put what had been hitherto the primary expression of God's presence in question. All in all, this attitude is based on the conviction that topographical, ethnic and social distinctions are no longer relevant.

6

SUMMARY AND CONCLUSIONS

6.1 Concluding remarks

It is appropriate now to summarise briefly some of our findings of the preceding chapters and to draw together the threads of the study as a whole. In general, it may fairly be claimed that the theme of the connections between Jewish attitudes toward the Gentiles and ethnic reconciliation has not been given sufficient attention in previous studies of Christian origins in general, and, not least, of 'Pauline Christianity' in particular. The present study of the dynamic between Jewish attitudes toward the Gentiles and ethnic reconciliation according to Ephesians 2 has attempted to fill that gap. Indeed, we will not fully understand the significance of ethnic reconciliation until we have grasped something of these attitudes.

We began our introductory chapter by surveying the previous scholarship which has been hampered by too rigid an understanding of 'Pauline Christianity'. This can be attributed substantially to scholarly tradition whose hermeneutical 'grid' has been derived from the philosophy of dialectics or the Protestant Reformation. The 'new perspective(s) on Paul', however, shifts our perspective back to first-century Judaism and enables us to penetrate fully into the historical context of first-century Jews and Judaism. Because we cannot fully appreciate what the author is affirming (or repudiating) unless we recognise the importance of that 'context', we have taken pains to describe in chapter 2 some of the relevant Jewish features and demonstrated them by focusing particularly on Ephesians 2.1–10 and attempting to set it as fully as possible into its historical context. Indeed, the uncontroversial *a priori* of Jewish context conceals many explosive issues: how much was our author influenced by Jewish ideas? Does he wish to speak about his Gentile addressees from a Jewish perspective? Does his status as a Jew also create for him a convenient 'pre-text' so that he could reiterate the perspective of *other* Jews about the Gentiles in his representation of it? These questions, I believe, have been sufficiently addressed in this study.

We have paid sufficient attention to the question of 'representation' or characterisation and suggested that our understanding of Jewish attitudes toward the Gentiles and the characterisation of the latter can be understood only if we give the author's characteristically Jewish language, terminology, thought and ideas their due weight. We have also paid particular attention to the author's Jewish perspective in which he ably heightens the boundary between different human groups by attaching negative valence to the Gentiles (e.g., they *walked* according to the 'Aion of this world, according to the prince of the power of the air').[1] I have demonstrated that the language of 'powers' in Ephesians 2.2 had become for our author a means of dividing human groups, establishing the differences between them, suggesting wherein their 'otherness' lies. It is safe to say that ethnography provides a way into the author's statements about the Gentiles. His method of explanation is not altogether unparalleled in ancient historiographers: he has perceived the Gentiles from within Israel by articulating a well-established Jewish theology in which the particularism of Israel's election and the universalism of monotheism were closely integrated. His 'powers' language thus reveals as much about his Jewish perspective as about the Gentiles. It would be wrong, however, to surmise that the aim of his representation of the Gentiles is merely to pass a negative verdict on the Gentiles without reflecting the reality of Gentiles' hopelessness in their religion (2.1–2). Still less was there a penetration into Christian thinking of a mythological conception of syncretism which came to play an important part in Gnosticism (*contra* Sasse), for the Jews (according to the 'new perspective' which takes into account the thought world of first-century Judaism) were quite capable of borrowing various names of 'foreign' deities and putting them to the service of such religious convictions as monotheism and Israel's distinctiveness. I have also demonstrated in chapter 2 that the key to understanding the author's characterisation of the Gentiles is the recognition that the negative verdict on the Gentiles represents but a preamble to his arduous effort to surmount the social distance between Jews and Gentiles. This is made most evident in his rhetoric of admission/confession and (re)conciliation in which he lays bare the fact that the Jews (himself included) were in no better position than the Gentiles, although the idea of Israel's status was never put in question (2.3). His argument is to evoke the need for the promptings of divine grace and love toward humankind (2.4–10). His negation of both 'faith' and 'works' as sources of salvation is meant fundamentally to lead the Gentile readers on to the surpassingly rich grace of the one God and

[1] See my discussion of Eph. 2.2 in sections 2.3.1 and 2.3.2, respectively.

creator and to evoke thoughts of humility in them (2.8–10). It would be wrong therefore to suggest that Ephesians consists of a polemic against meritorious works. Rather, the author's rhetoric of negation is based on the assumption that human beings, their acceptance of God's salvation by 'faith', and 'works' – be they works as produced by human hands or 'works of the Law' – all owe their entire existence to the creator God. Human boasting, contriving or manipulation can therefore be dismissed on the sole ground of their creatureliness.

In chapter 3 we saw the author of Ephesians as adopting a more subtle approach in unravelling the Jewish dismissive attitudes toward the Gentiles. His characterisation (as mentioned above) provides not only a way into his own statements about the Gentiles (2.11a) but also a window into other Jewish perception of the non-Jewish world (2.11b–12). This is evident in his representation of the Gentiles in Ephesians 2.11–12, which reveals a distinctive perspective of other Jews, and, more importantly, tells us much about the Jews themselves. We have taken pains to describe the self-understanding of the 'circumcision'/Jews as being God's chosen, distinguished and separated from the 'uncircumcision'/Gentiles. We have paid particular attention to the estrangement between Jew and Gentile, which can be best explained by the hypothesis that the Gentiles were perceived by the Jews through the 'grid' of covenantal ethnocentrism. I have suggested that covenantal ethnocentrism be used as a descriptive title for the Ephesians' understanding of the functioning of a certain stream of Judaism. The formulation outlined in Ephesians 2.11–13 is animated by a kind of covenant theology which unveils the covenantal confidence in which God's gracious promise to ethnic Israel/Jew is assured, even though it narrows the scope of the divine grace and so limits membership of what constitutes the 'body politic' ethnocentrically to include only ethnic 'Israel'/Jews or a much smaller group than the whole of mankind.

Indeed, covenantal ethnocentrism had become the principal basis on which the Gentiles were deemed to be outside the orbit of the elect of God and Israel's God-given grace. We concluded in the same chapter that the task of the author is not so much to reclaim Israel's blessings on behalf of his Gentile recipients as to exhibit his deconstructive strategy which provides a resolution to one of the thorniest issues regarding two ethnic groups: *can Jew and Gentile, the two estranged human groups, be one (people of God) in the divine 'oikonomia' which is marked by concord in the cosmos (Eph. 1.9–10)? And if so, how?* He has set out to answer this question by arguing that the Messiah Jesus is *the* antidote to the alienation between Jews and Gentiles (*pace* Merklein). But before this could happen, it is necessary to deconstruct the marginal status of the Gentiles who were deemed to lie at the fringe of the Jewish world, i.e., by dismantling the divisive factors which are ingrained in covenantal ethnocentrism. The issue, however, is not so much that the author no longer wishes to speak of the Gentiles as being included in Israel,[2] but rather that the insular nature of Judaism with which the author grapples, in which the identification between the Jewish ethnic group and their religious identity is far too close (thus covenantal ethnocentricity understood as the functioning of Judaism as a 'closed-ethnic religion'), has made Gentile inclusion impossible in a straightforward manner unless the notion of (God's) Israel is drastically redefined (see my discussion of the 'holy ones' in ch. 5, section 5.2). Given the fact that the Gentiles had been estranged from the 'body politic of Israel' by the 'circumcision'/Jews who practised ethnocentrism, it is not at all likely that anyone would speak of the inclusion of the Gentiles in Israel without also making the latter proselytes or second-class citizens in the ethnically based 'Israel'. This best explains why the author was reluctant in his later argument to speak unequivocally about the inclusion of Gentiles into 'Israel', for the not inconsiderable reason that the latter has turned ethnocentric and that the inclusion means the Gentiles are inevitably absorbed in an ethnocentric Judaism (*contra* Barth, Richardson).[3] The more important task for him is how to speak of Jews and Gentiles as one without giving the impression that the Gentiles are incorporated into an Israel which was defined and perceived by the Jews in a narrowly ethnic sense. Thus the meaning of an exclusive, ethnic-oriented 'body politic of Israel' would need to be transposed into an *inclusive* community-body (and a non-ethnic entity where there are no ethnic ties whatsoever required of its constituting members) before he could truly speak of the Gentiles and the 'holy ones'/Jews as being fellow-members of a single citizen-body

[2] See, e.g., Richardson, *Israel*, who, in writing: 'Within the Church, Gentiles in origin must always remember that they started out with a disadvantage and had to be drawn near to participate in the ancient privileges which Israel offered' (157), failed to account for the ethnic factor which led to the estrangement of Jews and Gentiles; cf. Baur, *History*, 124, who contends that the Gentiles have received a share in that which the Jews had received before, and thus Christianity is not the absolute religion in which Judaism and Paganism are alike absorbed.

[3] See further Runesson, 'Judaism', 62, who aptly observes that the diversity of Judaism's opinions about Gentiles is well documented by many scholars. He introduces categories such as 'closed-ethnic religion' (i.e., where a religion is completely closed to outsiders and no conversions are possible, and there is an identification between the ethnic group and religious identity) and 'open-ethnic religion' (where conversions are possible for outsiders not belonging to that particular ethnic group) to underscore the ethnic aspect of Judaism; see also Cohen, *Jewishness*, 109–10.

(v. 19). In chapter 4 we saw the metaphors of 'one new man' and 'one body' being introduced to achieve this particular end.

We also pointed out that a major weakness with previous treatments of Ephesians 2.14–18 has been a lack of appreciation for the close connections between the exclusive Jewish attitudes toward the Gentiles and the author's encomiastic statements about Christ. Indeed, previous scholarship has been substantially hampered by its attempt to 'discover' a preformed material in Ephesians 2.14–18, failing to recognise the discussion in Ephesians 2.11–13 which sets the parameters for understanding Ephesians 2.14–22. Rather than a 'parenthesis' or 'digression', which is tangential to the primary design of the author's argument, I suggested that vv. 14–18 cannot be fully understood in isolation from vv. 11–13. Indeed, Ephesians 2.14–18 represents the author's ingenious attempt to set in comparison with the magnanimity of Christ the Jewish attitudes toward the Gentiles (vv. 11b–12). What becomes immediately clear in his attempt to amplify Christ's magnanimity toward humankind is that this was prompted by the Jewish tendency to exclude, and this endeavour has two striking effects. At its heart lies the power of the author's language via *amplificatio* to induce the Gentile recipients for whom he writes to emulate the noble qualities of Christ, namely, Christ's undisguised inclusivism in which humankind can be made one. He maximises the expedient, noble act of Christ who brings peace to an estranged humanity, whose death has in his perception provided a new framework, i.e., *pax Christi*, within which mutual acceptance or 'the oneness of spirit' between Jews and Gentiles may then be filled out (v. 18; cf. 4.1–6). The author is obsessed with the *oneness* of Jews and Gentiles to the extent that the Jews' access to God cannot be considered as complete without the Gentiles (and vice versa). We will simply fail to grasp the import of Ephesians 2.14–18 unless we appreciate that the author wrote those encomiastic statements about Christ to be set in comparison with the small-mindedness of certain Jews or Judaism. The main aim of the encomium in vv. 14–18 is to reverse the Gentiles' hitherto disadvantaged status by removing the ethnic factor that has led to this. He has forged in this 'hymn-like' encomium a christological interpretation in which Christ is understood as one who campaigned to end ethnic estrangement and enmity and who restored both Jews and Gentiles to the common Father/God of all. Such community-enhancing metaphors as 'one new man', 'one body' and 'one spirit' signal the importance of ὁμόνοια and are introduced to do nothing more than to reinforce the oneness of Jews and Gentiles. Indeed, these metaphors are meant to put the exclusive Jewish 'body politic' and Jewish conception about humankind in question, but they never question the legitimacy of

Israel as God's choice. There are therefore no good grounds for suggesting that these metaphors are meant to replace Israel as the new people of God except to reconfigure, respectively, the exclusive 'body politic of Israel' which is based on a particular *ethnos* and the Jewish definition of humankind by marking off and separating the Jews from the nations.

In chapter 5 we saw some vital implications of Christ's reconciling work for the Christian Gentiles and, not least, for their relation to Israel. We have paid particular attention to the language that signals the author's all-embracing perspective in which an ideal community is (and should be) marked by inclusiveness and concord in Ephesians 2.19–22. We have demonstrated that he is obsessed not only with the *oneness* of Jews and Gentiles but also with the way in which this oneness can be forcibly expressed. The underlying assumption of his argument is, as we have demonstrated, that a genuine concordance could and should be made possible out of ethnic differences rather than similarities. To achieve this goal he has introduced, respectively, two major *topoi* from ancient political theorists and from the Jewish Temple to face down the 'us-them' divisions, to forge the idea of sameness and to consolidate a close relationship of Gentiles with other members of an inclusivistic community. It may be fairly claimed that no Greeks or Romans who recognised the city-state as the normative pattern of human existence and the primary framework of reference would have missed what the author was trying to do and achieve with his language of 'politics' in 2.19.[4] The same can be said about the *topos of* 'temple' which always generates an ambience of high pathos for most devout Jews, be it still standing or destroyed. The Gentiles, on the basis of Christ who surmounted human divisions that had kept different ethnic groups apart from one another, are on the same side with the 'holy ones'/Israel. Although we in no way know whether the 'circumcision' who excluded the Gentiles from their 'body politic' would embrace the author's ideal community, we cannot rule out that he has in mind the 'circumcision' as belonging to the 'holy ones'. Although the author can readily suggest that Gentiles have become fellow-citizens with 'Israel' (2.19), he nevertheless refrains from making this suggestion. The fact is that the meaning of Israel has been transcoded and turned into an ethnically based 'body politic' (ἡ πολιτεία τοῦ Ἰσραήλ). But with the 'holy ones', the author can now redefine the relationship of the Gentiles to the Israel of God afresh – a point missed by almost all commentators.

[4] See esp. de Ste Croix, *Class Struggle*, 9–10; McKechnie, *Outsiders*, 16–33; Whitehead, *Metic*; Meeks, *Christian Morality*, here 12–13, 37–51.

Indeed, it was possible for our author to speak and think of a renewed or expanded Israel in continuity with the old, with his claim here as one of several competing claims within the first century. In short, we will simply fail to grasp the import of Ephesians 2.19–22 and of the author's inclusivistic perspective unless we bear in mind that his main aim is to promote an anti-*politeia* (a *sympoliteia*?) or 'temple'-community which is marked by undisguised inclusivism, and that he does so with the exclusive Jewish attitudes toward Gentiles fresh in mind. Indeed, we cannot fully appreciate his language of inclusion in 2.19–22 without giving due weight to the Jewish tendency to exclude the Gentiles from Israel and Israel's God-given grace (*contra* Lincoln). While Jewish attitudes had to a great extent desocialised the Gentiles by reinforcing the marginal status of the latter (i.e., the Gentiles were 'far off') as at the fringe of Israel and Israel's blessing on the bases of an *ethnos* and covenantal ethnocentrism, the author firmly articulates on the basis of *pax Christi* that the boundaries between Jew and Gentile have been made redundant: both Gentiles and Jews are on the same side of the *one* community-*body* and have become fellow-citizens. Hence we must content ourselves with the conclusion that our study has highlighted what was one of the most thorny and inescapable questions in the beginnings of Christianity: *Who are the people of God?* To this we must say that the question lies at the heart of the author's inclusivistic perspective and, not least, of his self-understanding in which the ethnocentricity of Jews (and Judaism) is repudiated. Until the 'holy ones'/Jews and Gentiles become fellow-citizens and perceive themselves as *the* one people of God, the vision of our passage in Ephesians 2.19–22 cannot be completely fulfilled (cf. Rom. 15.8–12).

6.2 Exegetical implications

This understanding of the author's argument in Ephesians 2 carries with it a number of exegetical implications. It is unnecessary to repeat the specific conclusions drawn at the end of each chapter. There are, however, a number of important points worth noting:

(1) As far back as 1906 A. Jülicher raised a question regarding what *Sitz im Leben* of the first-century church prompted the writing of Ephesians.[5] Since then there has been no dearth of attempts variously undertaken over the generations to address the question of the particular situation to which Ephesians was directed. Was there a particular historical situation

[5] Jülicher, *Einleitung*, 127, writes: 'Aber eine klare Vorstellung über die Situation, in der ein Paulus redivivus den Eph. verfaßt hat, ist bisher nicht beschaffen worden.'

or circumstance that prompted the writing of the epistle?[6] Was there a particular problem which the author must resolve in the body of the letter?[7] If so, where can we most probably reconstruct this situation? I have set forth an alternative hypothesis in this study – a hypothesis that could potentially contribute to a more precise understanding of the nature and purpose of Ephesians. I suggest that one of the main issues – if not the most important issue – that shapes the thought of Ephesians is the author's concern about the place of the Gentiles within the purpose of God, and that Jewish attitudes toward them should be our starting point for reconstructing the *general* setting of the readers (*contra* Arnold). The author's statements about and references to the 'situation' are, most probably, being addressed in 2.1–22. The passage is meant to be an answer to the two basic questions: *Why didn't humankind, as designated by Jew and Gentile, become one people of God, and, how could the two ethnic groups become one?* Ephesians (a circular letter?) was written to the churches in Asia Minor consisting of a predominantly Gentile audience needing to be informed not only of what had happened to (and between) Jews and Gentiles when the Gentiles were 'without' Christ and why their place in the purpose of God was thwarted, but also of their true identity in that purpose in relation to Jews and other members who constitute the inclusive community.

(2) The talk of Jews and Gentiles being enthroned in the 'heavenly places' reflects not so much the believers' present eschatological situation as the author's effort to destigmatise the Gentiles' defective status: namely the Jewish perspective that the Gentiles are 'sub-let' to the 'prince', whose residence is the 'air'. The motif of heavenly enthronement suggests that the Gentiles no longer share the same space with the 'prince' but are enthroned in the domain to which Christ is exalted, 'far above all rule and power and dominion' (1.20–1; 3.10; 6.12). The heavenly enthronement is also a way of speaking of God's grace toward humankind, namely that human life could transcend death by passing to the higher heavenly sphere, an idea which is seen most often in Jewish apocalyptic writings.

(3) There is now a broad consensus that the author of Ephesians presents us with a cosmic vision of the church. However, we have demonstrated

[6] See, e.g., Köster, *Introduction*, who writes: 'In contrast with Colossians, Ephesians is not a true letter, though the two works otherwise have much in common. Ephesians was not written to a specific church and never alludes to a particular problem or situation of any specific church or circle of churches' (268); cf. Käsemann, 'Epheserbrief', 517.

[7] Perkins, *Reading*, argues that 'it is not possible to say that there is a particular problem which the author must resolve in the body of the letter' (195).

in this study that the church-body language in Ephesians can be best understood as a community-enhancing metaphor and that 'one body' has nothing to do with the church which is alleged to become the 'true Israel' (2.16). To be sure, the 'body' language is introduced largely to cope with the problem and results of *Jewish* covenantal ethnocentrism. Israel's status as God's choice was not an issue at all.

(4) As far as we can tell, the designation 'one new man' in 2.15 does not refer to a corporate personality into whom Jew and Gentile are incorporated, but is a society-redefining metaphor which stands in stark contrast to the Jewish conception about mankind and the social ramifications which follow from it. It is meant to underscore a new humanity that overcomes the polarisation of the 'us'/'circumcision' and the 'them'/'uncircumcision'. One cannot therefore fully appreciate the language of oneness without reference to the Jewish perception about the Gentiles, and, more importantly, to the author's strenuous effort to integrate (in principle) two ethnic groups into one unified whole.

(5) It may fairly be claimed on the basis of our study that the author of Ephesians has not entirely lost sight of Jews (and Judaism), but it has to be asked which picture of Judaism he has conjured up. He speaks in subtle terms of the Jews (thanks to the insights brought about by the 'new perspective(s)' and modern sociolinguists) who had kept a very high view of their covenantal status but who also viewed the world in ethnocentric terms. The author of Ephesians does not abandon Judaism in favour of 'Gentile Christianity'. There is also no concrete evidence for Gentile triumphalism over ethnic Israel in Ephesians (*contra* Käsemann, Martin, Roetzel and others). Rather, the author's language is of a renewed and expanded Israel/'holy ones' in which a 'Gentile Christianity' cannot understand itself except in terms of the category of Israel and of Israel's blessing.

6.3 Some questions for further research

Our analysis of Jewish attitudes toward the Gentiles and ethnic reconciliation according to Ephesians 2 also raises a number of important issues for further investigation. First, *does the author perceive Israel and the church as two separate entities?*; second, *can the 'code of household duties' be seen as an extended discussion of the motif 'household of God'?*; third, *how does the language of 'powers' correlate with the author's effort to consolidate the new identity of the Gentiles?* These questions deserve a full-scale enquiry in their own right, but we may at least suggest some tentative directions in which such an investigation might look.

6.3.1 Israel *and* the 'Church'(?)

One of the unfortunate features in the Christian history of interpretation is that Ephesians has often been taken as a pretext for the view that the 'Church' has parted company with Israel (e.g., Schnackenburg, Lincoln, et al.). It may be fairly claimed that the designation 'Israel *and* the church' is a theological misnomer – at least in Ephesians. The designation reflects more of a theological presupposition of much modern New Testament scholarship than of the perspective of our author. This theological presupposition may substantially account for the tendency to perceive the 'Church' as stepping in to become the 'true Israel'. The problem, however, is that those who embrace this particular theological presupposition have often failed to recognise that the meaning of Israel can be hijacked, transcoded and defined in a narrowly exclusivistic ethnic sense. This study has set out to argue at some length that what has been put in question is not the Israel of God, but the Jewish 'body politic' which is so confused with Israel that the Gentiles could hardly become part of it. The idea of the 'one *body*' (2.16; cf. 1.23), which the author introduces to rectify the exclusive 'body politic', is not a replacement of Israel but an anti-*politeia*. For scholars who see the parting of Israel and the church in Ephesians, the rationale must therefore be sought elsewhere. Still more importantly, this means that future research on the ecclesiology of Ephesians would need to take into account the function of the 'Church' as an anti-*politeia* rather than as a new entity outside Israel.

6.3.2 The 'household of God' and the Ephesian *Haustafel*

The passage in Ephesians 5.21–6.9 represents one of the fullest expressions of NT household codes (or *Haustafeln*, so named since Luther),[8] and a great deal of effort has gone into attempts to identify the sources of the 'code' in the past decades.[9] The predominant historical-critical

[8] See also Col. 3.18–4.1; 1 Tim. 2.8–15; 6.1–2; Titus 2.1–10; 1 Pet. 2.13–3.7; and subsequent Christian literature, *Did.* 4.9–11; *Barn.* 19.7; *1 Clement* 1.3; 21.6–9; Polycarp, *Phil.* 4.2–3; Ignatius, *Pol.* 4.1–5.2.

[9] Useful surveys of scholarship can be found in Balch, *Wives*; cf. Balch, 'Household Codes'. Dibelius, *Epheser*, 48–50, contends that the early church had taken over a 'schema' that was originally Stoic and that its household duties were slightly Christianised. The adoption meant that 'the early church had started to try to come to grips with the world' and to forget about the imminent end. Dibelius's theory is followed by Berger, 'Hellenistische Gattungen', esp. 1081, who adds that the influence that popular gnomic traditions have had on the *form* of the NT household codes must also be taken into account (1085); Kuhn, 'Ephesians', 131. Dibelius's theory has been rejected by Crouch, *Origin*, who argued that the codes were more Hellenistic Jewish in character with only minimal Stoic

mode of exegesis, for example, has put admirable effort into linguistic and historical matters such as the parallels in the religious environment of the first century CE. The function of the 'form' in earlier extra-Biblical settings is brought across to its discussions.[10] Although the *Haustafel* in Ephesians 5.21–6.9 has been subjected to quite intense study in the past,[11] the attempts to see the way in which our 'code' has fitted into the argument

impact. See also Schrage, *Ethics*, esp. 244–56; cf. Schrage, 'Ethik,' 1–21; Schröder, 'Lists'. Barth, 'Traditions', 16, surmises that 'Eph. 5.21–33 may contain a factual, though critical dialogue with the Kybele-Artemis tradition' which promotes women's liberation. See also Osiek, *Social Setting*, 81–92; Towner, 'Households', 418; Dunn, 'Household Rules', here 49–53.

[10] The suggestion that there was in the ancient world an original or pure form, from which the NT 'codes' derived or from which they have deteriorated, has come under severe attack in recent studies, see, e.g., Hartmann, 'Household-Code Form', who concludes that 'most scholars who have discussed the household codes have done so diachronically, explaining the *Gattung*, form, schema, etc, of the different codes as the result of taking over, inheriting, being influenced, etc., from particular literary or cultural circles', but that 'the material that should enable us to conjecture the existence of the literary form household-code is very fragile, and when it comes to drawing conclusions about the history and thinking of the early church from this presumed literary form, the case must be even more fragile' (228, 230). We would need to note that the discovery of some wisdom-texts at Qumran also strengthens the view that household concerns should not be seen as the monopoly of the Graeco-Roman ethicists (Harrington, *Wisdom Texts*, esp. 40–8; cf. Dunn, 'Household Rules', 51–3). The way in which family/household relations should be ordered and preserved was a widespread concern among Jewish writers: see, e.g., the wisdom instruction in the Qumran library (4Q416, 417, 418 [= Sapiential Work A]) 3.14–4.15; also 1QSa 1.4–12; CD 7.6–9; Sir. 41.15–42.8/Masada 3.18–4.15). These Jewish writings always looked back to the Torah to undergird their teaching. See also Sir. 3.1f.; Josephus, *C. Ap.* 2.198–210; Philo, *Hypoth.* 7; notably, the three divisions found in *Ps.-Phocylides* 175–227: marriage (175–206); parents–children (207–22); master–slave (223–7). See further van der Horst, *Essays*, 48, who suggests that Ps.-Phocylides is 'a compendium of *misvot* for daily life which could help Jews in a thoroughly Hellenistic environment to live as Jews without having to abandon their interest in Greek culture' (48); Collins, *Wisdom*, 62–74, 112–21, 166–73. The format of the addressee-injunction-motivation model in the 'codes' of Ephesians concurs with Jewish wisdom traditions, see esp. Nel, *Structure*.

[11] See also more recently the work of Marlis Gielen, *Haustafelethik*, esp. 68–86, 204–315. Gielen contends that the 'household' (οἶκος) is the bed-rock of social unity in ancient society (68), and that the earliest Christian movement could not even begin without the household. Gielen is influenced by the work of Lührmann, 'Ökonomie', esp. 91, 93–5. Lührmann's major thesis is that the *Haustafeln* in Ephesians and Colossians were taken over from the οἰκονομία-tradition, i.e., 'concerning household management', of the Greek world (94). Nevertheless, neither Lührmann nor Gielen has given sustained analysis of the οἶκος words in Ephesians and the way in which the author has understood the idea of divinely ordained οἰκονομία, and no real attention has been given to the way in which the theme of 'household of God' interacts with that of the *Haustafel*. Lührmann's 'three-phases' development of the οἰκονομία-tradition has borne its mark upon the work of MacDonald, *Pauline Churches*, 115–22, 136–7, who contends that the NT *Haustafeln* are influenced by the ethics of Graeco-Roman society as exhibited in the *topos* 'concerning household management' (121). See also Balch, 'Household Codes'; Best, 'Haustafel'; Lohse, *Ethics*, 138–45, 146–55; Barclay, 'Family', esp. 76–7.

of the entire epistle are slight.[12] Since there has been no sustained analysis of the household relations in light of the context of the rest of the primary text, a fresh attempt at a full enquiry into the Ephesian *Haustafel* is made all the more necessary in the future. The following questions may need to be addressed before we can make our 'response responsible' or avoid being disrupted by our own 'appropriative comprehension'.[13] Do our author and the contemporary writers operate within the same conceptual framework, assuming that the 'household' is a basic unit or microcosm of the city-state?[14] Was the city-state of the Graeco-Roman world the chief model for our author's reflection on the 'code', or must the Ephesian 'code' simply be seen as a *para*-οἰκονομία, a 'household-management' but grounded on a rationale of a different order?[15] Can we take the 'code' to illustrate the dialogue of early Christianity with its wider environment and therefore the (cultural) struggle of the early Christian movement in defining its own identity? Does the author conceive of his 'code' as primarily a microcosm of God's household (2.19), that it should reveal the essence of the author's thinking about an *ideal* community?[16] A fresh attempt at a reassessment of the extent of the transformation the author has made when he engaged with other 'models' is perhaps necessary.

As we mentioned in our study, the Gentiles are designated as the 'members of the household of God' (οἰκεῖοι τοῦ θεοῦ, 2.19, see my discussion in 5.3.1). To be sure, the designation was employed first and foremost to forge a new identity for the Gentiles who were *excluded* by the Jews. The designation thus lays bare first and foremost the idea of an inclusive household.[17] We may also note that the author of Ephesians has used other οἶκος words to reinforce the identity of the Gentiles and the

[12] The few exceptions are Schrage, *Ethics*, who contends that 'the heavily christianized *Haustafel* of Ephesians uses the Christ event to orient earthly life in the framework of secular institutions' (251); Fiorenza, *Memory*, esp. 266–70, here 268.

[13] Steiner, *Babel*, 318. [14] See esp. Lacey, 'Patria Potestas'.

[15] Lührmann, 'Ökonomie', who advances the thought in his comparative study of the οἰκονομία texts in the philosophical discussions and the NT texts, concluding that the Ephesian *Haustafel* 'takes over' the οἰκονομία-tradition of the Greeks (94). However, we may need to note that the tendency to redefine or 'transcode' (to use Bakhtin's expression) the existing social structure has already been under way in the earlier Paul when he writes: 'But our *politeuma* is in heaven, and from it we await a Saviour, the Lord Jesus Christ' (Phil. 3.20). According to Col. 1.25, Paul was entrusted to a divine οἰκονομία. The author of 1 Timothy has also begun to see the household as a church (rather than the 'state'!) in microcosm, see esp. Barclay, 'Family', 77; cf. Philo, *Ios.* 38–9; *Praem.* 113.

[16] Cf. Philo, *QG* 2.60; Plutarch, *Alex. fort.* 329A–B; Cicero, *Nat. d.* 2.154; *SVF* I, 262.

[17] See further Saller, 'Familia', who concludes that the *familia* was a focus of honour for the Romans: '[T]he honour of the *paterfamilias* depended on his ability to protect his household, and in turn the virtue of the household contributed to his prestige' (353).

community-body to which they belong.[18] Given the frequency and pervasiveness of the 'household' language in Ephesians,[19] it is not altogether surprising to ask whether he also intends his 'household code', in which various roles were given according to one's place in the οἶκος, to be read primarily within the framework of *God's household*, which is marked by its inclusiveness and oneness.[20] Since the language of God's household is brought into the picture when the author addresses issues related to an

[18] See section 5.3.1 in chapter 5. One of the most natural explanations for the frequency of οἶκος words is that earliest Christians congregated at private homes, and that the author used the motif of οἶκος to blend with his understanding of the Christian community (vv. 20–2; cf. 1 Tim. 3.5, 12; Mark 11.17; John 2.16; Ezra 7.15; Isa. 56.7; 1QS 5.6; 8.5, 9; 9.6). In our case, the οἶκος words aid our author not only to consolidate identity for the Gentiles but also to cement their connections with other members of God's 'house' (2.20–2). The household concept has also influenced the way in which our author perceived the nature of apostolic and prophetic ministry, which he described as ἡ οἰκονομία τοῦ μυστηρίου, i.e., the 'stewardship' or 'household-administration' in connection with the mystery of Christ (3.9, cf. 3.4). To be sure, the οἰκονομία is entrusted by God to Paul to make sure that the Gentiles also become '*fellow-heirs*, members of the same body, and partakers of the promise in Christ Jesus through the gospel', i.e., by implementing the decision made by God (3.6–7, cf. 1.10; cf. 4.1; 1 Cor. 4.1–2; Col. 1.25; Titus 1.7). We may also add that the idea of οἰκονομία has already been echoed in the beginning of our epistle, at which the ultimate goal of God's will is 'for the οἰκονομία of the fulness of time, namely to unify all things in the Messiah' (εἰς οἰκονομίαν τοῦ πληρώματος τῶν καιρῶν κτλ., 1.10). In addition to this, the author also uses household/family words to depict God in his prayer as the Father (πατήρ), whose household encompasses every 'family' in the heavenly place and on earth (Τούτου χάριν κάμπτω τὰ γόνατά μου πρὸς τὸν πατέρα, ἐξ οὗ πᾶσα πατριὰ ἐν οὐρανοῖς καὶ ἐπὶ γῆς ὀνομάζεται, 3.14–15; cf. Exod. 6.14, 15, 17, 19, 25). The point here is the greatness of God as a name-giver, namely, he is the beginning from which every family drew its birth rather than 'the sanctification of *lineage* as a divinely-ordained gift' (*pace* Barclay, 'Family', 76), cf. Philo, *Leg.* 2.15; Plato, *Cratylus* 401B; Cicero, *Tusc.* 1.62, etc. Another οἶκος term, κατοικέω (lit. 'to dwell in, to inhabit'), was used to designate the relationship between Christ and the Gentiles: κατοικῆσαι τὸν Χριστὸν διὰ τῆς πίστεως ἐν ταῖς καρδίαις ὑμῶν (3.17); cf. Gen. 9.27; *P. Fay* 12.27. The same author has also used οἶκος words to speak of the 'building up' of the community (4.12, 16, 29; cf. Rom. 14.19; 15.2; 1 Cor. 8.1; 14.3–5, 12, 17; 2 Cor. 10.8; 1 Thess. 5.11). However, household terminology used for a religious group predates our author, see, e.g., Jer. 38.33; Amos 5.25; 1QS 8.5; 9.6 (בית קודש); 1 Cor. 16.19, par. Rom. 16.3–5; Gal. 6.10; Philem. 2; cf. Acts 2.46; Col. 4.15; 1 Tim. 5.8. See further Banks, *Community*; Klauck, *Hausgemeinde*; Branick, *House Church*, here 13–17; Moxnes, 'Family', esp. 20–6; Towner, 'Households', esp. 418; Michel, 'οἶκος'; Kuhli, 'οἰκονόμος'. For discussion of the composition and definition of the Roman household, see esp. Gardner and Wiedmann, *Roman Household*, 1–29; Rawson, *Family*, 1–57, 170–200.

[19] Cf. Colossians in which its 'code' of household duties does not 'obviously connect to what goes before or what comes after' (Barclay, *Colossians and Philemon*, 68); cf. Best, 'Haustafeln', 195; Crouch, *Origin*, 9.

[20] Barclay rightly observes that it is in the Ephesian *Haustafel* that instructions are given about the Christian socialisation of children for the first time in Christian literature ('Family', 76). One must, however, add that it is the undisguised inclusivism of God's household that best explains why it is necessary to address not only the 'superiors' but also the inferiors – a point which has not been adequately addressed in recent NT scholarship on the Ephesian *Haustafel*. For a discussion on the 'lower-class children' in the Roman

alienated humanity and in particular when he reinforces the oneness of the people of God (vv. 19–22), it will not be out of step to ask whether the 'code' of household duties in 5.21–6.9 may well be a stretched-out discussion about the reintegration of peoples of different *social* pedigrees, roles and responsibilities in the community of God, and whether the oneness of God's household on earth is part of God's wider 'economics' (i.e., the 'οἰκονομία of the fulness of time'). *In nuce*, the reintegration of 'all things' and particularly of restoring humanity *per se* is an obvious motif in Ephesians (e.g., 1.10; 3.2, 9) and we are more likely to make good sense of the significance of the *Haustafel* in the light of the οἶκος motif. A fresh line of enquiry may be opened up in future research, one that is likely to confirm that the management of household is the way in which *inclusiveness* and *oneness* could be strengthened.[21] Could it be that the Ephesian *Haustafel* is a *para*-οἰκονομία which is sensitive to what is appropriate within the traditional order of the οἶκος and thus to the constraints of the time,[22] but which would transform itself from within this accepted social reality by subordinating itself to the sovereignty of Christ, i.e., 'in the Lord'?[23]

familia, see esp. Rawson, *Family*, 170–200, who concludes that 'the Roman *familia* did serve as a community which could accommodate not only the nucleus family but a range of quasi-familial and other relationships and in which children seem to have had some intrinsic value and were able not only to survive but even to prosper' (197); cf. Rawson, 'Adult-Child', esp. 17–23; Bradley, *Slavery*, esp. 81–106.

[21] Dio, for example, has already drawn into use the *topos* of household-management in his political oration to urge for unity or oneness in a state-body, see esp. *Or.* 38.15; *Or.* 5.348–51. Dio's underlying assumption is that the oneness of the household is always the foundation of a healthy state; the household helps precisely to maintain the order of the state. The same position is also held by Aristides, who claims that the way a household is preserved – by which he means the inferiors must obey the superiors – is the same as the way a state-body is preserved (e.g., *Or.* 24.32–5); see also Philo, *Ios.* 38–9.

[22] It is very unlikely that the Ephesian *Haustafel* is a defensive reaction directed against a fanatical overemphasis on the nearness of the eschaton (*contra* Käsemann). The suggestion of Barth, 'Traditions', namely that 'Eph. 5.21–33 may contain a factual, though critical dialogue with the Kybele-Artemis tradition which promotes women's liberation' (16), is nowhere near the mark.

[23] The theory of Lührmann, 'Ökonomie', 94, who speaks of 'die *Übernahme* der οἰκονομία-Tradition in den Haustafeln . . .') and thinks that the Ephesian *Haustafel* is a wholesale 'take-over' of the Greek tradition of οἰκονομία ('concerning household-management'), needs reappraisal. See further Hays, *Moral Vision*, who suggests that the conventional authority structures of the ancient household are subverted while they were left in place (64); Schrage, *Ethics*, who concludes that 'it is . . . the eschatological Lord who appears behind earthly authorities and social structures' (248); Lohse, who comments: 'There is no call for a revolutionary reformation of society, neither the legal equality of men and women nor the freeing of slaves. But powerful expression of the concept of partnership is given by the love commandment. The present social structures remain valid, but the conduct required within them is now subjected to the authority of the Lord' (*Ethics*, 144).

6.3.3 The language of warfare and consolidation of the Gentiles' new identity

The author of Ephesians is concerned about matters 'on earth' and 'in the heavenlies'. For him the 'powers' in the heavenly places are considered as an important element in God's wider 'economics' (1.10; 3.9–10; cf. 1.20–2; 2.2).[24] As we mentioned in this study, the 'powers' (although 'real') in Ephesians could become a means of dividing human groups, establishing the differences between them, suggesting wherein their 'otherness' lies. This indication may well imply that our interpretation of such passages as Ephesians 6.10–17 would need to take into consideration the use of the language of 'powers' in defining and reinforcing one's identity. If the Gentiles are no longer under the grip of the 'powers', who are they under now? How could the new identity of the Gentiles be forcibly expressed? Instead of seeing the final section of our epistle as consisting of some 'concluding remarks'[25] or 'instruction' on how to resist the continuing powerful influence of the evil forces,[26] it may prove fruitful if a different set of questions is asked: does the author use the language of 'warfare' to fortify the identity of his Gentile readers as the people of God (6.12)? Given that the Gentiles have been transposed from the realm of the 'powers' into the realm of God (2.6, cf. 2.19), could the language of warfare serve as a tell-tale *sign* that the Gentiles have indeed parted company with the 'powers'? Could it be that the panoply[27] (i.e., a catalogue of virtues) which the Gentile readers are urged to put on is simply a display of their *distinguishing identity-markers* worthy of the identity they have acquired in Christ?[28] In any case, the Gentiles and the 'powers' are not in the same domain. A fruitful line of enquiry may well be opened up

[24] See also Str-B, III, 594; Michel, 'πατήρ', here 55; cf. Michel, 'οἰκοδομη'.

[25] So Lincoln, 'Stand', who contends that the author has created an effective *peroratio* to bolster his readers' confidence: vv. 10–18 consist of an exhortation on 'valour', a quality of a soldier; cf. Lincoln, *Ephesians*, 430–41. Lincoln depends heavily upon the work of Burgess, 'Epideictic Literature', esp. 209–14, who concludes that warfare furnishes a theme for speeches common to almost all writers in history and that the conditions under which a general's speech is supposed to be delivered are those of an army at the moment of conflict.

[26] Arnold, *Ephesians*, 69, argues that all Christians are engaged in a dangerous struggle with evil spirits who stand contrary to God's purposes and the welfare of God's people; Cargal, 'Heavenlies', 818. Dudorf, 'πάλη', suggests that the author of Ephesians draws upon the figure of a fully armoured soldier who also happens to be an accomplished wrestler. The use of πάλη helps to impress upon the reader's mind that the battle being described is one in which a close-quarter struggle is involved.

[27] For a helpful discussion on the panoply of the Roman army, see, e.g., Polybius, *Hist.* 6.22–4, 26, 31, 33, 34, 37–9; Livy, *Ab urbe.*, 42.34; Josephus, *B. J.* 3.71–97, 104, 105, 107, 108. See further Shelton, *Romans*, esp. 249–69.

[28] See further Hobbs, 'Warfare' 259–73, who writes: 'Armour is not only a protective coat for the body, but a public display of rank and status' (266).

when due attention is given to the connections between the language of warfare and the maintenance of one's identity (cf. 1QM 15).[29]

Wherever our future explorations may take us, it is my hope that the lasting impression of this study will be that the substantial content of Christianity is Jewish. Our assessment of Ephesians within the 'new perspective' which helps us to gain a clearer view of the first-century Jews and Judaism has shown abundantly clearly that the theme of Jewish attitudes toward the Gentiles and ethnic reconciliation cannot be fully appreciated unless we give the enduring Jewish character of Christianity which is represented in Ephesians its due weight. It may be fairly claimed that the 'Christianity' represented by the author of Ephesians is a movement of renewal breaking through the boundaries within one Judaism (not all) of the first century which is marked characteristically by covenantal ethnocentrism. That being said, it would be wrong to suggest that Ephesians represents the abandonment of Judaism in favour of Gentile triumphalism over ethnic Israel. Rather, we should speak of a Jewish messianic inclusivistic movement which transcends covenantal ethnocentrism: the Messiah Jesus, who is portrayed as a peace-maker in Ephesians, has come to preach peace to the 'far off' *and* the 'near'. He has surmounted the social distance between Jews and Gentiles so that 'both' can gain access to the God of Israel in a common spirit.

[29] The warfare language in Ephesians is not without palpable antecedents, see, e.g., Isa. 59.17; 1 Macc. 3.3; Wis. 5.15–23; 1QM 15.6–8; 1 Thess. 5.8, etc. See further Neufeld, *Armour*, whose thesis is that the author of Ephesians has transformed the ancient tradition of the armed deity at war with the human community into a creative Christian exhortation (i.e., the saints as divine warriors are now engaged in the battle of the gods).

SELECT BIBLIOGRAPHY

All references will appear in the footnotes by the surname(s) of the author followed by a shortened version of the title and appropriate page numbers. English translations of the Greek classical writers are based on the Loeb Classical Library series. Unless otherwise stated all other English translations of other languages are my own.

Aalders, *Plutarch* = G. J. D. Aalders, *Plutarch's Political Thought* (Amsterdam/Oxford/New York: North-Holland Publishing Company, 1982)

Abbott, *Ephesians* = T. K. Abbott, *The Epistles to the Ephesians and to the Colossians* (Edinburgh: T & T Clark, 1991)

Adai, *Geist* = J. Adai, *Der Heilige Geist als Gegenwart Gottes in den einzelnen Christen, in Kirche und in der Welt: Studien zur Pneumatologie des Epheserbriefes*, RST 31 (Frankfurt: Peter Lang, 1985)

Aerts, *Periphrastica* = W. J. Aerts, *Periphrastica: An Investigation into the Use of* εἶναι *and* ἔχειν *as Auxiliaries or Pseudo-Auxiliaries in Greek from Homer up to the Present Day* (Amsterdam: A. M. Hakkert, 1965)

Alexander, 'Galen' = L. Alexander, 'Paul and the Hellenistic School: The Evidence of Galen', in T. Engberg-Pedersen (ed.), *Paul in his Hellenistic Context* (Edinbugh: T & T Clark, 1994), 60–83

Allan, 'In Christ' = J. A. Allan, 'The "in Christ" Formula in Ephesians', *NTS* 5 (1958–9), 54–62

Allison, '4Q403' = D. C. Allison, '4Q403 Fragm. 1, Col. 38–46 and the Revelation of John', *RevQ* 47 (1986), 409–14

Anderson, 'Ruah' = A. A. Anderson, 'The Use of "Ruah" in 1QS, 1QH and 1QM', *JSS* 7 (1962), 293

Applebaum, 'Communities' = A. Applebaum, 'The Organization of the Jewish Communities in the Diaspora', in S. Safrai et al. (eds.), *The Jewish People in the First Century*, CRINT I-1 (Assen, Amsterdam: van Gorcum, 1974), 464–502

Arnold, 'Exorcism' = C. E. Arnold, 'The "Exorcism" of Ephesians 6.12 in Recent Research', *JSNT* 30 (1987), 71–87

Ephesians = C. E. Arnold, *Ephesians: Power and Magic: The Concept of Power in Ephesians in Light of its Historical Setting* (Grand Rapids, Michigan: Baker, 1992)

'Head' = C. E. Arnold, 'Jesus Christ: "Head" of the Church (Colossians and Ephesians)', in J. B. Green and M. Turner (eds.), *Jesus of Nazareth: Lord*

and Christ. Essays on the Historical Jesus and New Testament Christology (Grand Rapids, Michigan: Eerdmans, 1994), 346–66
Aune, 'Apocalypticism' = D. E. Aune, 'Apocalypticism', in *DPL*, 25–35
'Archon' = D. E. Aune, 'Archon', *DDDB*, 153–9
Revelation 1–5 = D. E. Aune, *Revelation 1–5* (Texas: Word, 1997)
Austin, *Hellenistic World* = M. M. Austin, *The Hellenistic World from Alexander to the Roman Conquest: A Selection of Ancient Sources in Translation* (Cambridge: Cambridge University Press, 1981)
Avi-Yonah, *Hellenism* = M. Avi-Yonah, *Hellenism and the East: Contacts and Interrelations from Alexander to the Roman Conquest* (Ann Arbor, Michigan: University Microfilms for the Institute of Languages, Literature and the Arts, The Hebrew University, 1978)
Bailey, *Poet* = K. E. Bailey, *Poet and Peasant, and Through Peasant Eyes: A Literary-Cultural Approach to the Parables of Luke* (Grand Rapids, Michigan: 1983)
Bakhtin, *Imagination* = M. M. Bakhtin, *Dialogic Imagination* (Austin, Texas: University of Texas, 1984)
Balch, *Wives* = D. L. Balch, *Let Wives be Submissive: the Domestic Code in 1 Peter*, SBLMS 26 (Chico, California: Scholars Press, 1981)
'Household Codes' = D. L. Balch, 'Household Codes', in D. E. Aune (ed.), *Greco-Roman Literature and the New Testament*, SBLSBS 21 (Atlanta: Scholar Press, 1988), 25–50
Baldry, 'State' = H. C. Baldry, 'Zeno's Ideal State', *JHS* 79 (1959), 3–15
Unity = H. C. Baldry, *The Unity of Mankind in Greek Thought* (Cambridge: Cambridge University Press, 1965)
Balsdon, *Aliens* = J. P. V. D. Balsdon, *Romans and Aliens* (London: Duckworth, 1979)
Balz, 'προετοιμαζέιν' = H. Balz, 'προετοιμαζέιν', *EDNT*, III (1993), 155
Banks, *Community* = R. Banks, *Paul's Idea of Community: The Early House Churches in their Historical Setting* (Sydney: Anzea Publishers, 1979)
Barbour, 'Creation' = R. S. Barbour, 'Creation, Wisdom and Christ', in W. A. McKinney (ed.), *Creation, Christ and Culture*, FS T. F. Torrance (Edinburgh: T & T Clark, 1976), 22–42
Barclay, *Truth* = J. M. G. Barclay, *Obeying the Truth: A Study of Paul's Ethics in Galatians* (Edinburgh: T & T Clark, 1988)
Jews = J. M. G. Barclay, *Jews in the Mediterranean Diaspora: From Alexander to Trajan (323 BCE–117CE)* (Edinburgh: T & T Clark, 1996)
'Family' = J. M. G. Barclay, 'The Family as the Bearer of Religion in Judaism and Early Christianity', in H. Moxnes (ed.), *Constructing Early Christian Families: Families as Social Reality and Metaphor* (London: Routledge, 1997), 66–80
Colossians and Philemon = J. M. G. Barclay, *Colossians and Philemon*, NTG (Sheffield: Sheffield Academic Press, 1997)
Barnes, 'Ephesians' = A. Barnes, *Notes on the New Testament: Ephesians, Philippians, and Colossians* (Grand Rapids, Michigan: Baker, 1840)
Barrett, *Paul* = C. K. Barrett, *Paul: An Introduction to His Thought* (London: Geoffrey Chapman, 1994)
Barth, 'Boundaries' = F. Barth, 'Introduction', in F. Barth (ed.), *Ethnic Groups and Boundaries: The Social Organization of Cultural Difference* (Oslo: Universitetsforlaget/London: G. Allen and Unwin, 1969), 9–38

Barth, *Wall* = M. Barth, *The Broken Wall* (London: Collins, 1960)
'Conversion' = M. Barth, 'Conversion and Conversation: Israel and the Church in Paul's Epistle to the Ephesians', *Int* 17 (1963), 3–24
Ephesians 1–3 = M. Barth, *Ephesians 1–3*, AB 34 (New York: Doubleday, 1974)
People = M. Barth, *The People of God*, JSNTSS 5 (Sheffield: JSOT Press, 1983)
'Traditions' = M. Barth, 'Traditions in Ephesians', *NTS* 30 (1984), 3–25
Barthes, *Challenge* = R. Barthes, *The Semiotic Challenge*, ET R. Howard (Berkeley/Los Angeles: University of California Press, 1988)
Bauckham, 'James' = R. Bauckham, 'James and the Jerusalem Church', in R. Bauckham (ed.), *The Book of Acts in its Palestinian Setting*, IV (Carlisle: Paternoster Press/Grand Rapids, Michigan: Eerdmans, 1995), 417–27
'Throne' = R. Bauckham, 'The Throne of God and the Worship of Jesus', in C. C. Newman et al. (eds), *The Jewish Roots of Christological Monotheism*, Papers from the St Andrews Conference on the Historical Origins of the Worship of Jesus, SJSJ 63 (Leiden/Boston/Cologne: E. J. Brill, 1999), 43–69
Bauder, 'παράπτωμα' = W. Bauder, 'παράπτωμα', *NIDNTT*, III (1976), 585–6
Bauder and Link, 'ἐγγύς' = W. Bauder and H.-G. Link, 'ἐγγύς', *NIDNTT*, II (1976), 53–5
Bauer, 'Amplificatio' = B. Bauer, 'Amplificatio', in G. Üding (ed.), *Historisches Wörterbuch der Rhetorik*, I (Darmstadt: Wissenschaftliche Buchgesellschaft, 1992), 445–71
Bauer, 'χωρίς' = J. B. Bauer, 'χωρίς', *EDNT*, III (1993), 492–93
Baumbach, 'Schöpfung' = G. Baumbach, 'Die Schöpfung in der Theologie des Paulus', *Kairos* 21 (1979), 196–205
Baumgarten, 'Exclusions' = J. Baumgarten, 'Exclusions from the Temple: Proselytes and Agrippa I', *JJS* 33 (1982), 215–25
Baur, *Paul* = F. C. Baur, *Paul: The Apostle of Christ*, 2 vols., ET A. Menzies (London: Williams & Norgate, 1875)
History = F. C. Baur, *The Church History of the First Three Centuries*, ET A. Menzies (London: Williams and Norgate, 1878–9)
Bayer, 'ἐλπις' = M. Bayer, 'ἐλπις', *EDNT*, I (1990), 437–41
Beale, 'Reconciliation' = G. K. Beale, 'The Old Testament Background of Reconciliation in 2 Corinthians 5–7 and its Bearing on the Literary Problem of 2 Corinthians 6.14–17', *NTS* 35 (1989), 550–81
Beare, 'Ephesians' = F. W. Beare, 'The Epistle to the Ephesians: Introduction and Exegesis', in *IB*, X (New York: Abingdon, 1953), 597–749
Beck and Brown, 'εἰρήνη' = H. Beck and C. Brown, 'εἰρήνη κτλ.', *NIDNTT*, II (1976), 776–83
Beck, *Mature Christianity* = N. A. Beck, *Mature Christianity: The Recognition and Repudiation of the Anti-Jewish Polemic of the New Testament* (Selinsgrove: Susquehanna University Press, 1985)
Beker, *Heirs* = J. C. Beker, *Heirs of Paul: Their Legacy in the New Testament and the Church Today* (Grand Rapids, Michigan: Eerdmans, 1991)
Benoit, *Jesus* = P. Benoit, *Jesus and the Gospel*, 2 vols., ET-B. Weatherhead (New York: Herder and Herder, 1973)
Berger, 'Hellenistische Gattungen' = K. Berger, 'Hellenistische Gattungen in Neuen Testament', *ANRW* 2.25.2 (1984), 1032–1431

Berkhof, *Powers* = H. Berkhof, *Christ and the Powers*, ET J. H. Yoder (Scotdale: Herald, 1977)

Bertram, 'ἔθνος' = G. Bertram, 'ἔθνος κτλ.', *TDNT*, II (1964) 364–9

'ἔργον' = G. Bertram, 'ἔργον κτλ.', *TDNT*, II (1964) 635–55

Best, *Body* = E. Best, *One Body in Christ: A Study in the Relationship of the Church to Christ in the Epistles of the Apostle Paul* (London: SPCK, 1955)

'Ephesians i.1' = E. Best, 'Ephesians i. 1', in E. Best and R. McL. Wilson (eds.), *Text and Interpretation*, FS M. Black (Cambridge: Cambridge University Press, 1979), 29–41

'Trespasses' = E. Best, 'Dead in Trespasses and Sins (Eph. 2.1)', *JSNT* 13 (1981), 9–25

'Credal' = E. Best, 'The Use of Credal and Liturgical Material in Ephesians', in M. J. Wilkins and T. Paige (eds.), *Worship, Theology and Ministry in Early Church. Essays in Honor of R. Martin* (Sheffield: Sheffield Academic Press, 1992), 53–69

'Judaism' = E. Best, 'Ephesians 2.11–22: A Christian View of Judaism', in R. P. Carroll (ed.), *Text as Pretext*, FS R. Davidson (Sheffield: Sheffield Academic Press, 1992), 47–60

Ephesians[1] = E. Best, *Ephesians*, NTG (Sheffield: JSOT Press, 1993)

'Haustafeln' = E. Best, 'The Haustafeln in Ephesians,' *IBS* 16 (1994), 146–60 [= *Essays*, 189–203]

Essays = E. Best, *Essays on Ephesians* (Edinburgh: T & T Clark, 1997)

Ephesians[2] = E. Best, *Ephesians*, ICC (Edinburgh: T & T Clark, 1998)

Betz, 'ἀκροβυστία' = O. Betz, 'ἀκροβυστία', *EDNT*, I (1990), 55

'περιτέμνω' = O. Betz, 'περιτέμνω κτλ.', *EDNT*, III (1993), 79–80

Bickermann, 'Inscription' = E. J. Bickermann, 'The Warning Inscription of Herod's Temple', *JQR* 37 (1946–7), 387–405

Jews = E. J. Bickermann, *The Jews in the Greek Age* (Cambridge, Massachusetts: Harvard University Press, 1988)

Black, 'Creation' = M. Black, 'The New Creation in 1 Enoch', in W. A. McKinney (ed.), *Creation, Christ and Culture*, FS T. F. Torrance (Edinburgh: T & T Clark, 1976), 13–21

Blank, 'Israel' = J. Blank, 'Das Mysterium Israel', in W. Stolz (ed.), *Jüdische Hoffnungskraft und christlicher Glaube* (Freiburg: Herder, 1971), 133–90

Blässer, 'ἀπειθέω' = P. Blässer, 'ἀπειθέω', *EDNT*, I (1990), 118–19

Böcher, 'Däemonen' = O. Böcher, 'Däemonen, I', in *TRE* 8 (1981), 270–4

This Jesus = M. N. A. Bockmuehl, *This Jesus: Martyr, Lord, Messiah* (Edinburgh: T & T Clark, 1994)

Bockmuehl, *Revelation* = M. N. A. Bockmuehl, *Revelation and Mystery in Ancient Judaism and Pauline Christianity*, WUNT 36 (Tübingen: J. C. B. Mohr, 1990)

'αἷμα' = O. Böcher, 'αἷμα', *EDNT*, I (1990), 37–9

Boeft, *Fate* = J. D. Boeft, *Calcidius on Fate: His Doctrine and Sources*, PA 18 (Leiden: Brill, 1977)

Demons = J. D. Boeft, *Calcidius on Demons: Commentarius Ch. 127–136*, PA 33 (Leiden: E. J. Brill, 1977)

Borgen, 'Synagogue' = P. Borgen, 'The Early Church and the Hellenistic Synagogue', in his *Paul Preaches Circumcision and Pleases Men, and Other Essays on Christian Origins* (Trondheim, Norway: Tapir, 1983), 55–77

'Unity' = P. Borgen, 'Thoughts on Christian Unity in the New Testament', in his *Paul Preaches Circumcision and Pleases Men, and Other Essays on Christian Origins* (Trondheim, Norway: Tapir, 1983), 131–41

'Heavenly Ascent' = P. Borgen, 'Heavenly Ascent in Philo: An Examination of Selected Passages', in J. H. Charlesworth and C. A. Evans (eds.), *The Pseudepigrapha and Early Biblical Interpretation*, JSPPS 14 (Sheffield: Sheffield Academic Press, 1993), 246–68

Bouttier, *Éphésiens* = M. Bouttier, *L'Épître de Saint Paul aux Éphésiens*, CNT 9b (Geneva: Labor et Fides, 1991)

Boyer, 'Participle' = J. L. Boyer, 'The Classification of Participle: A Statistical Study', *GTJ* 5 (1984), 163–79

Bradley, *Slavery* = K. Bradley, *Slavery and Society at Rome* (Cambridge: Cambridge University Press, 1994)

Brandon, 'Time as God' = S. G. F. Brandon, 'Time as God and Devil', *BJRL* 47 (1964–5), 12–31

Deity = S. G. F. Brandon, *History, Time and Deity* (Manchester, 1965)

Branick, *House Church* = V. Branick, *The House Church in the Writings of Paul* (Wilmington, Delaware: Michael Glazier, 1989)

Bratcher and Nida, *Ephesians* = R. Bratcher and E. Nida, *A Translator's Handbook on Paul's Letter to the Ephesians* (London/New York/Stuttgart: United Bible Societies, 1982)

Braun, *Qumran* = H. Braun, *Qumran und das Neue Testament*, I (Tübingen: J. C. B. Mohr, 1966)

'ποιέω' = H. Braun, 'ποιέω κτλ.', *TDNT*, VI (1968) 458–84

Brenk, 'Moon' = F. E. Brenk, 'In the Light of the Moon: Demonology in the Early Imperial Period', *ANRW* II.16.3 (1986), 2068–145

Brown, *Semitic Background* = R. E. Brown, *The Semitic Background of the Term 'Mystery' in the New Testament*, FBBS 21 (Philadelphia: Fortress, 1968)

Bruce, *Development* = F. F. Bruce, *New Testament Development of Old Testament Themes* (Grand Rapids, Michigan: Eerdmans, 1968)

Ephesians = F. F. Bruce, *The Epistles to the Colossians, to Philemon, and to the Ephesians*, NICNT (Grand Rapids, Michigan: Eerdmans, 1988)

Büchsel, 'ἄλλος' = F. Büchsel, 'ἄλλος κτλ.', *TDNT*, I (1964), 264–7

'ἀποκαταλλάσσω' = F. Büchsel, 'ἀποκαταλλάσσω', *TDNT*, I (1964), 258–9

Bullinger, *Figures* = E. W. Bullinger, *Figures of Speech Used in the Bible* (Grand Rapids, Michigan: Baker, 1986^{10})

Bultmann, 'ἐλπις' = R. Bultmann, 'ἐλπις κτλ.', *TDNT*, II (1964), 517–23, 529–35

Burchard, 'Joseph and Aseneth' = C. Burchard, 'Joseph and Aseneth', in *OTP*, II, 177–247

Burger, *Versöhnung* = Chr. Burger, *Schöpfung und Versöhnung: Studien zum liturgischen Gut im Kolosser und Epheserbrief*, WMANT 46 (Neukirchen-Vluyn: Neukirchener Verlag, 1975)

Burgess, 'Epideictic Literature' = T. L. Burgess, 'Epideictic Literature', *SCP* 3 (1902), 89–261

Caird, *Principalities* = G. B. Caird, *Principalities and Powers* (Oxford: Clarendon Press, 1956)

Letters = G. B. Caird, *Paul's Letters from Prison: Ephesians, Philippians, Colossians, Philemon*, NCIB (Oxford: Oxford University Press, 1976)

Theology = G. B. Caird, *New Testament Theology*, ed. L. D. Hurst (Oxford: Clarendon Press, 1994)

Campbell, *Gospel* = W. S. Campbell, *Paul's Gospel in an Intercultural Context*, SIGC 69 (Frankfurt/Berne/New York/Paris: Peter Lang, 1991)

Caragounis, *Mysterion* = Chrys. C. Caragounis, *The Ephesian Mysterion* (Lund: CWK Gleerup, 1977)

Cargal, 'Heavenlies' = T. B. Cargal, 'Seated in the Heavenlies: Cosmic Mediators in the Mysteries of Mithras and the Letter to the Ephesians', *SBL Seminar Papers* 1994, 804–21

Carr, *Angels* = W. Carr, *Angels and Principalities: The Background, Meaning and Development of the Pauline Phrase hai archai kai hai exousiai*, SNTSMS 42 (Cambridge: Cambridge University Press, 1981)

Carroll and Green, *Death* = J. T. Carroll and J. B. Green, *The Death of Jesus in Early Christianity* (Peabody, Massachusetts: Hendriksen, 1995)

Carson, *Variegated Nomism* = D. A. Carson et al. (eds), *Justification and Variegated Nomism*, I: *The Complexities of Second Temple Judaism* (Tübingen: Mohr/Grand Rapids, Michigan: Baker Academic, 2001)

Carson and Williamson, *It is Written* = D. A. Carson and H. G. M. Williamson (eds.), *It is Written: Scripture Citing Scripture*, FS B. Lindars (Cambridge: Cambridge University Press, 1988)

Chadwick, 'Absicht' = H. Chadwick, 'Die Absicht des Epheserbriefes', *ZNW* 51 (1960), 145–53

'Ephesians' = H. Chadwick, 'Ephesians', in *PCB*, 980–4

Charlesworth, 'Dualism' = J. H. Charlesworth, 'A Critical Comparison of the Dualism in 1QS III, 13-IV, 26 and the "Dualism" Contained in the Fourth Gospel', *NTS* 15 (1968), 389–418

'Scrolls' = J. H. Charlesworth, 'The Dead Sea Scrolls and the Historical Jesus', in J. H. Charlesworth (ed.), *Jesus and the Dead Sea Scrolls: The Controversy Resolved* (New York: Doubleday, 1992), 1–74

Chilton, 'Father' = B. D. Chilton, 'God as "Father" in the Targumim, in non-Canonical Literatures of Early Judaism and Primitive Christianity, and in Matthew', in J. H. Charlesworth and C. A. Evans (eds.), *The Pseudepigrapha and Early Biblical Interpretation*, JSPSS 14 (Sheffield: JSOT Press, 1993), 151–69

Chilton and Neusner, *Judaism* = B. D. Chilton and J. Neusner, *Judaism in the New Testament: Practice and Beliefs* (London: Routledge, 1995)

Christiansen, *Ritual Boundaries* = E. J. Christiansen, *The Covenant in Judaism and Paul: A Study of Ritual Boundaries as Identity Markers*, AGAJU 27 (Leiden: E. J. Brill, 1995)

Clavel-Lévêque, 'Strabon' = M. Clavel-Lévêque, 'Les Gaules et les Gaulois: pour une analysis du fonctionnement de la *Géographie* de Strabon (1)', *DHA* 166 (1974), 75–93

Clements, *Deuteronomy* = R. E. Clements, *Deuteronomy* (Sheffield: JSOT Press, 1989)

Cohen, *Maccabees* = S. J. D. Cohen, *From the Maccabees to the Mishnah*, LEC 7 (Philadelphia: Westminster Press, 1987)

'Boundary' = S. J. D. Cohen, 'Crossing the Boundary and Becoming a Jew', *HTR* 82 (1989), 13–33

'Mishnah' = S. J. D. Cohen, 'Judaism to the Mishnah: 135–220', in H. Shanks (ed.), *Christianity and Rabbinic Judaism* (London: SPCK, 1993), 195–223
'Jews' = S. J. D. Cohen, '"Those Who Say They Are Jews and Are Not": How Do You Know a Jew in Antiquity When You See One?', in S. J. D. Cohen and E. S. Frerichs (eds.), *Diasporas in Antiquity* (Atlanta: Scholars Press, 1993), 1–45
'ἸΟΥΔΑΙΟΣ' = S. J. D. Cohen, 'ἸΟΥΔΑΙΟΣ ΤΟ ΓΕΝΟΣ and Related Expressions in Josephus', in F. Parente and J. Sievers (eds.), *Josephus and the History of the Graeco-Roman Period*, FS Morton Smith, SPB 41 (Leiden: E. J. Brill, 1994), 23–38
Jewishness = S. J. D. Cohen, *The Beginnings of Jewishness: Boundaries, Varieties, Uncertainties* (Berkeley: University of California Press, 1999)
Collins, 'Apocalyptic Eschatology' = J. J. Collins, 'Apocalyptic Eschatology as the Transcendence of Death', *CBQ* 36 (1974), 21–43
'Prince' = J. J. Collins, 'Prince', in *DDDB*, 1249–52
Wisdom = J. J. Collins, *Wisdom in the Hellenistic Age* (Edinburgh: T&T Clark, 1989)
Imagination = J. J. Collins, *Apocalyptic Imagination: An Introduction to the Jewish Matrix of Christianity* (New York: Crossroads, 1995)
Colpe, *Schule* = C. Colpe, *Die Religionsgeschichtliche Schule: Darstellung und Kritik ihres Bildes vom Gnostischen Erlösermythus*, FRLANT 78 (Göttingen: Vandenhoeck & Ruprecht, 1961)
Comfort, 'Temple' = P. W. Comfort, 'Temple', in *DPL*, 923–5
Conzelmann, *Epheser* = J. Becker, H. Conzelmann and G. Friedrich, *Die Briefe an die Galater, Epheser, Philipper, Kolosser, Thessalonicher und Philemon*, NTD 8 (Göttingen: Vandenhoeck & Ruprecht, 1976), 86–124
Polemics = H. Conzelmann, *Gentiles, Jews, Christians: Polemics and Apologetics in the Greco-Roman Era* (Minneapolis: Fortress, 1992)
Cotterell and Turner, *Linguistics* = P. Cotterell and M. Turner, *Linguistics and Biblical Interpretation* (Downers Grove, Illinois: InterVarsity Press, 1989)
Coutts, 'Ephesians 1.3–14' = J. Coutts, 'Ephesians 1.3–14 and I Peter 1.3–12', *NTS* 3 (1956–7), 115–27
Crawford, 'Citizenship' = M. H. Crawford, 'Citizenship, Roman', in *OCD*, 334–5
Crouch, *Origin* = J. E. Crouch, *The Origin and Intention of the Colossian Haustafel* (Göttingen: Vandenhoeck & Ruprecht, 1972)
Cruse, *Lexical Semantics* = D. A. Cruse, *Lexical Semantics* (Cambridge: Cambridge University Press, 1986)
Dahl, 'Adresse' = N. A. Dahl, 'Adresse und Prooemium des Epheserbriefes', *TZ* 7 (1951), 241–64
'Creation' = N. A. Dahl, 'Christ, Creation and the Church', in W. D. Davies and D. Daube (eds.), *The Background of the New Testament and its Eschatology* (Cambridge: Cambridge University Press, 1956), 422–43
Auslegung = N. A. Dahl, *Kurze Auslegung des Epheserbriefes* (Göttingen: Vandenhoeck & Ruprecht, 1965)
'Geheimnis' = N. A. Dahl, 'Das Geheimnis der Kirche nach Eph. 3, 8–10', in E. Schlink and A. Peters (eds.), *Zur Auferbauung des Leibes Christi*, FS P. Brunner (Kassel: Stauda-Verlag, 1965), 63–75

'Cosmic Dimensions' = N. A. Dahl, 'Cosmic Dimensions and Religious Knowledge (Eph 3:18)', in E. E. Ellis and E, Gräβer (eds.), *Jesus und Paulus*: FS W. G. Kümmel (Göttingen: Vandenhoeck & Ruprecht, 1975), 57–75

'Gentiles' = N. A. Dahl, 'Gentiles, Christians, and Israelites in the Epistle to the Ephesians', in G. W. E. Nickelsburg and G. W. MacRae (eds.), *Christians Among Jews and Gentiles*, FS K. Stendahl (Philadelphia: Fortress, 1986), 31–9

Christ = N. A. Dahl, *Jesus the Christ: Historical Origins of Christological Doctrines*, ed. D. H. Juel (Minneapolis: Fortress, 1991)

Darcus, 'Daimon' = S. Darcus, '*Daimon* as a Force Shaping *Ethos* in Heraclitus', *Phoenix* 28 (1974), 390–407

Davidson, *Angels* = M. J. Davidson, *Angels at Qumran: A Comparative Study of 1 Enoch 1–36, 72–108 and Sectarian Writings from Qumran*, JSPSS 11 (Sheffield: Sheffield Academic Press, 1992)

Davies, 'Polis' = J. K. Davies, 'The Origins of the Greek *Polis*: Where Should We Be Looking?', in L. G. Mitchell and P. J. Rhodes (eds.), *The Development of the Polis in Archaic Greek* (London: Routledge, 1997), 24–38

'Citizenship' = J. K. Davies, 'Citizenship, Greek', in *OCD*, 333–4

de Lacey, 'One Lord' = D. R. de Lacey, '"One Lord" in Pauline Christology', in H. H. Rowdon (ed.), *Christ the Lord*, FS D. Guthrie (Leicester: Inter-Varsity Press, 1982), 191–203

de Ste Croix, *Class Struggle* = G. E. M. de Ste Croix, *The Class Struggle in the Ancient Greek World* (London: Duckworth, 1981)

Deichgräber, *Gotteshymnus* = R. Deichgräber, *Gotteshymnus und Christushymnus in der frühen Christenheit: Untersuchungen zu Form, Sprache und Stil der frühchristlichen Hymnen*, SUNT 5 (Göttingen: Vandenhoeck & Ruprecht, 1967)

Delling, 'ἄρχω' = G. Delling, 'ἄρχω κτλ.', *TDNT*, I (1964), 488–9

Dentith, 'Language' = S. Dentith, 'Voloshinov and Bakhtin on Language', in his *Bakhtinian Thought: An Introductory Reader* (London: Routledge, 1995), 22–40

Dibelius, *Geisterwelt* = M. Dibelius, *Die Geisterwelt im Glauben des Paulus* (Göttingen: Vandenhoeck & Ruprecht, 1909)

Dibelius and Greeven, *Epheser* = M. Dibelius and H. Greeven, *An die Kolosser, Epheser, an Philemon* (Tübingen: J. C. B. Mohr, 1953)

Dietrich, *Fate* = B. C. Dietrich, *Death, Fate, and the Gods: The Development of a Religious Idea in Greek Popular Belief and in Homer* (London: Athlone, 1967)

Dihle, 'Response' = A. Dihle, 'A Response', in A. Bulloch et al. (eds.), *Images and Ideologies: Self-Definition in the Hellenistic World* (Berkeley: University of California Press, 1993), 287–95

Dodd, *Scriptures* = C. H. Dodd, *According to the Scriptures: The Substructure of New Testament Theology* (London: Nisbet & Co., 1952)

Drachmann, *Atheism* = A. B. Drachmann, *Atheism in Pagan Antiquity* (London: Gyldendal, 1922)

Drijvers, 'Aion' = H. J. W. Drijvers, 'Aion', in *DDDB*, 24

Du Toit, 'Vilification' = A. Du Toit, 'Vilification as a Pragmatic Device in Early Christian Epistolography', *Bib* 75 (1994), 403–12

Dudorf, 'πάλη' = M. E. Dudorf, 'The Use of πάλη in Eph. 6: 12', *JBL* 117 (1998), 331–5

Dunn, 'Death' = J. D. G. Dunn, 'Paul's Understanding of The Death of Jesus', in R. Banks (ed.), *Reconciliation and Hope: New Testament Essays on Atonement and Eschatology*, FS L. L. Morris (Grand Rapids, Michigan: Eerdmans, 1974), 125–41

Jesus = J. D. G. Dunn, *Jesus and the Spirit* (London: SCM, 1975)

Christology = J. D. G. Dunn, *Christology in the Making: A New Testament Inquiry into the Doctrine of the Incarnation* (London: SCM, 1989^2)

'Monotheistic Faith' = J. D. G. Dunn, 'Was Christianity a Monotheistic Faith from the Beginning?', *SJT* 35 (1982), 303–36

Romans 1–8 = J. D. G. Dunn, *Romans 1–8* (Texas: Word, 1988)

Romans 9–16 = J. D. G. Dunn, *Romans 9–16* (Texas: Word, 1988)

Unity = J. D. G. Dunn, *Unity and Diversity: An Inquiry into the Character of Earliest Christianity* (London: SCM/Philadelphia: TPI, 1990^2)

'New Perspective' = J. D. G. Dunn, 'New Perspective on Paul', in his *Jesus, Paul and the Law* (London: SPCK/Philadelphia: Westminster, 1990), 183–214

'Sacrifice' = J. D. G. Dunn, 'Paul's Understanding of the Death of Jesus as Sacrifice', in S. W. Sykes (ed.), *Sacrifice and Redemption: Durham Essays in Theology* (Cambridge: Cambridge University Press, 1991), 35–56

Partings = J. D. G. Dunn, *The Partings of the Ways between Christianity and Judaism and their Significance for the Character of Christianity* (London: SCM, 1991)

'Circumcision' = J. D. G. Dunn, 'What was the Issue between Paul and "Those of the Circumcision"?', in M. Hengel and U. Heckel (eds.), *Paulus und das antike Judentum*, WUNT 58 (J. C. B. Mohr, 1991), 295–313

'Anti-Semitism' = J. D. G. Dunn, 'Anti-Semitism in the Deutero-Pauline Literature', in C. A Evans and D. A. Hagner (eds.), *Anti-Semitism and Early Christianity: Issues of Polemic and Faith* (Minneapolis: Fortress, 1993), 151–65

'Echoes' = J. D. G. Dunn, 'Echoes of Intra-Jewish Polemic in Paul's Letter to the Galatians', *JBL* 112 (1993), 459–77

Galatians = J. D. G. Dunn, *The Epistle to the Galatians* (London: A. C. Black, 1993)

'Apologia' = J. D. G. Dunn, 'The Colossian Philosophy: A Confident Jewish Apologia', *Bib* 76 (1995), 153–81

1 Corinthians = J. D. G. Dunn, *1 Corinthians*, NTG (Sheffield: Sheffield Academic Press, 1995)

'Deutero-Pauline Letters' = J. D. G. Dunn, 'Deutero-Pauline Letters', in J. Barclay and J. Sweet (eds.), *Early Christian Thought in Its Jewish Context*, FS Morna D. Hooker (Cambridge: Cambridge University Press, 1996), 130–44

Colossians and Philemon = J. D. G. Dunn, *The Epistles to the Colossians and to Philemon*, NIGTC (Carlisle: Paternoster/Grand Rapids, Michigan: Eerdmans, 1996)

'Household Rules' = J. D. G. Dunn, 'The Household Rules in the New Testament', in S. C. Barton (ed.), *The Family in Theological Perspective* (Edinburgh: T & T Clark, 1996), 43–63

Christ = J. D. G. Dunn, *The Christ and the Spirit*, vol. I: *Christology* (Grand Rapids, Michigan: Eerdmans, 1998)
TPA = J. D. G. Dunn, *The Theology of Paul the Apostle* (Grand Rapids, Michigan/Cambridge, UK: Eerdmans, 1998)
'Works of the Law' = J. D. G. Dunn, 'Whatever Happened to "Works of the Law"', in J. Keřkovský (ed.), *ΕΠΙΤΟΑΥΤΟ*, FS P. Pokorný (Prague: Mlýn, 1998), 107–20
Dupont, *Life* = F. Dupont, *Daily Life in Ancient Rome* (London: Blackwell, 1989)
Dyson, *Community* = S. L. Dyson, *Community and Society in Roman Italy* (Baltimore/London: The Johns Hopkins University Press, 1992)
Ebel, 'περιπατέω' = G. Ebel, 'περιπτέω', *NIDNTT*, III (1976), 943–5
Ellis, *Use* = E. E. Ellis, *Paul's Use of the Old Testament* (Grand Rapids, Michigan: Baker, 1957)
Ellul, *Subversion* = J. Ellul, *The Subversion of Christianity*, ET = G. W. Bromiley (Grand Rapids, Michigan: Eerdmans, 1986)
Endres, *Jubilees* = J. C. Endres, *Biblical Interpretation of Jubilees*, CBQMS 18 (Washington, D.C.: Catholic Biblical Association of America, 1987), 236
Ernst, 'Epheser' = J. Ernst, *Die Briefe an die Philipper, an Philemon, an die Kolosser, an die Epheser* (Regensburg: F. Pustet, 1974)
Evans, *Noncanonical Writings* = C. A. Evans, *Noncanonical Writings and New Testament Interpretation* (Massachusetts: Hendrickson, 1995)
Fanning, *Verbal Aspect* = B. M. Fanning, *Verbal Aspect in New Testament Greek* (Oxford: Clarendon Press, 1990)
Fascher, 'Gottlosigkeit' = E. Fascher, 'Der Vorwurf der Gottlosigkeit in der Auseinandersetzung bei Juden, Griechen und Christen', in O. Betz et al. (eds.), *Abraham unser Vater*, FS O. Michel (Leiden: E. J. Brill, 1963), 78–105
Faust, *Pax* = E. Faust, *Pax Christi et Pax Caesaris: Religionsgeschichtliche, traditionsgeschichtliche und sozialgeschichtliche Studien zum Epheserbrief*, NTOA 24 (Göttingen: Vandenhoeck & Ruprecht, 1993)
Feldman, 'Groups' = L. H. Feldman, 'Jews and Christians as Groups in a Pagan World', in J. Neusner and E. S. Frerichs (eds.), *To See Ourselves as Others See Us: Christians, Jews, 'Others' in Late Antiquity* (Chico: Scholars Press, 1985), 247–62
Jew = L. H. Feldman, *Jew and Gentile in the Ancient World: Attitudes and Interactions from Alexander to Justinian* (Princeton, New Jersey: Princeton University Press, 1993)
Fiedler, 'ἁμαρτία' = P. Fiedler, 'ἁμαρτία', *EDNT*, I (1990), 65–9
Finley, *Politics* = M. I. Finley, *Politics in the Ancient World* (Cambridge: Cambridge University Press, 1983)
Fiorenza, *Memory* = E. S. Fiorenza, *In Memory of Her: A Feminist Theological Reconstruction of Christian Origin* (London: SCM, 1983)
Fischer, *Tendenz* = K. M. Fischer, *Tendenz und Absicht des Epheserbriefes*, FRLANT 111 (Göttingen: Vandenhoeck & Ruprecht, 1973)
Fitzmyer, '4QTestimonia' = J. A. Fitzmyer, '"4QTestimonia" and the New Testament', *TS* 18 (1957), 513–37
'Quotations' = J. A. Fitzmyer, 'The Use of Explicit Old Testament Quotations in Qumran Literature and in the New Testament', in his *Essays on the Semitic*

Background of the New Testament, SBLSBS 5 (Missoula, Montana: Scholars Press, 1971), 3–58

Theology = J. A. Fitzmyer, *Paul and His Theology: A Brief Sketch* (Englewood Cliffs, New Jersey: Prentice Hall, 1989)

Paul = J. A. Fitzmyer, *According to Paul: Studies in the Theology of the Apostle* (New York: Paulist Press, 1993)

Flusser, 'Psalms' = D. Flusser, 'Psalms, Hymns and Prayers', in M. E. Stone (ed.), *Jewish Writings of the Second Temple Period: Apocrypha, Pseudepigrapha, Qumran Sectarian Writings, Philo, Josephus*, CRINT II.2 (Assen: van Gorcum/Philadelphia: Fortress, 1984), 551–77

Foerster, 'ἀήρ' = W. Foerster, 'ἀήρ', *TDNT*, I (1964), 165–6

'εἰρήνη' = W. Foerster, 'εἰρήνη κτλ.', *TDNT*, II (1964), 406–20

'κτίζω' = W. Foerster, 'κτίζω κτλ.', *TDNT*, III (1965), 1000–35

Fohrer, 'σοφία' = G. Fohrer, 'σοφία κτλ', *TDNT*, VII (1971), 476–526

Fowler, *City-States* = W. W. Fowler, *The City-States of the Greeks and Romans* (London: Macmillan, 1911)

Frankemölle, 'ἀποκτείνω' = H. Frankemölle, 'ἀποκτείνω', *EDNT*, I (1990), 134

Freund, 'Decalogue' = R. A. Freund, 'The Decalogue in Early Judaism and Christianity', in C. A. Evans and J. A. Sanders (eds.), *The Function of Scripture in Early Jewish and Christian Tradition*, JSNTSS 154 (Sheffield: Sheffield Academic Press, 1998), 124–41

Friedrich, 'εὐαγγελίζομαι' = G. Friedrich, 'εὐαγγελίζομαι κτλ.', *TDNT*, II (1964), 707–37

Friedrich, 'ξένος' = J. H. Friedrich, 'ξένος', *EDNT*, II (1991), 486

Furnish, 'Ephesians' = V. P. Furnish, 'Ephesians, Epistle to the', in *ABD*, II, 535–42

Gager, 'Judaism' = J. G. Gager, 'Judaism as Seen by Outsiders', in R. A. Kraft and W. E. Nickelsburg (eds.), *Early Judaism and its Modern Interpreters* (Philadelphia: Fortress/Atlanta: Scholars, 1986), 99–116

García-Martínez, DSS = F. García-Martínez, *Dead Sea Scrolls Translated: The Qumran Texts in English*, ET W. G. E. Watson (Leiden/New York/Cologne, E. J. Brill, 1994)

Gardner and Wiedmann, *Roman Household* = J. F. Gardner and T. Wiedmann, *The Roman Household: A Sourcebook* (London/New York: Routledge, 1991)

Garland, *Deformity* = R. Garland, *The Eye of the Beholder: Deformity and Disability in the Roman World* (London: Duckworth, 1995)

Gärtner, *Temple* = B. Gärtner, *The Temple and the Community in the Qumran and the New Testament: A Comparative Study in the Temple Symbolism of the Qumran Texts and the New Testament*, SNTSMS 1 (Cambridge: Cambridge University Press, 1965)

Gaster, *Scriptures* = T. H. Gaster, *The Dead Sea Scriptures* (New York: Doubleday, 1976)

Gaston, *Stone* = L. Gaston, *No Stone on Another: Studies in the Significance of the Fall of Jerusalem in the Synoptic Gospels*. SNovT 23 (Leiden: E. J. Brill, 1970)

Giavini, 'Structure' = G. Giavini, 'La Structure Littéraire d'Eph. 2.11–22', *NTS* 16 (1970), 209–11

Gibbs, *Creation* = J. G. Gibbs, *Creation and Redemption: A Study in Pauline Theology*, SNovT 26 (Leiden: E. J. Brill, 1971)

Gielen, *Haustafelethik* = Marlis Gielen, *Tradition und Theologie neutestamentlicher Haustafelethik: Ein Beitrag zur einer christlichen Auseinandersetzung mit gesellschaftlichen Normen*, BBB 75 (Frankfurt: Anton Hain, 1990)

Gilbert, 'Wisdom' = M. Gilbert, 'Wisdom Literature', in M. E. Stone (ed.), *Jewish Writings of the Second Temple Period*, CRINT II.2 (Assen: Gorcum/Philadelphia: Fortress, 1984), 283–324

Giles, 'Ethnicity Markers' = H. Giles, 'Ethnicity Markers in Speech', in K. R. Scherer and H. Giles (eds.), *Social Markers in Speech* (Cambridge: Cambridge University Press, 1979), 251–89

Giovannini, 'Commonwealth' = A. Giovannini, 'Greek Cities and Greek Commonwealth,' in A. Bulloch et al. (eds.), *Images and Ideologies: Self Definition in the Hellenistic World* (Berkeley/Los Angeles/London: University of California Press, 1993), 265–86

Gnilka, *Epheserbrief* = J. Gnilka, *Die Epheserbrief*, HKNT 10/2 (Freiburg/Basel/Vienna: Herder, 1990)

Goldenburg, 'Scythian-Barbarian' = D. Goldenburg, 'Scythian-Barbarian: The Permutation of a Classical Topos in Jewish and Christian Texts of Late Antiquity', *JJS* 49 (1998), 87–102

Gonda, *Moods* = J. Gonda, *The Character of the Indo-European Moods, with Special Regard to Greek and Sanskrit* (Wiesbaden: Harrassowits, 1956)

Goodman, 'Jewish Proselytizing' = M. Goodman, 'Jewish Proselytizing in the First Century', in J. Lieu and T. Rajak (eds.), *The Jews among Pagans and Christians in the Roman Empire* (London: Routledge, 1992), 53–78

Goodspeed, *Meaning* = E. J. Goodspeed, *The Meaning of Ephesians* (Chicago: University of Chicago, Press, 1933)

Grant, *Greeks and Romans* = M. Grant, 'Appendix I: Foreigners', in his *Greeks and Romans: A Social History* (London: Weidenfeld and Nicolson, 1992)

Grassi, 'Ephesians' = J. A. Grassi, 'The Letter to the Ephesians', in *JBC*, 341–9

Groß, 'Geschöpf' = H. Groß, 'Der Mensch als neues Geschöpf (Jer 31; Ez 36; Ps 51)', in R. Mosis and L. Rupert (eds.), *Der Weg zum Menschen: Zur philosophischen und theologischen Anthropology*, FS A. Deissler (Freiburg/Basel/Vienna: Herder, 1989), 98–109

Grudem, *Prophecy* = W. A. Grudem, *The Gift of Prophecy in the New Testament and Today* (Illinois: Crossway Books, 1988)

Gruenwald, *Merkavah Mysticism* = I. Gruenwald, *Apocalyptic and Merkavah Mysticism* (Leiden: E. J. Brill, 1980)

Grundmann, 'δεξιος' = W. Grundmann, 'δεξιος', *TDNT*, II (1964), 37–40

Günther, 'ἁμαρτία' = W. Günther, 'ἁμαρτία', *TDNT*, I (1964), 577–85

Gutbrod, 'Ἰσραήλ' = W. Gutbrod, 'Ἰσραήλ κτλ.', *TDNT*, III (1965), 383–8

Haarhoff, *Stranger* = T. J. Haarhoff, *The Stranger at the Gate: Aspects of Exclusiveness and Co-operation in Ancient Greece and Rome, with Some Reference to Modern Times* (Oxford: Blackwell, 1948)

Hadas, *3–4 Maccabees* = M. Hadas, *The Third and Fourth Books of Maccabees* (New York: Harper & Brothers, 1953)

Hahn, 'Circumcision' = H.-C. Hahn, 'Circumcision', *NIDNTT*, I (1976), 307–12

Hall, *Barbarian* = Edith Hall, *Inventing the Barbarian: Greek Self-Definition through Tragedy* (Oxford: Clarendon Press, 1989)

Hall, *Identity* = J. M. Hall, *Ethnic Identity in Greek Antiquity* (Cambridge: Cambridge University Press, 1997)

Hall, 'Other' = S. Hall, 'The Spectacle of the "Other"', in S. Hall (ed.), *Representation: Cultural Representation and Signifying Practices* (London: Sage, 1997), 225–79

Halperin, 'Ascension' = D. J. Halperin, 'Ascension or Invasion: Implications of the Heavenly Journey in Ancient Judaism', *Religion* 18 (1988), 47–67

Hamerton-Kelly, *Pre-existence* = R. G. Hamerton-Kelly, *Pre-existence, Wisdom and the Son of Man: A Study of the Idea of Pre-existence in the New Testament*, SNTSMS 21 (Cambridge: Cambridge University Press, 1973)

Handelman, 'Ethnicity' = D. Handelman, 'The Organization of Ethnicity', *EthG* 1 (1977), 187–200

Hanson, *Unity* = S. Hanson, *The Unity of the Church in the New Testament: Colossians and Ephesians* (Uppsala: Almquist & Wiksells, 1946)

Harnack, *Vorwurf* = A. Harnack, *Der Vorwurf des Atheismus in der ersten Jahrhunderten*, TU 18.4 (Leipzig: Hinrichs, 1905)

'Pseudo-Philo' = D. J. Harrington, 'Pseudo-Philo', in *OTP*, II, 297–377

Wisdom Texts = D. J. Harrington, *Wisdom Texts from Qumran* (London: Routledge, 1996)

Harris, *Testimonies* = J. R. Harris, *Testimonies*, 2 vols (Cambridge: Cambridge University Press, 1916, 1920)

Harris, 'Prepositions' = M. J. Harris, 'Prepositions and Theology in the Greek New Testament', *NIDNTT*, III (1976), 1171–215

Colossians and Philemon = M. J. Harris, *Colossians and Philemon*, EGGNT (Grand Rapids, Michigan: Eerdmans, 1991)

Hartmann, 'Household-Code Form' = L. Hartmann, 'Some Unorthodox Thoughts on the Household-Code Form', in J. Neusner et al. (eds.), *The Social World of Formative Christianity and Judaism* (Philadelphia: Fortress, 1988), 219–32

Hartog, *Mirror* = F. Hartog, *The Mirror of Herodotus: The Representation of the Other in the Writing of History* (Berkeley: University of California Press, 1988)

Odysseus = F. Hartog, *Memories of Odysseus: Frontier Tales from Ancient* Greece, ET J. Lloyd (Chicago: University of Chicago Press, 2001).

Harvey, *True Israel* = G. Harvey, *The True Israel: Uses of the Names Jew, Hebrew and Israel in Ancient Jewish and Early Christian Literature*, AGAJU 35 (Leiden/New York/Cologne: E. J. Brill, 1996)

Hatch, *Essays* = E. Hatch, *Essays in Biblical Greek* (Oxford: Oxford University Press, 1889)

Haupt, *Gefangenschaftsbriefe* = E. Haupt, *Die Gefangenschaftsbriefe*, KEK 8 (Göttingen: Vandenhoeck & Ruprecht, 1902[8])

Hay, *Ps. 110* = D. M. Hay, *Glory at the Right Hand: Psalm 110 in Early Christianity*, SBLMS 18 (Nashville: Abingdon, 1973)

Hays, *Moral Vision* = R. B. Hays, *Moral Vision of the New Testament: A Contemporary Introduction to New Testament Ethics* (Edinburgh: T & T Clark, 1996)

Hayward, *Temple* = C. T. R. Hayward, *The Jewish Temple: A Non-Biblical Sourcebook* (London: Routledge, 1996)

Healey and Healey, 'Participles' = Phyllis Healey and Alan Healey, 'Greek Circumstantial Participles: Tracking Participants with Participles in the Greek New Testament', *OPTAT* 4 (1990), 177–259

Heiligenthal, 'ἔργον' = R. Heiligenthal, 'ἔργον', *EDNT*, II (1981), 49–51

Hellholm, 'Amplificatio' = D. Hellholm, 'Amplificatio in the Macro-Structure of Romans', in S. E. Porter and T. H. Olbricht (eds.), *Rhetoric and the New Testament: Essays from the 1992 Heidelberg Conference*, JSNTSS 90 (Sheffield: JSOT Press, 1993), 123–51

Hengel, *Judaism* = M. Hengel, *Judaism and Hellenism: Studies in Their Encounter in Palestine During the Early Hellenistic Period*, 2 vols. (London: SCM, 1974)

'Enthronement' = M. Hengel, 'Sit at My Right Hand!: The Enthronement of Christ at the Right Hand of God and Psalm 110.1', in his *Studies in Earliest Christology* (Edinburgh: T & T Clark, 1995), 119–225

Judentum = M. Hengel, *Judentum und Hellenismus* (Tübingen: J. C. B. Mohr, 1998)

Himmelfarb, 'Heavenly Ascent' = M. Himmelfarb, 'Heavenly Ascent and the Relationship of Apocalypses and the *Hekhalot* Literature', *HUCA* 59 (1988), 73–100

Ascent = M. Himmelfarb, *Ascent to Heaven in Jewish and Christian Apocalypses* (New York/Oxford: Oxford University Press, 1993)

Hinkle, *Peace* = M. E. Hinkle, *Proclaiming Peace: The Use of Scripture in Ephesians* (unpublished Ph. D. Thesis, Duke University, Durham, NC, 1997)

Hobbs, 'Warfare' = R. Hobbs, 'The Language of Warfare in the New Testament', in P. F. Esler (ed.), *Modelling Early Christianity: Social Scientific Studies of the New Testament in its Context* (London: Routledge, 1995), 259–73.

Hofius, 'Erwählt' = O. Hofius, '»Erwählt vor Grundgerung der Welt« (Eph 1 4)', *ZNW* 62 (1971), 123–8

'Eine altjüdische Parallele' = O. Hofius, 'Eine altjüdische Parallele zu Röm. IV. 17b', *NTS* 18 (1971–2), 93–4

'πατήρ' = O. Hofius, 'πατήρ', *NIDNTT*, II (1976), 615–21

Holmes, *Sociolinguistics* = Janet Holmes, *An Introduction to Sociolinguistics* (London/New York: Longman, 1992)

Horgan, *Pesharim* = M. P. Horgan, *Pesharim: Qumran Interpretations of Biblical Books*, CBQMS 8 (Washington, D.C.: The Catholic Biblical Association, 1979)

Horsley, 'δόγμα' = G. H. R. Horsley, 'δόγμα', *NDIEC*, IV (1987), 146

Houlden, 'Christ' = J. L. Houlden, 'Christ and the Church in Ephesians', *SE* 6 [= TU 112] (1969), 267–73

Letters = J. L. Houlden, *Paul's Letters from Prison: Philippians, Colossians, Philemon and Ephesians* (London: Penguin, 1970)

Hübner, *Biblische Theologie* = H. Hübner, *Biblische Theologie des Neuen Testaments*, II: *Die Theologie des Paulus und ihre neutestamentliche Wirkungsgeschichte* (Göttingen: Vandenhoeck & Ruprecht, 1993), 363–75

Vetus Testamentum = H. Hübner, *Vetus Testamentum in Novo*, II: *Corpus Paulinum* (Göttingen: Vandenhoeck & Ruprecht, 1997)

Hui, *Holy Spirit* = A. W. D. Hui, *The Concept of the Holy Spirit in Ephesians and Its Relation to the Pneumatologies of Luke and Paul* (unpublished Ph. D. thesis, University of Aberdeen, 1992)

Hurtado, *One God* = L. W. Hurtado, *One God, One Lord: Early Christian Devotion and Ancient Jewish Monotheism* (London: SCM, 1988)
Jacques, *List* = X. Jacques, *List of Septuagint Words Sharing Common Elements. Supplement to Concordance or Dictionary*, SB 1 (Rome: Biblical Institute Press, 1972)
Jaeger, *Paideia* = W. Jaeger, *Paideia: The Ideals of Greek Culture*, 3 vols. (Oxford: Oxford University Press, 1948)
Jeal, *Theology and Ethics* = R. R. Jeal, *The Relationship between Theology and Ethics in the Letter to the Ephesians* (unpublished Ph. D. thesis, University of Sheffield, 1990)
Jenkins, *Identity* = R. Jenkins, *Social Identity* (London: Routledge, 1996)
Ethnicity = R. Jenkins, *Rethinking Ethnicity: Arguments and Explorations* (London: Sage, 1997)
Jeremias, 'Eckstein' = J. Jeremias, 'Der Eckstein', *Angelos* 1 (1925), 65–70
'Eckstein-Schlussstein' = J. Jeremias, 'Eckstein-Schlussstein', *ZNW* 36 (1937), 154–7
'ἀκρογωνιαῖος' = J. Jeremias, 'ἀκρογωνιαῖος', *TDNT*, I (1964), 792–3
Johnson, *Writings* = L. T. Johnson, *The Writings of the New Testament: An Interpretation* (London: SCM, 1986)
'Slander' = L. T. Johnson, 'The New Testament Anti-Jewish Slander and the Conventions of Ancient Polemic', *JBL* 108 (1989), 419–41
Jones, *Plutarch* = C. P. Jones, *Plutarch and Rome* (Oxford: Clarendon Press, 1971)
Dio = C. P. Jones, *The Roman World of Dio Chrysostom* (Cambridge, Massachusetts: Harvard University Press, 1978)
Judge, *Pattern* = E. A. Judge, *The Social Pattern of the Christian Groups in the First Century: Some Prolegomena to the Study of New Testament Ideas of Social Obligation* (London: Tyndale Press, 1960)
Juel, *Messianic Exegesis* = D. Juel, *Messianic Exegesis: Christological Interpretation of Old Testament in Early Christianity* (Philadelphia: Fortress, 1988)
Jülicher, *Einleitung* = A. Jülicher, *Einleitung in das neue Testament* (Freiburg: Herder, 1894, 1906)
Käsemann, *Leib* = E. Käsemann, *Leib und Leib Christi*, BHTh 9 (Tübingen: J. C. B. Mohr, 1933)
Versuche = E. Käsemann, 'Epheser 2, 17–22', in his *Exegetische Versuche und Besinnungen*, I (Göttingen: Vandenhoeck & Ruprecht, 1964), 280–3
'Epheserbrief' = E. Käsemann, 'Epheserbrief', in *RGG*^{3}, II, 517–20
Essays = E. Käsemann, *Essays on New Testament Themes* (London: SCM Press, 1964)
'Ephesians' = E. Käsemann, 'Ephesians and Acts', in L. E. Keck and J. L. Martyn (eds.), *Studies in Luke-Acts*, FS P. Schubert (Nashville: Abingdon Press, 1966), 288–97
Questions = E. Käsemann, *New Testament Questions of Today* (London: SCM, 1969)
Perspectives = E. Käsemann, *Perspectives on Paul* (London: SCM Press, 1971)
Kasher, *Struggle* = A. Kasher, *The Jews in Hellenistic and Roman Egypt: The Struggle for Equal Rights* (Tübingen: J. C. B. Mohr, 1985)

'Angelology' = A. Kasher, 'Angelology and the Supernatural Worlds in the Aramaic Targums to the Prophets', *JSJ* 27 (1996), 168–91

Kaufmann, 'Circumcision' = K. Kaufmann, 'Circumcision', *JE*, IV, 93

Kee, 'Membership' = H. C. Kee, 'Membership in the Covenant People at Qumran and in the Teaching of Jesus', in J. H. Charlesworth (ed.), *Jesus and the Dead Sea Scrolls: The Controversy Resolved* (New York: Doubleday, 1992), 104–22

Kellermann, 'συναρμολογουμένη' = U. Kellermann, 'συναρμολογουμένη', *EDNT*, III (1993), 298–9

Kirby, *Pentecost* = J. C. Kirby, *Ephesians, Baptism and Pentecost: An Inquiry into the Structure and Purpose of the Epistle to the Ephesians* (London: SPCK, 1968)

Kirk, *Heraclitus* = G. S. Kirk, *Heraclitus: The Cosmic Fragments* (Cambridge: Cambridge University Press, 1954)

Iliad = G. S. Kirk, *The Iliad: A Commentary*, vol. I, Books 1–4 (Cambridge: Cambridge University Press, 1985)

Kitchen, *Anakephalaiosis* = M. Kitchen, *The Anakephalaiosis of all Things in Christ: Theology and Purpose in the Epistle to the Ephesians* (unpublished Ph.D. thesis, University of Manchester, 1988)

'Status' = M. Kitchen, 'The Status of Law in the Letter to the Ephesians', in B. Lindars (ed.), *Law and Religion: Essays on the Place of the Law in Israel and Early Christianity* (Cambridge: J. Clarke & Co., 1988), 141–7, 187

Ephesians = M. Kitchen, *Ephesians* (London: Routledge, 1994)

Kittel, 'δόγμα' = G. Kittel, 'δόγμα κτλ.', *TDNT*, II (1964), 230–2

Klauck, *Hausgemeinde* = H.-J. Klauck, *Hausgemeinde und Hauskirche in Frühen Christentum*, SBS 103 (Stuttgart: Verlag Katholisches Bibelwork, 1981)

Knibb, *Qumran Community* = M. Knibb, *The Qumran Community*, CCWJCW 2 (Cambridge: Cambridge University Press, 1987)

Knight, *Pastoral Epistles* = G. W. Knight III, *Commentary on the Pastoral Epistles*, NIGTC (Grand Rapids, Michigan: Eerdmans/Carlisle, UK: Paternoster, 1992)

Knox, *St Paul* = W. L. Knox, *St Paul and the Church of the Gentiles* (Cambridge: Cambridge University Press, 1939; repr. 1961)

Kobelski, 'Ephesians' = P. J. Kobelski, 'Ephesians', in *NJBC*, 883–90

Koch, *Schrift* = D.-A. Koch, *Die Schrift als Zeuge des Evangeliums: Untersuchungen zur Verwendung und zum Verstännis der Schrift bei Paulus*, BHTh 69 (Tübingen: J. C. B. Mohr, 1986)

Kok, *Truth* = Ezra H.-S. Kok, '*The Truth of the Gospel*': *A Study of Gal. 2.15–21* (unpublished Ph.D. thesis, University of Durham, 1993)

Konstan, *Friendship* = D. Konstan, *Friendship in the Classical World* (Cambridge: Cambridge University Press, 1997)

Köster, 'φύσις' = H. Köster, 'φύσις', *TDNT*, IX (1974), 272

Introduction = H. Köster, *Introduction to the New Testament: History and Literature of Early Christianity*, II (Philadelphia: Fortress, 1982)

Krämer, 'γωνία' = H. Krämer, 'γωνία', *EDNT*, I (1990), 267–9

Kruse, *Paul* = C. G. Kruse, *Paul, the Law and Justification* (Leicester: Apollos, 1996)

Kuhli, 'Ἰσραήλ' = H. Kuhli, 'Ἰσραήλ', *EDNT*, II (1991), 202–4

'οἰκονόμος' = H. Kuhli, 'οἰκονόμος', *EDNT*, II (1991), 498–500

Kuhn, 'Ἰσραήλ' = K. G. Kuhn, 'Ἰσραήλ. κτλ', *TDNT*, III (1965), 359–73
'Ephesians' = K. G. Kuhn, 'The Epistle to the Ephesians in the Light of the Qumran Texts', in J. Murphy-O'Connor (ed.), *Paul and Qumran: Studies in New Testament Exegesis* (London: Geoffrey Chapman, 1968), 115–31
Kümmel, *History* = W. G. Kümmel, *The New Testament: the History of the Investigation of its Problems*, ET S. M. Gilmour (London: SCM, 1973)
Introduction = W. G. Kümmel, *An Introduction to the New Testament* (Nashville: Abingdon, 1975)
Kunin, 'Judaism' = S. Kunin, 'Judaism', in J. Holm and J. Bowker (eds.), *Sacred Space* (London/New York: Pinter, 1994), 115–48
Lacey, 'Patria Potestas' = W. K. Lacey, 'Patria Potestas', in B. Rawson (ed.), *The Family in Ancient Rome: New Perspective* (London: Routledge, 1992), 122–44
Larsen, *Federal States* = J. A. O. Larsen, *Greek Federal States: Their Institutions and History* (Oxford: Clarendon Press, 1968)
Larsen and Rhodes, 'Federal States' = J. A. O. Larsen and P. J. Rhodes, 'Federal States', *OCD*, 591–2
Laubach, 'αἷμα' = F. Laubach, 'αἷμα', *NIDNTT*, I (1976), 220–4
Lausberg, *Handbuch* = H. Lausberg, *Handbuch der literarischen Rhetorik*, 2 vols. (Munich: Heuber, 1960[1])
Elemente = H. Lausberg, *Elemente der Literarischen Rhetorik* (Munich: Heuber, 1967)
Lee, 'Powers' = J. Y. Lee, 'Interpreting the Demonic Powers in Pauline Thought', *NovT* (1970), 54–69
Levine, *Caesarea* = L. I. A. Levine, *Caesarea Under Roman Rule* (Leiden: E. J. Brill, 1975)
'Judaism' = L. I. A. Levine, 'Judaism from the Destruction of Jerusalem to the End of the Second Jewish Revolt: 70–135 CE', in H. Shanks (ed.), *Christianity and Rabbinic Judaism* (London: SPCK, 1993), 125–49
'Temple' = L. I. A. Levine, 'Josephus' Description of the Jerusalem Temple: *War*, *Antiquities*, and other Sources', in F. Parente and J. Sievers (eds.), *Josephus and the History of the Greco-Roman Period*, SPB 41 (Leiden: E. J. Brill, 1994), 233–46
Levinson, *Pragmatics* = S. C. Levinson, *Pragmatics* (Cambridge: Cambridge University Press, 1983)
Licht, 'Two Spirits' = J. Licht, 'An Analysis of the Treatise of the Two Spirits in DSD', in C. Rabin and Y. Yadin (eds.), *Scripta Hierosolymitana*, IV: *Aspects of the Dead Sea Scrolls* (Jerusalem: Magnes Press, 1965[2]), 88–100
Limbeck, 'ἐντολή' = M. Limbeck, 'ἐντολή', *NIDNTT*, I (1990), 459–60
Lincoln, 'Heavenlies' = A. T. Lincoln, 'A Re-examination of "the Heavenlies" in Ephesians', *NTS* 19 (1972–3), 468–83
'Use' = A. T. Lincoln, 'The Use of the OT in Ephesians', *JSNT* 14 (1982), 16–57
'Church' = A. T. Lincoln, 'The Church and Israel in Ephesians 2', *CBQ* 49 (1987), 605–24
Ephesians = A. T. Lincoln, *Ephesians*, WBC 42 (Dallas, Texas: Word, 1990)
Paradise = A. T. Lincoln, *Paradise Now and Not Yet: Studies in the Role of the Heavenly Dimension in Paul's Thought with Special Reference to His Eschatology* (Grand Rapids, Michigan: Baker, 1991)

'Theology' = A. T. Lincoln, 'The Theology of Ephesians', in A. T. Lincoln and A. J. M. Wedderburn, *The Theology of the Later Pauline Letters* (Cambridge: Cambridge University Press, 1993), 73–166

'Liberation' = A. T. Lincoln, 'Liberation from the Powers: Supernatural Spirits or Societal Structures?', in M. D. Carroll et al. (eds.), *The Bible in Human Society*, FS J. Rogerson (Sheffield: Sheffield Academic Press, 1995), 335–54

'Stand' = A. T. Lincoln, '"Stand, Therefore . . . ": Ephesians 6:10–20 as *Peroratio*', *BI* 3 (1995), 99–114

Lindemann, *Aufhebung* = A. Lindemann, *Die Aufhebung der Zeit: Geschichtsverständnis und Eschatologie im Epheserbrief*, SNT 12 (Gütersloh: G. Mohn, 1975)

'Bermerkungen' = A. Lindemann, 'Bemerkungen zu den Adressaten und zum Anlaβ des Epheserbriefes,' *ZNW* 67 (1976), 235–51

Epheserbrief = A. Lindemann, *Der Epheserbrief*, ZBNT 8 (Zurich: Theologischer Verlag, 1985)

Linderski and Rhodes, 'Isopoliteia' = J. A. O. Linderski and P. J. Rhodes, 'Isopoliteia', *OCD*, 771

Lohse, 'χειροποίητος' = E. Lohse, 'χειροποίητος κτλ.', *TDNT*, IX (1974), 436–7

'Rules' = E. Lohse, 'The Rules for the Household', in his *Colossians and Philemon* (Philadelphia: Fortress, 1975), 154–7

Ethics = E. Lohse, *Theological Ethics in the New Testament* (Minneapolis: Fortress, 1988)

Lona, *Eschatologie* = H. E. Lona, *Die Eschatologie im Kolosser- und Epheserbrief*, FB 48 (Würzburg: Echter Verlag, 1984)

Louw and Nida = J. P. Louw and E. A. Nida, *Greek-English Lexicon of the New Testament Based on Semantic Domains*, 2 vols. (New York: United Bible Societies, 1989)

Lüderitz, 'Politeuma' = G. Lüderitz, 'What is the Politeuma?', in J. W. Henten and P. van der Horst (eds.), *Studies in Early Jewish Epigraphy* (Leiden: E. J. Brill, 1994), 183–225

Lührmann, 'Ökonomie' = D. Lührmann, 'Neutestamentliche Haustafeln and antike Ökonomie', *NTS* 27 (1980–1), 83–97

MacDonald, *Pauline Churches* = Margaret Y. MacDonald, *The Pauline Churches: A Socio-historical Study of Institutionalization in the Pauline and Deutero-Pauline Writings*, SNTSMS 60 (Cambridge: Cambridge University Press, 1988)

MacGregor, 'Wrath' = G. H. C. MacGregor, 'The Concept of the Wrath of God in the New Testament', *NTS* 7 (1960–1), 101–9

Mach, *Engelsglauben* = M. Mach, *Entwicklungstadien des jüdischen Engelsglauben in vorrabbinischer Zeit*, TSAJ 34 (Tübingen: J. C. B. Mohr, 1992)

MacMullen and Lane, *Paganism* = R. MacMullen and E. N. Lane (eds.), *Paganism and Christianity 100–425 C.E.: A Sourcebook* (Minneapolis: Fortress, 1992)

Madvig, 'μεσότοιχον' = D. H. Madvig, 'τὸ μεσότοιχον', *NIDNTT*, III (1976), 795

Malherbe, *Exhortation* = A. J. Malherbe, *Moral Exhortation: A Greco-Roman Sourcebook* (Philadelphia: Westminster, 1986)

Manville, *Citizenship* = P. B. Manville, *The Origins of Citizenship in Ancient Athens* (Princeton: Princeton University Press, 1990)

Marcus, 'Circumcision' = J. Marcus, 'The Circumcision and the Uncircumcision in Rome', *NTS* 35 (1989), 67–81

Marcuse, 'Walls' = P. Marcuse, 'Walls in the City: Is the Goal a Wall-less City?', in D. Crow (ed.), *Geography and Identity* (Washington, D.C.: Maisonneuve Press, 1990), 211–25

Markus, *Christianity* = R. A. Markus, *Christianity in the Roman World* (London: Thames and Hudson, 1974)

'Self-Definition' = R. A. Markus, 'The Problem of Self-Definition: From Sect to Church', in E. P. Sanders (ed.), *Jewish and Christian Self-Definition: The Shaping of Christianity in the Second and Third Centuries*, I (London: SCM, 1980), 1–15, 217–19

Marshall, 'Salvation' = I. H. Marshall, 'Salvation, Grace and Works in the Later Writings in the Pauline Corpus,' *NTS* 42 (1996), 339–58

Martin, *Reconciliation* = R. P. Martin, *Reconciliation: A Study of Paul's Theology* (London: Marshall, Morgan & Scott, 1981)

May, 'Cosmological Reference' = H. G. May, 'Cosmological Reference in the Qumran Doctrine of the Two Spirits and in the Old Testament Imagery', *JBL* 82 (1963), 1–14

McCarter, 'Patriarchal Age' = P. K. McCarter, Jr, 'The Patriarchal Age: Abraham, Isaac and Jacob', in H. Shanks (ed.), *Ancient Israel: A Short History from Abraham to the Roman Destruction of the Temple* (London: SPCK, 1989), 1–29

McEleney, 'Conversion' = N. J. McEleney, 'Conversion, Circumcision and the Law', *NTS* 20 (1974), 328–33

McKay, *Syntax* = K. L. McKay, *A New Syntax of the Verb in New Testament Greek: An Aspectual Approach*, SBG 5 (New York: Peter Lang, 1994)

McKechnie, *Outsiders* = P. McKechnie, *Outsiders in the Greek Cities in the Fourth Century BC* (London: Routledge, 1989)

McKelvey, 'Cornerstone' = R. J. McKelvey, 'Christ the Cornerstone', *NTS* 8 (1962), 352–9

Temple = R. J. McKelvey, *The New Temple: The Church in the New Testament* (Oxford: Oxford University Press, 1969)

McKnight, *Light* = S. McKnight, *A Light Among the Gentiles: Jewish Missionary Activity in the Second Temple Period* (Minneapolis: Fortress, 1991)

McLean, 'Atoning Sacrifice' = B. H. McLean, 'The Absence of an Atoning Sacrifice in Paul's Soteriology', *NTS* 38 (1992), 531–53

McVay, *Ecclesial Metaphor* = J. K. McVay, *Ecclesial Metaphor in the Epistle to the Ephesians from the Perspective of a Modern Theory of Metaphor* (unpublished Ph. D. thesis, University of Sheffield, 1995)

Meeks, 'Unity' = W. A. Meeks, 'In One Body: The Unity of Humankind in Colossians and Ephesians', in J. Jervell and W. A. Meeks (eds.), *God's Christ and His People*, FS N. A. Dahl (Oslo: Universitetsforlaget, 1977), 209–21

Urban Christians = W. A. Meeks, *The First Urban Christians: The Social World of the Apostle Paul* (New Haven: Yale University Press, 1983)

Christian Morality = W. A. Meeks, *The Origins of Christian Morality: The First Two Centuries* (New Haven/London: Yale University Press, 1993)

Merkel, 'Diskussion' = H. Merkel, 'Der Epheserbrief in der neueren exegetischen Diskussion', in *ANRW* II.25.4 (1982–8), 3157–246

'καταλλάσσω' = H. Merkel, 'καταλλάσσω κτλ.', *EDNT*, II (1991), 261–3

Merklein, *Christus* = H. Merklein, *Christus und die Kirche: Die theologische Grundstrucktur des Epheserbriefes nach Eph. 2: 11–18*, SBS 66 (Stuttgart: Verlag Katholisches Bibelwerk, 1973)

Amt = H. Merklein, *Das Kirchliche Amt nach dem Epheserbrief*, SANT 33 (Munich: Kösel-Verlag, 1973)

'Komposition' = H. Merklein, 'Zur Tradition und Komposition von Eph 2: 14–18', *BZ* 17 (1973), 79–102

'Rezeption' = H. Merklein, 'Paulinische Theologie in der Rezeption des Kolosser- und Epheserbriefes', in K. Kertelge (ed.), *Paulus in den Neutestamentlichen Spätschriften zur Paulusrezeption im Neuen Testament*, QD 89 (Freiburg/Basel/Vienna: Herder, 1981), 26–69

'ἀήρ' = H. Merklein, 'ἀήρ', *EDNT*, I (1990), 34

Metzger, *Textual Commentary* = B. M. Metzger, *A Textual Commentary on the Greek New Testament* (Stuttgart: United Bible Societies, 1975)

Meuzelaar, *Leib* = J. J. Meuzelaar, *Der Leib des Messias* (Assen, Amsterdam: van Gorcum, 1961)

Meyer, *Ephesians* = H. A. W. Meyer, *Critical and Exegetical Handbook to the Epistle to the Ephesians* (New York: Funk & Wagnalls, 1884)

Meyer, 'Dtn. 32: 8f., 43 (4Q)' = R. Meyer, 'Die Bedeutung von Deuteronomium 32 8f, 43 (4Q) für die Auslegung des Moses Liedes', in A. Kuschke (ed.), *Verbannung und Heimkehr* (Tübingen: J. C. B. Mohr, 1961), 197–209

'λαός' = R. Meyer, 'λαός', *TDNT*, IV (1967), 39–50

'πάροικος' = R. Meyer, 'πάροικος', *TDNT*, V (1967), 850–1

Michaelis, 'παράπτωμα' = W. Michaelis, 'παράπτωμα', *TDNT*, VI (1968), 170–2

Michel, *Römer* = O. Michel, *Der Brief an die Römer*, KEK 5 (Göttingen: Vandenhoeck & Ruprecht, 1963^{12})

'οἶκος' = O. Michel, 'οἶκος κτλ.', *TDNT*, V (1967), 119–59

'οἰκοδομή' = O. Michel, 'οἰκοδομή', *TDNT*, V (1967), 144–7

'πατήρ' = O. Michel, 'πατήρ', *EDNT*, II (1993), 53–7

Middleton, *Greek Article* = T. F. Middleton, *The Doctrine of the Greek Article* (London: Luke Hansard & Son, 1808)

Missiou, *Andokides* = Anna Missiou, *The Subversive Oratory of Andokides: Politics, Ideology and Decision-Making in Democratic Athens* (Cambridge: Cambridge University Press, 1992)

Mitchell, *Reconciliation* = M. M. Mitchell, *Paul and the Rhetoric of Reconciliation: An Exegetical Investigation of the Language and Composition of 1 Corinthians* (Louisville, Kentucky: Westminster/John Knox Press, 1991)

Mitton, *Ephesians* = C. L. Mitton, *The Epistle to the Ephesians: Its Authorship, Origin, and Purpose* (Oxford: Clarendon Press, 1951)

Moo, 'Law' = D. J. Moo, 'The Law of Christ as the Fulfilment of the Law of Moses: A Modified Lutheran View', in G. L. Bahsen et al., *Law, the Gospel, and the Modern Christian* (Grand Rapids, Michigan: Zondervan, 1993), 319–76

Romans = D. J. Moo, *The Epistle to the Romans*, NICNT (Grand Rapids, Michigan: Eerdmans, 1997)

Moore, 'Ephesians' = M. S. Moore, 'Ephesians 2.14–16: A History of Recent Interpretation', *EvQ* 54 (1982), 163–8

Morgan, *Nicknames* = Jane Morgan et al., *Nicknames: Their Origins and Social Consequences* (London: Routledge & Kegan Paul, 1979)

Moritz, *Mystery* = T. Moritz, *A Profound Mystery: The Use of the Old Testament in Ephesians*, SNovT 85 (Leiden/New York/Cologne: E. J. Brill, 1996)

Morris, 'Sacrifice' = L. Morris, 'Sacrifice', in *DPL*, 856–8

Moule, *Idiom* = C. F. D. Moule, *An Idiom Book of New Testament Greek* (Cambridge: Cambridge University Press, 1959²)

Birth = C. F. D. Moule, *The Birth of the New Testament* (London: Blackwell, 1981³)

Mouton, 'Communicative Power' = E. Mouton, 'The Communicative Power of the Epistle to the Ephesians', in S. E. Porter and T. H. Olbricht (eds.), *Rhetoric, Scripture and Theology: Essays from the 1994 Pretoria Conference*, JSNTS 131 (Sheffield: Sheffield Academic Press, 1996), 280–307

Moxnes, 'Family' = H. Moxnes, 'What is Family?: Problems in Constructing Early Christian Families', in H. Moxnes (ed.), *Constructing Early Christian Families: Families as Social Reality and Metaphor* (London: Routledge, 1997), 13–41

Murray, 'Polis' = O. Murray, 'Polis', *OCD*, 1205–6

Mußner, *Christus* = F. Mußner, *Christus, das All und die Kirche*, TThS 5 (Trier: Paulinus Verlag, 1955)

'Geschichtstheologie' = F. Mußner, 'Die Geschichtstheologie des Epheserbriefes', *BibLeb* (1964), 8–12 [= AnBib 17–18 (1963), 59–63]

'Contributions' = F. Mußner, 'Contributions Made by Qumran to the Understanding of the Epistle to the Ephesians', in J. Murphy-O'Connor (ed.), *Paul and Qumran: Studies in New Testament Exegesis* (London: G. Chapman, 1968), 159–178

'Modell' = F. Mußner, 'Eph 2 als Ökumenisches Modell', in J. Gnilka (ed.), *Neues Testament und Kirche*, FS R. Schnackenburg (Freiburg/Basel/Vienna: Verlag Herder, 1974), 325–36

'Epheserbrief' = F. Mußner, 'Epheserbrief', in *TRE*, IX, 743–53

Epheser = F. Mußner, *Der Brief an die Epheser*, ÖTKNT 10 (Gütersloh: Verlagshaus G. Mohn/Würzburg: Echter-Verlag, 1982)

Tractate = F. Mußner, *Tractate on the Jews: The Significance of Judaism for Christian Faith*, ET L. Swidler (Philadelphia/London: Fortress/SPCK, 1984)

Nel, *Structure* = P. J. Nel, *The Structure and Ethos of the Wisdom Admonitions in Proverbs*, BZAW 158 (Berlin/York: de Gruyter, 1982)

Neufeld, *Armour* = T. R. Y. Neufeld, *Put on the Armour of God: The Divine Warrior from Isaiah to Ephesians*, JSNTSS 140 (Sheffield: Sheffield Academic Press, 1995)

Neufeld, *Confessions* = V. H. Neufeld, *The Earliest Christian Confessions*, NTTS 5 (Grand Rapids: Eerdmans, 1963)

Neusner, *Metaphors* = J. Neusner, *Judaism and Its Social Metaphors* (Cambridge: Cambridge University Press, 1989)

Newman, *Glory-Christology* = C. C. Newman, *Paul's Glory-Christology: Tradition and Rhetoric*, SNovT 69 (Leiden: E. J. Brill, 1992)

Nicholson, *Covenant* = E. W. Nicholson, *God and His People: Covenant and Theology in the Old Testament* (Oxford: Clarendon Press, 1986)

Nickelsburg, *Jewish Literature* = G. W. E. Nickelsburg, *Jewish Literature between the Bible and the Mishnah* (Philadelphia: Fortress, 1981)

'Stories' = G. W. E. Nickelsburg, 'Stories of Biblical and Early Post-Biblical Times', in M. E. Stone (ed.), *Jewish Writings of the Second Temple Period*, CRINT II.2 (Assen: Van Gorcum/Philadelphia: Fortress, 1984), 33–87

Nickelsburg and Stone, *Faith* = G. W. E. Nickelsburg and M. E. Stone, *Faith and Piety in Early Judaism: Texts and Documents* (Philadelphia: Fortress, 1983)

Nida and Taber, *Theory* = E. Nida and C. R. Taber, *The Theory and Practice of Translation* (Leiden: E. J. Brill, 1969)

Nitzan, '4QBerakhot^{a-e}' = B. Nitzan, '4QBerakhot^{a-e} (4Q286–290): A Covenantal Ceremony in the Light of Related Texts', *RevQ* 64 (1995), 487–506

Nock, 'Mandulis Aion' = A. D. Nock, 'A Vision of Mandulis Aion', *HTR* 27 (1934), 53–104

Nolland, 'Uncircumcised Proselytes' = J. Nolland, 'Uncircumcised Proselytes?', *JSJ* 12 (1979–81), 173–94

O'Brien, *Thanksgivings* = P. T. O'Brien, *Introductory Thanksgivings in the Letters of Paul*, SNT 49 (Leiden: E. J. Brill, 1977)

'Unusual Introduction' = P. T. O'Brien, 'Ephesians I: An Unusual Introduction to a New Testament Letter', *NTS* 25 (1979), 504–16

'Principalities' = P. T. O'Brien, 'Principalities and Powers: Opponents of the Church', in D. A. Carson (ed.), *Biblical Interpretation and the Church* (Exeter: Paternoster, 1984), 110–50

'Mystery' = P. T. O'Brien, 'Mystery', in *DPL*, 621–3

O'Connell, 'Greek Versions' = K. G. O'Connell, 'Greek Versions', *IDBSup* (1976), 377–81

O'Neil, 'Leagues' = J. L. O'Neil, 'The Political Elites of the Achaian and Aetolian Leagues', *AS* 15–17 (1984–6), 33–61

Osiek, *Social Setting* = C. Osiek, *What Do They Say about the Social Setting of the New Testament?* (New York: Paulist Press, 1992)

Paassen, *Geography* = C. van Paassen, *The Classical Tradition of Geography* (Groningen/Djakarta: J. B. Wolters, 1957)

Page, *Satan and Demons* = S. H. T. Page, *Powers of Evil: A Biblical Study of Satan and Demons* (Grand Rapids, Michigan: Baker, 1995)

Parker, 'Aion' = R. C. T. Parker, 'Aion', *OCD*, 48

'Atheism' = R. C. T. Parker, 'Atheism', *OCD*, 201

Patzia, *Ephesians* = A. G. Patzia, *Ephesians, Colossians, Philemon*, NIBC 10 (Peabody, Massachusetts: Hendrickson/Carlisle, UK: Paternoster, 1995)

Paulsen, 'φραγμός' = H. Paulsen, 'φραγμός κτλ.', *EDNT*, III (1993), 437–9

Percy, *Probleme* = E. Percy, *Die Probleme der Kolosser- und Epheserbrief* (Lund: C. W. K. Gleerup, 1946)

'Probleme' = E. Percy, 'Zu den Probleme der Kolosser- und Epheserbriefes', *ZNW* 43 (1950–1), 178–94

Perkins, *Reading* = P. Perkins, *Reading the New Testament: An Introduction* (New York: Paulist, 1978)

Gnosticism = P. Perkins, *Gnosticism and the New Testament* (Minneapolis: Fortress, 1993)

Perschbacher, *Syntax* = W. J. Perschbacher, *New Testament Greek Syntax* (Chicago: Moody Press, 1995)

Pettazoni, *Aion-(Kronos) Chronos* = R. Pettazoni, *Aion-(Kronos) Chronos in Egypt: Essays on the History of Religions* (Leiden: E. J. Brill, 1954)

Pfammatter, *Bau* = J. Pfammatter, *Die Kirche als Bau* (Rome: Pontificiae Universitatis Gregorianae, 1960)

Epheserbrief = J. Pfammatter, *Epheserbrief, Kolosserbrief*, NEBNT 10/12 (Würzburg: Echter Verlag, 1987)

Pfeiffer, 'Polemics' = R. H. Pfeiffer, 'The Polemics Against Idolatry in the Old Testament', *JBL* 43 (1924), 229–40

Pokorný, 'Mysterien' = P. Pokorný, 'Epheserbrief und gnostischen Mysterien', *ZNW* (1962), 160–94

Gnosis = P. Pokorný, *Der Epheser und die Gnosis* (Berlin: Evangelische Verlagsanstalt, 1965)

Epheser = P. Pokorný, *Der Brief des Paulus an die Epheser*, THNT 10/II (Leipzig: Evangelische Verlagsanstalt, 1992)

Polanyi, *Personal Knowledge* = M. Polanyi, *Personal Knowledge: Toward a Post-Critical Philosophy* (London: Routledge & Kegan Paul, 1969[3])

Porter, *Verbal Aspect* = S. E. Porter, *Verbal Aspect in the Greek of the New Testament, with reference to Tense and Mood*, SBG 1 (New York/Berne/Frankfurt/Paris: Peter Lang, 1989)

Idioms = S. E. Porter, *Idioms of the Greek New Testament*, BL 2 (Sheffield: JSOT Press, 1992)

'Myths' = S. E. Porter, 'Two Myths: Corporate Personality and Language/ Mentality Determinism', *SJT* 43 (1990), 289–307

Καταλλάσσω = S. E. Porter, *Καταλλάσσω in Ancient Greek Literature, with Reference to the Pauline Writings*, EFN 5 (Cordoba: Ediciones el Almendro, 1994)

'Use' = S. E. Porter, 'The Use of the Old Testament in the New Testament: A Brief Comment on Method and Terminology', in C. A. Evans and J. A. Sanders (eds.), *Early Interpretation of the Scriptures of Israel*, JSNTSS 148 (Sheffield: Sheffield Academic Press, 1997), 79–96

Porter and Clarke, 'Perspective' = S. E. Porter and K. D. Clarke, 'Canonical-Critical Perspective and the Relationship of Colossians and Ephesians', *Biblica* 78 (1997), 57–86

Preisker, 'μακράν' = H. Preisker, 'μακράν κτλ.', *TDNT*, IV (1967), 372–4

Preuss, *Theology* = H. D. Preuss, *Old Testament Theology*, I (Louisville, Kentucky: Westminster/John Knox, 1995)

Pryke, 'Spirit and Flesh' = J. Pryke, '"Spirit" and "Flesh" in the Qumran Documents and Some New Testament Texts', *RevQ* 19 (1965), 345–60

Quell, 'πατήρ' = G. Quell, 'πατήρ', *TDNT*, V (1967), 959–74

Rader, *Hostility* = W. Rader, *The Church and Racial Hostility: A History of Interpretation of Eph. 2:11–22*, BGBE 20 (Tübingen: J. C. B. Mohr, 1978)

Radl, 'μεσότοιχον' = W. Radl, 'μεσότοιχον κτλ.', *EDNT*, II (1991), 412–14

'ποιέω' = W. Radl, 'ποιέω', *EDNT*, III (1991), 124

Räisänen, *Law* = H. Räisänen, *Paul and the Law*, WUNT 29 (Tübingen, J. C. B. Mohr, 1983)

Rajak, 'Charter' = T. Rajak, 'Was There a Roman Charter for the Jews?', *JRS* 74 (1984), 107–23

'Community' = T. Rajak, 'The Jewish Community and its Boundaries', in J. Lieu et al. (eds.), *The Jews among Pagans and Christians in the Roman Empire* (London: Routledge, 1992), 9–28

Ramaroson, 'Éphésiens 1, 15–2, 10' = L. Ramaroson, 'Une lecture de Éphésiens 1, 15–2, 10', *Biblica* 58 (1977), 388–410

Rawlinson, *Herodotus* = G. Rawlinson, *Herodotus: The Histories* (London: Everyman, 1997)

Rawson, *Family* = B. Rawson (ed.), *The Family in Ancient Rome: New Perspectives* (London: Routledge, 1992)

'Adult-Child' = B. Rawson, 'Adult-Child Relationships in Roman Society', in B. Rawson (ed.), *Marriage, Divorce, and Children in Ancient Rome* (Oxford: Clarendon Press, 1996), 7–30

Reitzenstein, *Erlösungsmysterium* = R. Reitzenstein, *Das iranische Erlösungsmysterium*, Religionsgeschichtliche Untersuchungen (Bonn, 1921)

Concordance = K. H. Rengstorf, *A Complete Concordance to Flavius Josephus* (Leiden: E. J. Brill, 1973)

Rese, 'Vorzüge' = M. Rese, 'Die Vorzüge Israels in Rom 9,4f. und Eph 2,12: Exegetische Anmerkungen zum Thema Kirche und Israel', *TZ* 31 (1975), 211–22

'Church' = M. Rese, 'Church and Israel in the Deuteropauline Letters', *SJT* 43 (1990), 19–32

Rhodes, *City States* = P. J. Rhodes, *The Greek City States: A Sourcebook* (Norman, Oklahoma: University of Oklahoma Press, 1986)

'Poleis' = P. J. Rhodes, 'The Greek *Poleis*: Demes, Cities and Leagues', in M. H. Hansen (ed.), *The Ancient Greek City-States* (Copenhagen: Munksgaard, 1993), 161–82

Richardson, *Iliad* = N. Richardson, *The Iliad: A Commentary*, vol. VI, Books 21–4, ed. G. S. Kirk (Cambridge: Cambridge University Press, 1993)

Richardson, *Israel* = P. Richardson, *Israel in the Apostolic Church*, SNTSMS 10 (Cambridge: Cambridge University Press, 1969)

Ridderbos, *Paul* = H. Ridderbos, *Paul: An Outline of His Theology*, ET: J. Richard De Witt (Grand Rapids, Michigan: Eerdmans, 1975)

Ringgren, 'עשה' = H. Ringgren, 'עשה', *TWAT*, VI (1989), 414–31

Rist, 'Daimonion' = J. M. Rist, 'Plotinus and the *Daimonion* of Socrates', *Phoenix* 17 (1963), 13–24

Roberts, 'Enigma' = J. H. Roberts, 'The Enigma of Ephesians: Rethinking Some Positions on the Basis of Schnackenburg and Arnold', *Neotestamentica* 27 (1993), 93–106

Roberts, 'Instrumental ἐν' = J. W. Roberts, 'Instrumental ἐν in the New Testament', *ResQ* 6 (1962), 143–6

Robertson and Dietrich, 'Fate' = N. Robertson and B. C. Dietrich, 'Fate', *OCD*, 589–90

Robinson, *Ephesians* = J. A. Robinson, *St Paul's Epistle to the Ephesians* (London: Macmillan, 1904)

Robinson, *Body* = J. A. T. Robinson, *The Body: A Study in Pauline Theology* (London: SCM, 1952)

Roetzel, 'Διαθῆκαι' = C. J. Roetzel, 'Διαθῆκαι in Romans 9, 4', *Bib* 51 (1970), 377–90

'Relations' = C. J. Roetzel, 'Jewish Christian – Gentile Christian Relations: A Discussion of Ephesians 2.15a, 15', *ZNW* 74 (1983), 81–9

Conversations = C. J. Roetzel, *The Letters of Paul: Conversations in Context* (Louisville, Kentucky: Westminster/John Knox Press, 1991[3])
Rogerson, 'Personality' = J. W. Rogerson, 'The Hebrew Conception of Corporate Personality: A Reexamination', *JTS* 21 (1970), 1–16
Anthropology = J. W. Rogerson, *Anthropology and the Old Testament* (Sheffield: JSOT, 1984)
Rokeah, *Jews* = D. Rokeah, *Jews, Pagans and Christians in Conflict*, SPB 33 (Jerusalem: The Magnes Press/Leiden: E. J. Brill, 1982)
Roloff, *Kirche* = J. Roloff, *Die Kirche im Neuen Testament*, GNT 10 (Göttingen: Vandenhoeck & Ruprecht, 1993)
Romm, *Edges* = J. S. Romm, *The Edges of the Earth in Ancient Thought* (Princeton: Princeton University Press, 1992)
Rubin, 'Prepuce' = N. Rubin, 'On Drawing Down the Prepuce and Incision of the Foreskin (*Pericah*)', *Zion* 54 (1989), 105–17
Runesson, 'Judaism' = A. Runesson, 'Particularistic Judaism and Universalistic Christianity', *Studia Theologica* 53 (1999), 55–75
Rykwert, *Town* = J. Rykwert, *The Idea of a Town: The Anthropology of Urban Form in Rome, Italy and the Ancient World* (London: Faber and Faber, 1976)
Sabine and Smith, *Commonwealth* = G. H. Sabine and S. B. Smith, *On the Commonwealth: Marcus Tullius Cicero* (Columbus, Ohio: Ohio State University, 1929)
Sahlin, 'Beschneidung Christi' = H. Sahlin, 'Die Beschneidung Christi: Eine Interpretation von Eph 2, 11–22', *SBU* 12 (1950), 5–22
Sakellariou, *Polis-State* = M. B. Sakellariou, *The Polis-State: Definition and Origin*, ΜΕΛ 4 (Athens: Research Centre for Greek and Roman Antiquity National Hellenic Research Foundation, 1989)
Saller, 'Familia' = R. P. Saller, '*Familia, Domus*, and the Roman Conception of the Family', *Phoenix* 38 (1984), 336–55
Sampley, *One Flesh* = J. P. Sampley, *'And the Two Shall Become One Flesh': A Study of Traditions in Ephesians 5:21–33*, SNTSMS 16 (Cambridge: Cambridge University Press, 1971)
Sanders, *Paul* = E. P. Sanders, *Paul and Palestinian Judaism: A Comparison of Patterns of Religion* (Minneapolis: Fortress, 1977)
Law = E. P. Sanders, *Paul, the Law, and the Jewish People* (Minneapolis: Fortress, 1983)
Judaism = E. P. Sanders, *Judaism: Practice and Belief 63BCE–66CE* (London: SCM, 1992)
Sanders, 'Elements' = J. T. Sanders, 'Hymnic Elements in Ephesians 1–3', *ZNW* 56 (1965), 214–32
Hymns = J. T. Sanders, *The New Testament Christological Hymns*, SNTSMS 15 (Cambridge: Cambridge University Press, 1971)
Ethics = J. T. Sanders, *Ethics in the New Testament: Change and Development* (London: SCM, 1975)
Schismatics = J. T. Sanders, *Schismatics, Sectarians, Dissidents, Deviants: The First One Hundred Years of Jewish-Christian Relations* (London: SCM Press, 1993)
Sandvoss, 'Asebie' = E. Sandvoss, 'Asebie und Atheismus im klassischen Zeitalter', *Saeculum* 19 (1969), 312–29

Sasse, 'αἰών' = H. Sasse, 'αἰών κτλ.', *TDNT*, I (1964), 197–209
Sayer, 'Space' = A. Sayer, 'The Difference that Space Makes', in D. Gregory and J. Urry (eds.), *Social Relations and Spatial Structures* (London: Macmillan, 1985), 49–66
Schafer, 'Paroikos' = H. Schafer, 'Paroikos', in *RECA* XVIII.4, 1695–707
Schäfer, 'ἀκρογωνιαῖος' = K. T. Schäfer, 'Zur Deutung von ἀκρογωνιαῖος Eph 2,20', in J. Blinzler et al. (eds.) *Neutestamentliche Ausfsätze*, FS J. Schmid (Regensburg, Verlag F. Pustet, 1963), 218–24
Schäfer, *Aufstand* = P. Schäfer, *Der Bar Kokhba-Aufstand* (Tübingen: J. C. B. Mohr, 1981)
Judeophobia = P. Schäfer, *Judeophobia: Attitudes toward the Jews in the Ancient World* (London/Cambridge, Massachusetts: Harvard University Press, 1997)
Schille, *Hymnen* = G. Schille, *Frühchristliche Hymnen* (Berlin: Evangelische Verlagsanstalt, 1965)
Schlatter, *Briefe* = A. Schlatter, *Die Briefe an die Galater, Epheser, Kolosser und Philemon*, ENT 7 (Stuttgart: Calwer Verlag, 1963)
Schlier, *Christus* = H. Schlier, *Christus und die Kirche im Epheserbrief* (Tübingen, J. C. B. Mohr, 1930)
Epheser = H. Schlier, *Der Brief an die Epheser* (Düsseldorf: Patmos Verlag, 1968^6)
Schmidt, 'ἔθνος' = K.-L. Schmidt, 'ἔθνος κτλ', *TDNT*, II (1964), 369–72
Schmidt, 'πάροικος' = K.-L. and M. A. Schmidt, 'πάροικος κτλ.', *TDNT*, V (1967), 841–50
Schnabel, 'Wisdom' = E. J. Schnabel, 'Wisdom', in *DPL*, 967–73
Schnackenburg, 'Politeia' = R. Schnackenburg, 'Die Politeia Israels in Eph 2, 12', in M. Carrez et al. (eds.), *De la Tôrah au Messie: Études d'exégèse et d'herméneutique bibliques*, FS H. Cazelles (Paris: Desclée, 1981), 467–74
'Bau' = R. Schnackenburg, 'Die Kirche als Bau: Epheser 2.19–22 unter ökumenischen Aspekt', in Morna D. Hooker and S. G. Wilson (eds.), *Paul and Paulinism*, FS C. K. Barrett (London: SPCK, 1982), 258–72
'Exegese' = R. Schnackenburg, 'Zur Exegese von Eph 2, 11–22: Im Hinblick auf das Verhältnis von Kirche und Israel', in W. C. Weinreich (ed.), *The New Testament Age*, FS Bo Reicke, II (Macon, Georgia: Mercer University Press, 1984), 467–91
Ephesians = R. Schnackenburg, *Ephesians: A Commentary*, ET Helen Heron (Edinburgh: T & T Clark, 1991)
Schneider, 'μεσότοιχον' = C. Schneider, 'μεσότοιχον', *TDNT*, IV (1967), 625
Schneider, 'δῶρον' = G. Schneider, 'δῶρον', *EDNT*, I (1990), 365
'τέκνον' = G. Schneider, 'τέκνον', *EDNT*, III (1993), 341–2
Schnelle, *History* = U. Schnelle, *The History and Theology of the New Testament Writings*, ET M. E. Boring (London: SCM, 1998)
Schofield, *Stoic Idea* = M. Schofield, *The Stoic Idea of the City* (Cambridge: Cambridge University Press, 1991)
Schrage, 'Ethik' = W. Schrage, 'Zur Ethik der neutestamentlichen Haustafeln', *NTS* 21 (1974), 1–22
Ethics = W. Schrage, *The Ethics of the New Testament*, ET D. E. Green (Philadelphia: Fortress, 1988)

Schreiner, 'Völker' = J. Schreiner, 'Segen für die Völker in der Verheissung an die Väter', *BZ* 6 (1962), 1–31
Schrenk, 'ἐντολή' = G. Schrenk, 'ἐντολή', *TDNT*, II (1964), 545–66
'πατήρ' = G. Schrenk, 'πατήρ κτλ.', *TDNT*, V (1967), 945–59, 974–1015
Schröder, 'Lists' = D. Schröder, 'Lists, Ethical', in *IDBSup*, 546–7
Schürer, *HJPAJC* = E. Schürer, *The History of the Jewish People in the Age of Jesus* Christ, *175 BC–135 AD*, 5 vols. (Edinburgh: T & T Clark, 1973–)
Schwartz, 'Descent' = D. R. Schwartz, 'On Two Aspects of a Priestly Descent at Qumran', in L. H. Schiffman (ed.), *Archaeology and History in the Dead Sea Scrolls*, JSPSS 8 (Sheffield: JSOT Press, 1990), 157–79
Schweizer, 'Kirche' = E. Schweizer, 'Die Kirche als Leib Christi', *Neot* (1963), 294–316
'σῶμα' = E. Schweizer, 'σῶμα κτλ.', *TDNT*, VII (1971), 1066–94
'Christianity' = E. Schweizer, 'Christianity of the Circumcised and Judaism of the Uncircumcised', in R. Hammelton-Kelly and R. Scroggs (eds.), *Jews, Greek and Christians*, FS W. D. Davies (Leiden: E. J. Brill, 1976), 245–60
Sealey, *History* = R. Sealey, *A History of the Greek City States 700–338 BC* (California: University of California, 1976)
Searle, *Expression* = J. R. Searle, *Expression and Meaning: Studies in the Theory of Speech Acts* (Cambridge: Cambridge University Press, 1979)
Seesemann, 'πατέω' = H. Seesemann, 'πατέω', *TDNT*, V (1967), 943–5
Segal, *Two Powers* = A. F. Segal, *Two Powers in Heaven: Early Rabbinic Reports about Christianity and Gnosticism* (Leiden: E. J. Brill, 1977)
'Ruler' = A. F. Segal, 'Ruler of this World: Attitudes about Mediator Figures and the Importance of Sociology for Self-Definition', in E. P. Sanders et al. (eds.), *Jewish and Christian Self-Definition*, II (London: SCM, 1981), 245–68, 403–13
Rebecca's Children = A. F. Segal, *Rebecca's Children: Judaism and Christianity in the Roman World* (Cambridge, Massachusetts/London: Harvard University Press, 1986)
Segal, 'Penalty' = P. Segal, 'The Penalty of the Warning Inscription from the Temple of Jerusalem', *IEJ* 39 (1989), 79–84
Sekki, *Ruah* = A. E. Sekki, *The Meaning of Ruah at Qumran*, SBLDS 110 (Atlanta: Scholars Press, 1989)
Sellin, 'Genitive' = G. Sellin, 'Über einige ungewöhnliche Genitive im Epheserbrief', *ZNW* 83 (1992), 85–107
Shanor, 'Master Builder' = J. Shanor, 'Paul as Master Builder: Construction Terms in First Corinthians', *NTS* 34 (1988), 461–71
Shelton, *Romans* = Jo-Ann Shelton, *As the Romans Did: A Sourcebook in Roman Social History* (Oxford/New York: Oxford University Press, 1988[1])
Sheppard, 'Homonoia' = A. R. R. Sheppard, '*HOMONOIA* in the Greek Cities of the Roman Empire', *AS* 15–17 (1984–6), 229–52
Sherwin-White, *Roman Citizenship* = A. N. Sherwin-White, *The Roman Citizenship* (Oxford: Clarendon Press, 1939)
Simon, *Christianisme* = M. Simon, *Le Christianisme antique et son contexte religieux, Scripta Varia*, I (Tübingen: J. C. B. Mohr, 1981)
Sinclair, *Democracy* = R. K. Sinclair, *Democracy and Participation in Athens* (Cambridge: Cambridge University Press, 1988)

Sjöberg, 'Wiedergeburt' = E. Sjöberg, 'Wiedergeburt und Neuschöpfung im palästinischen Judentum', *ST* 4 (1950), 44–85
'Neuschöpfung' = E. Sjöberg, 'Neuschöpfung in den Toten-Meer-Rollen', *ST* 9 (1955), 131–6
'πνεῦμα' = E. Sjöberg, 'πνεῦμα κτλ.', *TDNT*, VI (1968), 375–89
Skehan, 'Structure' = P. W. Skehan, 'The Structure of the Song of Moses in Deuteronomy', *CBQ* 13 (1951), 153–63
'Song of Moses' = P. W. Skehan, 'A Fragment of the "Song of Moses" (Deut. 32) from Qumran', *BASOR* 136 (1954), 12–15
Smallwood, 'Domitian's Attitude' = E. M. Smallwood, 'Domitian's Attitude towards the Jews and Judaism', *CP* 51 (1956), 1–13
'Circumcision' = E. M. Smallwood, 'The Legislation of Hadrian and Antoninus Pius against Circumcision', *Lat* 18 (1959), 334–47
Jews = E. M. Smallwood, *The Jews under the Roman Rule: From Pompey to Diocletian*, SJLA 20 (Leiden: E. J. Brill, 1976)
Smith, *Ethnic Origins* = A. D. Smith, *The Ethnic Origins of Nations* (London: Blackwell, 1986)
Smith, 'One' = D. [C]. Smith, 'The Two Made One. Some Observations on Eph. 2:14–16', *OJRS* 1 (1973), 34–54
'Heresy' = D. C. Smith, 'The Ephesian Heresy and the Origin of the Epistle to the Ephesians', *OJRS* 5 (1977), 78–103
Smith, 'Powers' = J. Z. Smith, 'Towards Interpreting Demonic Powers in Hellenistic and Roman Antiquity', in *ANRW* II.16.1 (1978), 425–39
'Fences' = J. Z. Smith, 'Fences and Neighbours: Some Contours of Early Judaism', in W. S. Green (ed.), *Approaches to Ancient Judaism*, II, BJS 9 (Chico, California: Scholars Press, 1980), 1–25
Smith, 'Ethnicity' = M. G. Smith, 'Plurality, Race and Ethnicity in Selected African Countries', in J. Rex and D. Mason (eds.), *Theories of Race and Ethnic Relations* (Cambridge: Cambridge University Press, 1986), 187–225
Snodgrass, *Stone Testimonia* = K. R. Snodgrass, *The Christological Stone Testimonia in the New Testament* (unpublished Ph.D. diss., University of St. Andrews, 1973)
Sperber and Wilson, *Relevance* = D. Sperber and D. Wilson, *Relevance: Communication and Cognition* (London/Cambridge, USA: Blackwell, 1995^2)
Stählin, 'ξένος' = G. Stählin, 'ξένος κτλ.', *TDNT*, V (1967), 1–36
Stambaugh, *Sarapis* = J. E. Stambaugh, *Sarapis under the Early Ptolemies* (Leiden: E. J. Brill, 1972)
Stanley, 'Conflict' = C. D. Stanley, '"Neither Jew nor Greek": Ethnic Conflict in Graeco-Roman Society', *JSNT* 64 (1996), 101–24
Stauffer, 'ἄθεος' = E. Stauffer, 'ἄθεος', *TDNT*, III (1965), 120–1
Steiner, *Babel* = G. Steiner, *After Babel: Aspects of Language and Translation* (Oxford: Oxford University Press, 1998^3)
Stemberger, *Talmud* = G. Stemberger, *Introduction to the Talmud and Midrash*, ET M. Bockmuehl (Edinburgh: T & T Clark, 1991)
Stern, *GLAJJ* = M. Stern, *Greek and Latin Writers on Jews and Judaism*, 3 vols. (Jerusalem: Israel Academy of Sciences and Humanities, 1974, 1980, 1984)
Stern, *Jewish Identity* = S. Stern, *Jewish Identity in Early Rabbinic Writings*, AGAJU 28 (Leiden: E. J. Brill, 1994)

Stewart, *Myths* = J. A. Stewart, *The Myths of Plato* (London: Macmillan and Co., 1905)
Strathmann, 'πόλις' = H. Strathmann, 'πόλις κτλ.', *TDNT*, VI (1968), 516–35
Stuckenbruck, *Angel Veneration* = L. T. Stuckenbruck, *Angel Veneration and Christology: A Study in Early Judaism and in the Christology of the Apocalypse of John*, WUNT 70 (Tübingen: J. C. B. Mohr [P. Siebeck], 1995)
Stuhlmacher, 'Peace' = P. Stuhlmacher, '"He is our Peace" (Eph. 2:14): On the Exegesis and Significance of Eph. 2: 14–18', in his *Reconciliation, Law, and Righteousness* (Philadelphia: Fortress, 1986), 182–200
Swartley, 'War' = W. M. Swartley, 'War and Peace in the NT', in *ANRW* II.26.3 (1992), 2298–489
Tachau, *Einst* = P. Tachau, *"Einst" und "Jetzt" im Neuen Testament: Beobachtungen zu einem urchristlichen Predigtschema in der neutestamentlichen Briefliteratur und zu seiner Vorgeschichte* (Göttingen: Vandenhoeck & Ruprecht, 1972)
Thielman, *Paul* = F. Thielman, *Paul and the Law: A Contextual Approach* (Downers Grove, Illinois: InterVarsity Press, 1994)
Thomas, *Interaction* = Jenny Thomas, *Meaning in Interaction: An Introduction to Pragmatics* (London/New York: Longman, 1995)
Thompson, *Blacks* = L. A. Thompson, *Romans and Blacks* (London: Routledge/Oklahoma: Oklahoma University Press, 1989)
Thompson, *Clothed with Christ* = M. Thompson, *Clothed with Christ: The Example and Teaching of Jesus in Romans 12.1–15.13*, JSNTSS 59 (Sheffield: Sheffield Academic Press, 1991)
Thomson, *Chiasmus* = I. H. Thomson, *Chiasmus in the Pauline Letters*, JSNTSS 111 (Sheffield: Sheffield Academic Press, 1995)
Thomson, *Geography* = J. P. Thomson, *History of Ancient Geography* (Cambridge: Cambridge University Press, 1948)
Thrall, *Greek Particles* = M. E. Thrall, *Greek Particles in the New Testament: Linguistic and Exegetical Studies*, NTTS 3 (Leiden: E. J. Brill, 1962)
Thrower, 'Atheism' = J. Thrower, *A Short History of Western Atheism* (London: Pamberton, 1971)
Tobin, *Creation* = T. H. Tobin, *The Creation of Man: Philo and the History of Interpretation*, CBQMS 14 (Washington, D.C.: The Catholic Biblical Association of America, 1983)
Tomson, 'Names' = P. J. Tomson, 'The Names Israel and Jew in Ancient Judaism and in the New Testament: Part II', *Bijdragen* 47 (1986), 266–89
Towner, *Goal* = P. H. Towner, *The Goal of Our Instruction*, JSNTSS 34 (Sheffield: JSOT, 1989)
'Households' = P. H. Towner, 'Households and Household Codes', in *DPL*, 417–19
Trebilco, *Communities* = P. Trebilco, *Jewish Communities in Asia Minor*, SNTSMS 69 (Cambridge: Cambridge University Press, 1991)
Treves, 'Two Spirits' = M. Treves, 'The Two Spirits of the Rule of the Community', *RevQ* 3 (1961), 449–552
Troiani, 'ΠΟΛΙΤΕΙΑ' = L. Troiani, 'The ΠΟΛΙΤΕΙΑ Israel in the Graeco-Roman Age', in F. Parente and J. Sievers (eds.), *Josephus and the History of the Graeco-Roman Period*, FS M. Smith, SPB 41 (Leiden: E. J. Brill, 1994), 11–22

Tuan, *Topophilia* = Y.-F. Tuan, *Topophilia: A Study of Environmental Perception, Attitudes, and Values* (Englewood Cliffs, New Jersey: Prentice Hall, 1974)
Turner, *Syntax* = N. Turner, *A Greek Grammar of New Testament Greek: Syntax* (Edinburgh: T & T Clark, 1963)
Style = N. Turner, *Style*. Vol. IV, in J. H. Moulton (ed.), *A Grammar of New Testament Greek* (Edinburgh: T & T Clark, 1976)
Urry, 'Space' = J. Urry, 'Social Relations, Space and Time', in D. Gregory and J. Urry (eds.), *Social Relations and Spatial Structures* (London: Macmillan, 1985), 20–48
van Buren, *Jewish-Christian Reality* = P. M. van Buren, *A Theology of the Jewish-Christian Reality*, Part 2 (San Francisco: Harper & Row, 1987)
van der Horst, *Essays* = P. van der Horst, *Essays on the Jewish World of Early Christianity* (Schweiz: Universitätsverlag Freiburg/Göttingen: Vandenhoeck & Ruprecht, 1990)
'Throne Vision' = P. van der Horst, 'Moses' Throne Vision in Ezekiel the Dramatist', in his *Essays on the Jewish World of Early Christianity* (Schweiz: Universitätsverlag Freiburg/Göttingen: Vandenhoeck & Ruprecht, 1990), 63–71
Epitaphs = P. van der Horst, *Ancient Jewish Epitaphs*, CBET 2 (Kampen: Kok, 1991)
van Henten, '4 Macc 17: 8–10' = J. W. van Henten, 'A Jewish Epitaph in a Literary Text: 4 Macc 17: 8–10', in J. W. van Henten and P. van der Horst (eds.), *Studies in Early Jewish Epigraphy*, AGAJU 21 (Leiden: E. J. Brill, 1994), 44–69
van Roon, *Authenticity* = A. van Roon, *The Authenticity of Ephesians*, SNT 29 (Leiden: E. J. Brill, 1974)
Vasaly, *Representations* = Ann Vasaly, *Representations: Images of the World in Ciceronian Oratory* (Berkeley, California: University of California Press, 1993)
Versnel, 'Daimôn' = H. S. Versnel, 'Daimôn', *OCD*, 426
Vielhauer, *Oikodome* = P. Vielhauer, *Das Bild vom Bau in der christlichen Literatur vom Neuen Testament bis Clemens Alexandrinus* (Munich: Kaiser, 1979)
von Rad, 'εἰρηνη' = G. von Rad, 'εἰρηνη', *TDNT*, II (1964), 402–6
Deuteronomy = G. von Rad, *Deuteronomy*, OTL (London: SCM Press, 1966)
Wallace, *Grammar* = D. B. Wallace, *Greek Grammar Beyond the Basics* (Grand Rapids, Michigan: Zondervans, 1997)
Wallbank, *Polybius* = F. W. Wallbank, *A Historical Commentary on Polybius* (Oxford: Oxford University Press, 1979)
Wallman, *Ethnicity* = S. Wallman (ed.), *Ethnicity at Work* (London: Macmillan, 1979)
Walter, 'δόγμα' = N. Walter, 'δόγμα', *EDNT*, I (1990), 339–40
'ἔθνος' = N. Walter, 'ἔθνος', *EDNT*, I (1990), 381–3
Wedderburn, *Baptism* = A. J. M. Wedderburn, *Baptism and Resurrection: Studies in Pauline Theology against its Graeco-Roman Background*, WUNT 44 (Tübingen: J. C. B. Mohr, 1987)
Weiss, 'χρηστότης' = K. Weiss, 'χρηστότης', *TDNT*, IX, 489–92
Wengst, *Lieder* = K. Wengst, *Christologische Formeln und Lieder des Urchristentums*, SNT 7 (Gütersloh: Mohn, 1973^{2})

Pax = K. Wengst, *Pax Romana and the Peace of Christ* (London: SCM, 1987)
Werner-Møller, 'Two Spirits' = P. Werner-Møller, 'A Reconsideration of the Two Spirits in the Rule of the Community (1Q Serek III, 13-IV, 26)', *RevQ* 3 (1961), 413–41
Westcott, *Ephesians* = B. F. Westcott, *St Paul's Epistle to the Ephesians* (Minneapolis: Klock & Klock, 1978)
Westermann, *Praise* = C. Westermann, *The Praise of God in the Psalms* (London: Epworth, 1966)
Whitaker, 'συναρμολογούμενον' = G. H. Whitaker, 'συναρμολογούμενον και συνβιβαζόμενον. Eph iv.16', *JTS* 31 (1930), 48–9
Whitehead, *Metic* = D. Whitehead, *The Ideology of the Athenian Metic*, PCPhSS 4 (Cambridge: Philological Society, 1977)
Whittaker, *Graeco-Roman Views* = M. Whittaker, *Jews and Christians: Graeco-Roman Views*, CCWJCW 6 (Cambridge: Cambridge University Press, 1984)
Wilckens, 'σοφία' = U. Wilckens, 'σοφία κτλ.', *TDNT*, VII (1971), 465–76
Wilhelmi, 'Versöhner-Hymnen' = G. Wilhelmi, 'Der Versöhner-Hymnen in Eph 2.14ff', *ZNW* 78 (1987), 145–52
Wilken, 'Christians' = R. L. Wilken, 'The Christians as the Romans (and Greeks) Saw Them', in E. P. Sanders (ed.), *Jewish and Christian Self-Definition: The Shaping of Christianity in the Second and Third Centuries*, I (London: SCM, 1980), 100–25, 234–6
Wills, *Repetition* = J. Wills, *Repetition in Latin Poetry: Figures of Allusion* (Oxford: Clarendon, 1996)
Wilson, 'We' = R. A. Wilson, '"We" and "You" in the Epistle to the Ephesians', *SE* 2 (1964), 676–80
Wink, *Naming* = W. Wink, *Naming the Powers: The Language of Power in the New Testament* (Philadelphia: Fortress, 1984)
Unmasking = W. Wink, *Unmasking the Powers: The Invisible Forces that Determine Human Existence* (Philadelphia: Fortress, 1986)
Engaging = W. Wink, *Engaging the Powers: Discernment and Resistance in a World of Domination* (Minneapolis: Fortress, 1992)
Winston, *Wisdom* = D. Winston, *The Wisdom of Solomon*, AB 43 (New York: Doubleday, 1979)
Wintle, 'Justification' = B. C. Wintle, 'Justification in Pauline Thought', in D. A. Carson (ed.), *Right With God* (Carlisle: Paternoster/Grand Rapids, Michigan: Baker: 1992), 51–68
Wolter, *Rechtfertigung* = M. Wolter, *Rechtfertigung und zukünftiges Heil: Untersuchungen zu Röm 5:1–11*, BZNW 43 (Berlin: de Gruyter, 1978)
'παράπτωμα' = M. Wolter, 'παράπτωμα', *EDNT*, III (1993), 33–4
Wright, 'Barbarians' = T. E. J. Wright, 'Barbarians', *OCD*, 233
Wuellner, 'Rhetoric' = W. Wuellner, 'Greek Rhetoric and Pauline Argumentation', in W. R. Schoedel and R. L. Wilken (eds.), *Early Christian Literature and the Classical Intellectual Tradition*, FS R. M. Grant, TH 5 (Paris: Éditions Beauchesne, 1979), 177–88
Yoder, *Politics* = J. H. Yoder, *The Politics of Jesus* (Grand Rapids, Michigan: Eerdmans, 1994^2)
Zanker, 'Enargeia' = G. Zanker, 'Enargeia in the Ancient Criticism of Poetry', *RheM* 124 (1981), 297–311

Zeitlin, 'Names' = S. Zeitlin, 'The Names Hebrew, Jew, and Israel', *JQR* 43 (1952–3), 365–79

2 Maccabees = S. Zeitlin, *The Second Book of Maccabees*, ET S. Tedesche (New York: Harper & Brothers, 1954)

Zepf, 'Aion' = M. Zepf, 'Der Gott Aion in der hellenistischen Theologie', *ARW* 25 (1927), 225–44

Zerwick, *BG* = M. Zerwick, *Biblical Greek* (Rome: Editrice Pontificio Istituto Biblico, 1963)

GA = M. Zerwick, *Grammatical Analysis* (Rome: Editrice Pontificio Istituto Biblico, 1988)

Zmijewski, 'καχησις' = J. Zmijewski, 'καχησις', *EDNT*, II (1991), 276–9

Zuckermann, 'Politeumata' = C. Zuckermann, 'Hellenistic *Politeumata* and the Jews: A Reconsideration', *SCI* 8–9 (1988), 171–85

Zuntz, 'Aristeas' = G. Zuntz, 'Aristeas Studies II: Aristeas on the Transmission of the Torah', in his *Opuscula Selecta: Classica, Hellenistica, Christiana* (Manchester: Manchester University Press, 1972), 126–43

Aion = G. Zuntz, *Aion, Gott des Römerreichs*, AHAWPHK (Heidelberg: Carl Winter, 1989)

SUBJECT INDEX

INDEX OF SCRIPTURES AND OTHER ANCIENT WRITINGS

The Old Testament

Apocrypha, Pseudepigrapha and other Jewish writings

Apocrypha

Rabbinic literature

Other ancient and early Christian writings

Inscriptions and papyri